THE ETHICS OF INTERPERSONAL
RELATIONSHIPS

THE ETHICS OF INTERPERSONAL RELATIONSHIPS

Robert W. Firestone
and
Joyce Catlett

KARNAC

First published in 2009 by
Karnac Books Ltd
118 Finchley Road
London NW3 5HT

British Library Cataloguing in Publication Data

A C.I.P. for this book is available from the British Library

ISBN-13: 978-1-85575-605-2

Typeset by Vikatan Publishing Solutions (p) Ltd., Chennai, India

www.karnacbooks.com

To Stuart Boyd, teacher and life-long friend, in appreciation for his brilliance, his humor and overall effect on my life. Most importantly, he not only taught me well but allowed me to forge ahead and develop my own theoretical ideas. For this, I'm deeply grateful.

Robert W. Firestone

CONTENTS

ACKNOWLEDGEMENTS

We wish to express our appreciation to Tamsen Firestone for her major contribution to this work, which included re-writing and editing as well as her advice and guidance in developing the final manuscript. We are grateful to Jo Barrington, Susan Short, and Sara Bartlett for their outstanding editing skills. We also wish to thank Anne Baker, who helped us research and reference the literature on psychological issues related to moral reasoning and conduct and recent developments in the neurosciences and psychoanalytic theory. We extend thanks to Jina Carvalho, who is responsible for disseminating an expanding number of written and filmed works through the Glendon Association.

We express our gratitude to the men and women whose stories illustrate the challenges involved in moving toward more humane and ethical ways of being and living. We acknowledge their honesty and courage in revealing their personal struggles and appreciate their ongoing participation in our common endeavor. They have been strongly motivated to make the insight and understanding that they have gained over the past three decades available so that others might benefit from their experiences. Finally, we thank Oliver Rathbone, Managing Director of Karnac Books, for recognizing the importance and timeliness of this work and Christelle Yeyet-Jacquot for her interest and help in completing this project.

The names, places, and other identifying facts contained herein have been fictionalized and no similarity to any people, living or dead, is intended.

The ethics of interpersonal relationships

"He who is too busy doing good finds no time to be good."
Rabindranath Tagore

Why is it so difficult to do what we think is right? Living ethically should be a common occurrence in all households. I don't know about you, but I feel I should be closer to friends and families, donate more money to the needy, take better care of my body with only good foods and regular exercise, volunteer at the nursing home, and the list goes on. I guess I lack courage?

In graduate school I was fascinated by the work of Lawrence Kohlberg and his theory of moral development. I even attended a training seminar with him at Harvard University in the interest of learning to live by what I consider higher values. When I finished the program I was even more challenged to navigate life's different stages of development and to live a life based on principles.

In *The Ethics of Interpersonal Relationships*, Robert Firestone and Joyce Catlett identify the source of the ethical dilemmas that occur when trying to live a principled life. I am impressed with their candor in describing how we hurt those we love most and keep ourselves from the happiness we seek. This book provides a major shift

xi

in understanding why people are mean, unethical and not compassionate. As the authors state, "this work is an attempt to explain the
source of human destructive behavior, how it manifests itself in personal relationships and suggests a treatment modality for coping with
negative, acting-out behavior."

Defenses are ways of thinking and acting which we believe will
protect us from being hurt. However, they ultimately bring what they
were meant to guard against. We can see this in the person who wants
love but does not believe people can be trusted. Or the person who
wants to get close but is afraid of being taken advantage of. Or even
the person who grows up in the alcoholic family, vowing they will
never do the same, only to marry an alcoholic or to become an alcohol
dependent person.

The basic premise of this book is the theory that is outlined in two of
Dr. Firestone's earlier works, *The Fantasy Bond* and *Voice Therapy*. The
Fantasy Bond and Voice Process are the primary defense mechanisms
that interfere with our ability to live by ethical principles, values, and
ideals. Because the problem is psychological, this book approaches
the subject of ethics from a point of view that is compassionate and
understanding rather than one that is judgmental.

Robert Firestone and Joyce Catlett live by the ideals and principles
that they put forth. A few years ago I was invited to Bob's home for
dinner and I found myself in the midst of a circle of family and friends.
Everyone present (men, women and children) actively participated in
the evening: hosting, cooking, setting up and serving, and then clean-
ing up. After dinner, most of them gathered in the living room for an
evening discussion, and I was invited to join them. Apparently, they
meet often to talk about anything they want--from issues that they
are personally struggling with to problems they are having with each
other to just reporting how their day was. Participants were urged to
speak openly and, when feelings arose, they were encouraged to feel
them. As I sat observing, many issues were addressed and resolved in
a short period of time. I left the evening I spent amongst Bob and his
family and friends with feelings of admiration and respect for these
courageous people. I had witnessed them actively involved in the
process of living by the ethical principles that they aspired to.

It is my hope that this book receives a wide readership as it offers
a major breakthrough as to how to make our lives principled through

understanding psychological (not moral) processes. Thank you, Bob and Joyce, for your contribution to humanity.

In closing, remember the wise words of Mark Twain, "Always do right—this will gratify some and astonish the rest."

Jon Carlson, PsyD, EdD, ABPP
Distinguished Professor
Governors State University
Author, *Adlerian Therapy* & *Inclusive Cultural Empathy*

The ethics of interpersonal relationships

Our inspiration for writing this book springs from a deep feeling for people and a grave concern that without a proper understanding of the reasons for their inhumanity in relation to one another and the development of a compassionate world view, it is likely that human beings may eventually destroy themselves and life on the planet. Despite all of the advances in science and technology, if one takes a proper look at the world situation today, one must consider it to be utter madness. Millions go hungry, genocide reaches epic proportions, ethnic strife and prejudice are omnipresent, there is mass killing in the name of religion, and warfare remains a widely accepted solution to humankind's differences. With better, more efficient weapons, and less reason, and with technology outrunning rationality, there can only be dire consequences.

This work is an attempt to explain the source of destructive behavior and how it manifests itself in personal relationships between men, women, couples, and families, and in the social arena. Faced with a similar concern regarding antisocial behavior, Sigmund Freud (1925/1959) postulated a death instinct, an innate destructive side to human nature. Modern theorists have criticized Freud's death instinct theory for its lack of empirical evidence. The authors also disagree with Freud's conclusion and postulate that aggressive manifestations in human beings are primarily a result of frustration and personal torment.

Our thesis is that people's immorality in relation to others derives from the defensive manner in which they deal with interpersonal and existential pain. There is no way to be personally defended without hurting others, particularly those people closest to us, especially our children. This conclusion reflects a clinical accounting rather than a moralistic condemnation. This paradox is complex and multifaceted. It is important to understand how and why defenses are formed, where they originate and why they are endemic. It is logical that faced with pain and frustration in our developmental years, we form psychological defenses to alleviate our discomfort. Existential issues of aloneness and the awareness of our eventual demise add to our anxieties and further predispose defensive denial of feeling. The tragedy is that the same defenses that enable us to survive the emotional pain of our childhood are not only maladaptive in adulthood, limiting our personal potential for living a full life, but they also inevitably lead to negative behavior toward others, thereby perpetuating a cycle of destructiveness.

Feeling and compassion are a significant part of our human heritage, but when faced with overwhelming primal pain, we develop defenses to eliminate the ensuing suffering. However, we cannot shut down our emotions selectively. In attempting to do so, we necessarily limit our capacity to feel love and joy as well. To the extent that we rely on psychological defenses, we tend to become emotionally deadened and lose spirit. Once cut off from feelings, we are desensitized toward ourselves and become not only more self-destructive but more likely to act out aggression toward others. Furthermore, we tend to become hostile whenever our defenses are threatened. This aggression can be triggered by positive life events as well as negative events. Because of past wounds, we are often frightened or distrustful when we experience positive recognition or loving responses. We react by withholding positive personality traits, lashing out or distancing ourselves to maintain our psychological equilibrium. Sadly, our defenses usually take priority over a genuine regard for the people close to us. Our friends, our partners, and our children are expendable in the face of our self-protective attitudes.

Damage to our psyche during our developmental years bends us out of shape and leaves us demoralized. It not only fosters aggressive responses, but also leads to toxic character traits that injure other people's self-esteem. Character traits such as dishonesty, intrusiveness, superiority, narcissism, tightness, domineering behavior, a martyred or victimized orientation, paranoid or suspicious attitudes, and outright hostility are destructive manifestations that take a toll on other people. These could well be described as human rights violations in the interpersonal sphere.

Life can be conceptualized as a series of weaning experiences or separations, beginning with separation from the breast or mother and later from one's parents, going to school, leaving home, forming a serious relationship, marriage, starting one's own family, and eventually aging and dying. These separation experiences are sources of anxiety and discomfort. Even under ideal developmental conditions, people are likely to form defenses to cope with the stress brought about by these experiences.

Along with these existential realities, family life does not always provide for the healthy emotional nurturance of children. Many parents are emotionally immature, critical, rejecting, even hostile or punitive, causing the child considerable anxiety and distress. The fantasy bond (R. Firestone, 1985), which originates as an imagined connection to one's mother or caregiver, is the primary defense that attempts to offer comfort and heal the fracture brought about by experiences of separation and deprivation. This imaginary bond involves a self-parenting process in which people compensate for the frustration and emotional trauma of their childhoods by nurturing and punishing themselves in thought and action, much as their parents once did. The degree of self-parenting is proportional to the degree of emotional deprivation experienced. As such, it leads to addictive propensities such as eating disorders, drug and alcohol abuse, and to a variety of other self-nurturing behaviors as well as punishing, critical or hostile thought processes directed toward self and others.

To support the fantasy bond, one must idealize the family of origin at the expense of one's self and, in the process, internalize critical rejecting parental attitudes. In addition, parents' negative traits are displaced and projected onto other individuals and the world at large, predisposing a defensive, distrustful, or angry posture toward others. Although the fantasy bond serves the purpose of helping to avoid anxiety, it predisposes a faulty adjustment that leads to alienation on an interpersonal level, as well as animosity and aggressive attitudes toward other groups.

The more fearful or insecure people become, the more they rely on a fantasy bond with their in-group and project hostility toward the out-group. The animosity and increase in social distance lead to destructive unethical attitudes and behaviors toward those people with different beliefs and lifestyles. A frightened population can easily be led by an unscrupulous leader to perform acts against humanity that breach their moral codes. In this regard, the authors write about leadership, power, and society from an ethical perspective, noting the destructive authoritarian nature of both pathological leaders and their constituents. We consider society to be a largely defensive organization, involving a pooling of individual psychological defenses. Because of this negative aspect of society, one should be wary of the dangers of submission and conformity to such a system.

To summarize the dynamics of defense formation, early separation experiences and interpersonal pain lead to the development of self-protective defense mechanisms, and these defenses are reinforced as children gradually become aware of their mortality. Thereafter, people adapt to death anxiety by defensive denial, addictive propensities, and by restricting their lives to varying degrees.

It is important to emphasize that individuals respond to the dread of death on a preconscious or unconscious level by adopting defensive ways of living with little or no awareness (Arndt, Greenberg, Pyszczynski, & Solomon, 1997; R. Firestone, 1994b, 1997a). In the tradition of Otto Rank (1936/1972) and Ernest Becker (1973/1997), researchers in terror management theory were aware of the impact of existential dread on individual defense formation and culture, and went on to support this thesis with experimental evidence (S. Solomon, Greenberg, & Pyszczynski, 2000). As noted, the ways in which people defend themselves become imbedded within the conventional social patterns of a given society.

However, when a person relinquishes defenses, disrupts illusions of connection, becomes more individuated, freer, more personally successful and expands his or her life, unconscious fears about death and dying emerge into conscious awareness. Any experience that reminds an individual that he or she is fully alive and responsive or particularly valued or acknowledged will make him/her not only acutely conscious of his/her life but also of its eventual loss (R. Firestone, 1990a).

This book approaches the subject of ethics from a unique psychological perspective that is not meant to be judgmental or moralistic.[1] The authors are not prescribing, setting standards, or listing moral principles to be lived up to. We are not blaming, but accounting for destructive, unethical conduct. Our effort is directed toward explaining the source of this behavior, making clear its manifestations, and suggesting a treatment modality for coping with negative, acting-out behavior.

Our hope is that by understanding these dynamics and methods for altering unethical ways of living, people can transform themselves and develop better, more successful modes of relating. This morality is based on sound mental health principles. For example, we are not simply advising people to be generous or act kindly; we are teaching them that these actions help challenge negative attitudes toward self and thereby make people feel better emotionally. Living a life characterized by honesty, generosity, and love for those closest to us, and then extending those feelings outward has an optimal effect on one's sense of well-being. It is selfish in the best sense of the word.

This book explains the origin of psychological defenses in family interactions as well as existential concerns, and elaborates on the way in which the very defenses that initially protected us come to predispose alienation from ourselves and other people. It describes a multitude of toxic character traits and reveals their impact on children, couples, families, and nations. Unfortunately, much real damage is acted out in the name of love, family, God, and country. The authors contrast negative traits and behaviors that are commonplace in the world today with a description of an ideal ethical mode of living. We present a preliminary version of a scale to evaluate these toxic traits.

We describe how most people live a life of defensive equilibrium and how the withholding of positive personality traits operates to keep people apart. This dynamic helps to explain why people are refractory to a better, more fulfilling life of love, admiration, respect, warmth, and close companionship after they have been hurt. Most people profess to offer love and say that they want to be loved but few can tolerate a truly loving relationship.

We present a position that offers a hope of altering the destiny of humankind's unethical behavior through better psychological understanding and education. We elucidate the concept of the destructive voice process: a series of angry, critical thoughts toward self and others that is in essence the language of the defensive process (R. Firestone, 1988). This alien element of the personality is at the core of unethical behaviors. Insight into this negative thought process helps to identify destructive tendencies, understand their source, and promote actions to change damaging practices. Understanding the source of a person's aggressiveness in defending the fantasy bond and learning to cope with the voice process have strong implications for child-rearing and better mental health practices. Identifying destructive behaviors and faulty programming in family life and society, developing insight into the relationship between defenses and aggressive responses, and offering a method to counteract destructive trends constitute a challenge to what many people consider to be humankind's basically unethical nature.

Organization of the book

The Ethics of Interpersonal Relationships is divided into five sections. Part I, "An Innovative Approach to Ethics," describes the history and dimensions of the friendship circle, which serves as a living example of an ethical society and is the primary source of the personal accounts related throughout the book. The chapters also address questions such as, "What qualities would the ideal ethical individual possess?" and "What behaviors would one consider to be unethical in terms of their effects on individuals, their relationships, family life, and society-at-large?" The authors offer their views regarding these unethical behaviors, in particular those that are subtle, covert, or effectively disguised through mystification and hypocrisy to such an extent that many people remain unaware of their potential destructiveness.

Part II, "Coping with Unethical Ways of Living," explains how to deal most effectively with angry emotions and delineates a method for identifying and changing toxic personality traits. Mastering anger is a primary concern for a person who is attempting to live a life of integrity; therefore, considerable attention is devoted to elucidating both healthy and unhealthy manifestations of aggression. There is a discussion of the primal elements inherent in anger and a description of a methodology that can be used to identify and deal with destructive thoughts or voices that influence maladaptive aggressive behavior. In the chapter on toxic personality traits, there is a preliminary version of a scale that can be used to assess where an individual falls along a continuum of personality characteristics, with positive traits at one end and negative, toxic traits at the other.

In Part III, "Dynamics Underlying Unethical Behaviors," the chapters describe the key concepts of the authors' theoretical approach (1) the fantasy bond—an illusion of connection to the mother or primary caregiver; and (2) the voice process—a secondary defense—that supports the fantasy bond. We explain the origin of psychological defenses in the child's attempt to protect him/herself against interpersonal pain and existential anxiety and describe how these defenses predispose the acting out of aversive behaviors in intimate relationships and family life. The chapter "The Fantasy Bond in Couple and Family Relationships" explores manifestations of the fantasy bond in these relationship constellations and focuses on how partners tend to use each other for security and imagined safety, a process that gradually reduces each member's sense of independence and leads to a deterioration of feeling.

The chapters in Part IV, "Destructive Lifestyles," outline and describe the diverse ways in which individuals act out unethical behaviors in their everyday lives through addiction, withholding, self-denial, a victimized orientation, vanity, and narcissism. The authors focus on the negative effects that these behaviors have on one's mate, children, friends, and coworkers. Personal accounts from, and interviews with, people in the friendship circle provide examples of these psychologically debilitating behaviors and illustrate the destructive thoughts or voices that regulate them.

In Part V, "Ethical and Unethical Societal Practices," Chapters 12 and 13 address broad social issues including the ethics of business and politics, the nature of power, and toxic leadership. The authors offer a new perspective on the origins of ethnic warfare. We argue that war is the inevitable outcome of a leadership that plays on its constituents' fear of death to enlist them in carrying out aggressive, violent acts toward those who hold different religious beliefs or world views. Chapter 14 suggests the elements that contribute to living a truly ethical life on an everyday basis. There is an in-depth description of social, economic, and political life in the friendship circle. The fact that this three-generational experience in applied psychology has had a positive outcome in terms of increased harmony in interpersonal relating lends support to the authors' belief that people can alter damaging practices in their relationships and, on a broader scale, struggle for positive societal change as well.

An Appendix is presented that encapsulates the authors' point of view.

Note

1. The authors' approach to ethics is similar in many respects to that of the philosopher Peter Singer (1986/1994), who pointed out that the term "morality"

   Brings with it a particular, and sometimes inappropriate, resonance today. It suggests a stern set of duties that require us to subordinate our natural desires—and our sexual desires get particular emphasis here—in order to obey the moral law. A failure to fulfil our duty brings with it a heavy sense of guilt. Very often, morality is assumed to have a religious basis. These connotations of "morality" are features of a particular conception of ethics, one linked to the Jewish and Christian traditions, rather than an inherent feature of any ethical system. Ethics has no necessary connection with any particular religion, nor with religion in general (p. 5).

PART I

AN INNOVATIVE APPROACH
TO ETHICS

CHAPTER ONE

The friendship circle

By Robert W. Firestone

This is a community of some 100 or more persons—women, men, children—who seem to have achieved the better life together with a minimum of dogma, political authority, withdrawal, mysticism, insulation, isolation, dispossession of the goods and comforts of modern technology. There is no golden lie, no coercion, no constitution, no turning out at the expense of in, no turning in at the expense of out. It is not, nor claims to be, Utopia.

> Dr. Stuart Boyd (1982), *Analysis of the Friendship Circle*[1]

The first step in the evolution of ethics is a sense of solidarity with other human beings.

> Albert Schweitzer

Most people believe that ethics is inextricably tied to religion or spiritual considerations. Many feel that a society or social process without religion would lead to immorality, chaos, and destruction. Yet throughout history, religion and religious practices have led to antisocial, discriminatory behavior or even violence and bloodshed toward non-believers or different believers. The authors believe that ethics and an ethical society

3

can evolve separate from organized religious practices and belief systems about immortality or conceptions of an afterlife.[2] Furthermore, people living together, leading humane and ethical lives of personal service, generosity, and compassion toward one's fellows can reach inspiring and spiritual proportions.

The ethics of interpersonal relationships includes a wide range of ethical considerations that pertain to individual, couple, and family interactions as well as to group dynamics and the politics of nations. Although literally thousands of books have been written about ethics, values, and morals,[3] this book derives from a unique and moving personal experience between myself, my associates, my friends, and our families. The story behind this work begins with a brief description of our adventurous life into uncharted territories of the mind.

In the early 1970s, I was one of a number of mental health professionals who, with our spouses and friends, were involved in seminars and discussion groups in which we talked about our most intimate problems in life, expressed our deepest feelings and, in the process, formulated a new lifestyle based on the impact that this experience had on our understanding of psychology. This extended group psychotherapy endeavor not only transformed our personal lives, but provided considerable information about the emotional and behavioral factors that negatively affect a person's development as an individual.

My friends and I wanted to eliminate destructive acting-out behaviors in our relationships, particularly in regard to our children. We wished to end the perpetuation of psychological abuses through the generations. We not only hoped to stop the cycle of damage to each individual's self-esteem and self-concept, but also to further positive behaviors that were conducive to healthy, happy psychological functioning. Out of this psychological incubator in which people struggled with their core defenses came an implicit morality and a unique approach to ethical living. It was the beginning of what has amounted to an unusual, unintentional experiment in applied psychology that has spanned several generations. At the present time, this experiment has lasted for over thirty-five years.

Evolution of the friendship circle

It all began with a dream, a dream that so many people hold in their hearts yet rarely realize. It is a dream of a better life, a life of peace and enlightenment where people could live and work together with honesty, compassion, and generosity. Perhaps this dream was more vivid for those individuals who played a significant part in the formation of what eventually developed into an unintentional community. But even for them, there were only faint stirrings and little hope for their idea to materialize in the real world. Yet, through their shared struggle to live life honestly, they were able to catalyze each other to turn their dreams into reality.

The sharing of three diverse endeavors was central to the evolution of this group of friends. The first was the rebuilding of a sailing schooner which led to exciting sea voyages and eventually to a circumnavigation. The second was the mutual participation in several business enterprises. Both of these served as vehicles for the third and most important endeavor, which was a strong desire to understand themselves. Each person had a driving interest in his/her personal development and in that of his or her family members and friends. The essential ingredient that made all these endeavors possible was the honest communication with each other and the compassionate atmosphere that prevailed in the ongoing discussions.

Beginnings

What started out as a small number of spirited friends with no conscious intent to form a community or any structured way of living has grown into a kind of mini-society. They were intelligent people—lawyers, psychologists, engineers, teachers, and business people, a doctor, a scientist—who shared interests in philosophy, psychology, sailing, and travel. Each exhibited a powerful sense of individualism. The friends came from a variety of religious, racial, geographic, socioeconomic, and educational backgrounds.

The desire for honest and forthright communication has been the defining characteristic of this social milieu from its inception. At first, talks about personal issues and life in general would spring up in conversations characterized by serious thought and a good deal of humor. These early talks took place in living rooms, campgrounds, baseball fields, and hotel rooms, generally occurring at times of leisure.

The marathon weekends

During the late 60s and early 70s, encounter groups, leadership seminars, and marathons were commonplace in the practice of psychotherapy. My associates and friends expressed an interest in participating in weekend retreats away from the city to further understand themselves and facilitate deep emotional expression. I anticipated that the prolonged contact would help break down defensive barriers and allow people to reach a deeper sense of themselves. During these meetings, which lasted for as long as eight or ten hours at a stretch, participants became more open with one another. As the atmosphere grew progressively more accepting and sensitive, many members of the group reached a depth of feeling they had never experienced before.

As each person told his or her story, others identified in some way with the painful childhood memories that were revealed. I was struck by the unmistakable commonality of experience. The degree of anguish reflected by all of the participants perplexed me. Were their families essentially different from those of other people? Was my family any different? What about my own children? The flood of ideas and feelings was disquieting, yet the thoughts persisted. In the future, I would come to understand how these pieces of the puzzle fit together.

After each meeting, the participants felt relaxed and had clear insights about how their suppressed feelings affected their current lives. As a typical weekend progressed, a transformation took place in the participants. People's faces, initially etched with stress and anxiety and lined with the cumulative effect of character defenses, began to change. By the end of the weekend retreat, the same faces were flushed with feeling and aliveness. Afterward, many people expressed appreciation for what they felt had been a meaningful experience. We were all aware that during these weekends, we had been living an entirely different lifestyle.

However, upon returning home, most of us gradually lost this edge of feeling and communion with ourselves and became defended again. We were disappointed to have reverted to "normal" life in such a short time. It was clear that during the weekend marathons, we had become emotionally alive, whereas in our everyday lives we regressed to a familiar, less feeling existence, characterized to varying degrees by role-playing, toughness, and other emotionally cut-off states. To a certain extent we had lost touch with ourselves and with our real experience, a fact that we would have been unaware of were it not for the unique emotional experiences during the weekends away.

In an effort to preserve the authentic way of being we had experienced during those weekends, we began to change our routine, habitual lifestyles. We discussed these changes openly in group meetings. We benefited from the feedback we received from friends and family members; we often heard valuable information about how our defenses were hurting others as well as ourselves.

Over the years, my friends and I gradually gave up many of our addictive habit patterns and defensive styles of interacting with our mates and family members. As we became increasingly more responsive to our own feelings, we developed more sensitivity and compassion for others. Any dishonesty or intrusiveness that had been present in previous interactions was diminished to a considerable extent. Motivated by our experiences in the marathons and other group interactions, the participants in the friendship circle have, to a large degree, achieved the goal of bringing the warmth and aliveness of those weekends into their everyday lives.

The young people's discussion group

Still another source of our insights and discoveries was a discussion group with our teenagers. In 1971, we discovered that several of our children were becoming involved in using drugs that were potentially dangerous. We were concerned with their overall emotional well-being. As a result, we asked one of the fathers, a businessman who had an unusually good rapport with the teenagers, to lead a discussion group for them. Interestingly, even though many members of the group were professional psychologists, we chose a nonprofessional to lead the group because of his sensitivity and respect for the young people.

The eleven children (who were between 10 and 13 years old at the time) met once a week to talk about their thoughts and feelings, their goals in life, their relationships with their parents, and their emerging sexual feelings. After talking together for a short time and taking a stand against drugs, the youngsters found that they had other issues they wanted to resolve, and invited their parents to these talks. It was sad when our children first started talking to us because we became aware of many ways that we had hurt them. Even though we were psychologically sophisticated people, we had had little insight into the true pain of our children until they were able to speak in that group. As one of the parents, I felt a deep sadness, like no other, when my children exposed their hurt. I was grateful to my group of friends for the unique opportunity to address these issues.

The honest exchange of perceptions and expression of feelings during these meetings between parents and children gradually dissolved the generational boundaries. Parental roles began to be discarded and the adolescents related to their parents on a more equal basis. As the young people became friends with each other and openly related to their parents, they challenged the hypercritical, judgmental attitudes they had grown up with, spoke out against condescending, disrespectful treatment, and began to ask for real acknowledgment and respect from the adults in their lives.

Later, these teenagers became involved in the sailing adventure as crew, acquiring their own power and expertise during the journey and, as a result, became self-sufficient adults who contributed significantly to the community. Now thirty years later, they are still friends and work together on a daily basis.

The circumnavigation

In 1972, one of the couples in the friendship circle was getting a divorce, and the husband was interested in buying a boat to live on. One of the friends suggested that all of us chip in and buy a larger boat that the newly separated husband could live on, one that we could all work on and sail together. We soon found an unfinished, eighty-foot staysail schooner, the Vltava, which we bought for forty thousand dollars, the total savings we had at the time. We threw ourselves into the project of finishing the yacht. At the same time, as many of the friends became skilled in sailing, we began to extend our boundaries. After overcoming our fears and testing the schooner in voyages to San Francisco, Mexico, and an ocean crossing to Hawaii, we decided to sail the Vltava around the world. During the 17-month journey, we visited Mexico, Costa Rica, Panama, the

West Indies, Miami, New York City, the Azores, Tangiers, Europe, Africa, India, the Philippines, Hong Kong, Japan, and Hawaii before returning home.

During the circumnavigation, the permanent crew was made up of our teenage children, who were 14 to 19 years old when the voyage began. The adults would join the trip as their work permitted. Conditions on the boat were crowded and primitive. There was fresh water only for drinking, baths were drawn from the sea in buckets, and we used dry ice in place of refrigeration for our perishables. In spite of the hardships, we loved the experience. For many of us, life aboard the ship was the best time of our lives.

We learned to live together. There were ongoing talks where people were free to bring up any topic—psychological, philosophical, or practical. The few squabbles that did arise were addressed and resolved in these talks. Living closely under a multitude of sea conditions and dangers, we learned to face adversity and work together. And from this shared venture, our friendships deepened.[4] When the Vltava returned to the States, there were many marriages and soon many new small faces appeared on the scene. Interestingly, some of our adult children later married one another and those of us who started out as friends and acquaintances became in-laws and family members. In addition, the sailing odyssey that began with the Vltava thirty years ago led to another circumnavigation, more than 200,000 miles of ocean experience, and to new and larger vessels.

Coming home

We loved life aboard the Vltava and, as with the marathon weekends, we wanted to continue the adventure of sharing life together while at home. We wanted to work together in shared business ventures and live more closely as well. Soon we started three small business enterprises, people moved closer geographically and socialized more, and eventually we bought an apartment house where many people chose to live. All along, we were making new friends, while sailing and conducting business, talking openly about our personal lives and enjoying the camaraderie. Those who were drawn to the friendliness, enjoyed the shared activities, and were receptive to the honest communication became life-long friends.

The circle of friends now numbers over 120 members. Several businesses grew into multimillion dollar corporations and expanded the wealth of the participants. Personal and group talks became a regular weekly occurrence and included such subjects as plans for the businesses, proposed sailing adventures, living arrangements, finances, and, most importantly, our personal lives and the well-being of our children. We were concerned that what had hurt us in our psychological development not be passed on. From our talks, an implicit morality developed with an emphasis on being inclusive, compassionate, and generous, and a negative loading on behaviors that were hostile, manipulative, dishonest, prejudiced, vain, status-oriented, intrusive, or selfish.

In spite of all of its positive attributes, this environment has never claimed to be a Utopia, nor does it spare the individual from suffering. Indeed, the process of overcoming neuroses and psychological defenses fosters a basic dilemma because overcoming inner demons leaves one face-to-face with the agonizing existential realities of aloneness, sickness, and death.

In the process of growing and developing personally, these people challenged and altered well-established core defenses, thereby changing basic ways of perceiving themselves and the world around them. These changes entailed years of conflict and personal struggle as each person fought against his or her fundamental resistances. Since no search for truth, personal growth, or major character change can occur without experiencing considerable anxiety, the early days of the group were fraught with painful emotions, instability, distrust, and paranoia. People who are struggling to work out their problems and challenging core defenses are not necessarily friendly and cause each other a certain amount of suffering. Well-meaning people, long-time friends, felt hurt when their honest responses or feedback were misunderstood or received with outright hostility. There was fear as participants looked beyond their conventional views and challenged the status quo in couples and families. Recognizing pathological elements in nuclear family life broke down the idealization process, threatened the fantasy bond, and left people feeling frightened, temporarily disoriented, and alone. It was also painful when people held on to addictive behaviors and routines that destroyed their dignity and limited their lives. In this challenging atmosphere, people suffered when others backed away from honest disclosure, went against themselves and best interests, and became distant. It was hard not to become cynical. There have also been external pressures. Many people in the larger society are prejudiced against those who lead a different lifestyle such as ours. Because they do not understand it, they often do not trust it.

It is true that most of our friends are generally happy and excited about life. There has been much fun, travel, adventure, and success in our lives, but real life is both painful and exhilarating: it includes aging, sickness, deterioration—it includes dying. In coming to love and care for one another, our friends have become increasingly vulnerable emotionally to these misfortunes. We have lost precious people who were close to us and that has been very painful. Caring more about people has exposed us to the pain of life on a daily basis. This problem is both qualitative and quantitative as there are so many people to be concerned about. On any given day, there is always both good and bad news to respond to. This is basically a life of meaning and struggle, but a worthwhile life full of everything that is human—both joy and pain. In an atmosphere of honesty, compassion, deep feelings, and an ethical framework, life's painful issues can be effectively faced.

Further developments

In 1979, I was asked by this group of people to close my psychotherapy practice and devote myself full-time as a participant-observer and consultant to this new lifestyle. In consenting, my goal was to investigate those aspects of daily living that are conducive to good mental health—that is, the attitudes, actions, activities, and conditions that would enhance people's lives. I wanted to explore the dimensions of a meaningful life that my friends, colleagues, and I had created, gather the relevant data, and discover whether or not people could put their principles and values into practice on an everyday basis. More personally, I wished to write about my observations of the new lifestyle, the morality it predisposed, and its impact on my own life and ideas.

As the years have passed, we have found ourselves talking on a deeper level and even more candidly about our relationships and interactions with our children. In these discussions, the right of each person to speak his or her mind freely and to express deep feelings has been cherished and protected. Participation in the talks has enabled people to work together in a harmonious way and the normal, routine bickering of everyday life has diminished to a considerable degree. The process of maintaining a forum for the exchange of perceptions and feelings, without fear of retaliation for what one has said, has made it possible for these individuals to live together with a minimum of friction. Over a period of many years, a set of implied values began to emerge from these discussions. Based on a deeper understanding of what had hurt us in childhood, these values were supported by ongoing efforts to remove unnecessary obstacles to straightforward communication.

Currently we are striving to perpetuate our way of living, our values, and to further integrate these principles into our daily lives. We want to preserve the emotional environment that has sustained us so well, we want our children and grandchildren to grow up and flourish in it. To a large extent, it appears that we have succeeded in overcoming the destructive effects of our own childhoods, and have interrupted the negative defensive process that is generally passed on to succeeding generations. Although no one deliberately set out to establish a new way of living, it is now a reality. For however long it may last, it is gratifying to know that a place exists, not merely in a dream but in reality, where so many people share life in harmony, with a high level of honesty, deep feeling, and concern for others and their happiness.

Early discoveries

> How the community lives raises some very interesting issues for moral and ethical philosophy but as far as "conventional" morality is concerned it's no contest—truth versus hypocrisy; manifest improvement in happiness and stability versus anxiety and broken, hating relationships (Boyd, 1982).

My involvement with this group of friends over the past 35 years has strengthened my realization that people's natural strivings toward growth and individuation emerge within a positive social structure, the dimensions of which can be made explicit in a way that might well benefit others. During our longitudinal study of these individuals, my associates and I have assembled and documented considerable information about the emotional damage that individuals sustain as children and how their defenses and reactions to stress perpetuate their suffering throughout their lives. Our investigations have led to conclusions regarding both the type and quality of experience that is conducive to the well-being of individuals and therefore growth-enhancing, as well as those experiences that are destructive and limiting.

For example, we discovered the importance of honesty in personal communications and noted that mixed messages and duplicitous communication have a significantly negative effect on a child's mental health. Damaging a person's sense of reality is extremely harmful to his/her development and therefore becomes a moral issue. Conversely, parents' emotional honesty and integrity foster a sense of trust and an open attitude toward life in their children.

We learned that most people do not want what they say they want and that they are refractory to a better life. Paradoxically, they cannot tolerate their dreams becoming a reality and unconsciously work against their best interests. The majority of the participants in the friendship circle found that they had difficulty accepting warmer, richer emotional lives than they had experienced as children. We found that people establish a defensive equilibrium as children in relation to emotional deprivation and stress in their developmental years and later react adversely to experiences that are more positive. Perversely, they may act out destructively toward people who threaten their defenses by contradicting their early experiences.

Another significant discovery was that most people tend to unconsciously recreate the painful circumstances of their childhood in their current relationships. To achieve this, they often manipulate those close to them by projecting negative characteristics onto them, distorting their intentions, or provoking negative reactions from them.

We also observed that many people have difficulty with their anger. In the process of developing themselves personally, these friends achieved insight into the sources of their anger and learned effective ways of dealing with aggression. They recognized that anger is a natural response to frustration and that it is proportional to the degree of a person's wanting. In that sense, anger is an irrational emotion; the more we want something, the more we are angry at any impediments, regardless of rational considerations.

People also learned the value of experiencing their angry feelings unconditionally, without practical or moral implications. On the other hand, how they expressed anger outwardly was subject to reality concerns and ethical consideration. The friends recognized that when they avoided and rationalized angry feelings, they tended to internalize these emotions and were more likely to be self-attacking or hostile. As Freud suggested: "A thought murder a day keeps the doctor away," meaning that by accepting our angry feelings uncritically, we would remain free of repression and subsequent psychological symptom formation. A thought murder is innocent in that it harms no one, whereas a simple act of sarcasm may cause pain to another.

In learning to express their anger in more appropriate ways, people were better able to refrain from playing the victim, acting as a martyr, expressing paranoid attitudes, controlling through weakness, or engaging in other passive-aggressive behaviors that are destructive. Based on their childhood experiences, many individuals were cognizant that perhaps the most damaging people in family life are those who act out self-destructive, microsuicidal, or actual suicidal behaviors (R. Firestone, 2000; R. Firestone & Seiden, 1987). They were painfully aware that entire families can be controlled and manipulated by these individuals to the detriment of all persons involved.

In addition, people dealt openly with their competitive feelings. They learned to distinguish between irrational competitiveness (where one's focus is not on the goal or person being pursued, but only on competing or winning) and genuine competitiveness (incidental competitive feelings that arise in the course of pursuing one's goals). They observed that when they retreated from experiencing their competitive feelings, they tended to hurt themselves psychologically and often became more hostile toward others.

From observing couples in the friendship circle, we noted that there were often negative trends in behavior following major life events such as marriage, buying a home, or having a child. It appeared that, at critical times, people were terrified of achievements in life that signified full maturity and adulthood because they symbolized separation from parental figures and movement toward old age and death (R. Firestone, 1985). Therefore, events that are expected to bring people happiness and fulfillment can often have the opposite effect on a person's sense of well-being.

There have also been numerous discussions about problematic issues within contemporary society. The friends were aware that in family life there was a tendency to elevate a family's particular set of values over those of another and to express critical, condescending attitudes toward outsiders. These attitudes set up a tension between "us and them" that was characteristic of the culture at large. Many of us talked about stereotyping and the destructiveness of racial, religious, or cultural superiority. The friends objected to prejudice and status, and to material measures of success and achievement. They discussed the destructive use of power and favored humanistic concerns. They believed that a moral life is determined by an individual's daily existence rather than by intangible abstract principles. In the process of putting their own ideals and principles into practice, these people have extended these personal concerns outward, offering what they could to anyone who crossed their path.

Based on the lessons I have learned within the friendship circle, it is my contention that people's problems in relating to one another and unethical behaviors in interpersonal relationships, can be understood and transformed through dedication and understanding. Over the years, the participants in the friendship circle have worked with me to produce more than thirty documentary films for the psychology profession, and several for the general public, revealing this process of self-inquiry and personal development. In the films, these friends expose personal problems and work on improving their lives with both ideational content and depth of feeling.[5] This book is a continuation of their contribution and reflects their wish to further share their experiences. Many personal examples included in the text came from their group discussions and interactions. I am forever grateful for the openness, honesty, and forthrightness of the men, women, and children who have participated and continue to live this lifestyle of integrity.

Notes

1. In 1982, Dr. Stuart Boyd, clinical psychologist and liberal arts scholar, to whom this book is dedicated, visited the friends for a period of three months. He recorded his impressions of these people in a daily journal and subsequently wrote an analysis comparing their way of

life to the ideas, dreams, and efforts of others throughout history, to create the "good society" and a better life for human beings. This chapter and Chapter 14 contain excerpts from his journal and analysis.

2. See Richard Kilburg's (2006) descriptive account of the historical development of ideas regarding the origins of morality, ranging from Socrates, Aristotle, Plato, and Confucius, who all "argued passionately that morality and honor in the world rest on the shoulders of people of virtue" (p. 214), through Augustine who taught that "the laws of God as delineated in Holy Scripture constitute the only true map to human goodness and right behavior" (p. 214). In contemporary life, there has been an "emergence of 'neo-classic virtue advocates' who are once again challenging what could be called the 'religious rule-givers.' Psychological research and practice are now mirroring these developments in philosophy" (p. 215). This latter movement has also been described by Derek Parfit (1984/1994).

3. There are far too many books dealing with the topic of ethics and ethical behavior in relation to mental health issues, developmental and social psychology, and psychotherapy to mention here. However, a few important and timely works can be listed: *The Social Psychology of Prosocial Behavior* by John F. Dovidio, Jane A. Piliavin, David A. Schroeder, and Louis A. Penner (2006); *Soul Searching: Why Psychotherapy Must Promote Moral Responsibility* by William J. Doherty (1995); *Concern for Others: A New Psychology of Conscience and Morality* by Tom Kitwood (1990); *The Values of Psychotherapy* by Jeremy Holmes and Richard Lindley (1989); *The Mystery of Goodness and the Positive Moral Consequences of Psychotherapy* by Mary W. Nicholas (1994); and *The Modes and Morals of Psychotherapy* (2nd ed.) by Perry London (1964).

4. See the Los Angeles Times article by Beverly Beyette (1978), "Vltava's Voyage to Understanding," and a documentary film, *Voyage to Understanding* (Parr, 1983).

5. These films are available from the Glendon Association (www.glendon.org).

CHAPTER TWO

A concept of the ethical personality

Human dignity cannot be achieved in the field of technology, in which human beings are so expert. It can be achieved only in the field of ethics, and ethical achievement is measured by the degree in which our actions are governed by compassion and love, not by greed and aggressiveness.

Arnold Toynbee (Gage, 1976, p. 368)

The simple fact is that the ethical cannot be detached from reality, and consequently continual progress in learning to appreciate reality is a necessary ingredient in ethical action.

Dietrich Bonhoeffer (1949/1955, p. 360)

What is involved in living an ethical life? There are countless ways of addressing the subject of morals and ethics, and each person must seek his or her own guidelines.[1] In this chapter, we will attempt to delineate the personality traits and behaviors that we feel would characterize the "ideal" ethical individual. This approach to ethics is psychologically based and, therefore, ethical behaviors are those that have positive rather than negative effects on a person's sense of well-being. These behaviors counter people's self-critical, self-depreciating attitudes, increase their self-esteem, and tend to improve their adjustment. The values and ethical standards described in this work are derived from a sensitive understanding of human nature and an awareness of the destructive forces that impinge on a healthy psychological development. The attempt to live according to one's ideals and principles is a difficult, yet noble endeavor. As Michael Josephson (2004) succinctly put it:

> Ethics is not for wimps ... . It's not easy to be honest when it might be costly ... . It's not easy to stand up for our beliefs and still respect different viewpoints ... . It's not easy to stop feeling like a victim, to resist cynicism ... . It's not easy to be consistently kind, to think of others first ... to give the benefit of the doubt. It's not easy to be grateful or to give without concern for reward or gratitude ... . That's why it's such a lofty goal (pp. 1–2).

Living a principled life involves a fundamental choice between striving to lead an honest life of feeling, meaningful activity and compassion for oneself and others or settling for a lifestyle characterized by maintaining illusions, defenses, and deadening habit patterns. Living without self-deception, fantasized connections, and self-protective mechanisms necessarily leaves a person facing a state of uncertainty and ambiguity. For this reason, most people cling to security behaviors and rely on fantasy bonds that offer form over substance in their personal relationships.

Cursed with the conscious awareness of the existential realities of aloneness and death, humans are a frightened species. They are reluctant to face the fact that life is terminal, that anguish and suffering are inherent in the human condition, and that their relations with others are often painful. As S. Freud (1930/1961) observed:

> We are threatened with suffering from three directions: from our own body, which is doomed to decay and dissolution and which cannot even do without pain and anxiety as warning signals; from the external world, which may rage against us with overwhelming and merciless forces of destruction; and finally from our relations with other men (p. 77).

The way that people learn to cope with these painful issues largely determines the course of their psychological, moral, and spiritual life. Because of their unique anticipation of death's finality, people must choose between living a life of denial and self-protection or remaining open and vulnerable, thereby maintaining a feeling for life in spite of its painful realities. If they shy away from these existential issues, they lose feeling for themselves and others.

However, this is not a philosophical decision where the advantages and disadvantages are being carefully considered from a mature, rational mind-set. This is a choice that a child faces early in life, often as early as age three or four. The extent of psychological damage to the developing child and his or her need for defense formation combine with emotional immaturity to prevent the child from being aware of the conflict or of the fact that a choice is being made. According to Ernest Becker (1973/1997):

> There can be no clearcut victory or straightforward solution of the existential dilemma he [the child] is in. It is his problem right from the beginning almost of his life, yet he is only a child to handle it ... . What we call the child's character is a *modus vivendi* achieved after the most unequal struggle any animal has to go through; a struggle that the child can never really understand because he doesn't know what is happening to him, why he is responding as he does, or what is really at stake in the battle (pp. 28–29).

The greater the pain in the early years before the child's realization of death's inevitability, the more elaborate the defenses he or she will develop (Mikulincer, Florian, Birnbaum & Malishkevich, 2002).[2] Nonetheless, even children who were raised under ideal conditions would still develop defenses in relation to the death issue. Because of both interpersonal frustrations and existential terrors, most children turn away from the basic strivings essential to living an ethical life. Defenses formed early in life predispose attitudes and behaviors that are antithetical to the ability to consistently live by one's values and ideals.

The choice to live a relatively undefended and ethical lifestyle presents each person with an essential paradox. On the one hand, people who are not repressed and remain close to their feelings are better able to cope in life. They are able to respond with appropriate affect to both good and bad personal experiences. Because they are open, they are able to tolerate sadness, anger, competitive or other "unacceptable" feelings, and therefore are not compelled to act out these feelings on others. These people tend to have a positive influence on family and friends. Moreover, living less defensively and according to one's values and principles tends to be counter-depressive.[3]

However, responding emotionally to real events in life rather than retreating to a self-protective posture makes one more susceptible to real suffering. Freud spoke about this dilemma when he noted that curing a patient of his neurosis left him face to face with the horrors of real life.

We have found that "emotionally healthy, mature individuals are acutely sensitive to events in their lives that impinge on their sense of well-being or that adversely affect the people closest to them" (R. Firestone, 1988, p. 259). Pursuing a life of integrity requires remaining vulnerable to all aspects of living—sadness as well as joy, pain as well as comfort, fear as well as courage, insecurity as well as confidence. It also involves making a commitment to an ongoing search for personal meaning and transcendent goals (R. Firestone, Firestone, & Catlett, 2003). With full recognition of this basic dilemma, in this chapter we will attempt to portray the characteristics of an ethical person and the challenges that one must face in order to live a principled existence.

The challenge of living a life of integrity

What are the prerequisites for becoming a person of integrity? People who are honest and trustworthy would represent themselves accurately to others as well as to themselves. However, to achieve this level of integrity requires considerable self-knowledge. The pursuit of self-knowledge and self-understanding implies a willingness to recognize aspects of one's personality that are unpleasant or destructive as well as accepting one's positive traits. Ideally one would choose to alter negative characteristics rather than attack oneself for one's weaknesses or shortcomings.

Although honesty is an ethical ideal, many people are hampered in their capacity to be genuinely honest. When people are hurt early in life they tend to turn against their wants and needs and, as a result, are unable to be honest about their motivations. Later, they have difficulty trusting or even tolerating a better life or allowing for the satisfaction of their wants and needs. Real accomplishment and successes can interrupt fantasy processes and cause distress. For this reason many people unconsciously avoid success; others dishonestly rationalize their failures, blaming them on external circumstances or other people.

When people fail to pursue their goals, they cannot communicate honestly about them. If they deny having a specific want or desire, they are being dishonest because people's wants and desires are a fundamental part of their identity as human beings. On the other hand, if they formulate a goal but are not taking the appropriate actions, they are also being dishonest. In either case, their communications will necessarily be duplicitous and confusing to other people.

Another challenge in maintaining one's integrity comes from living within a society that is largely dishonest and that discriminates against certain groups of people. Societal pressures strongly reinforce tendencies to be self-protective, secretive, or indirect in one's communications. Social bias, prejudice, and stereotyping have resulted in disenfranchisement and stigmatization of many groups of people in our culture, making it difficult for them to directly express their wants and desires or to honestly state their thoughts and opinions. As Babbitt (1996) pointed out, "The problem with the accounts of personal integrity discussed so far ... is a failure to recognize that some social structures are of the wrong sort altogether for some individuals to be able to pursue personal integrity" (p. 117).

Characteristics of the ideal individual from an ethical perspective

> The person who lives according to practical wisdom attains *eudaimonia* [spiritual contentment], and is accounted virtuous, where the virtues are such traits of character as courage, temperance, liberality, justice and honesty. A person in whom these virtues are cultivated is said by Aristotle to therefore have the special virtue of magnanimity, the possession of a "great soul" (Grayling, 2003, p. 33).

What behaviors and personality traits would characterize the "ideal" or truly ethical individual? Obviously, there is no such person; no one is perfect, yet all of us can improve and develop ourselves. Many of the personal qualities described below represent fundamental human virtues that have been elucidated by ancient philosophers as well as modern philosophers and ethicists.[4]

Personal integrity

Integrity has been defined as: "Firm adherence to a code ... incorruptibility ... a quality or state of being complete or undivided" (Woolf, 1981, p. 595). Being true to oneself and one's values contributes to an inner state or feeling of being unified, whole, and integrated. Being in touch with one's self on a feeling level is fundamental to this sense of being integrated. Such a person tends to be at ease with him/herself, whether alone or in the company of others.

According to Boss (2004), Gostick and Telford (2003), and other ethicists, integrity is a unifying principle, a basic disposition overriding the other virtues. As Boss has noted, "Without integrity, we are not truly virtuous because there is still disharmony within ourselves" (p. 411). Furthermore, "rather than keeping their innermost self intact by use of immature defense mechanisms and resistance, virtuous people organize their innermost self based on integrity" (p. 412). In discussing integrity from both an ethical and a psychological perspective, Babbitt (1996) proposed that:

> Personal integrity [can] be defined in terms of paths of development, where the determination of the right sorts of paths of development depends on moral imagination, on general beliefs about what *ought* to be possible for human beings in terms of autonomy, self-respect, and dignity (p. 105).

Babbitt went on to comment that a high level of self-differentiation and emotional emancipation from one's' family-of-origin are prerequisites for developing a high level of integrity: "A notion of being 'true to oneself' cannot by itself explain intuitions about personal integrity for people who are not individuated as people at all" (p. 114).

Rogers (1961) contended that integrity (or inner congruence) occurs when "the feelings ... [a person] is experiencing are available to his awareness, and he is able to live these feelings, be them, and able to communicate them if appropriate" (p. 61).[5] Ellyn Bader (personal communication, 1999) described the internal fortitude required to attain this level of integrity and personal honesty as comparable to the courage and bravery one would need to climb Mount Everest. She observed that in an intimate relationship especially, one must be brave enough to thoroughly know oneself, including one's deepest self-doubts and inner demons, and courageous enough to directly communicate these feelings to one's partner.

Although integrity is considered an overarching virtue in many philosophical systems, in Peterson and Seligman's (2004) classification of character strengths, integrity is a disposition that is subsumed under "Courage." Being courageous is dependent on "emotional strengths that involve the exercise of will to accomplish goals in the face of opposition, external or internal" (p. 29).[6]

Honesty

Honesty is closely related to the concept of integrity. It is defined by Webster's Dictionary as "Fairness and straightforwardness of conduct ... adherence to the facts: sincerity ... uprightness of character or action" (Woolf, 1981, p. 544). On the other hand, philosophers have stressed the fact that honesty is not a universal or absolute moral duty. Moreover, being dishonest can be a virtue in unusual circumstances. During World War II, for instance, a number of individuals in occupied European countries acted according to a value superordinate to that of honesty, and lied to German Gestapo officers to protect Jewish families hiding in their homes. With respect to this ethic, the philosopher Comte-Sponville (1996/2001) contended that truthfulness "is less important than justice, compassion, and generosity and certainly less important than love; to put it another way, truthfulness, as love of truth, is less important than love of one's fellowman, or charity" (p. 204).

In discussing moral dilemmas involving indirect forms of dishonesty or lying through omission, Comte-Sponville posed the question:

> Should one tell a dying person the truth of his condition? ...
> Telling a dying person the truth, if he inquires and is able to
> bear it, can be a way of helping him to die lucidly (to lie to a

dying person, is, as Rilke says, to rob him of his death); it can help him die as he lived and wanted to live, in peace and dignity and truth, not amid illusions and denials (pp. 204–205).

Many people who are truthful in most areas of their life are dishonest in others. For example, some people who claim to be basically honest cheat on their income tax, break the speed limit, tell "little white lies" to avoid conflict, or shop the Internet during working hours.

What do truthfulness and honesty demand of us? Dietrich Bonhoeffer (1949/1955) has asserted that "Telling the truth … is not solely a matter of moral character; it is also a matter of correct appreciation of real situations and of serious reflection upon them … . Telling the truth is, therefore, something which must be learnt" (p. 359).

As we have seen, life presents all of us with serious moral dilemmas in relation to "telling the truth" as well as to adapting our other values and ideals to the reality of specific situations without violating our basic principles. Philosophers have debated the moral pros and cons of these conflictual situations for centuries.[7] However, the kind of honesty we are describing here is more personal than intellectual, more psychological than philosophical, and more heartfelt than thought out. It applies most directly to interpersonal communications in close relationships.

Lack of duplicity

Integrity also implies congruence between an individual's words and actions. Individuals who live a life of integrity are not duplicitous; they place a high value on making their behaviors correspond to their stated goals and priorities. People who are not duplicitous do not mislead or confuse others with double messages. They are not hypocritical, preaching one thing and doing something else. Their posture, facial expression, and other bodily cues are also congruent with their verbal statements. They do not utilize positive statements to cover over hostile, negative feelings. If they notice themselves making an insincere or false statement about their intentions or goals, they experience some degree of discomfort or distress. Their subjective reaction in these situations may be likened to that of a musician who winces when he or she accidentally hits a wrong note.

Research shows that in marriages where verbal communications contradict nonverbal cues, partners report a high degree of marital dissatisfaction (Canary, Cupach & Messman, 1995; Gottman, 1979). In these studies, partners were observed contradicting their positive statements with nonverbal negative messages through frowns, sneers, expressions of disgust, a tense or impatient tone of voice, inattention, and leaning away from, rather than toward, the other person. In parent-child relations, double messages can be even more devastating (Bateson, 1972). The greater the discrepancy between the manifest content of a parent's communication and its underlying meaning, the greater the potential for disturbance in the child. Mixed messages damage one's sense of reality, interfere with reality testing, and, as such, play a role in psychopathology.

Living ethically implies that people make every effort to make their words accurately reflect their internal feeling state. This effort is rewarding in terms of increasing a person's overall mental health as well as favorably affecting loved ones.

Consistency and reliability

Consistency and reliability are traits that are manifested by an evenness in temperament, non-melodramatic responses to events in one's life, and the lack of erratic swings in one's mood or state of mind. People who live with integrity feel at harmony within themselves, and this inner peace of mind enables them to maintain an evenness and regularity in their mood and responses to others. A reliable parent, for example, offers his or her children responses that are consistent and contingent on meeting their needs, thereby permitting them to develop a secure attachment with that parent and a basic trust in life (Main & Hesse, 1990; D. Siegel & Hartzell, 2003). Reliability also evokes trust in other people, which is important in sharing projects and working toward a common goal.

Directness and willingness to self-disclose

Direct communication and self-disclosure are important elements in maintaining friendships and close relationships. People who have the courage to directly state their thoughts, opinions, feelings, and beliefs are more trustworthy than those who are indirect, inward, or secretive about their inner experience or perceptions.

We are not talking about unnecessarily punitive frankness that serves no purpose but to hurt other people's feelings. What we are describing is a more appropriate or positive form of honesty, one that involves dealing with troublesome issues directly rather than allowing them to develop into grudges. In conveying one's true feelings, there must be as high a value placed on practicing kindness and compassion as there is on honesty and forthrightness. This process involves communicating the necessary information to keep the people closest to us informed about issues that are important in our lives, and in theirs. Being direct and revealing of oneself involves taking full responsibility for one's feelings. For example, one would not complain or "dump" one's problems on an interested listener.

Being indirect or vague in how one expresses one's thoughts and feelings is confusing and tends to alienate people. Passive brooding, sulking, sarcasm, ridicule, or gossip hurt relationships and create feelings of resentment and reactive anger. Generally speaking, the secrecy and deception that permeate many relationships in the larger society fragment and often erode a person's belief in the veracity of his or her perceptions and subjective experience. Laing (1976) underscored the consequences of these breaches in the ethic of truthfulness:

> I'm sure that truth deprivation can wreak as much havoc to some people as vitamin deprivation. We *need* truth. Truth and reality seem sometimes virtually indistinguishable, sometimes separable, but always most intimately related … . To live correctly, my genes need to know what is the case (p. 145).

Nondefensiveness

Nondefensiveness is a personality trait that is essential to maintaining an ethical lifestyle. It implies an objective, balanced perspective in relation to oneself and others. People are defensive when they respond to feedback or criticism by becoming angry, punitive, retaliatory, insulated, or by manipulating through falling apart emotionally. This defensive process limits a person's chance for personal development and growth and adversely affects others.

Conversely, a person who responds to inputs by weighing personal information objectively, evaluating whether criticisms are valid or not and acting appropriately, can be described as open or nondefensive. The proper response to criticism is, after careful scrutiny, to either reject the information if it proves to be false or to face up to one's faults or inadequacies if the criticism is valid. It is never functional to attack oneself; it is far better to accept the criticism and resolve to make the appropriate changes. When one is turned against oneself, there is little chance for development. Being nondefensive not only improves one's adjustment but significantly affects how well people get along with others.

Most people are overly sensitive to information about themselves in certain areas, while being open to feedback about other subjects. In close relationships, people quickly learn which topics to exclude from their communications because of the other person's angry or hurt reactions. This predisposes withdrawal in the other person or can lead to escalation of conflict.

Defensiveness in the workplace seriously limits productivity. Both managers and employees who react angrily or retaliate after receiving realistic feedback about their performance can be intimidating. Their negative reactions effectively shut off the lines of communication that are necessary for the smooth operation of a business enterprise.

Defensiveness also manifests itself in emotional resistance or being stubborn about changing negative traits. Openness encompasses attitudes and actions that go beyond simple receptivity to feedback and implies having a genuine interest in learning and challenging one's self-protective, limiting behaviors and routine habit patterns. People who are open and nondefensive tend to be freer and more willing to take appropriate risks in life. They feel motivated to expand their boundaries and broaden their range of experiences. They are accepting of a changing identity rather than a fixed identity.

With respect to ethics, people who are defensive are both self-destructive and offensive to others. Defensiveness is one of the most insidious character traits that disrupt harmony between people.

Love and compassion

So far as ethics is concerned, where love of one's neighbor, affection, kindness and compassion live, we find that ethical conduct is automatic. Ethically wholesome actions arise naturally in the context of compassion (Dalai Lama, 1999, p. 131).

Love implies internal feelings of affection and concern as well as external manifestations of kindness, sensitivity, thoughtfulness, physical affection, and respect. It is unreasonable to describe a relationship as loving when these observable manifestations are absent or when they are in fact contradicted. Actions that are disrespectful, dishonest, hostile, overly possessive or manipulative, cold or distant cannot be considered loving yet they are often manifested in ostensibly loving relationships. Genuine love or regard implies responsible and ethical behavior toward spouses, family, and friends and extends to people beyond one's immediate surroundings.

In a romantic relationship, sexuality is a key component and is an extension of physical affection. It involves offering sexual satisfaction to one's partner as well as being fully receptive to sexual fulfillment. The giving and receiving of sexual pleasure without constraint is an intimate offering to one another. On the other hand, withholding physical affection or one's sexuality conflicts with a genuine experience of love.

Compassion has been defined as concern with the distress of others as well as "a desire to alleviate it" (Woolf, 1981, p. 227).[8] The concept of compassion needs to be distinguished from sympathy, which is defined as "a feeling for or a capacity for sharing in the interests or distress of another" (p. 1172). However, sympathy is "value-blind," according to Comte-Sponville (1996/2001) who emphasized that:

> To sympathize is to feel or experience along with someone … . But *what* we are sympathizing *with* still needs to be taken into account. To participate in another person's hatred is to be full of hate. To participate in another person's cruelty is to be cruel (p. 105).

A sympathetic person's commiserations can make someone in distress feel worse rather than better and can make a victimized person feel even more victimized. In contrast, a compassionate person would show understanding and respond to the best of his or her ability with the appropriate helpfulness.

In addition, the ability to feel compassion for another person is largely dependent on the ability to feel for oneself and give value to oneself and one's experience. Painful childhood experiences tend to impede the development of compassionate attitudes and narrow a person's focus.[9]

In expressing compassion, an individual would be warm, affectionate, and sensitive in his or her relationships, particularly toward those people who are closest to him or her. In addition, there would be a deep concern with the suffering of all people and an attempt made to alter their unfavorable circumstances. A person behaving in a compassionate manner looks for no reward beyond the gratification inherent in the act itself. Expressing love or kindness toward others is selfish in the best sense. When we take other people seriously, offer affection and show concern for their needs separate from ourselves, we tend to have more positive self-regard. Feelings of love and compassion reflect back on those who offer love.

Empathy

Empathy involves being sensitively attuned to another person; it was defined by D. Siegel and Hartzell (2003) as "Understanding the internal experience of another person … . This is a cognitively complex process that involves mental capacities to imagine the mind of another" (p. 224).[10]

Laing (1985) described an empathic exchange as a meeting in which the interpersonal contact resonates phenomenologically with the intrapersonal. A person responds by reaching into him/herself and reaching out to the other. Simultaneously maintaining internal feelings for oneself and external feelings toward the other allows for real communication and rapport, "compresence." Laing specified that this condition is an essential ingredient of a positive therapeutic encounter.[11] This type of emotional attunement toward others is at the core of empathy. In an ideal relationship, mutually empathic individuals would communicate in a sensitive manner that prevents loved ones from feeling unnecessarily hurt, demoralized, or pained.

Generosity

Altruism and generosity are the behavioral components of compassion and empathy. Compassion is basically an emotion, a feeling response to another's suffering; empathy adds a cognitive element that makes it possible for one to be sensitively attuned to what the other person is experiencing, whereas altruism and generosity are actions through which compassion and empathy are expressed.

Generosity is a sensitive, feeling response to another person's wants and needs. Generous actions provide others with what is necessary in an understanding and timely manner. When acts of kindness are performed insensitively or from a position of superiority or for the purpose of elevating oneself, they do not reflect a genuine giving attitude and can be destructive to both giver and receiver. Offering help in a way that causes another to feel small or indebted cannot be thought of as authentic generosity.

In the context of ethical living, an ideal exchange between people involves the capacity to both give and receive love. In such an exchange, the recipient is open and gracious in accepting affection and acts of kindness or assistance. The authors have formulated three steps involved in an appropriate response to a generous act. The first is being open to accepting help and permitting someone else to meet one's needs; the second involves expressing genuine appreciation verbally; and the third entails finding ways to respond or give back with thoughtful or loving actions. In this regard, it is not necessary to respond in kind but rather in a manner that reflects one's own nature and capabilities and the specific needs or concerns of the recipient (R. Firestone, et al, 2003).

Involving oneself in each step of this cyclical process of giving and receiving counteracts negative ruminations and critical voices about oneself. The concept of altruism is not only a sound mental health principle; research has shown that it can also have a beneficial effect on an individual's physical health. For example, one study by Brown, Nesse, Vinokur, and Smith (2003) showed that people who provided emotional support to their spouses lived longer than those who received emotional support.

True generosity not only involves looking after one's loved ones and their priorities but also extends to others in the larger society. For example, kind people will go out of their way to do a favor for a friend or run a timely errand for someone. They look forward to opportunities to respond to another person's need.

Independence

> Personal relatedness can exist only between beings who are
> separate but who are not isolates (Laing, 1960/1969, p. 25).

Independence can be considered a virtue because it is an energy
source, offering vitality rather than draining energy from others and the society at large. Overly dependent individuals place
a burden and responsibility on other people, particularly their
partners and families. In regard to ethics, independence must be
looked at in the context of how and for what purpose that energy
is directed.

Only when people have a sense of their own identity and are truly
individualistic are they able to sustain healthy give-and-take relationships. They have a greater potential for intimacy than those who
rely on others for affirmation of self. To be close to another person,
one has to be separate and autonomous.

A person who is independent has achieved a high level of self-
differentiation (Bowen, 1978). Autonomy involves emancipating
oneself from one's family of origin and other external influences. An
autonomous person is neither submissive nor defiant in relation to
those influences. As a result, independent people gradually evolve
and formulate their own value systems, conceptualizing their own
goals and priorities in life.

Within couples, a lack of independence in one or both partners
predisposes the formation of a fantasy bond rather than a genuinely
loving relationship. On some level, most people imagine that by fus-
ing, submitting their individuality to a stronger, more dominant person, or giving up their own independence and unique point of view,
they will achieve a modicum of safety and security.

Family systems theorist Murray Bowen (1978) described the consequences of this lack of self-differentiation in partners:

> In the average nuclear family ... , the spouses are ... emotion-
> ally 'fused' with each other and with the children, and it is dif-
> ficult to get far beyond the fusion or to do more than react and
> counterreact emotionally (p. 545).

People's tendencies to form dependency ties are fostered by conventional attitudes and assumptions about life. For example, in

modern society, most people expect far more security from an intimate relationship or marriage than it is possible to extract. The burden that these anticipations put on relationships is extreme; obviously no one person can fulfill such unrealistic expectations or live up to this idealized image. When partners expect to fulfill all of their needs in their relationships or marriages, the original equality, genuine companionship, and spontaneous affection they experienced when they originally fell in love are diminished to a considerable degree.

Ideally, the independent person would be neither domineering nor submissive; parental nor childish. Both polarities are unreal and unequal; they detract from an adult posture in life and hurt other people. Instead the autonomous individual would accept responsibility for his/her own life and problems rather than prevailing upon others. Complaining, maintaining a cynical attitude, feeling victimized, omnipotent, or superior all take their toll on close relationships. It is difficult enough to sustain one's own life, remain cheerful and effective, without taking on other people's personal issues.

People are truly alone in life, and can never attempt to merge their identity with others without negative consequences for all parties involved. Ethically speaking, individuals who take power over their own lives, whose value systems are inner rather than outer directed, and who function more or less autonomously generally have a positive effect on the interpersonal world that surrounds them.

Vulnerability

> To live with ambiguity is to accept vulnerability (Lifton, 2003, p. 198).

Traditionally, invulnerability is defined as assurance, impenetrability, strength. A psychological definition of invulnerability implies taking a defended stance and attempting to be impenetrable to emotional hurt. Random House Dictionary (Flexner, 1998) defines the word vulnerable as being "capable of or susceptible to being wounded or hurt ... open to moral attack" (p. 2134). Most people agree with this definition, seeing vulnerability as a negative and conducting their lives in a manner to avoid exposure. In contrast, the authors conceptualize vulnerability in positive terms and describe being open to the possibility of being emotionally hurt as a strength, rather than a weakness. Remaining vulnerable to feeling and exposure is actually an adaptive and powerful position to take in life because it implies self-acceptance, inner strength, and the capacity to deal with frustration. Much energy is consumed in leading a defended life, shutting off emotions and suppressing unpleasant thoughts or memories.

Because of the ways they were hurt in their childhoods, most individuals are reluctant to take the emotional risk involved in loving or being loved. As children, most people utilize repression or other defense mechanisms to cope with their original pain and in the process lose accessibility to their innermost feelings. As adults, they must manipulate the interpersonal environment so that pain from the past will not resurface.

Children are completely vulnerable to impingements from the environment due to their core dependency, innate fragility, and immaturity. However adults are no longer dependent to the extent that they were as children and can cope with adversity. Having necessarily defended themselves as children, adults must learn how to be open and vulnerable again.

People who learn to be more vulnerable are able to take appropriate risks by pursuing their goals and asking directly for what they want in the face of possible rejection, disappointment, or frustration. People who are open and vulnerable are not idealistic or overly optimistic about having their needs gratified; instead they evaluate situations realistically. In contrast, defended individuals rarely take chances or ask for what they want, thereby limiting their opportunities.

When people are in a vulnerable state, their openness is readily observable in their facial expression, posture, and gestures. For example, when embracing another person, one can actually feel the rigidity of someone's defenses in the tenseness of their muscles as compared with the relaxed affection of someone in a more vulnerable state. Being vulnerable leaves people lively and energetic, strongly invested in life, and more likely to achieve fulfillment. They are more available for deep, meaningful relationships and have a more positive effect on other people's well-being.

Flexibility, relaxed, easy style, and good sense of humor

A flexible, relaxed way of being has implications in terms of interpersonal ethics. In general, people who possess these personality traits have a positive effect on others. Good-natured, enthusiastic people who are not rigid and who feel relatively free from the constraints of formality add life and energy to others. People with a sense of humor make life's situations more pleasant. A well-developed sense of humor has a counter-depressive effect. This trait has been listed by both men and women as among the top qualities they are seeking in a mate (Feingold, 1992; G. Miller 2000). In his book *The Mating Mind*, Geoffrey Miller observed:

> One of the strongest and most puzzling findings from evolutionary psychology research has been the value that people around the world place on a good sense of humor. Indeed, this is one of the few human traits important enough to have its own abbreviation (GSOH) in personal ads …. A capacity for comedy reveals a capacity for creativity … . It circumvents our tendencies towards boredom … . Humor is attractive, and that is why it evolved (pp. 415–416).

Although these three qualities are not acts of conscious willfulness, they are worth considering in an examination of ethical behavior because of the role they play in how people affect one another.

In relation to child-rearing, parents who are more relaxed and easy-going with infants and children tend to provide their offspring with an environment that is conducive to healthy psychological development. On the other hand, studies have shown that an anxious, ill-at-ease parent transmits his or her feeling state directly to the child through touch and eye contact that has a residual effect on neuron development in the brain (Schore, 1994; D. Siegel, 1999; D. Siegel & Hartzell, 2003).[12] Bowen (1978) described how an anxious mother sets up an insidious cycle of projection and overprotection that is detrimental to the child.

> The process begins with anxiety in the mother. The child responds anxiously to mother, which she misperceives as a problem in the child. The anxious parental effort goes into

sympathetic, solicitous, overprotective energy, which is directed more by the mother's anxiety than the reality needs of the child. It establishes a pattern of infantilizing the child, who gradually becomes more impaired and more demanding (p. 381).

When people are relaxed, those in their presence feel an unconscious sense of support for being themselves. Being relaxed and free of anxiety are side effects of a good adjustment and are therefore desirable in their own right; however, they have an additional ethically positive effect on friends, partners, and family members.

Search for meaning and transcendent goals

Most people have an intuitive sense that there is "something more" to life than food, shelter, and material success. In fact, the search for meaning and purpose in life is as fundamental to human beings as their drive for self-preservation. There is a core need for social affiliation, a striving for self-actualization and values that transcend one's personal fulfillment. As Frankl (1946/1959) asserted, human beings are meaning-seeking creatures. When a person's defenses preclude this pursuit, he or she often suffers from a form of emotional poverty, feels empty, without a center, and exists in a state of despair, a despair that Kierkegaard (1849/1954) believed was endemic to the human condition.[13]

In seeking personal meaning, individuals tend to go beyond their basic needs and wants and engage in activities and causes that they regard as having a greater significance for themselves, society, and the future. Throughout history, a number of individuals have lived lives of dedication and service to mankind. Examples from the 20th century are: Anwar Sadat, Nelson Mandela, the Dalai Lama, Martin Luther King, Jr., Mother Teresa, etc. On the American political scene, after his defeat in the 2000 presidential election, former Vice President Al Gore invested in a cause that he believed was of great consequence and vital for the survival of the planet. His book and film about global warming transcended his concern for popularity or future political power. In a similar vein, the late former President Gerald Ford, during his first month in office, pardoned Richard Nixon for his role in the Watergate scandal in an effort, as he put it, to "heal the nation." According to many political pundits, the formal pardon, extremely unpopular at the time, was primarily responsible for Ford's loss to Jimmy Carter in the 1976 presidential election. And in his farewell address in January 1961, Dwight D. Eisenhower warned of the unethical dangers of the growing, powerful military-industrial complex, in spite of his long-standing military career and the uproar that his comments caused.

According to Rollo May (1983), the pursuit of a transcendent goal, separate from one's self-interest, requires the ability to use one's imagination to move beyond the immediate concrete situation. It implies a sense of "caring" or, more accurately, "the capacity to stand outside and look at oneself and the situation and to assess and guide oneself by an infinite variety of possibilities" (p. 147).

The authors agree with Viktor Frankl's (1946/1959) concept of self-transcendence and his view that people cannot pursue happiness directly, but rather that happiness is a by-product of investing in transcendent goals that give one's life personal meaning.

> Self-actualization is possible only as a side effect of self-transcendence (p. 133). I therefore admonish my students in Europe and America: Don't aim at success—the more you aim at it and make it a target, the more you are going to miss it. For success, like happiness, cannot be pursued; it must ensue, and it only does so as the unintended side effect of one's personal dedication to a cause greater than oneself or as the by-product of one's surrender to a person other than oneself (pp. 16–17).

In a previous work, the first author (R. Firestone, 1988) stated:

> We must conclude that there is no hidden significance to life that may be discovered; rather it is only each individual's investment of himself, his feelings, his creativity, his interests, and his personal choice of people and activities, that is special. Indeed, we imbue experience with meaning through our own spirit rather than the opposite, and our priorities express our true identity (p. 272).

There are countless ways that people find meaning in life—through their personal relationships, work, creativity, dedication to a humanitarian cause, or through love. For example, people in the friendship circle have found meaning in expressing their altruism through acts of kindness to individuals both in and outside of their immediate families and group of friends. They have also found meaning in their love for one another, a love that is manifested daily in their sensitivity and generosity. The compassion and empathy that they express in their talks often give rise to a transcendent feeling that makes each individual aware of his or her uniqueness as well as the commonalities of human experience. People rarely feel so close or so alone. There is an extraordinary blending of joy with existential sorrow. At these moments, they approach a spiritual sense of themselves in relation to their interpersonal world and an awareness of the significance that life has for them.

Tolerance and inclusiveness

> Man is made for cooperation. To act against one another then is contrary to nature; and it is acting against one another to be vexed and to turn away. And he [humankind] remembers also that every rational animal is his kinsman, and that to care for all men is according to man's nature (Marcus Aurelius, *Meditations*).

Being tolerant implies open-mindedness, understanding, benevolence, and good-will toward one's fellows. Tolerance begins with an accepting attitude toward oneself and implies that a person accept his/her own feelings uncritically. This refers to an acceptance of feelings free from rational or ethical considerations as contrasted with actions that require both forms of scrutiny. It also implies being free enough from vanity and illusions of omnipotence to be able to make mistakes without self-recrimination or destructive self-attacks. Paradoxically individuals are ethical to the extent that they tolerate all of their emotions, even competitive feelings or feelings of anger or hatred.

People who are accepting of themselves tend to be more accepting of others. They are more inclusive and likely to be free of prejudice, biases, and sexual stereotyping. Living ethically requires taking a strong position against sexist, religious, and racist attitudes, which lead to discrimination and cause emotional and physical suffering to large numbers of innocent people. Attitudes held in families often encourage prejudice toward other families, groups, and cultures that approach life differently. These distinctions support core beliefs that individuals who do not look "like we do," who do not act "like we do" are inferior, worthless, immoral, or even dangerous. The result of this form of programming and its extension into societies has a drastic negative effect on relationships and sets groups of people against one another. The destructive effect of these policies on the world scene and the consequent madness appear daily on the front page of newspapers everywhere. In a previous work, the first author described this dynamic of group identification:

> Identification with a particular ethnic or religious group is at once a powerful defense against death anxiety and a system of thought and belief that can set the stage for hatred and bloodshed. Conformity to the belief system of the group, that is, to its collective symbols of immortality, protects one against the horror of facing the objective loss of self. In merging his or her identity with that of a group, each person feels that although he or she may not survive as an individual entity, he or she will live on as part of something larger that *will* continue to exist after he or she is gone (R. Firestone, 1997a, p. 281).

Few people have developed a sufficient level of tolerance, acceptance, or compassion for others. Furthermore, many people seek safety and security in merging their identity with that of a particular group, religion, or nation, which predisposes intolerance, stereotypic attitudes, and prejudice. They tend to be exclusive in terms of categorizing people as belonging to an "in-group" (their group) or an "out-group." They feel superior to and denigrate members of any group, religion, or nation that do not agree with or share their particular beliefs, customs, myths, or solutions to ultimate existential questions. People are even willing to sacrifice themselves in war to preserve their nation's or religion's symbols of immortality.

Exclusiveness is a dangerous posture to adopt, especially in our modern world. As Henry Miller (1947) observed: "Wherever there is the jealous urge to exclude there is the menace of extinction. I see no nation on earth at present which has an all-inclusive view of things" (p. xxii).

The philosopher Peter Singer (2002) envisioned an inclusive, one-world view when he wrote about:

> A nation as an "imagined political community,"[14] one that lives in the minds of those who see themselves as citizens of the same nation .... We need to ask whether it will, in the long run, be better if we continue to live in the imagined communities we know as nation-states, or if we begin to consider ourselves as members of an imagined community of the world (pp. 170–171).

Tolerance and inclusiveness are ethical principles of paramount importance in that the future of our civilization may well depend on our developing a nonprejudicial, nonbiased view of people who have different beliefs, customs, and ethnic backgrounds. Building a peaceful world would require a rejection of illusions of belonging to the best family, living in the greatest nation, or believing in the true religion. It would also require rejecting all aspects of our superiority or omniscience. In the words of Camus, "To live and die as human beings we need to refuse to be a god ... . He who does not know everything cannot kill everyone" (quoted by Lifton, 2005. p. 15).[15] In relation to death, all men are equal.

Conclusion

People who adopt the ethical principles delineated in this chapter exhibit a depth of compassion and a basic trust in others that have a powerful effect on their relationships. They manifest a minimum of negative, intrusive behaviors in their personal interactions and thus have a positive influence on their mates, friends, and families, rather than having a deleterious effect. They are vulnerable and relatively undefended and retain an excitement about living because they have remained connected to their feelings. They are aware of their wants and aspirations, direct their actions toward fulfilling these goals, and live within their own value system. They face death straightforwardly and feel sad about the future loss of self and loved ones. Understanding that all people ultimately share the same fate, they see no person as categorically inferior or superior, nor do they invest any person with greater or lesser status.

By taking an approach that is compassionate and humane rather than moralistic or prescriptive, people can gradually learn to overcome defenses that act as barriers to ethical living. They can develop their own values and principles and seek their own solutions to life and living. They can cultivate a concern for human rights issues in their personal relationships and learn to value self-fulfillment, freedom, and independence for all people. Living by these ethical principles is necessary for insuring the survival of humankind.

Notes

1. Re: diverse approaches to the study of ethics, Amelie Rorty (1993), philosopher of education, pointed out that "Of course, philosophical systems of morality are complex enterprises, conjoining a number of different tasks ... . All of them involve a theory about what is best and worst in human nature, an account of how to bypass or transform the worst so as to allow the best to flourish" (p. 29).

   For a brief and concise overview of a number of these theories and diverse approaches to ethics in everyday life, see Chapter 1 of *Do the Right Thing: Living Ethically in an Unethical World* by Thomas G. Plante (2004). Peter Singer's *Ethics* (1994), an anthology of ethical ideas compiled from writings encompassing the past two and a half millenniums, is another rich resource. Singer (1986/1994) wrote: "Ethics is about how we ought to live. What makes an action the right, rather than the wrong, thing to do?" (p. 3). Also see *Virtue and Psychology* by Blaine J. Fowers (2005). In a parenthetical comment, Fowers noted: "There is a substantial consensus that the extant Ethics Code is insufficient to guide psychologists in unequivocal ways through the great variety of situations that we face" (p. 178). Similarly, Tjeltveit (2004) has criticized aspects of the American Psychological Association's Ethics Code. In another article, Tjeltveit (2006) wrote: "Divergent views about the good life will accordingly inform how therapists, clients, and others understand beneficence [the optimal ideal in the APA 2002 ethical code] and conceive of optimal therapy goals and outcomes" (p. 189). In his writing, C. Taylor (1989) has emphasized the importance of committing whole-heartedly to one's ethical heritage.

2. This prediction has been supported by studies conducted by Mikulincer, et al, (2002). These researchers found that individuals classified as having an anxious attachment pattern with a parent

expressed more death fears than those who were classified as having a secure attachment pattern.

3. In treating depression, several clinicians found that when patients focused on developing character strengths and virtues, they were often able to effectively challenge and overcome symptoms of depression (Seligman & Csikszentmihalyi, 2000; Wong, 2006). Also see Yip's (2005) article, "A Strengths Perspective in Understanding and Working with Clients with Psychosis and Records of Violence."

4. The traits or personal qualities discussed here are frequently described in the context of a "virtues" approach to ethics, one that asks the question: "What kind of a person ought I to be" rather than "how ought I to live?" This approach focuses on characteristics that an individual would strive to develop in him or herself that would facilitate living according to ethical principles. The virtues approach to ethics is, however, only one among a number of approaches. According to Browning (2004):

> Ethics of virtue can be found in the well-known writings of Alasdair MacIntyre (1981) and Stanley Hauerwas (1981). They insisted that simple rational principles [ethics of principles] are not enough to either resolve conflicts or guide action toward the future. The dynamics of modernity, according to them, need to be anchored, if not countered, by tested traditions of habits and virtues (pp. 241–242).

Erik Erikson (1964) linked the development of virtues to the eight stages of psychosexual development. In *Insight and Responsibility*, he defined "virtue" as "the combination of *strength, restraint,* and *courage* (p. 113). Also see Peterson and Seligman's (2004) historical and psychological analysis of the study of strengths, virtues and positive character traits (pages 53–88).

5. Rogers (1961) described the concept of internal congruence in relation to psychotherapy as well as everyday life:

> Each of us knows individuals whom we somehow trust because we sense that they are being what they are, that we are dealing with the person himself, not with a polite or professional front (p. 61).

6. See Rushworth Kidder's (2007) "Moral Courage" (the "Common Threads of Courage" section, Chapter 1, para. 3) and *The Mystery of Courage*, by William Ian Miller (2000).

7. Moral dilemmas generally involve choices between two courses of action, each of which may be based on an ethical principle (e.g. telling the truth vs. saving a person's life). According to the Social Intuitionist approach, people react to such dilemmas with an automatic evaluation based on intuitions, whereas according to the Rationalistic approach, moral judgments are caused by moral reasoning and reflection. "Moral emotions such as sympathy may sometimes be inputs to the reasoning process, but moral emotions are not the direct causes of moral judgments" (Haidt, 2001, p. 814). Also refer to Albert Bandura's (1991) social cognitive theory of morality, Lawrence Kohlberg's (1981) *Essays on Moral Development* and Carol Gilligan's (1982) *In a Different Voice*. Research studies (Jaffee & Hyde, 2000; Pratt, Skoe & Arnold, 2004; Wark & Krebs, 1996) on both Kohlberg's and Gilligan's models have pointed to certain limitations in their methodology and interpretations. In "The Moral Philosopher and the Moral Life," William James (1891/1948) acknowledged the difficulties involved in resolving ethical dilemmas outside of the laboratory, in the real world.

8. Paul Gilbert (2005) proposed that:

> Compassionate relating emerges from complex interaction between motives to be concerned for and improve the well-being of others, and competencies to be sensitive to others' distress with sympathy for, and understanding of, their positions—with a complex array of cognitive competencies. At the same time one must be able to tolerate distress in others and in self to avoid defensive withdrawal or over-control … . Other characteristics for compassion may include strength … . Compassion also involves abilities for gratitude, generosity and forgiveness (pp. 52–53).

9. In discussing how compassion develops in a child, D. Siegel and Hartzell (2003) suggested that the ability to feel compassion "may depend on mirror neuron systems, which evoke an emotional state in us that mirrors that of another person, enabling us to feel another person's pain" (p. 224). Also see Theoret and Pascual-Leone's (2002) discussion of the role that mirror neurons play in the development of empathy. According to Oberman, et al (2005) and Williams, Whiten, Suddendorf and Perrett (2001), "Autism might be the clinical manifestation of the congenital dysfunction of the mirror cell system" (p. R737).

A convergence of findings from attachment research, neuro-science, and psychoanalysis has expanded clinicians' understanding of the mechanisms underlying the negative impact that early aversive childhood experiences have on the child's developing mind and on his or her evolving ability to feel compassion and empathy, emotions that are necessary for moral development (Cozolino, 2002, 2006; Fonagy, 2001; Schore, 1994, 2003; D. Siegel, 1999; 2006; D. Siegel & Hartzell, 2003).

10. Decety and Jackson (2006) described three primary components of empathy:

(a) an affective response to another person, which often, but not always, entails sharing that person's emotional state; (b) a cognitive capacity to take the perspective of the other person; and (c) emotional regulation … . Self-regulatory processes are at play to prevent confusion between self- and other feelings (p. 54).

Also see *Empathy Reconsidered* (Bohart & Greenberg, 1997) and "The Empathic Brain and Its Dysfunction in Psychiatric Populations" by Decety and Moriguchi (2007), describing the neurological basis of several emotional disorders reflecting deficits in empathy.

11. For a demonstration of "compresence" see "Existential Psychotherapy" videotaped psychotherapy session conducted by R.D. Laing December, 1985, Evolution of Psychotherapy Conference, Phoenix, Arizona.

12. Attunement, an important component in mother-infant interaction, has been described by Stern (1985, 1995), and the effects of parental misattunement have been delineated by Schore (1994, 2003), D. Siegel (1999), and Cozolino (2006). Stern's work (1985) has shown how a tense, rigid, or overly anxious mother interacts with her infant. He has also described the diverse negative effects of such misattuned or noncontingent responses on the infant. See Stern's description of a detailed videotaped example of qualitative research into parent-infant interactions on pp. 65–69 in *The Motherhood Constellation* (Stern, 1995). Lyons-Ruth and Jacobvitz (1999) reported a study by Hamn, Castino, Jarosinski, and Britton (1991) demonstrating disorganized attachment patterns between a group of mothers and toddlers.

13. Kierkegaard (1849/1954), in *The Sickness Unto Death*, Chapter 3, "The Forms of This Sickness, i.e. of Despair," noted that "The despairing man who is unconscious of being in despair is, in comparison with

him who is conscious of it, merely a negative step further from the truth and from salvation" (cited by Religion-Online, 2007, Despair Viewed Under the Aspect of Consciousness section, para. 4).

14. Singer was referring to Benedict Anderson's (1991) thesis as presented in *Imagined Communities: Reflections on the Origins and Spread of Nationalism*.

15. Camus' statement was also cited by Lifton (2003) in *Superpower Syndrome: America's Apocalyptic Confrontation with the World*, Lifton asserted that "As Albert Camus, the French writer who struggled with these issues throughout his life put it, to live and to die as humans we need "to refuse to be a god," which means embracing "thought which recognizes limits" (p. 199). "Without the need for invulnerability, everyone would have much less to be afraid of" (p. 191).

CHAPTER THREE

A moral perspective on personal relationships

The founders and the later exponents of the higher religions and philosophies have spelled out, within the last twenty-five centuries, the standards of conduct that, in the atomic age, are required of everybody if mankind is to save itself from self-destruction. But these higher standards of behavior have been actually achieved in practice only by a tiny minority.

Arnold Toynbee (Gage, 1976, p. 330)

Most books about ethics are based on religious beliefs, spiritual insights, or philosophical ideas and offer guidelines or prescriptions to help readers lead more spiritual or moral lives (Beckwith, 2002; Boss, 2004).[1] This book is not derived from religious doctrine or a philosophical system, nor does it necessarily provide specific prescriptions for living a more moral or spiritual existence. Nevertheless, it points to a more satisfying and effective mode of existence, a lifestyle based on a nondefended, vulnerable, and feelingful approach to life.

The authors have not taken a moralistic perspective in relation to people's behaviors and lifestyles; instead we approach the

45

subject from a psychological perspective, describe the major barriers to leading an ethical life, and demonstrate that living with integrity, according to one's values and ethics, is a sound mental health principle.[2]

Defining ethics in operational terms

What criteria should be used to distinguish between ethical and unethical actions, particularly when their effects, in terms of destructiveness, are sometimes subtle, difficult to identify, or successfully hidden?[3]

It is useful to consider a specific action or communication as ethical when it respects, supports, and nurtures the basic human potentialities of another. For example, at any given moment, personal exchanges can be appraised as being either supportive of the "real self" of both parties or as interfering with each person's ongoing, optimal sense of self and personal development. Unethical actions would be those behaviors that limit or damage fundamental human qualities or interfere with personal fulfillment. Although human rights issues in relationships are rarely considered, they are as relevant to a person's well-being as food, medical care, and shelter.

The basic qualities of our human heritage that distinguish our species from the other animals are the unique ability to love and feel compassion for oneself and others, the capacity for abstract reasoning and creativity, the capability to set goals and develop strategies to accomplish them, an awareness of existential concerns, the desire to search for meaning and social affiliation, and the potential to experience the sacredness and mystery of life.[4] As fundamental as these qualities are, the process of attaining them is fraught with dangers, and human potentialities can easily be distorted, sidetracked, or even eliminated. Blows to our sense of identity, independence, uniqueness, creativity, gender identification, self-concept, and self-esteem act to induce us to cut off feeling for ourselves and others and thereby deprive us of our birthright.

When individuals are compelled by negative circumstances in their upbringing to become hostile or develop a basic distrust of others, or when they are forced to become self-protective and cut off feeling for themselves and other people, they lose the part of themselves that is most alive and human. Regardless of other considerations, if any of our uniquely human attributes are damaged by society or family life, it is logical to consider the circumstances under which the damage occurred to be abusive and, as implied by our definition, unethical. In examining parent-child relations, we must define parental behaviors as abusive whenever they have long-term debilitating effects on their child's self-concept, relationships, or career, or lead to a condition of general unhappiness (R. Firestone, 1997a).[5] However, the object of this work is not to judge or attach blame but rather to establish insight into and accountability for negative behavior in relationships. Much of the behavior that constitutes emotional abuse in family life is both unconscious and unintentional.

The first author (R. Firestone, 1990b) has described emotional child abuse as a violation of children's right to life which fosters a form of psychological death—a death of the spirit or soul:

> Regrettably, the socialization process in the nuclear family categorizes, standardizes, and puts the stamp of conformity on most children. It imposes a negative structure, a self-regulating system that cuts deeply into the child's feeling reactions and conditions his thoughts and behaviors to meet certain accepted standards. Thereafter, the child continues to impose the same structure and programming on himself … .
>
> The results are double-edged. Once a human being is "processed" in this way and deprived of individuality, he is reduced to an animal level of existence. However, the child retains his capacity to suffer, and his condition is now worse than that of an animal; he has been deprived of his human qualities, yet still retains the propensity for experiencing emotional pain and misery (p. 318).

Ethical principles were derived originally from man's deep reverence for life; therefore the ethics of a specific behavior can be evaluated in terms of whether it enhances or diminishes life both qualitatively and materially. Ethical behavior protects the rights of both children and adults, including the right to develop as an autonomous individual and the right to personal freedom and equality (Erikson, 1963; Greenspan, 1997; Katzman, 2005).

According to philosopher Simone Weil (1949/1952), the attempt to meet the vital needs of all people, that is, to fulfill the requirements for survival and for sustaining life, falls under the rubric of an "obligation" or a moral duty. She contended, "It is an eternal obligation towards the human being not to let him suffer from hunger when one has the chance of coming to his assistance" (p. 6). Weil believed that violations of people's human rights were just as serious as failures to fulfill one's moral obligation to feed, clothe, and house people, to protect them from violence, and to provide them with necessary medical care. These needs are "like our physical needs, a necessary condition of our life on this earth." When these are not met:

> We fall little by little into a state more or less resembling death, more or less akin to a purely vegetative existence ... . Everyone knows that there are forms of cruelty which can injure a man's life without injuring his body. They ... deprive him of a certain form of food necessary to the life of the soul (p. 7).[6]

At the societal level, behaviors can be considered as ethical when they help create the conditions necessary for the evolution of a humanistic society with concern for the well-being and fulfillment for all people, whereas behaviors and communications that interfere with or prevent the evolution of the "good" society must be considered unethical. Ethical behaviors cannot be simplified or measured in quantitative terms alone because the process of developing an ethical lifestyle or way of being in the world is unique to each person's ability and circumstance. Practicing one's principles and values in the real world where ethical dilemmas abound and agonizing choices are sometimes required necessarily involves being knowledgeable and informed, possessed of considerable self-awareness and self-understanding as well as a compassionate feeling for other people.

Destructive behaviors in intimate relationships

> If you find the ideal love and try to make it the sole judge of good and bad in yourself, the measure of your strivings, you become simply the reflex of another person. You lose yourself in the other, just as obedient children lose themselves in the family (Becker, 1973/1997, p. 166).

Close, personal relationships have the potential for causing emotional pain and hurt as well as creating harmony and happiness. They can be risky ventures and people feel especially vulnerable to the possibility of being hurt by an intimate partner.

Some of the most hurtful behaviors, commonplace in relationships, are those that individuals act out in an attempt to ward off loving responses from their partner. Authors and playwrights have written volumes about people's distrust of love that prevents them from accepting it as a reality in their lives. The authors have described this phenomenon in a previous work (Firestone & Catlett, 1999): "An unavoidable truth about human beings is that very often the beloved is compelled to punish the lover who appreciates his or her positive qualities" (p. 3). Defended individuals tend to maintain the negative identity they acquired within the family context and are resistant to being seen in a more positive light. Changing their basic self-concept would threaten their defense system and arouse considerable anxiety, so they unconsciously strive to alter their lover's positive responses.

As described in Chapter 1, the participants in the friendship circle became aware that, in trying to avoid anxiety, they often hurt the people who loved them the most, without meaning to. One way that they damaged the feelings of a loved one was by holding back the positive traits and behaviors he or she had especially admired. These patterns of withholding, based on an intolerance of being loved, were particularly evident in their closest relationships, and less so in their friendships.

A good deal of the harm that people inflict on each other in their relationships involves disrespect or disregard for each person's autonomy. Relationship partners often treat each other in ways they would never treat an acquaintance, coworker, or friend. Researchers have called attention to the fact that individuals tend to commit the most egregious human rights violations in their closest, most intimate associations (Felson, 2002; Spitzberg & Cupach 1998; Tedeschi & Felson, 1994).[7]

In his work with couples, psychologist John Gottman (Gottman, 1979; Gottman & Krokoff, 1989; Gottman & Silver, 1999) found four behaviors that were identifiable as diagnostic predictors of eventual divorce: defensiveness, stonewalling or filibustering, criticality, and contempt. The researchers found that contempt was the most serious indicator of potential divorce and could be clearly identified after observing couples for only a few minutes. Contempt implies relating to the other so as to denigrate and judge from a superior position.

A person behaving in a contemptuous manner is smug, hyper-critical, and belittling, making the recipient of his or her behavior feel small, and causing a good deal of psychological pain. He or she speaks in an authoritarian, parental tone of voice that reflects a vain attitude or higher status.

> For example, Ron, a young man in our circle of friends, became angry with his girlfriend, Karen, while the couple was having dinner with mutual friends. From his perspective, Karen was talking too loudly, joking too much, and calling too much attention to herself. Generally, Ron's behavior toward Karen was characterized by an attitude of superiority in which he more or less consistently played the role of helper. The next day, assuming his usual parental stance, Ron confronted Karen in a group discussion. In a condescending, analytical tone of voice, he said, "The way you acted last night was totally inappropriate! Men would think you were coming on to them. We've talked about this before, it's so immature!"
>
> Someone in the group pointed out to Ron that his superior tone and manner of talking to Karen were disrespectful and judgmental. Others encouraged him to speak about his feelings rather than condemn her. When he did, Ron revealed that the possibility that some of the men at the table might have thought that Karen was flirting with them made him feel jealous. He felt threatened when they seemed to be enjoying Karen's company and she was enjoying the attention. As Ron spoke personally, it became apparent that his parental stance masked feelings of insecurity and fear of loss.

In general, when one member of a couple is analytical and plays the role of helper, the prognosis for a satisfying relationship is poor. The symptoms associated with this particular style of relating tend to appear early on and lead to more difficulty as the relationship progresses. In this situation, both partners are insecure and fear rejection. The ways in which they defend themselves against the anticipated rejection lead to further polarization within the couple, with one partner compensating through more parental, superior behavior and the other playing more the part of the compliant or defiant child (R. Firestone & Catlett, 1999).

Defensiveness is another harmful behavioral manifestation that causes a good deal of damage in personal relationships. Within many couples, one or both partners may habitually respond angrily to any criticism, true or false, mild or harsh, by either attacking back or falling apart. One partner will become cold or give the other the "silent treatment" as punishment for the other's attempt to be candid or honest. Some partners filibuster or stonewall with overpowering arguments and a loud voice that intimidates and effectively silences the other. These overreactions and punishing responses also render certain subjects taboo in the couple's ongoing dialogue. All of these defensive reactions gradually lead to a shutting down of lines of communication within the couple.

Within many couples, partners tend to be hypercritical regarding each other's habits, shortcomings, weaknesses, or simple human foibles. Researchers (Leary & Springer, 2001; Leary, Springer, Negel, Ansell & Evans, 1998) reported that criticism accounted for the greatest proportion of cases of hurt feelings in their study of couples. Gottman and Silver (1999) observed that confrontations that involve criticisms rather than simple statements of dissatisfaction with a partner's behavior were perceived as particularly aversive. In many cases, this criticality involved serious distortions of the other person, who was perceived as being more negative, troublesome, or unappealing than he or she actually was.

> At first, when Martin and Veronica got married, their friends were impressed by the nature of their relationship. They were highly independent people who were respectful of each other. Rather than criticize one another's idiosyncrasies, they valued each other's individuality. They did not make demands on one another but instead appreciated what each offered the other in their relationship.
>
> Martin and Veronica wanted to have a child. However, it took a long time for Veronica to conceive and she had a physically difficult pregnancy. As it progressed, she withdrew and became increasingly disrespectful, hostile, and critical of

Martin. Veronica was irritated by behaviors that previously had elicited either compassion or amusement. She acted as though she could barely tolerate Martin. Martin was hurt and angry. Without realizing it, Veronica was sabotaging their relationship.

Their friends were alarmed by the increasing hostility in the relationship, and were worried for them and for their baby. Several of them voiced their concerns. As Martin and Veronica began to talk, it became obvious that the communication between them had broken down. As Veronica spoke of her feelings, she realized that she felt fear and anxiety about the impending birth of her child. In her self-protective, cut-off state, she had been unaware of her abusive treatment of Martin. As the conversation progressed, she began to feel for Martin again. She felt sad when she realized how rejecting she had been.

Many partners project their own self-critical thoughts onto the other person and imagine that he or she is critical of them (R. Firestone & Catlett, 1999; Scharff & Scharff, 1991). They fight unnecessary battles with these externalized aspects of their own destructive thinking, seeing the partner as the enemy rather than facing the enemy within themselves.

In their conversations, partners often indicate underlying attitudes of disrespect by interrupting or speaking for the other person. Partners may speak as a unit, in terms like "we" or "us," thereby diminishing the sense of being two separate individuals. Others continuously seek reassurance that their partner really loves them and prefers them above anyone else. Many people imagine being so powerfully connected to their partners that they expect them to read their minds and resent having to ask directly for what they want. Subsequently, they feel hurt when their partners fail to respond to their unspoken desires. Others refuse to be equal companions in sharing life; instead, they become parental and authoritarian or dependent and childish, manipulating each other either through domineering or submissive behavior.

Often, people take a proprietary interest in their mates that is disrespectful of the other's freedom. Some act out feelings of possessiveness and jealousy in explosive angry outbursts, feeling completely justified and self-righteous in doing so. Others react by feeling hurt, victimized, or falling apart.

As noted earlier, people are often duplicitous and lack integrity in their closest relationships: that is, there is a discrepancy between their actions and their words. Duplicity and dishonesty are widespread in couples and in family life. People lie about money issues, addictive patterns, and, in particular, about extramarital affairs. In such cases, the breach of trust is often more destructive to the relationship than the "infidelity" (R. Firestone, Firestone & Catlett, 2006; S. Glass, 2003). Most people are unaware of the extent to which they are dishonest with each other. They are often reluctant to reveal their deceptions to their mates for fear of losing the relationship altogether. Yet deception seriously limits the feeling of trust between partners and leads to a buildup of guilt feelings that tends to further alienate them.

Before Frank met Anna, he enjoyed his freedom and dated many women. Even though he was having fun, his relationships were primarily superficial and short-lived. He longed for a deeper, more meaningful relationship with a woman with whom he could eventually have a child. Frank recognized that his fear of intimacy was keeping him from achieving this goal.

When Frank and Anna began dating, Frank realized that this was a woman he wanted to take seriously. He decided to stop dating other women and focus his attention on Anna. He expressed his intention to be faithful to her. This commitment caused him anxiety and he struggled with feelings of wanting to get away. Even though he no longer saw other women, he continued flirtatious e-mail correspondences with women he had previously dated. He told himself that these communications were harmless because they were not directly sexual.

One day, he left one of these e-mails up on his computer screen and Anna read it. She was angry and felt deceived. At first, Frank felt misunderstood and innocent. However, when they were discussing it among friends, people pointed out that even though Frank had not consciously meant any harm by e-mailing other women, it was not a meaningless act. Frank saw that the e-mails had been a way out, an emotional escape to relieve the anxiety that he felt from being close to Anna. He realized that the "minor" deception had disturbed his girlfriend's sense of trust in him and he felt remorseful. Subsequently, he reaffirmed his desire to be faithful and more importantly, swore that he would never be dishonest with her again.

There are many destructive behaviors acted out in the course of the average couple's day. They occur routinely: in unpleasant exchanges about finances and child-rearing, in hurtful interactions in the privacy of the bedroom, in depreciating comments made publicly in front of family, friends, and strangers, and in arguments that disrupt the harmony of a shared activity. Even when blatant, these negative behaviors often remain on the periphery of the offending partner's consciousness while he/she maintains a fantasy of being loving and responsive.

Many couple relationships are characterized by disrespectful reactions, including those that effectively intimidate or control the other person through defensive maneuvers or manipulations. These manipulations, power plays, and other strategies of control are manifested in various ways: through domination, bullying, and the use of force; through self-destructive threats that cause fear reactions; and through manipulations that trigger guilt feelings in the other person.

In some relationships, there is a form of social terrorism that makes one partner accountable or responsible for the unhappiness of the other. The tyranny of weakness, helplessness, and self-hatred exerted by self-denying, addictive, or self-destructive individuals has a profoundly manipulative effect (R. Firestone, 2000; R. Firestone & Catlett, 1999; R. Firestone & Seiden, 1987). For example, a man's habitual drug use, sullenness, or depression can control his wife's behavior. A woman's tears, self-hatred, or emotional breakdowns frequently establish submission to her will on the part of her husband and children. Some people consciously or unconsciously use self-destructive behaviors to gain leverage over an intimate partner. Threats of self-harm, bizarre risk-taking behavior, or actual suicide attempts are especially frightening. These maneuvers effectively imprison both parties. The more insecure the partner is, the more the need to control and manipulate the other. Similarly, the extent to which the other person submits to this control is proportional to the degree to which he or she feels insecure, fearful, and guilty. Although obligations, restrictions, and coercion are often effective in controlling the behavior of one's partner, the individuals involved with these maneuvers lose a sense of dignity and self-respect.

The people in the friendship circle have struggled over the years to expose negative power plays and manipulations of partners and attempted to define ethical behavior in couple relations. As children, many of them had experienced a family life that was characterized by a false sense of togetherness and an image of merged identity that were detrimental to their development as separate and autonomous individuals. They observed their parents treating each other in many of the negative ways noted above. As a result, they were determined to avoid treating their mates and children in a similar manner. They learned to show respect for the boundaries, wants, and priorities of their mates, and supported their goals and interests even when they were different from their own. Becoming aware of these destructive influences made it possible for them to alter noxious behaviors and develop better relationships characterized by mutual respect. Developing insight into the reasons why they often punished others who especially acknowledged them enabled them to accept more love and affection in their lives.

Ethical concerns in family life and child-rearing practices

> At birth and throughout their later upbringing, we instill in them [children] the necessity to love, honor, and respect us, to do their best for us, to satisfy our ambitions—in short, to give us everything our parents denied us. We call this decency and morality.
>
> Children rarely have any choice in the matter. All their lives, they will force themselves to offer their parents something that they neither possess nor have any knowledge of, quite simply because they have never been given it: genuine, unconditional love (A. Miller, 2005 pp. 37–38).

An examination of the ethics of family life is vital because children are our heritage, the legacy we leave behind, and our hope for the future. Traditionally, in our culture there is a tendency to idealize the couple and family, which limits or prohibits open scrutiny of family practices. In breaking through this barrier and coming to terms with parental behaviors that are detrimental to a child's well-being, the object is not to criticize or denigrate the institution of the family, but rather to explore and better understand issues of child development and find optimal ways of improving parent/child relationships. Parents who were damaged in their upbringing will inadvertently pass on this damage to their children in spite of their best intentions unless they work through their own developmental issues. Both parents and children should be viewed with compassion (R. Firestone, 1997a; Fraiberg, Adelson & Shapiro, 1975/1980; Lieberman & Zeanah, 1999).

Years of clinical experience with patients and their families as well as observations of and interactions with the families of my friends and colleagues have convinced the first author (R. Firestone) that many common behaviors and conditions in family life have an adverse effect on both children and parents. My interest has always been to understand the causes of personal suffering and maladjustment. In the course of this effort, I had to gradually relinquish my own inclination to idealize the family. I was forced to look at a myriad parental attitudes and behaviors that were injurious to children's well-being. It became increasingly apparent that the majority of psychological symptoms and personal suffering in my patients was directly traceable to harmful operations within the traditional family structure (R. Firestone, 1997a).

Typical abuses and their effects on children

The neglect and the physical and sexual abuse that children suffer in the course of a "normal" upbringing are more prevalent, and the effects far more destructive and long-lasting, than was previously recognized (Briere, 1992). Yet, there are also other more subtle behaviors that impact children and interfere with their ability to develop their full potential (Garbarino & Gilliam, 1980; Garbarino, Guttmann & Seeley, 1986). In a previous work (R. Firestone, 1997a), the first author defined emotional child abuse as:

> Damage to the child's psychological development and emerging personal identity, primarily caused by parents' or primary caretakers' immaturity, defended lifestyle, and conscious or unconscious aggression toward the child ... . Although personal deficiencies and limitations in adult functioning are at times a result of biological or hereditary factors, in our experience, they

have been more closely related to, even overdetermined by, abuses suffered in the process of growing up (pp. 19–20).

Verbal abuse

Parents' hostile attitudes are often communicated to a child through sarcastic, derisive, or condescending comments. Derogatory statements directed toward children about their appearance, performance, and mannerisms are debilitating to children's self-esteem and self-confidence. In addition, many parents repeatedly make unfavorable comparisons with siblings or peers. Many times, children are ridiculed in situations where they are particularly vulnerable. For example, parents sometimes tease, criticize, or push a child away who is expressing spontaneous affection toward them.

Parents and other adults often mistakenly believe and make statements implying that children are intrinsically bad and must learn how to be good. Children treated in this manner develop a negative image of themselves, maintaining a sense of guilt and "badness" throughout their lives. Once this negative self-image has been established, children tend to act accordingly, provoking anger and criticism from others, which in turn, reinforces their negative self-image. It is very difficult for children raised in such a negative cycle to develop into ethical adults.

Most adults tend to view children in diminutive terms, as being less capable and competent than they really are. Condescending attitudes toward children are manifested in a variety of situations. Parents, teachers, doctors, and nurses often treat children as inferiors and talk down to them: "Now it's time to take 'our' bath." Or "How are 'we' doing?" More often than not, these communications are delivered in a pedantic, phony or disrespectful style that infantilizes children and increases their feelings of unworthiness and incompetence.

Harsh mistreatment during the socialization process

During the socialization process, adults often mistreat children in myriad ways, ranging from mild irritability to sadism and brutality. Many parents believe that to be properly socialized, children must be made to submit to parental authority "for their own good." Societal attitudes and legal sanctions often reinforce their beliefs (Garbarino & Gilliam, 1980).[8] Parents who attempt to force their child to submit, who issue unreasonable ultimatums, or who take a rigid stance in relation to unnecessary rules are responsible for setting up situations that inevitably lead to destructive power struggles. During a direct confrontation or "battle of wills" parents often express fierce, punitive attitudes and even rage, reactions which stand in contrast to their typically more reasonable responses. These explosive outbursts intimidate and terrify children, who perceive their parents as dangerously out of control. Many parents equate discipline with punishment and feel justified in using harsh, forceful measures to enforce "good" behavior. This faulty approach to child-rearing tends to be supported by our society.

Some parents exert more subtle forms of control over children through rules that emphasize obligation over choice and image over real concern. Psychological control is exerted through covert and overt constraints exercised by the parents. Dampening the child's enthusiasm for life, invalidating his or her experiences, withdrawing love, inducing guilt, blaming the child for other family members' problems, questioning his or her loyalty to the family, and vacillating between caring and criticizing the child are all examples of this form of psychological control.

Many parents fail to provide conditions in which the child's personality and unique qualities can emerge. Instead they try to bring the child into their own defensive structure and, in many unconscious ways, limit the development of the child's individual potential. Parents also tend to expect respect and loyalty from their children, whether it is deserved or not. They mistakenly perceive the evolving independence of the toddler or young child as disrespect for them and their authority, and feel compelled to stifle these expressions. It is logical that children who are properly nurtured, loved, and respected would be respectful and loving toward their parents.

Overprotectiveness, intrusiveness, and lack of respect for the child's boundaries

Overprotective parents limit a child's experience and ability to cope with life and instill an abnormal form of dependency. Parents who lack an understanding of a child's need to grow and individuate tend to discourage or even oppose their child's independent interests and pursuits. In being overly concerned with his or her physical health, they induce excessive fear reactions and tendencies toward hypochondria. In over-identifying with their child's pain, such parents soothe, reassure, coddle, or oversympathize, all of which limit the development of ego strength in the child.

> David and Liz were first-time parents in their mid-twenties. Both had looked forward to having a baby and both had experience taking care of infants. Liz had worked as a nanny and David had grown up in a large family with young siblings and cousins. However, both were surprised by the thoughts that they had after their daughter, Lisa, arrived.
>
> Each of them was tortured by thoughts of harm coming to Lisa. At night David would be afraid that she might have stopped breathing and he would get up to check her in her crib. When Liz was away from her baby, she would imagine that Lisa would be hurt because someone had been careless with her. They would imagine her in a car crash, being dropped from a height, drowning in a bathtub.
>
> David and Liz spoke about their "ridiculous" fears in a group discussion. Even though they knew that these thoughts were "only in our heads," they were worried about reacting to them by become nervous and overprotective of Lisa. David and Liz continued to discuss their torturous thoughts with their friends. Eventually, the power of these thoughts subsided. David and Liz began to relax and feel more confident as parents.

Some parents may attempt to isolate their children from peers or other extrafamilial influences that might have a negative impact. However, when carried to an extreme, such exclusion limits the child in his or her exposure to a variety of different attitudes and approaches to life and is detrimental to a child's trust in other people and ability to function in the world.

Intrusive behaviors on the part of parents seriously damage the spirit and personality of the child (Barber, 2002). Many parents over-step the personal boundaries of their children in various ways: by inappropriately touching them, going through their belongings, reading their mail, and requiring them to perform for friends and relatives. Parental intrusiveness seriously limits children's personal freedom and autonomy. Many mothers and fathers believe that their offspring "belong" to them. They tend to speak for their children, take over their productions as their own, brag excessively about their accomplishments, and attempt to live vicariously through them. These parents have an unconscious need to take love from a child rather than to give love. The authors refer to this need as "emotional hunger" (R. Firestone, 1990b).

Emotional Hunger

Emotional hunger, a strong emotional need and dependency based on parents' immaturity, must be distinguished from genuine love for the child. Yet it is often confused with love because emotionally hungry parents have intense feelings toward their children, are very concerned about them, and spend a good deal of time with them. Because of this confusion, both on the part of parents and outside observers, much innocent damage is perpetrated on children in the name of love.

If parents are genuinely loving, they nurture the child, which has a positive effect on his or her development. That child will tend to be securely attached, harmonious in his/her relationships, and tolerant of intimacy as an adult. In contrast, contact with an emotionally hungry parent leaves a child emotionally impoverished, anxiously attached, and hurting. The more contact between this type of parent and the child, the more the parent is damaging to the child's security and comfort. This style of relating—excessive touching, overconcern for the child or overinvolvement in the child's life—not only violates the child's boundaries but also promotes withholding responses in the youngster. This can result in serious limitations in both the child's later career and personal life, can threaten his or her sense of self and autonomy, and can be more damaging than more obvious abuses.

> When Susan's son, Peter, was born, she wanted to make sure that his childhood was a happy one. She did not want him to have the lonely, unhappy childhood that she had had. She doted on him and was highly sensitive to any slight or deprivation that he might suffer. She hovered over him and interceded

on his behalf whenever she felt that he was being overlooked or missing out. Peter was angry; he threw tantrums and could not be consoled. He hit other kids and could not control his temper.

Then Peter went on a trip with his father and family friends without Susan. Everyone noticed that Peter was a different child: he was calm, relaxed, and happy. He did not get angry; there was no sign of a temper that needed to be controlled. When they returned, everyone spoke with Susan about the difference in Peter's behavior. Someone wondered if Peter's anger was connected to the way that Susan treated him.

Susan decided to try to recreate the independent circumstances of Peter's trip. She made a conscious decision to "back off" for a while and give her son some room. Peter became happier immediately. However, Susan was surprised that she had a strong reaction: she became depressed. As she examined these feelings in a talk, she felt deep sadness. It had become apparent to her that Peter had not needed her special focus and attention. He was happier living without it. Susan realized that she had been the one who had needed comfort, not Peter. In tending to Peter, she had really been tending to herself as a child.

Parents who are emotionally hungry act compulsively in relation to their children in much the same manner as an addict. They not only fail to nourish but actually drain the child of his/her resources. In this manner, their exaggerated attention and involvement have an ongoing negative impact on the child's development. These parents often find it difficult to reduce the intensity of their contact even when they recognize that the contact is damaging.

Deprivation, lack of genuine affection, interest, or concern

Deprivation may be manifested through either physical or emotional neglect. Children who are not provided with the necessary age-appropriate supervision are involved in more accidents and sustain more physical injuries than other children. Later, as adolescents and adults, they tend to be more accident prone and self-destructive (Orbach, 1988). In his summary of research on the effects of neglect, Orbach stated, "Neglect appears to amplify the destructive impact of abuse. The parents' apathy creates a feeling of superfluity in the child. At the most simple and direct level, the child learns that she is an unwanted burden" (p. 93). Similarly, children raised by "psychologically unavailable" parents often develop symptoms of "nonorganic failure to thrive" such as apathy, lethargy, or developmental delays.

Parents who themselves were deprived of love during their formative years often lack the emotional resources to offer love and affection to their child. The first author has termed the central ingredients for adequate nurturance as "love-food" (R. Firestone, 1957, 1984). The concept of love-food refers to the desire as well as the capability on the part of the parent to provide for need-gratification of the infant, which includes love, affection, necessary care, direction, and appropriate control or structure. Love-food is necessary for survival in both the physical and psychological sense.

Many parents imagine that they care deeply for their children, while, in fact, they make little real meaningful contact with them on a daily basis. A frequently cited finding by Szalai (1972) showed that the average parent spent only 5.4 minutes a day genuinely relating with his or her child. Parents often try to deny this reality by reassuring their children with statements such as "We really care about you but we're not the physically affectionate kind of people," or "We love you so much, that's why we're so tough on you."

Lack of sensitivity to the child, excessive permissiveness, and inconsistency

Parents who are cut off emotionally are necessarily insensitive to the needs of their children. They may be inappropriate in scheduling feedings, delay their responses to their baby's cries of hunger, or overfeed or force-feed the child. Some are incapable of feeding and caring for an infant without arousing undue anxiety or frustration in the child. Parents who lack sensitivity to their child's behavioral cues or emotional state often overstimulate their babies. Such parents are responding to their own inner state or agenda rather than adjusting their responses to their infants' mood.

Excessive permissiveness can be considered a form of neglect because the child fails to develop appropriate internal controls over acting-out behavior. Immature parents are usually unable to provide sufficient direction or structure for their children. The result is that children who are not properly socialized become anxious as adults because they are unable to successfully regulate or manage their emotions, particularly aggression. Consequently, they tend to act out irresponsibly, develop negative attitudes toward themselves, and feel considerable self-hatred (Shengold, 1991).

Many parents respond inconsistently in relation to their children breaking rules or otherwise misbehaving; they are sometimes harshly punitive and at other times indifferent. This leaves children confused as to what is right and wrong, and how they should behave. One particularly destructive pattern of inconsistency occurs when a personal interaction with the child threatens a parent's tolerance for love and intimacy. The parent may react by being especially punishing toward the child after sweet exchanges. This pattern of closeness followed by cruelty confuses children and predisposes feelings of distrust. As adults, these children continue to be distrustful of love and are particularly wary following close, loving, or intimate moments.

Parental role-playing and dishonesty

Fathers and mothers who role-play, offering "proper" responses rather than authentic reactions, tend to mislead and confuse their children. Talking and behaving in a manner that differs from their true feeling state has an adverse effect on the child's sense of reality. Many child-rearing books, in teaching how to relate to children, inadvertently encourage parents to offer these mixed messages and in that sense do more harm than good.

> When Andrea and Bruce had a daughter, Maggie, Andrea devoted herself completely to the role of being a mother. Her days were entirely consumed with practical tasks: organizing, cleaning, and transporting the child. Her focus on Maggie was so intense and her involvement in the details of her life so extensive that Maggie actually seemed to be frightened and overwhelmed by her mother.
>
> Bruce's style of relating to Maggie had the opposite effect; she was relaxed and happy in his presence. Bruce had no preconceived notions about the role of being a father, so he was

just himself with her. He did not restructure his life and become excessively "child centered." Instead, he included Maggie in the activities that he enjoyed: he liked to fish, so he took her along with him on fishing trips. He liked to cook, so he cooked with her. He liked to build, so he took her to the shop with him. He was genuinely interested in her and because he liked her and listened to her, his responses were appropriate and respectful. The child felt comfortable and affectionate toward the father and anxiously attached to the mother.

When parents are role-playing, children suffer from the absence of a genuine person in their lives. What they need are authentic adults who relate to them directly in terms of honest emotions. Children need a personal human response. When they look into the faces of adults, they want to see real feeling and real people being real people. They need the human beings that their parents are behind the roles. Furthermore, parents who are honest and vulnerable are more open to feeling and more likely to be lovable. Children need to be able to love their parents. When children are unable to feel this love or are actually provoked into feeling hatred toward their parents, they feel like they are bad and often carry this negativity about themselves into their adult lives.

Lack of positive role models

Children learn more from example than by what they are explicitly taught. When parents fail to provide an adequate role model their verbal prescriptions carry little meaning. If they want their children to develop into moral, honest adults with personal integrity, they must personify these characteristics in their own lives. Parents necessarily pass on to their offspring their own defenses and inadequacies as well as their implicit systems of dealing with life. In doing so, they unintentionally teach their children maladaptive and/or unethical attitudes and behaviors to the extent that they themselves manifest such attitudes and behaviors.[9]

Child-rearing in the friendship circle

To help future generations of children, people must try to overcome their tendency to deny the widespread condition of child abuse in our society. To protect our children we must objectively examine subtly dehumanizing child-rearing approaches. Children who are abused are more likely to be abusive, thereby perpetuating this unethical behavior through the generations. For these reasons, parents in the friendship circle have an ongoing interest in child-rearing practices. In the compassionate environment of the talks, they offer each other constructive criticism, advice, and the opportunity to understand and develop themselves personally.

The approach to parenting in these talks has a dual focus (R. Firestone, 1989). Parents discuss their specific concerns about their children, but more importantly they also focus on their own developmental issues. We have found that, in attempting to resolve their trauma by understanding and working through their own thoughts and emotions, parents can begin to have more compassion for their children as well as for themselves. This appears to be the key element that enables parents to alter their child-rearing practices in a positive direction.[10] We have come to realize that the most important thing that parents could do for their children is to improve their own emotional lives and learn to live more fully. With this realization, we continue to challenge our defenses, develop our understanding of self and others, and try to become better people and therefore better parents.

People in the friendship circle aspire to offer their children an environment that supports the development of their unique potentialities, with a minimum of unnecessarily destructive elements, during the socialization process. Hopefully, our values and ethical principles are being passed on to the children by our example as we endeavor to live lives of decency, honesty, and kindness. Our guiding principle for raising children has been that they owe us nothing while we owe them everything. We brought them into the world and are responsible for their existence; therefore, we must strive to further their goals and avoid interfering with the emergence of their uniqueness, their true nature (R. Firestone, et al, 2003).

Conclusion

Attitudes in relation to human decency, values, and ethics should be a fundamental consideration in an analysis of couples, family relationships, child-rearing practices, and social institutions. This type of inquiry would lead to a painstaking examination of our priorities in relation to traditional family values. Only by investigating the painful issues that would be made evident, can we begin to change negative behavioral patterns that damage children as well as ourselves.

As our friends and colleagues examined the forces that had caused them pain and suffering in the course of their development, they were able to distinguish personality traits and behaviors that were toxic and aversive from those that were positive or reinforcing of good feelings. They were motivated to overcome tendencies to act out behaviors that were detrimental to themselves and others.

Although this group of friends holds strong values regarding ethical issues and has put them into practice, their approach is nonintrusive. There is no mandate to change others and people are "left alone" in the best sense. The respectful and supportive environment has helped us to achieve more autonomy, reach our professional and career goals, create more fulfilling relationships, and live a harmonious way of life. These positive developments have led to a feeling of optimism in our circle of friends about the human potential for growth and change. We believe that other people can be inspired by our experience. They can be motivated to challenge their defensive behaviors and go on to fulfill their own destiny in life, rather than living out the life for which they were programmed by their families and the greater society.

Notes

1. Re: various theories about the source of ethical principles, Baumeister (2005) asserted: "The source of moral rules is a subject of debate .... Religions in particular, have emphasized moral action as one requirement for spiritual advancement" (p. 336). Philosopher Peter Singer (1993) claimed that "ethics is not something intelligible only in the context of religion" (p. 3). And E.O. Wilson (1998) in "The Biological Basis of Morality" declared: "I believe in the independence of moral values, whether from God or not, and I believe that moral values come from human beings alone, whether or not God exists" (para. 4).

   Olson (2007) called attention to the fact that "a body of empirical evidence reveals that the roots of prosocial behavior, including moral sentiments such as empathy, precede the evolution of culture" (para. 3). P. Singer (2006) further proposed that "Human nature is inherently social and the roots of human ethics lie in the evolved psychological traits and patterns of behavior that we share with other social mammals, especially primates" (p. 142). Also see a discussion of the evolutionary basis of ethics by Ober and Macedo (2006). One involuntary emotion identified by de Waal (2006) is empathy which he suggested was based on "emotional contagion."

2. The authors' approach to ethics is accepting in tone and spirit, much as was Andre Comte-Sponville's (1996/2001) approach in his book, *A Small Treatise on the Great Virtues.*

   Re: ethical living and mental health, Cicero (trans. 1971) in his discourse on the "good life" declared that "in order to live a happy life the only thing we need is moral goodness." Theorists and researchers in positive psychology have elucidated the relationship between ethical principles and good mental health (Keyes & Haidt, 2003; Peterson & Seligman, 2004). Piliavin (2003) cited studies showing that altruism and generosity improve people's mental health and well-being. In addition, recent brain-imaging experiments have investigated a number of neural structures hypothesized to be involved in feelings of well-being (Urry, et al, 2004).

3. Ethicists and philosophers have long debated the criteria that one should utilize in determining whether an action is ethical or unethical. Space does not permit an exposition of these criteria; however, in-depth descriptions of the various systems of ethics can be found in Beckwith (2002), Boss (2004), Bond (1996), Gibbs (2003), and Hauser (2006), among others. Importantly, Katzman (2005) emphasized the point that "moral relativism," like "cultural relativism," is an incorrect method for evaluating both character and action. See Beckwith (2002) for a discussion of *utilitarian* ethicists who believe that the moral rightness or wrongness of an act can be objectively or impersonally judged by its non-moral results and *deontological* ethicists who "stress the intrinsic moral rightness or wrongness of a particular act, motive, virtue, habit, or moral rule" (p. xiv). Deontological ethical systems are based on Kant's (1959) categorical imperative (cited by Browning, 2004, p. 244) Also see Hauser's (2006) overview of theories of moral judgment and action as set forth by deontological ethicists, among them Kant, Hume and Rawls.

   William James (1891/1948) stated that an important question in ethics is the psychological question which asks about "the historical *origin* of our moral ideas and judgments" (p. 66). Also see Agnes Heller (1996) existential/transcendental theory of ethics in *An Ethics of Personality.* Gibbs (2003), in interpreting Kohlberg's highest (7th) stage of moral development also placed importance on existential concerns: "From that vantage point (Stage 7), one transcends existential despair and experiences inspiration from a deeper reality for living in the light of love and justice—albeit in a world often dark with self-centered, angry distortion and injustice" (p. 195).

4. A convergence of recent findings from neuroscience, anthropology, evolutionary psychology and attachment theory points to still another fundamental human potentiality, the ability to make moral judgments. Flugel (1945) initially proposed that the determinants of moral action are *"our biological nature and our innate psychological equipment"* (p. 231) (italics added). Also see Hauser (2006) who asserted that "When we judge an action as morally right or wrong, we do so instinctively, tapping a system of unconsciously operative and inaccessible moral knowledge" (pp. 418–419). Hauser proposed that infants are born with the potentiality to form moral concepts, just as they are born with the potentiality to learn language, a thesis which contradicts Piaget's and Kohlberg's ideas about the moral development of children, that is, that it follows definite stages. Hauser explained that the child's innate ability to make moral judgments differs from Hume's and Hoffman's thesis that moral behavior is motivated by emotions such as empathy and the ability to take the other's perspective. In fact, Hauser suggested that the ability to judge between right and wrong may be what arouses these emotions in certain situations.

Evidence for an innate human potential for moral judgments and behaviors can also be found in the attachment literature. For example, on the basis of several research studies, Gillath, Shaver, and Mikulincer (2005) proposed that:

> Unlike 'selfish gene' theories (e.g. Dawkins, 1976), which discourage us from imagining that evolution equipped *Homo sapiens* with a capacity for compassion and care, attachment theory suggests that the same caregiving behavioral system [an innate behavioral system] that evolved to assure adequate care for vulnerable, dependent children can be extended to include care and concern for other people in need, perhaps even compassion for all suffering creatures—an important Buddhist ideal (p. 140).

See Mikulincer, et al (2003) regarding research findings supportive of this developmental hypothesis.

As noted, evolutionary theory provides further support for Hauser's thesis. A number of evolutionary biologists and psychologists (Joyce, 2006; Katz, 2000; Ridley 1996; Sober & Wilson, 1998) have hypothesized that "humans are by nature moral animals ... meaning that the process of evolution has designed us to think in moral terms, that biological natural selection has conferred upon us the tendency to employ moral concepts" (Joyce, 2006, p. 3). See Krebs' (2000b) discussion in Katz's (2000) volume *Evolutionary Origins of Morality* regarding mechanisms responsible for the evolution of generosity and of helping behavior. Krebs (2000a) has also pointed out that the selective: "benefits of cooperation contain the key that will unlock the door to an explanation of the evolution of morality ... If everyone cooperated, there would be no conflict within groups and everyone would come out ahead—the egalitarian moral ideal" (p. 142). Also see Ridley's (1996) *The Origins of Virtue: Human Instincts and the Evolution of Cooperation* and Richard Dawkin's (2006) *The God Delusion*. Dawkins suggested that "Altruistic giving may be an advertisement of dominance and superiority" (p. 218), traits that also enhance gene survival.

5. Emotional deprivation or neglect, as well as emotional, physical, and sexual abuse have been found to impair neuronal structures in the child's brain, which, in turn, negatively impact the development of moral judgment and ethical behavior (Schore, 1994, 2003; D. Siegel, 1999, 2001; D. Siegel & Hartzell, 2003). Siegel (2007) has identified morality as one of the nine functions of the middle prefrontal cortex. "This same region is active as we imagine ethical dilemmas and as we initiate moral action. We come to a sense of ourselves and of others, and a sense of right action and morality, through integrative circuitry in our neural core" (p. 322).

   Also see studies conducted by Koenigs, et al (2007) regarding the crucial role of emotions and an intact (undamaged) ventromedial prefrontal cortex in making moral judgments.

6. In his work, Erik Erikson (1963, 1969) agreed in substance with Weil's sentiments regarding the ethical obligation to meet a variety of human needs, physical, psychological, and spiritual. According to Browning (2004), Erickson's work exemplifies a "mixed deontological" model of moral obligation. In another work in which Erickson (1964) described the stages in child development (e.g. trust vs. mistrust, etc.), he emphasized the child's phylogenetic need for "mutual recognition of and by another face" (p. 94) as well as parents' obligation to try to meet that need.

7. Messman and Canary (1998) observed that couples and families "experience conflict as a routine aspect of relational life. However,

the routine nature of conflict renders fights, arguments, and confrontations no less hurtful to partners" (pp. 134–136).

8. Garbarino and Gilliam (1980) commented that:

> There is clear legal sanction for the use of physical force against children. The Texas legislature, for example, in 1974 enacted legislation containing the following statement: "The use of force, but not deadly force, against a child younger than 18 years is justified: (1) if the actor is the child's parent or stepparent ... (2) when and to the degree the actor believes the force is necessary to discipline the child" (p. 32).

9. With respect to teaching children unethical attitudes and behaviors through role-modeling, Katzman (2005) noted that: "The articles of the Convention [on the Rights of the Child] that appear to be incompatible with the teaching of children to hate include ... Article 3 ... the best interests of the child shall be the primary consideration"(p. 145).

10. The amount of time parents spend in attuned communication or misattuned interactions is not the most relevant factor influencing the emotional development of children; rather, the most significant factor is that parents attempt to repair ruptures that inevitably occur in interactions with the infant or child. As parents regained compassion for themselves in the parenting talks, they developed more compassion and sensitivity to their child, thereby facilitating the process of repair.

PART II
COPING WITH UNETHICAL WAYS OF LIVING

CHAPTER FOUR

Mastering anger

A man that does not know how to be angry does not know how to be good.
Henry Ward Beecher (1887) Proverbs from Plymouth Pulpit

Feeling angry is a universal human phenomenon. It is as basic as feeling hungry, lonely, loving, or tired.
Theodore Rubin (1969, p. 3)

The management of anger is a primary consideration in relation to ethical issues. The inappropriate acting out of anger and hostility in interpersonal relationships is pervasive and plays a destructive role within couples and in family life. It can lead to anti-social and criminal behavior and ultimately to national and ethnic violence (De Zulueta, 1993; Geen & Donnerstein, 1998; J. Gilligan, 1996b; Kecmanovic, 1996; Staub, 1989; Volavka, 2002; Waller, 2002).

Anger is an automatic response to frustration and stress (Bandura, 1973; N. Miller & Dollard, 1941). The acceptance of anger and the ability to tolerate angry feelings, whether rational or irrational, make anger accessible to control and regulation. Intolerance of

73

angry feelings leads to acting out behaviors and the internalization, projection, and displacement of anger.

Although there are obvious negative connotations associated with anger, it has a number of constructive and adaptive functions. During evolutionary times, the ability to experience anger was necessary for survival. Threats from predators and other enemies evoked fear and led to appropriate "fight or flight" reactions. The feeling of anger provided the energy and motivation required for the aggressive behavior necessary for self-protection (Kotulak, 1996)[1]. In modern society, anger and outrage at social injustices have provided the impetus behind many positive changes in the political and social arena. As Baumeister (2005) pointed out: "Aggression upholds a principle, or defends someone's honor, or solves a problem" (p. 359). Similarly, in personal relationships, anger, when expressed appropriately, can function to change aversive behavior and overcome barriers to intimacy (Bach & Deutsch, 1979; R. Firestone & Catlett, 1999; Gottman & Krokoff, 1989; Lerner, 1985; Potter-Efron, 1994).

Learning to accept angry emotions uncritically as they arise and to express them appropriately in personal interactions is vital to achieving harmony in close relationships. Indeed, maintaining contact with the full range of one's negative emotions—anger, sadness, fear, disgust, envy, and shame—is essential to maintaining a strong sense of identity, leading a life of integrity, and finding personal meaning in life (Oatley, 1996; Parrott & Harre, 1996).

Specific ethical considerations are associated with the consequences of mishandling anger. The failure to effectively communicate angry feelings in an intimate relationship leads to an increase in hostility and cynicism that damages both parties and creates distance. When people suppress their angry emotions, they are more likely to act them out destructively, either against themselves or against others (R. Firestone, 1985; A. Miller, 1980/1984; Prescott, 1975). Since one cannot selectively suppress feelings, blocking out anger and other "unacceptable" emotions seriously limits one's experience of positive emotions. More importantly, the intensity of suppressed anger can build up until it erupts into aggressive, explosive behavior that can lead to child abuse, violent acts, or homicide. The buried anger can also be turned against the self, leading to self-destructive acts or eventually suicide (Fonagy, 2004b; J. Gilligan, 1996b; McFarlane & van der Kolk, 1996).

Theories of human aggression

Aggression is not strictly a clinical term. "It is a lay term ... and it is used to describe a number of functionally different behaviors, all having in common the infliction of [verbal or physical] harm upon another person" (Geen, 1994, p. 1). In contrast to theories of aggression set forth by Sigmund Freud (1925/1959) and Melanie Klein (1948/1964), who asserted that infants possess innate aggression or a death instinct, the authors propose that human beings are not innately aggressive, destructive, or self-destructive. It is true that they have the capacity for violence[2] but this is different from an instinct for violence. "They become aggressive, violent, or harmful to self only in response to emotional pain, fear, rejection and deprivation" (R. Firestone, 1997a, p. 4). Furthermore, anger and self-destructive tendencies aroused in early interactions within the family are reinforced and intensified by the frustration and anguish brought about by the child's evolving knowledge of his or her personal death. Self-destructive tendencies based on anger that is turned against the self can be a defensive attempt to accommodate to death by deadening oneself in advance, by divesting oneself of an emotional investment in a life one must ultimately lose.

On a phenomenological level, the authors are in agreement with Freud's observation of people's self-destructiveness and destructiveness toward others. However, we emphasize that self-destructive tendencies and aggression are based more on frustration related to early interpersonal pain, in addition to the anxiety and despair intrinsic in the human condition, than any inherent tendencies.

Other theories of human aggression

Contemporary theories of aggression are still somewhat contradictory. In a review of current theories, Anderson and Bushman (2002) commented: "Research on human aggression has progressed to a point at which a unifying framework is needed" (p. 27).[3] In fact, there is still considerable debate regarding nature versus nurture—genetic versus environmental—antecedents of aggression. In her work, De Zulueta (1993) noted that "A brief survey of the writings on human aggression and violence may give the reader some insight into the difficulties involved in studying our own behaviour without subjecting our findings to our deeply held assumptions about human nature" (p. 28).[4]

Theorists and researchers do agree that there are two primary types of aggression: angry or *affective aggression* "in which harming the victim is the main motive for the act; and *instrumental aggression*, which may or may not involve strong emotions but is motivated by concerns more important to the aggressor than the harmdoing itself" (Geen, 2001, p. 4). As an example of instrumental aggression, some individuals engage in aggressive acts out of a need for self-protection, to support a drug habit, for monetary gain, or to enhance their standing as a gang member, and not necessarily out of an angry impulse to inflict bodily harm on anyone.

Blair (2001) distinguished reactive aggression from instrumental aggression. In reactive aggression, the individual perceives a threat and reacts by being aggressive. Instrumental and reactive aggression are associated with different development disorders. Borderline Personality Disorder is linked to reactive aggression, whereas psychopaths engage in high levels of both instrumental aggression and reactive aggression (R. Firestone & Firestone, 2008).

Aggression is a highly complex emotional phenomenon driven by diverse motivations (Eron, Gentry & Schlegel, 1994; Pepler & Slaby, 1994). For example, there is a great deal of difference in the emotions motivating domestic violence, physical, emotional, and sexual maltreatment of children, gang clashes, and warfare.

In some situations, aggression is culturally acceptable, while in others there are strong social sanctions against it. For example, aggressive assaults are often an integral part of an adolescent's identification with a gang which, in the context of an impoverished inner-city subculture, can be an appropriate adaptation or a survival strategy, as well as a rite of passage (J. Gilligan, 2001). However, gang activity obviously leads to antisocial acts, criminal activity, and, in some cases, homicide. Aggression in the service of defending one's country is socially acceptable and laudable, yet military action and wartime atrocities have killed millions of innocent civilians as well as members of the armed forces. Within most societies, criminal activity and aggression and physical mistreatment acted out in personal relationships are not only considered antisocial but are an indication of psychopathology.

Certain forms of passive-aggression or civil disobedience can achieve goals that are worthwhile and that are not necessarily at the expense of other people. Strategies of nonviolent disobedience used by Mahatma Ghandi and Martin Luther King Jr., and those exemplified in the civil rights and women's movements and in early phases of the labor union movement have contributed significantly to social reform and economic gains for many people. On the other hand, passive-aggressive behavior, when manifested as a means of control or manipulation in a personal relationship, is damaging to both individuals.

When verbally and physically aggressive behaviors are acted out in a close relationship, Geen (1998) argued that the most important question to ask is "What are the intervening processes that connect the instigating condition to the aggressive response?" Berkowitz (1993) asserted that anger plays a significant role in these intervening processes. He specified, however, that anger is not an antecedent condition but runs parallel to the impulsive aggression. Berkowitz also emphasized that an impulsive, "knee-jerk" reaction to frustration is "only a potential first stage in aggression" (p. 4). Beyond this point, he believed that cognitive processes play an important role in the way that aggression is acted upon. Thus identifying specific cognitions or thought processes that strongly influence aggressive behavioral responses could be crucial to the study of aggression and to a more accurate assessment of the potential for violence in high-risk individuals.

In our work, the authors have found it valuable to access and identify destructive thoughts or voices that strongly influence or control maladaptive aggressive and/or violent behavior. In our investigations, we found a close connection between negative, cynical, or paranoid thought processes and destructive behavior toward others. *The Firestone Assessment of Violent Thoughts (FAVT)* (R. Firestone & Firestone, 2008) was developed as an instrument to test this hypothesis and to provide mental health professionals and criminologists with a scale to determine an individual's violence potential. We found evidence that specific attitudes or "voices" were predictive of aggression and/or violence and conversely that one could deduce from an individual's violent behavior patterns the types of thoughts he or she was experiencing.[5]

A number of social psychologists, among them Zimbardo, Maslach, and Haney (1999), have investigated situational variables hypothesized to increase the probability that otherwise emotionally healthy individuals will engage in aggressive behaviors even when these acts violate their ethics and values. For example, the classic Stanford Prison experiment (Haney & Zimbardo, 1998; Zimbardo & White, 1972) was conducted using "normal" students who played the roles of guards and prisoners. The experiment had to be called off after only six days because of the emotional breakdown in "prisoners" and the aggressive, dehumanizing behavior of "guards" who became progressively more parental, authoritarian, and sadistic toward the prisoners. The experiment demonstrated that although people do not necessarily have an inborn instinct for aggression or violence, they have the potential to behave aggressively under certain conditions. According to Zimbardo, et al (1999), the behavior of the guards showed that:

> Good people can be induced, seduced, initiated into behaving in evil (irrational, stupid, self-destructive, antisocial) ways by immersion in "total situations" that can transform human nature in ways that challenge our sense of the stability and consistency of individual personality, character, and morality (p. 10).[6]

Causal factors

From a developmental perspective, overly aggressive and/or violent behaviors were found to be significantly correlated with disorganized attachment in early childhood (De Zulueta, 1993; Fonagy, 1999, 2004a, 2004b; Lyons-Ruth, Yellin, Melnick & Atwood, 2005; Main & Hesse, 1990; Seifert, 2003). Attachment research indicates that a parent's unresolved trauma and loss are predictive of the formation of a disorganized attachment pattern with the child. Early psychological stress, specifically from a severely misattuned maternal environment, which is related to a disorganized attachment pattern, can negatively impact brain development, including brain systems that regulate the production of a stress hormone—cortisol (Fonagy, 2004a). Schore (2002b) noted that "abused type D (disorganized) infants show higher cortisol levels than all other attachment classifications ... . Infants raised in a neglectful environment show a low cortisol pattern" (p. 17). These differential patterns lead respectively to hyperarousal and hypoarousal or dissociation.

Schore also found that severe hyperarousal is associated with a predisposition to reactive rage, whereas infant neglect is associated with severe hypoarousal and later fearless aggressive behavior and a predisposition to predatory rage.[7]

Several theorists, among them J. Gilligan (2001) and Dutton (1995a), contend that violent behavior is related to familial and social conditions that evoke unbearable feelings of shame. Gilligan emphasized that:

> It is not poverty, racism, sexism, or age-discrimination, as such, that actually cause violence. It is, rather, that each correlates with violence because each increases the statistical probability that individuals exposed to these social forces will be subjected to intolerable and potentially self-destroying intensities of shame, from which they do not perceive themselves as having any means of rescuing themselves except by violence (p. 66).

In a somewhat similar vein, Baumeister (1997; Bushman & Baumeister, 1998) suggested that violence is related to narcissistic wounds or "ego-threats" that often trigger feelings of shame. Baumeister (1997) proposed that "ego-threats, that is, the combination of high self-esteem [inflated self-esteem or vanity] and an external, unflattering evaluation—are the principal cause of violence" (p. 143).

Herzog (2001) found that toddlers who had suffered physical abuse and who had dissociated during the episodes, tended to repeat the abusive pattern with younger children. In such situations, "identification with the aggressor seemed to be the resultant patterning" (p. 90).

The authors agree with Herzog that at times of overwhelming stress, the child identifies with the aggressor (Ferenczi, 1933/1955; R. Firestone, 1997a; Fraiberg, et al, 1980; A. Freud, 1966). At the moment of crisis, the child finds it necessary to depersonalize and ceases to identify with him/herself as the helpless child and instead identifies with the all-powerful, angry, aggressive parent. Even a depressed parent who is self-hating and moody is often perceived by the child as angry or threatening. The defense helps to allay severe anxiety states and a feeling of fragmentation but in the process, the child internalizes the anger and hostility of the parent. Later on, in times of emotional stress, he/she is likely to unleash the same aggression toward self and others that he/she experienced. This concept explains the intergenerational transmission of child abuse. The incorporated parental anger can be manifested in the adult individual in many different ways: (1) it can be directed against other people; (2) it can be experienced as self-hatred and expressed in indirect or actual self-destructive behavior, depression, or psychosomatic symptomology; (3) it can be acted out in a manner that provokes abuse from others; or (4) it can be projected or externalized onto other people. In the latter situation, individuals disown anger in themselves, externalize it, and as a result, perceive others as being overly angry or aggressive toward them.

The authors' understanding of how aggression is transmitted through successive generations also takes into account social learning theory (Bandura & Walters, 1963), which proposes that children learn through example (role-modeling) to imitate a parent's or other family member's aggressive behavior. When the child grows up, he or she manifests the same aggressive patterns, most often through identification with and imitation of the behavior patterns characteristic of the parent of the same sex.

Maladaptive manifestations of aggression

> Perverted anger twisted into grotesque forms must eventually poison one's self as well as one's relationships with others (Rubin, 1969, p. 32).

In attempting to live according to their values and ideals, many people experience difficulty in dealing with anger. The key issue involved in the mishandling of anger is the imposition of rational constraints on emotions, which then limits one's ability to fully experience feelings on a conscious level. There are a number of reasons why people are reluctant to feel their anger or fail to even recognize that they are angry. For example, most children are punished or criticized for feeling angry. They are encouraged to deny or suppress their anger when it seems unreasonable. As adults, they continue to suppress angry feelings that they believe are unreasonable or too intense. However, anger is experienced in proportion to the degree of frustration a person feels regardless of whether it is rational or irrational.

Self-denying individuals are often confused and disoriented when their anger is aroused because, in spite of their self-protective posture, they still experience anger when their wants or needs are frustrated. The failure to clearly identify the source of their frustration contributes to inappropriate responses, such as irrational outbursts of irritability or self-defeating, passive-aggressive behaviors. Similarly, retreating from competitive situations intensifies feelings of jealousy, leading to chronic low-grade anger and, at times, to aggressive or violent acts of revenge.

Externalized anger

Some people project their anger onto others and perceive them as more threatening than they actually are. They then act out preemptively against those who are mistakenly identified as a source of frustration or humiliation and provoke the very aggression or abusive treatment they fear. This acts as a self-fulfilling prophecy and there is a spiraling effect that can culminate in overt aggression or violence. On a societal level, the negative consequences of this phenomenon are often profound.

In addition, anger may be displaced from one person or situation on to another when it is too threatening to be faced in the original context. Angry emotions toward relationships that are sources of security—that is, parents, family members, or spouses—are often redirected toward innocent substitutes. The anger may be acted out toward associates or friends, taking its toll in the work place, social settings, or in society at large. In particular, attitudes toward early authority figures are often transferred to new objects, leading to inappropriate responses toward people in leadership positions.

Displaced anger is also a serious factor in racial and religious prejudices. In this case anger involved in one's interpersonal relationships is diverted onto specific groups. This outlet is experienced as safe whereas the more personal expression of rage is either too threatening or too guilt provoking. The aggression connected with prejudice may be a prevailing cultural pattern that is considered acceptable or even laudable by members of the in-group.

"Externalizers" often develop a victimized or paranoid orientation toward life, responding with righteous indignation and rage to real or imagined slights, insults, or disappointments.

Individuals who are intolerant of angry feelings in themselves are likely to feel powerless, helpless, and victimized. They blame others for their problems, hold grudges, and have a desire for revenge. This maladaptive response leads to obsessive ruminating and storing up of anger that is unpleasant and dysfunctional and often culminates in uncontrollable outbursts. In particular, sustained anger toward others that focuses on taking revenge for having been hurt, wronged or treated unjustly may have long-term detrimental effects on one's mental health.[8]

In general, the tendency to externalize anger is more prominent in males than in females (Geen, 1998).[9] Dutton (1995b) has found that men who engage in interpersonal or domestic violence often do so as a reaction to abandonment anxiety. A man's extreme dependency on his wife or partner is usually masked by isolating strategies designed to make her dependent through intimidation, threats, and actual physical assault. According to Dutton, "sexual jealousy, especially to the extent that it involves delusions or distortions, may represent a form of chronic abandonment anxiety. Jealousy is frequently mentioned by battered women as an issue that incited violence" (p. 68). Narcissistic rage aroused by events perceived as threatening or devastating to the perpetrator's vanity or inflated self-esteem is also a factor in many cases of domestic and criminal violence (Baumeister, Smart & Boden, 1996; J. Gilligan, 2001).

Internalized anger

People who are afraid to feel or express anger or hostility directly often internalize their angry feelings and turn them against themselves. Many individuals indirectly express anger or hostility through passive-aggressive manipulations. Others develop a variety of physical symptoms or psychosomatic illnesses. For example, individuals who habitually suppress their anger may develop migraine headaches, ulcers, hypertension, arthritic conditions, asthma, or heart problems (Eaker, Sullivan, Kelly-Hayes, D'Agostino & Benjamin, 2007).[10] When anger is turned inward it often leads to feelings of depression and worthlessness. Psychoanalysts have traditionally described depression as primarily due to anger directed against the self.

In a certain sense, most aggression is related to anger toward the self. The hostility that many people feel toward others is a derivative of their own self-hatred and self-attacks. In these instances, the self is simply externalized in the acting out of aggression toward another person. In concentration camps, guards frequently acted out violence toward prisoners, punishing them as though they were bad children. Their tone often took on a parental quality. In terms of psychodynamics, they were brutally punishing their child selves akin to how they had been treated or disciplined as children. Some of the same dynamics were undoubtedly operating in the prisoner/guard experiment with college students described earlier.[11]

Violence and suicide

Violence, the extreme manifestation of externalized anger, and suicide, the ultimate expression of internalized anger, tend to overlap to a certain extent. According to Plutchik and van Praag (1990), about "30 percent of violent individuals have a history of self-destructive behavior, while about 10–20 percent of suicidal persons have a history of violent behavior" (p. 37). These researchers conducted investigations in an attempt to find out why some people turn to suicide and others to violence. Identifying specific negative thoughts or voices that are experienced by individuals who are at risk for suicidal or violent behavior can provide a partial answer to Plutchik and van Praag's question.

Furthermore, a number of symptoms exhibited by young children are predictive of either violent or self-destructive behavior later in life. For example, a child who has an oppositional behavioral disorder, who is agitated and hyperactive, who is aggressive toward peers, who has trouble regulating his or her emotions, or who exerts hostile control over parents and teachers, is more likely than other children to engage in aggressive or violent behavior as an adolescent and adult (Fonagy, Target, Steele & Steele, 1997; Jacobvitz & Hazen, 1999; Liotti, 1999; Perry, 1997). A child who is withdrawn, isolated, and appears depressed is more likely than another, more assertive child to become self-destructive or suicidal later on. Clearly, there are variations within each developmental pathway. For example, in some cases, Jacobvitz and Hazen (1999) observed an inflexible style of relating to peers in withdrawn children that can lead them to "seek out peer playmates that reinforce their negative views of self and other, such as the bullies" (p. 155). These researchers emphasized that "along with looking at aggressive and withdrawn behavior in more depth, considerably more attention should be given to odd, socially, and affectively disconnected behaviors and communication patterns that are out of sync with the ongoing peer interaction" (p. 154).

Violent and suicidal behaviors are both influenced by physiological or biological factors. In fact, researchers have suggested using certain biochemical indicators to evaluate the risk of suicide or recurrent impulsive violent behavior (G. Brown, Linnoila & Goodwin, 1990; Linnoila, Virkkunen, Roy & Potter, 1990). Imbalances in specific brain chemicals are known to be correlated with impulsivity and problems in regulating emotions, which, in turn, are recognized as risk factors for both suicidal and violent behavior.[12]

The role of alcohol and drugs in facilitating violent and/or suicidal behavior

The close association between excessive alcohol or drug use and incidents of violence and suicide has long been acknowledged. According to Roizen (1997), approximately 86 percent of homicide offenders, as well as 57 percent of men and 27 percent of women involved in marital violence, were drinking at the time of their offense.[13] It has been hypothesized that alcohol encourages aggression and/or violence by disrupting normal brain function. Drinking to excess weakens brain mechanisms that usually restrain impulsive behavior, including inappropriate aggression. Habitual use of alcohol also predisposes faulty information processing, causing people to misjudge social cues and overreact aggressively to a perceived threat or danger.

Many drugs, both legal and illegal, are associated with heightened aggressive responses. For example, several mild tranquilizers, including the benzodiazepines, may facilitate hostility in psychiatric patients (S. Taylor and Hulsizer, 1998). Agitation, anger, and aggressive behavior were observed in patients, with and without psychiatric histories, who took triazolam (Halcion), a benzodiazepine used to treat insomnia. Unfortunately, Halcion and other anti-anxiety drugs are routinely prescribed to relieve withdrawal symptoms in recovering alcoholics. At times, certain antidepressants, rather than preventing depression, have acted to precipitate a suicidal outcome.

Many crimes are committed in order to acquire illegal drugs. Many of these drugs, methamphetamines and crack cocaine, for example, have a strong potential for increasing violent behavior.[14] The fact that research findings show that drug or alcohol abuse exacerbate the acting out of aggressive, self-destructive, or suicidal behaviors underscores the destructive consequences of these types of addictions (El-Bassel, Gilbert, Wu, Go & Hill, 2005; Kingery, Pruitt & Hurley, 1992; Roth, 1994).

Pseudoaggression

Pseudoaggression refers to the type of anger that is used to provoke rejection, create distance, and restore psychological equilibrium. This end is achieved through acts of defiance and hostility, verbal aggression, and the acting out of withholding behavior patterns that provoke and alienate others. In this way, people control their interpersonal environment and preserve their psychological defenses at the expense of a more emotionally satisfying, fulfilling existence.

Pseudoaggression differs from anger that is a reaction to frustration in that it is often a response to the discomfort aroused by positive acknowledgment or being especially loved and valued in an intimate relationship. When individuals receive love or are admired in a way that contradicts their negative self-concept, their psychological equilibrium is threatened. Any disruption of one's defenses or any challenge to one's core identity in the family-of-origin tends to arouse anxiety. Unusually positive experiences often trigger deep sadness and other painful emotions which in turn predispose anger and hostility (R. Firestone, 1985, 1990a). When this happens, people try to numb the pain by manipulating, pushing away, or otherwise taking control over the other person's loving, admiring, or acknowledging responses.

> Judy S. was a case in point. At 25, she was the most successful salesperson in a new company that was experiencing rapid growth. She was highly regarded as a trainer and manager of her sales team, whose profits were the backbone of the company. Because of her record sales, the president of the company presented her with a large bonus at the firm's annual dinner. In his speech, he expressed appreciation for her substantial

contribution to the company and acknowledged her as top salesperson of the year. Judy was thrilled by the bonus and deeply touched by the personal recognition from her boss.

Later, however, Judy reacted negatively. She began arriving late for work and missed several important sales meetings with her team. She delegated "cold" sales calls to members of her team, even though making introductory calls to find new business was something she had found especially gratifying. The president of the company was initially puzzled, then angry, and responded to the decline in her performance by reducing her commission rate.

Alarmed, Judy talked with a friend who suggested that she might be reacting to the unusual recognition and personal response from her boss. In thinking over her friend's idea, Judy recalled that the bonus had not only made her happy, but also uncomfortable and anxious. Her boss' praise and appreciation stood out in her mind as being different from anything she had experienced in her family. In the weeks following the dinner, she had started to doubt her ability to continue working at the same level over the long haul. She began to put pressure on herself to live up to her previous sales record and felt resentful, imagining the pressure was coming from her boss. Her resentment and low-grade anger, which she suppressed, were expressed in her holding back the activities that had earned her the recognition. Understanding the source of her seemingly perverse reaction to success enabled Judy to gradually reverse the trend toward failure.

Maladaptive aggression in interpersonal relationships, family life, and society

Learning to handle anger constructively is paramount in establishing a code of ethics in couple and family relationships and in society at large. Uncontrolled aggression directed outward in personal interactions is obviously damaging to others but is harmful to the self as well. Ironically, although manifestations of outright aggression, including verbal or emotional violence, are clearly recognized as destructive expressions, the majority of people in most societies believe that corporal punishment is an important part of teaching children discipline (Felitti, et al, 1998; Gershoff, 2002; Greven, 1990; Prescott, 1996; Straus, 1996, 2001).[15]

Maladaptive aggression in interpersonal relationships

In an intimate relationship, when one person's negative, defensive behavior evokes an angry reaction from the other, the resulting conflict will generally escalate. On the other hand, some people are unable to respond with direct anger to such provocations; instead they brood, sulk, or act out passive-aggressive manipulations. Bach and Deutsch (1970) called attention to the harmful effects associated with each partner's failure to communicate angry responses to provocations from the other and suggested a way out of this impasse. They implied that acknowledging angry emotions can avert long-term misunderstandings and conflict in interpersonal relationships.

> [Most people are peace-loving.] They tend to overestimate how much one can swallow and forget ... . [However] aggressive assertion of one's real feelings can ... keep small hurts and annoyances, born of carelessness and misunderstanding, from becoming buried resentments that build up to block a pair from real intimacy (p. 179).

In some couples, behaviors on the part of a more passive or compliant individual precipitate angry responses in the other. When the childish, victimized behaviors of a passive-aggressive person provoke an aggressive response or abusive treatment from the more dominant, assertive individual, both parties are damaged psychologically in the exchange. Both people collude in this dynamic interaction. It is just as unethical to continue to accept abuse from a loved one as it is to act it out. This statement does not imply that one should blame the victim or excuse the perpetrator.[16]

Maladaptive aggression in child-rearing

In an examination of typical child-rearing patterns, there are numerous parenting situations that have the potential for arousing unnecessarily aggressive responses in both parents and children. Parents who are immature, defensive, or burdened, or who are hostile or emotionally rejecting, arouse intense anger and hostility in their offspring and these patterns usually persist into adult life.

Insensitive, harsh power plays on the part of parents are degrading and humiliating to children, creating painful feelings of shame. Shame has been found to be a precursor of violent behavior in many incarcerated men (J. Gilligan, 2001). Parents who unnecessarily suppress their children, humiliate them, or degrade them while proclaiming their love for them, offer a double message that contributes to the unhealthy suppression of aggression and reactive anger in their children. Bach and Goldberg (1974) described this "crazy-making" scenario as follows: "The child victim is trapped if there is no liberating outside intervention. The double-binding parent overcontrols, blocks out other influences and projects the image of a caring parent, which makes him that much more difficult to confront" (p. 256).

There are other environmental factors that contribute to the development of maladaptive forms of aggression and/or violent acting out behavior in adolescents and adults. For example, research shows that children who witness violence in their families or communities or who are physically, emotionally, or sexually abused are at increased risk of becoming violent later in life (Blair, Colledge, Murray & Mitchell, 2001; J. Gilligan, 2001; A. Miller, 1998; Schore, 1994; Whitfield, Anda, Dube & Felitti, 2003).[17]

The compulsion on the part of many parents to act out aggressive behavior in relation to a child is largely due to internalized anger from their own childhood and defenses they formed in relation to unresolved trauma and grief. According to D. Siegel (2001), during times of stress, the prefrontal cortex of such parents is "off-line," or more technically, in a "low-mode," and the flow of information from brain structures that control impulsive behavioral responses is interrupted. In this state of mind, parents are largely cut off from normal feelings of empathy, the ability to self-reflect (mindfulness), and considerations of morality. D. Siegel has described the emotional state of parents when they are in the "low-mode" of reacting:

> One aspect of unresolved trauma or grief is to make such a lower mode of processing more likely to occur … . Entry into such lower-mode states may produce excessive emotional reactions, inner turmoil, dread, or terror, as well as an ensuing sense

of shame and humiliation. In such conditions, the individual may be prone to "infantile rage" and aggressive, intrusive, or outright violent behavior (p. 88).

In other words, these parents are reacting in terms of fear responses and implicit nonverbal memories from the past and are generally unaware of the damage they are inflicting on their children. Moreover, they often fail to repair the disintegration in the relationship caused by their aggression, that is, they fail to soothe or reassure the child afterward, which only serves to exacerbate the child's trauma or distress (Siegel & Hartzell, 2003).

Societal suppression of anger and sexuality

There are a number of religions that promulgate a basic view of anger that is both inaccurate and, in a sense, immoral. This attitude equates thoughts and feelings with behaviors in terms of morality, that is, "bad" (angry or lustful) thoughts are as reprehensible and subject to condemnation as "bad" behavior. Equating thoughts with behavior is unethical. It is psychologically damaging to those people who, in attempting to live a good life, try to suppress any thought or feeling they judge as bad. As the authors have noted, thoughts and feelings should not be subjected to moral scrutiny; they are internal processes that do not hurt anyone. Only actions, including verbal actions, cause harm. Accepting and even enjoying "nasty," mean thoughts and fantasies are part of a healthy orientation. Acceptance of negative feelings leads to better control over these negative emotions and is therefore moral.

It also appears that dogmatic religious beliefs that are suppressive of sexuality and pleasure contribute indirectly to the expression of aggression and/or violence. Findings from anthropological research (Prescott, 1975, 1996; Stoller, 1975) have shown that politically, religiously, or sexually suppressive societies are especially restrictive in relation to anger and sexual behavior. These restrictions in turn lead to increased crime, sexual assault, rape, and deviant forms of sexuality. According to Prescott (1975) "Research supports the point of view that the deprivation of physical pleasure is a major ingredient in the expression of physical violence" (para. 2).

Dealing effectively with anger

> Inhibited aggression, as a major source of emotional symptoms,
> is to today's society what inhibited or repressed sexuality was
> as a creator of emotional problems during Freud's era (Bach &
> Goldberg, 1974, p. 155).

Mastering anger essentially involves a process of re-education: dispelling false assumptions about anger, and learning fundamental principles about aggression in relation to mental health issues. There is a logical approach to dealing with anger and aggressive feelings that the authors have used with their clients. They have emphasized (1) that anger is a normal and inevitable reaction to frustration; (2) that feelings must be allowed free reign in consciousness while actions are subject to moral considerations; and (3) that decisions regarding the outward expression of anger involve both reality issues and moral concerns. This approach addresses the question of whether acting out anger is in one's self-interest. For example, it is not in the interest of a person who values his/her job and wants to keep it to blow up at the boss. One would choose to feel the feelings of anger but not act them out.

In therapy, clients are encouraged to freely express their angry emotions. The therapist and client then evaluate the meaning or cause, explore the primal component, and discuss ways of dealing with anger in the real-life situation. The negative thought processes or voices that led up to the aggressive response are investigated. This approach to anger offers a client relief and an understanding of his or her emotions, enabling the client to act responsibly in relation to these feelings.

In some cases, venting angry feelings may not be necessary; simply recognizing and understanding angry emotions can be sufficient. For example, in his first session, a client told the first author that he felt like he was going crazy with anger and rage. During the previous year, his friend and business partner had betrayed him by embezzling funds from their company, refusing to admit guilt, and forcing my client out of the partnership. The client found himself obsessed with thoughts of murder and bodily harm, picturing mutilated limbs and blood. He was thoroughly shaken up by the intensity of his emotions. He was left feeling as though he were guilty of murder. During the session, we spoke about his anger and

I reassured him that he was not going insane. His angry reactions to being deceived and robbed were entirely appropriate and natural, and he had every right to feel as angry as he was at his partner. The only therapy that the client needed in this case was to understand his anger and to have his reality validated. He came to realize that there was a great deal of difference between angry thoughts, which have no outside consequences, and angry actions, which do.

Expressing anger in a close relationship

The ultimate purpose for engaging in an honest exchange of angry feelings in an intimate relationship is to heal the fracture, not worsen it. The goal is for people to feel free to communicate any aspect of emotional pain they might be experiencing, clarify the area in which they feel distress, and ask for what they want. The aim is to seek relief from agitated emotions and precipitate a desired change, and this is more readily achieved through negotiation rather than the escalation of angry diatribes.

In working with couples, the authors encourage partners to communicate their anger in a neutral, matter-of-fact tone of voice rather than in an accusatory or parental manner. If one person verbalizes his or her frustration angrily or emotionally, or expresses wants and needs as a demand, there is often a resultant angry response from the other that escalates the situation. We counsel partners to be specific in describing their frustration, hurt, or disappointment, i.e. the reasons they are angry, without implying that the other person is responsible for their angry feelings or actions. We stress the importance of people taking responsibility for how they handle or mishandle their aggression.

The concept of responsibility in relation to a person's maladaptive response to frustration and anger is difficult to assign, especially when an individual reacts by becoming self-destructive. For example, if a woman leaves her lover and he then commits suicide, is she responsible for his suicide? Although her rejection was a factor in his feeling hurt and angry, the way that he dealt with his anger is what led to his suicide; that was his responsibility, not hers. Ethically speaking, she had the right to pursue her own direction in life and was in no way responsible for his turning his anger inward against himself.

With couples whose arguments invariably escalate to vicious name-calling and denigration of each other, we often suggest that the individuals utilize a strategy referred to as "unilateral disarmament." One partner unilaterally makes a move toward reconciliation before the argument has gone too far, an act which requires considerable self-discipline at a time when emotions are running high. Applying this strategy does not mean that the person surrenders his or her point of view or gives in to the other. Instead, it represents a powerful expression of vulnerability and nondefensiveness and suggests that it is more important to restore harmony than prove one is right.

Maintaining a posture of nondefensiveness facilitates the development of a more sensitive understanding of the other person's hurt, anger, and other painful emotions. It involves having an objective, balanced view of oneself and one's partner as well as being receptive to feedback (R. Firestone & Catlett, 1999). In contrast, defensive individuals react with anger and hostility to criticism or confrontation by counterattacking rather than by exploring the veracity or falsity of the information they receive.

We also encourage couples to refrain from manipulating each other through guilt, weakness, or passive-aggressive behaviors that express an underlying hostility. We found that, prior to therapy, most couples were largely unaware of the communications and behaviors that had served the unconscious purpose of pushing their partner away and creating distance. Therefore, we help couples become familiar with the dynamics underlying destructive distancing responses and teach them methods to struggle and better cope with fears associated with intimacy.

Understanding the primal component of angry emotions

To help clients become aware of the effect of suppressed and unconscious aspects of anger, the authors help them to identify primal feelings from the past that influence and exaggerate angry reactions to present-day frustrations. These feelings are often triggered by situations in adult life that are similar to circumstances or events in childhood that originally caused distress. Because of their helplessness, extreme dependency, and comparatively small size in relation to adults, children's emotions are intense and their fear reactions are often experienced on a life-and-death level. For the most part, overly intense emotional reactions in adults have a distorting primal component based on early experiences that were originally perceived as threatening. The exceptions would be situations where their adult lives were seriously in jeopardy, and those conditions are relatively rare.

Becoming sensitive to the types of situations that arouse intense reactions of anger is valuable in making a distinction between primal and present-day emotions. Whereas the anger in the current situation may be appropriate, the intensity that accompanies it is not appropriate to the reality of the event. Thus, people can learn to recognize when their feelings are primal or highly-charged emotionally and spare themselves a good deal of suffering.[18] We have found that an awareness of the primal components of one's anger not only helps defuse the intensity of the feeling, but also allows time for rational self-reflection and a more thoughtful consideration of the consequences of one's actions.

Identifying destructive thoughts or voices that predispose aggressive behavior

Destructive actions occur when feelings of frustration are combined with negative cognitive processes. The first author has described the voice process as a series of destructive thoughts, alien to the self and others, that plays a significant part in influencing angry, aggressive responses (R. Firestone, 1988, 1997a).

The voice is the result of incorporating into oneself the critical, angry attitudes and responses that are directed toward a person by parents and family members during the developmental years. This concept is further elucidated in chapter 6, "The Source of Unethical Behavior."

When people filter events through this critical voice process, even innocuous incidents are imbued with a negative loading and heightened angry responses. Voice therapy is a technique in which individuals express the voice process in the second person as though they are being spoken to by someone else. Putting words to this voice process reveals the specific aggression underlying negative attitudes toward oneself and other people. It is valuable for people to learn to identify the specific hostile, cynical thoughts that intensify anger and lead to the acting out of aggression.

Most people tend to overreact to criticism regardless of whether it is harsh or mild, true or false. Their reactions are due to the fact that criticisms, regardless of their accuracy, may correspond to their own voice attacks, thereby triggering obsessive, destructive thought processes. Simply becoming aware that one is attacking oneself or others, even without objectively evaluating the content of the attacks, will render voice attacks less damaging to oneself and others.

Becoming aware of a build-up of cynical, critical voices toward others and recognizing this as a warning sign can help prevent such thoughts from being translated into destructive actions. People who learn to distinguish between projections based on their critical internal thoughts and realistic perceptions of another's traits are better able to communicate their angry feelings honestly and appropriately, and maintain harmonious relations (R. Firestone & Catlett, 1999). One can learn to identify when the shift in one's attitude (from positive to negative) takes place and understand the underlying meaning behind this change in perspective. This awareness provides an element of control over the acting out of maladaptive, aggressive behaviors.

Educational perspectives and prevention

Teaching children about anger is a vital part of helping them to adapt to life. Children need to learn about emotions as much as they need to learn about academic subject matter and the practical aspects of life. Every child should be taught about adaptive and maladaptive forms of aggression and become skilled at handling angry feelings.[19]

Over the years, the educational system has been negligent in relation to teaching children and young people about their emotions, especially about angry or sexual feelings. Religious and political biases have restricted this type of education to the family. Learning ways to deal with and avert maladaptive angry responses and violence should be part of an overall education in family values. Recently, with the advent of well-publicized school shootings, some school boards have adopted violence prevention programs to teach children and adolescents specific skills for dealing with their angry emotions as well as with the underlying feelings that precipitate angry responses, such as shame, sadness, and hurt.

Research has shown that even young children can readily learn to identify and give words to their emotions, handle their anger in constructive ways, feel empathy for their peers, and develop some of the skills necessary for resolving conflict (Coie, 1996; Coie, et al, 1993; Kam, Greenberg & Kusche, 2004; Kam, Greenberg & Walls, 2003; Kluger, 2006; Susman & Stoff, 2005). Currently a few programs have been established in public and charter schools to educate children and their families in these skills. For example, the Second Step Program (sponsored by the Committee for Children) provides schools with a violence prevention curriculum for children of preschool age through grade 8, as well as an anti-bullying program for preadolescents and adolescents. Evaluation and follow-up studies found an increase in prosocial behaviors and a significant decrease in hostile, aggressive behavior in children who participated in the program as compared with a control group (Grossman, et al, 1997).[20]

The primary prevention of destructive forms of aggression and violence begins with parenting. Parents who have the ability to handle angry feelings constructively are able to serve as positive role models for their children. They are far more effective than parents who merely lecture or apply disciplinary measures when children act up or act out. The processes of identification and imitation are more powerful than parents' words, rules, rewards, and punishment (R. Firestone, 1990b). Children need parents who accept and know how to manage their own anger. There is no better method for teaching a child to express angry feelings constructively than for parents to communicate their anger honestly and directly to each other, to their children, and to other people.

Few rules and restrictions are necessary to effectively socialize children and teach them self-control. The fewer rules the better. Yet it is important to consistently uphold and enforce the limited number of rules that parents have mutually agreed upon. Overpermissiveness is counterproductive because the child who is neglected in this way is denied the opportunity to learn self-discipline and self-control. Flattering a child or building up his or her vanity also interferes with optimal psychological development. Vain individuals are particularly vulnerable to feelings of shame and narcissistic rage when negative events threaten their inflated self-image.

Parents who have mastered their anger can use it effectively to discipline their children without becoming either harsh or weak and ineffective. For example, if their child misbehaves, they are able to convey both their anger and caring feelings through their actions and tone of voice. In this way, parents are able to make a strong, lasting impression without unduly frightening their children or making them feel like they are bad people.

Ideally, parents would accept their children's feelings, thoughts, and opinions uncritically, while teaching them to control undesirable, aggressive, provoking, or manipulative behaviors. To avoid raising children who become unethical, undesirable adults, parents need to teach young children not to whine, pout, sulk, or act out abusive responses. Children should know that it is helpful to cry when they are sad but they need to learn that using tears in an attempt to control through weakness is counterproductive. By helping their children express their emotions appropriately, parents are assisting them in developing better, more effective means of communication.

Emotionally mature parents can learn to help children get through a temper tantrum, a condition that, for the child, can be an uncontrollable, frightening "emotional storm" once it reaches a certain threshold. Parents can respond firmly, while at the same time being available, offering reassurance and security, and remaining close until the tantrum has run its course. At the same time, if the tantrum is an expression of a child's frustration in relation to a demand not being met, the parent should not give in to the child. Capitulating to children's wishes and demands under these circumstances teaches them that maladaptive methods for expressing anger are effective. In contrast, being firm and refusing to shield children from the inevitable frustrations of life helps them develop the ability to experience everyday frustration with equanimity.

Conclusion

Ethically speaking, the ability to cope with angry emotions is of major significance. The inability to do so plays a central role in people's inhumanity toward one another. For this reason, it is important to understand the initial frustration or primal feelings that trigger anger and the thought processes or inner voices that determine its mode of expression.

Aggression is not a basic instinct or innate human response; it is a response to frustration and shame. There are countless ways that people react to anger: anger can be manifested in violent acts against other people, turned against the self in the form of psychosomatic illness, depression, or suicide, or used unconsciously to avoid closeness in an intimate relationship. To avert these and other negative consequences, it is crucial that people learn to accept and manage their angry emotions.

Learning to deal effectively with anger does not mean suppressing it, swallowing it, or becoming "nice," submissive, or compliant, as many people assume (Bach & Goldberg, 1974). To the contrary, if one is able to experience angry feelings and is comfortable with them, one becomes a much stronger person. People who are not afraid of their anger possess an inner strength because they can allow themselves to feel as angry as they wish without losing control. They are able to choose when and where to express their anger and can amplify its expression if necessary.

Parents who have learned to deal with their own angry feelings are more accepting of anger in their children and encouraging of their movement toward self-expression, while discouraging the acting out of passive-aggressive or manipulative behavior. In this way, they teach their children valuable skills for managing their anger that are essential to living a truly ethical life.

Lastly, anger can be a source of energy and vitality when people understand its nature, accept angry feelings as an inherent part of their emotional makeup, and learn how to utilize aggression constructively. Mastering angry feelings is vital for good mental health, enhances personal power, and facilitates the pursuit of goals and priorities. Learning about core emotions, their function and appropriate expression, should be a basic part of every child's education in life. In a broad perspective, people developing healthy attitudes about feeling and controlling aggression can prevent much of the trouble in the world.

Notes

1. See *Inside the Brain: Revolutionary Discoveries of How the Mind Works* (Kotulak, 1996).
2. The authors agree in substance with De Zulueta's (1993) definition of violence: "The *Oxford English Dictionary* interprets the term 'violence' in several different ways, one of which is 'the treatment

or usage tending to cause bodily injury or forcibly interfering with personal freedom'" (pp. viii–ix).

3. In their review, Anderson and Bushman (2002) described several current theories of aggression: Cognitive Neoassociation Theory (Berkowitz, 1990, 1993), which has subsumed the early frustration-aggression hypothesis set forth by N. Miller & Dollard (1941); Social Learning Theory (Bandura, 1986, 2001); and Social Interaction Theory (Tedeschi & Felson, 1994). Also see Brennan's (1998) summary of theories of aggression and violence and Susman and Stoff's chapter, "Synthesis and Reconsiderations of the Psychobiology of Aggressive Behavior: A Conclusion."

4. De Zulueta (1993) has noted that "A common finding when reading the literature on human violence is the confusion that appears to exist between words referring to aggression and words referring to concepts such as violence or cruelty" (p. 28). See De Zulueta's comprehensive review of the literature on human aggression in *From Pain to Violence*, pp. 25–42.

5. Preliminary findings from the development of *The Firestone Assessment of Violent Thoughts (FAVT)* (R. Firestone & Firestone, 2008) demonstrated significant relationships between the concept of the internal voice and destructive behavior against self and others (Doucette-Gates, Firestone & Firestone, 1999). Items on the scale are composed of self-statements gathered from inmates, parolees, and domestic abusers. Five levels were found to be significantly correlated with violent behavior. They were labeled: (1) Paranoid/Suspicious; (2) Persecuted Misfit; (3) Self-Depreciating/Pseudo-Independent; (4) Overtly Aggressive; and (5) Self-Aggrandizing (Doucette-Gates, Firestone & Firestone, 1999). The rationale for Factor 5 is also supported by research conducted by Baumeister, et al (1996) showing that violence is related to vanity, and specifically "threatened egotism." The FAVT also contains two subscales: (1) the Instrumental/Proactive Aggression subscale and (2) the Hostile/Reactive Aggression subscale.

   See also the concept of "emotional scripts" described by DiGiuseppe, Eckhardt, Tafrate and Robin (1994) in relation to "dysfunctional anger," and Beck's (1999) description of cognitions or "automatic" thoughts underlying aggression and violence, as well as studies conducted by Eckhardt and Dye (2000).

6. Similarly, the classic experiment by Milgram (1974) in which many subjects, acting on instructions from the experimenter, were willing to deliver increasingly strong electric shocks to fellow subjects, had "disturbing results" according to the experimenter.

7. Early neglect, in particular psychological neglect, predisposes impairment in neuronal structures that are responsible for regulating the emotions and for accurately perceiving social cues regarding emotions in others. Research has shown that deficits in these areas often lead to a decreased ability to inhibit impulsivity with respect to the acting out of aggressive, violent behavior (Davidson, Putnam & Larson, 2000; Egeland, Sroufe & Erickson, 1983; Patterson, 1982). Also see Blair (2001) and Blair, et al (2001) as well as "The Developmental Roots of Violence in the Failure of Mentalization" by Peter Fonagy (2004b). Regarding the effects of early trauma on adult adjustment, see De Zulueta's (1993) chapter "The Traumatic Origins of Violence in Adults." Also see *Rage: A Step-by-Step Guide to Overcoming Explosive Anger* by Potter-Efron (2007).

8. Baumeister (1997) suggested that "The bottom line is that revenge can contribute to violence and cruelty because the avenger, who is perpetrating harm, acts with the clear conscience and self-righteous zeal of the victim … . Research has established that apologies do reduce victims' vindictive feelings" (p. 162). Emphasizing what he believed to be the potentially life-saving benefits of restorative justice, Desmond Tutu (1999) declared: "True forgiveness deals with the past, all of the past, to make the future possible" (p. 279).

9. See "Wife Killings Committed in the Context of a Lovers Triangle" by Shakelford, Buss and Weekes-Shackelford (2003) for an evolutionary perspective on domestic assault, homicide, and male sexual jealousy, and Rennison and Welchans (2000). According to Dutton (1995b), in the United States, nearly 1.5 million women seek medical attention each year because of physical assaults by their male partners. Also see Fonagy (1999, 2001) for an attachment theory perspective on partner violence.

   In recent years, violent tendencies in women have received increasing attention (Garbarino, 2006; Motz, 2001; Pearson, 1997; Welldon, 1988). A study conducted by published by Archer (2000) in *Psychological Bulletin* found that "women were slightly more likely … than men to use one or more acts of physical aggression and to use such acts more frequently" (p. 651).

10. For example, in *Psychosomatic Medicine*, Eaker, et al (2007) found that "Women who 'self-silenced' during conflict with their spouse, compared with women who did not, had four times the risk of dying" (p. 509) of coronary heart disease.

11. For descriptions of abusive child-rearing practices common in early twentieth-century Germany and Austria that have been hypothesized as predisposing this type of sadistic behavior on the

part of many SS guards, see Fromm (1941), A. Miller (1980/1984; 1998), and Robbins and Post (1997).

12. Low serotonin levels in the central nervous system (CNS), assessed through highly sophisticated blood tests, have been found in suicidal and violent individuals, as well as in alcoholics (Linnoila, et al, 1990).

13. Several studies have shown that alcohol is a potent antecedent and trigger of aggression (Conner et al, 2001; Haggard-Grann, Hallqvist, Langstrom & Moller, 2006; S. Taylor & Hulsizer, 1998). The Injury Prevention Network Newsletter (Violence Prevention Coalition of Greater Los Angeles, 1991) cited the following statistic: "Fifty percent of adolescent suicides are under the influence of alcohol at the time of their death" (p. 1).

14. Roth's (1994) survey found that "Criminals who use illegal drugs … commit robberies and assaults more frequently than do nonuser criminals, and they commit them especially frequently during periods of heavy drug use" (Correlations between violence and psychoactive substances, Para. 4).

15. Straus (1996) asserted that "the cross-cultural evidence suggests only that corporal punishment is associated with an increased probability of societal violence. A probabilistic relationship is typical of most disease vectors" (p. 837). In a more optimistic vein, Gershoff (2002) noted that: "A growing number of countries have adopted policies or laws that prohibit parents from using corporal punishment as a means of discipline (Austria, Croatia, Cyprus, Denmark, Finland, Germany, Israel, Italy, Latvia, Norway, and Sweden)" (p. 539).

16. Re: the stereotyping of men and women along perpetrator/victim dimensions, see Goldberg (1983).

17. Re: the effects of neglect, abuse and/or witnessing violence that are often manifested later during adolescence, see Blair, et al (2001). In a survey of violence worldwide, investigators for the United Nations' first comprehensive Report on Violence against Children (Pinheiro, 2006) found that:

> Between 133 and 275 million children worldwide are estimated to witness domestic violence annually. The exposure of children to violence in their homes on a frequent basis, usually through fights between parents or between a mother and her partner, can severely affect a child's well-being, personal development and social interaction in childhood and adulthood (p. 14).

18. See description of feeling release therapy in *The Fantasy Bond,* (R. Firestone, 1985). Follow-up showed that they had increased their tolerance for anger and sadness, developed better impulse control, and no longer felt compelled to act out irrational anger in their close relationships.

19. In a video documentary, *Teaching Our Children about Feelings* (Parr, 1985), the first author demonstrated ways of talking with children about experiencing and expressing anger.

20. See a description of the Second Step curriculum in Kluger, (2006). Other prevention programs include the CASEL program (Collaborative for Academic, Social, and Educational Learning) and the PATHS Program (Promoting Alternative Thinking Strategies), by Channing Bete Co. (2007).

For adolescents who are at risk, see Forgays and DeMilio's (2005) article on "Is Teen Court Effective for Repeat Offenders? A Test of the Restorative Justice Approach," and Borduin, et al's (1995) article on "Multisystemic Treatment of Serious Juvenile Offenders: Long-Term Prevention of Criminality and Violence."

For adults in the correctional system, on parole or in mandated anger management classes, there are programs based on the Restorative Justice Model "Resolve to Stop the Violence" (RSVP). See J. Gilligan and Lee (2004) for effectiveness studies. Another program, based on attachment theory and psychodynamic principles, has been in existence as a therapeutic community at Grendon Prison near Oxford, England since 1962. "Reconviction rates were lower for prisoners who stayed for at least 18 months" (R. Taylor, 2000, p. 1). Also see "Finding a Secure Base: Attachment in Grendon Prison" by Michael Parker and Mark Morris (2004), and "Concluding Comments: A Humane Approach to Working with Dangerous People" by David Jones and Richard Shuker (2004). Based on findings from one study, Skeem, Monahan, and Mulvey (2002) concluded that "psychopathic patients appear as likely as nonpsychopathic patients to benefit from adequate doses of treatment in terms of violence reduction" (p. 577).

CHAPTER FIVE

Addressing toxic personality traits

There are indeed people who are hazardous to others' mental, emotional, and physical health.

Lillian Glass (1995, p. 12)

Only by delving into the dark side of human behavior and discovering its functions are we likely to develop an informed sense of the possible moral issues implicit and explicit in social action.

Spitzberg & Cupach (1998, p. xvi)

Toxic personality traits are characteristic ways of being and behaving that are harmful to other people. They are deeply ingrained and relatively enduring patterns of thought, feeling, and behavior that cause considerable damage in interpersonal relationships, the workplace, and society. Glass (1995) used the term "toxic" in describing people who have a decidedly negative impact on the lives of others. "A toxic person is anyone who has poisoned your life, who is not supportive, who is not happy to see you grow, to see you succeed, who does not wish you well" (p. 12). In the corporate world, Lubit (2004) observed that "Toxic managers divert people's energy from the real work of the organization, destroy morale, impair retention, and interfere with cooperation and information sharing" (p. 1). In this sense, individuals who possess a preponderance of objectionable or "toxic" traits could be conceptualized as being psychologically corrosive or poisonous to others in a wide range of situations and settings.[1]

On a broader social scale, toxicity or a lack of toxicity in the personalities of national and political leaders is a critical issue with respect to international relations. Historically speaking, many destructive leaders have been narcissistic, dishonest, hypocritical, and quite a few have acted out sociopathic tendencies (Kellerman, 2004; Post, 2004; Robins & Post, 1997). Perhaps the most harmful act on the part of a toxic leader is the manipulation of the population through fear that is made possible by exaggerating an external threat and/or by reinforcing the followers' sense of helplessness and powerlessness (Lipman-Blumen, 2005). Most importantly, destructive leaders tend to emphasize the differences between people, an attitude that supports intolerance, prejudice, and a superior "us versus them" dichotomy (Staub, 1989, 2003). Lipman-Blumen (2005) has noted that this type of leader strives to maintain power through "playing to the basest fears and needs of followers" and by "identifying scapegoats and inciting others to castigate them" (pp. 19–20).[2] Toxic leaders may also treat "their own followers well, but persuade them to hate and/or destroy others" (p. 20). Such leaders appear to prefer aggression and actual warfare rather than diplomacy and negotiation.

In this chapter, the authors explain how individuals in the friendship circle were able to identify and modify toxic personality traits. In their discussion groups, participants learned how to be less defensive when they received negative feedback about these traits. As they became more aware of how their undesirable behaviors were hurtful to the well-being of family members and friends, they developed methods for changing them. They identified the negative internal thought processes or voices that governed these traits. They developed insight into the sources of these unacceptable attitudes and were able to regain feeling for themselves through understanding the connection between their negative characteristics and the pain and frustration they experienced in childhood. They became aware of specific defenses that functioned to cut off their feelings, developed corrective suggestions that countered the negative thought process, and focused on positive traits and behaviors that were conducive to good feeling and harmonious interactions. As an outgrowth of this process, the authors were able to identify many of the specific toxic traits that are the most detrimental to interpersonal relations.

Identifying toxic personality traits

Authors' investigation of toxic personality traits

As described in Chapter 1, the people in the friendship circle talked on an equal basis with spouses, bosses, employees, family members, and friends without interference. In their ongoing discussions, there was not only freedom to express ideas and perceptions of themselves and others, but there was freedom to express feelings as well. There was an implicit assumption that people were asking for honest feedback and would try to the best of their ability to listen to all that was said without taking offense and/or retaliating. The feedback in this group process was sensitive and compassionate, and rarely came from an attacking orientation.

Participants confronted behaviors in each other that they found to be personally unpleasant, noxious, or hurtful. They were especially critical of personality traits that were demeaning of others, such as attitudes of superiority, contempt, sarcasm, dishonesty, phoniness, and cynicism. Any attempt to manipulate the group process, for example, through domineering power plays or childish, victimized complaints, was unpopular and vigorously challenged. Individuals who manifested these and other negative traits were offered feedback about the specific ways that these characteristics were hurtful to others. As a result of this feedback, people were motivated to alter their destructive responses and developed better relationships.

The process of sharing everyday life, including work relationships and sailing, provided a crucible in which these negative traits were incidentally modified by living in close proximity. Many of the "rough edges" in people's personalities were smoothed out and behaviors that were abrasive at close quarters were gradually altered. The mutual participation in business ventures helped individuals discover and counteract unproductive work habits and offensive traits that interfered with their working as part of a team, and incidentally led to the development of better leadership skills.

Other investigations of toxic personality traits

There is a considerable body of literature, both professional and popular, offering descriptive accounts of negative or toxic personality traits and elucidating their effects on couple and family relationships (Barber, 2002; Boscan, et al, 2002a; Boscan, et al, 2002b; Carlson & Sperry, 1998; Carter, 2003; Cavaiola & Lavender, 2000; Forward, 1989, 2001; L. Glass, 1995; McLemore, 2003; Spitzberg & Cupach, 1998). A number of research studies have attempted to determine the relative toxicity of diverse traits that are considered damaging to people in both work and home environments (Babiak & Hare, 2006; Kowalski, 2001a; Spitzberg & Cupach, 1998). For example, some studies identified hostility and anger as being the most toxic traits of personality in terms of the potential psychological and/or physical damage that people who possess these qualities can inflict on others.

Other researchers investigating the effects of toxic traits on marital relationships stressed the fact that hostility, in the form of criticism and intrusiveness, leads to tension and stress within the couple (Betchen, 2005; Ruszczynski & Fisher, 1995). These tensions "have been associated with not only poor psychological health … but also with worse physiological outcomes, such as increased cardiovascular reactivity and depressed immune functioning" (Rook, 1998, p. 370).[3]

The aversive effect of a "toxic" person on the quality of an interaction is generally stronger than the beneficial effect of a person who has more positive characteristics. In explaining this phenomenon, Rook (1998) reported research findings demonstrating a "negativity effect" and cited evidence that "negative social exchanges show a far stronger negative correlation with a person's emotional well-being than do the correlations between positive social exchanges and well-being" (p. 371).[4] According to Rook this negativity effect has "been documented in relation to physiological, as well as psychological, outcomes" (p. 372). For example, Kiecolt-Glaser, et al (1993) found that "Couples who were more negative or hostile during a 30-min marital problem discussion also showed greater immunological change [decline] after 24 hours together in the CRC [Clinical Research Center]" (p. 406).

The child's first experiences with toxic individuals occur in family relationships. The effects of early negative family interactions lead to mental health problems as the child develops into adolescence and adulthood (Benjamin, 2003a; Briere, 1992; P. Gilbert, 1989; Main & Hesse, 1990, A. Miller, 1980/1984; Perry, 1997; D. Siegel, 1999). As one example of these continuing negative effects, in a study investigating the correlation between parents' negative traits and later emotional problems in their adult offspring, Segrin (1998) noted that "a close relationship with an overprotective, intrusive yet emotionally distant parent has been implicated in serious mental health problems" (p. 328). In several studies, Zeanah, et al (1993) found that negative personality traits in parents were associated with insecurity in infants and children.

Invalidation, a common toxic behavior (Carter, 2003; Linehan, 1993), is any act that puts "other people down to bring yourself up" (Leiter, 2003, p. xi). Invalidators tend to possess a number of toxic personality traits, including hostility, vanity, intrusiveness, insensitivity, contemptuousness, coldness, and a lack of feeling that seriously undermine the self-esteem and mental health of the people close to them. According to Carter (2003), these individuals utilize many methods to contradict and/or dismiss other people's feelings and thoughts, such as projection, overgeneralization, judgment, manipulation, double messages, and the double bind wherein "the invalidator puts you in a position where you are wrong if you do and wrong if you don't" (p. 17).[5]

Individuals who have many personality deficits and toxic traits may manifest behaviors and symptoms that meet the criteria for personality disorders (Choca, 2004; Kernberg, 1984; Masterson, 1981; Meissner, 1984, 1986; Millon & Davis, 1996). Cavaiola and Lavender (2000) defined personality disorders as "long-standing disturbances in personality that usually begin in late adolescence and continue throughout adulthood ... [and] cause a person to consistently act in disturbing patterns of behavior in both occupational and social relationships" (p. 4).

On the societal level, individual psychological defenses are pooled and combine to form the social mores, sanctions, standards, and institutions of a particular social structure. Social pressure exerted by negative cultural attitudes acts back on each member of society in a kind of feedback loop, with unfortunate consequences (R. Firestone, 1997a). The impact on children of the resultant social toxicity has been described by Garbarino (1995) in his book, *Raising Children in a Socially Toxic Environment*.

The social world of children, the social context in which they grow up, has become poisonous to their development … . They're [toxic elements] easy enough to identify: violence, poverty and other economic pressures on parents and their children, disruption of relationships, nastiness, despair, depression, paranoia, alienation—all the things that demoralize families and communities. These are the forces in the land that pollute the environment of children and youth. These are the elements of social toxicity (pp. 4–5).

Identifying toxic personality traits and their effects

Toxic personality traits often are not readily identifiable because many times they are considered ego-syntonic in that they resonate well with the individual who possesses them, causing little or no distress (Choca, 2004; Kernberg, 1975; Meissner, 1995).[6] For example, people who are stingy may see themselves as being frugal or thrifty. People may be proud of their self-denial when it may in fact be an indication of pathology.

People in the friendship circle found that hostile, aggressive tendencies and self-destructive tendencies were especially objectionable and damaging to relationships. The destructiveness of the former was obvious whereas the latter was less apparent. Individuals who acted out negative behaviors against themselves and their own best interests caused fear in others. Their self-destructive behavior acted as a powerful manipulation. By acting helpless or refusing to take responsibility for themselves, they placed a serious burden on their friends. When confronted, self-destructive individuals often responded defensively with anger and/or intensified their acting-out behaviors. Friends who intervened by challenging addictions or offering suggestions to counteract other self-defeating behaviors were responded to as though they were enemies. In spite of having caring intentions, these friends tended to question their own motives for confronting the person and attacked themselves for causing someone pain.

An individual who acts out self-destructively often sets into motion a contagion effect, reinforcing latent self-destructive tendencies in other people. The efforts that others exert in attempting to help or prevent negative consequences for the self-destructive person deplete their own energy and vitality. This complex ethical issue is prevalent in couple relationships, family constellations, the workplace, and other group settings, as well as in society-at-large.

An individual determines the emotional climate around him/herself and in a very real sense creates his/her own world. Many people live in a hostile social environment of their own making, without realizing the fact that they are responsible.

> When one man was told by his friends that he was intrusive and disrespectful in the way he related, he recalled that as a college student he had continually provoked his classmates by his lack of respect for their boundaries and by his questions and irrelevant chatter. He disclosed that after a while almost everybody avoided interacting with him. After graduation, he was invited to be a houseguest by his mentor, a well-liked university professor. However, during the first week of his visit, the professor and his wife were so provoked by him that they asked him to leave. In retrospect, the man recognized how quickly his disrespectful manner and pushiness had alienated the couple.

Those individuals who act out superior attitudes and are parental, contemptuous, or authoritarian in their interactions are hurtful because they make others feel small and incompetent. People treated in this manner find it difficult to deal with the anger and rage that are naturally aroused and they often become depressed and self-hating.

Submissiveness and subservience can be as damaging to relationships as being domineering or imperious. An acquiescent style of deferring is irritating and serves the function of pushing others away. People who are defended in this manner often provoke anger and hostility in others. Other traits, including insensitivity, dependency, childishness, phoniness, indifference, aloofness, coldness, and the tendency to respond impersonally also cause others emotional pain.

The degree of emotional damage that is caused by a "toxic" person varies and is affected by many factors. Toxic character traits are not necessarily consistent and may manifest themselves in some situations and not in others. For example, some people can be extremely toxic in interactions with coworkers and employees and less destructive in relating to family members (Cavaiola & Lavender, 2000).[7] Others may be relatively congenial and flexible at work, yet rigid and authoritarian at home. However, the general trend is for people to manifest the same offensive or disagreeable traits in a wide variety of situations and in the majority of their personal interactions (Forward, 1989).

The degree of destructiveness associated with a specific toxic trait is affected by the frequency and intensity with which it is manifest in one's social interactions. Some negative traits are so noxious that even when they occur infrequently, they can have long-lasting adverse effects (Cavaiola & Lavender, 2000; Kowalski, 2001b).

> One father, who was usually easy-going and even somewhat passive, would occasionally become extremely irritable and berate his wife and children for upsetting him. Weeks could pass without an outburst, then something minor would happen and he would lash out in an accusatory tirade, then slip into a depressed state. The entire family felt as though they had to "walk on eggshells" to avoid upsetting him. His wife cautioned the children to be quiet so as to not disturb their father. As a result of this man's intimidation, there was a continual atmosphere of tension and disharmony in this family despite the fact that the father's mood swings occurred only sporadically.

Interactions with a "toxic" person invariably arouse destructive voices in the other person. In any personal exchange, an individual's sense of self is either being supported or damaged (Forward, 1989; L. Glass, 1995, Kowalski, 2001b; Tedeschi & Bond, 2001; Tedeschi & Felson 1994). Each person is either reinforcing the other's life-affirming propensities or supporting tendencies to turn against the self and retreat from life.

An exchange with a critical, superior person will precipitate one's self-critical thoughts and attitudes. Similar dynamics are operating in interactions with individuals who are hostile, contemptuous, sarcastic, or offensive in other ways. Therefore, each social encounter carries either a positive or a negative valence depending on the effect that it has on a person's sense of worth or self-esteem. It has the potential for depleting or for enhancing the energy level and vitality in one or all participants.[8]

Therefore, in any interaction the specific positive and negative traits of the participants have a powerful impact, both on the outcome of their exchanges and on each party's emotional state. When positive traits are dominant, the exchange is beneficial and conducive to good feeling, whereas when toxic traits prevail in one (or both) parties, the exchange is inevitably harmful to both people. In *The Politics of Experience*, R.D. Laing (1967) described how both kinds of traits are manifested in personal interactions:

> Personal action can either open out possibilities of enriched experience or it can shut off possibilities. Personal action is either predominantly validating, confirming, encouraging, supportive, enhancing, or it is invalidating, denying, discouraging, undermining and constricting. It can be creative or destructive. In a world where the normal condition is one of alienation, most personal action must be destructive both of one's own experience and of that of the other (p. 34).

The authors developed a preliminary scale to measure where an individual falls on a continuum with positive traits at one extreme and negative, toxic traits at the other. (See Figure 5.1.) We determined the correlation between a socio-metric variable (where an individual was located on a continuum from very popular to unpopular with peers) and a checklist of positive and negative traits. Pending reliability and validity studies, our instrument could potentially be used to predict the outcome of marital as well as other relationships.[9]

Inwardness

When interactions with a toxic individual reinforce a person's destructive thought process, the person often retreats to a more inward, self-protective stance. Becoming inward and alienated from one's experience cuts one off from feelings of compassion and empathy for oneself and others. It represents a retreat into oneself, leading to varying degrees of a depersonalized state of mind. Inwardness involves a reluctance to engage in give-and-take exchanges and is characterized by an impersonal style of relating and a tendency to rely on painkilling habit patterns and substances (R. Firestone, 1997a).[10] Manifestations of "inwardness"

Where would you place yourself on a continuum that ranges from 5 (positive) to 1 (negative) in relation to each pair of personality traits listed below? Where do you think a judge would place you?

As an example, where would you place yourself on a continuum ranging between Happy and Miserable?

Example

5........................4........................3........................2........................1

Happy .... *Miserable*

Positive traits	Negative traits
1. Friendly	Hostile
2. Authentic	Phony
3. Nondefensive	Defensive
4. Warm, affectionate	Cold, unaffectionate
5. Flexible	Rigid
6. Generous	Ungenerous, tight
7. Honest	Deceptive
8. Independent	Dependent
9. Relaxed	Tense
10 Good-humored	Generally unhappy, down
11. Adult, responsible for oneself	Childish, victimized
12. Realistic self-appraisal	Narcissistic (vain)
13. Sexually alive	Repressed sexually
14. Outgoing	Inward
15. Respectful of boundaries	Intrusive
16. Free of addiction	Addictions (alcohol, drugs, routines)
17. Accepting	Judgmental
18. Good judgment	Impulsive
19. Attractive	Poor appearance, neglectful
20. Self-assertive	Self-denying
21. Active	Passive

Figure 5.1. Personality traits questionnaire.

also include: a preference for fantasy gratification at the expense of reality concerns, passivity, a victimized orientation toward life, and treating oneself as an object. In addition, it leads to increased tendencies toward isolation, withholding and self-denial, a negative self-image, cynicism toward other people, lack of direction in life, and a diminished sense of values. When people are removed from fully experiencing their lives and are indifferent to themselves and others, these negative propensitie become more dominant in their personality.

Many people exist for long periods of time in an inward state, observing themselves rather than experiencing their lives directly. They look inward instead of outward; therefore their actions are generally less adaptive. Their personal interactions are filtered through the distorted lens of the destructive voice process which has a negative emotional loading. They respond in a manner that hurts other people and pushes them away.

An inward, unfeeling state and a feelingful state can be conceptualized as endpoints on a continuum, as delineated in Figure 5.2. Between the two extremes lies an area in which most people live. When the voice process is ascendant over rational thought processes, people are more cut off from feeling and, as noted, are more likely to manifest toxic traits and behaviors in their personal interactions. However, most people are largely unaware that their negative traits and behaviors are strongly influenced by a system of unconscious, critical, and hostile attitudes toward self and others.

Psychodynamics

Childhood

People develop a system of defenses early in life in an attempt to alleviate interpersonal pain and death anxiety; thereafter, they exist in a psychological equilibrium that they seek to protect at all costs (R. Firestone, 1985). During their formative years, they gradually develop a number of negative personality traits and destructive behaviors, specifically adapted to their circumstances, as a way of maintaining this equilibrium. The cluster of traits and behaviors that comprise the inward process serve the unconscious function of preserving this homeostasis, yet at great expense to the individual. In other words,

Outward lifestyle	Inward lifestyle
Social involvement	Isolation
Active, assertive	Passive, victimized orientation
Maintaining a separate identity	Seeking a merged identity and fusion
Feeling state	Cutting off or withdrawal of affect; impersonal relating
Goal-directed behavior; self-fulfillment; self-affirmation	Seeking gratification in fantasy; self-denial; self-destructiveness
Lack of self-consciousness; realistic self-appraisal	Hypercritical attitudes toward the self; vanity
Adaptability	Nonadaptability
Facing up to pain and anxiety with appropriate affect and response	Using substances and routines as painkillers to avoid feeling
Self-fulfillment	Self-denial
Personal sexuality	Impersonal, masturbatory or addictive sexuality
Searching for meaning and transcending goals	Narrow focus

Figure 5.2. Outward lifestyle vs. inward lifestyle.

to protect themselves from pain and anxiety, people unintentionally cultivate noxious traits and styles of relating that disturb their relationships in order to maintain a modicum of comfort.

Often the negative characteristics that people develop are a direct imitation of a parent or parents' undesirable traits. In general, the idealization of one's parents can necessitate the imitation of their negative or toxic traits. People often take on as their own the qualities they disliked or hated in their parents as well as the traits and behaviors that caused them the most pain in their developmental years. Additionally, in preserving the idealized image of their parents and family, they must obscure or deny the existence of parents' negative traits and displace them onto other people in the interpersonal environment. They distort their mates, children, and friends in order to maintain this unrealistic view of their parents.

Intimate relationships

People are aware that love stirs up many different and complex emotions. However, they are largely unaware that the positive experience of being loved and appreciated can arouse painful, poignant emotions based on past personal trauma. Furthermore, love makes one aware of how precious life is and can increase one's anxiety about one's limitation in time and the reality of one's finite existence. In a previous work (R. Firestone, et al, 2003), the authors described this phenomenon:

> People are generally refractory to the love that they claim to desire, and the beloved often rejects or aggresses against the lover, thereby maintaining a safe amount of emotional distance. Indeed, love reminds us that we are truly alive and really do exist, and in embracing life and love we are forced to be cognizant of our personal death as well (p. 384).

Existential issues

The acting out of toxic personality traits and aversive behaviors in personal relationships provides the means for accomplishing the unconscious goal of remaining unaware of existential issues, particularly aging and dying. By creating trouble for themselves in their relationships, people are able to obscure other, more painful aspects of life (Schnarch, 1991).

People respond to the human condition, painful circumstances faced by all human beings, in a manner that is analogous to the situation faced by the prisoner on death row. Just as prisoners faced with the knowledge of the exact hour of their execution often attempt suicide to escape the unbearable anticipatory anxiety, "normal" individuals commit emotional or microsuicide in an attempt to accommodate to death anxiety (R. Firestone, 1994b; Firestone & Seiden, 1987). As they withdraw their emotional investment in meaningful relationships and give up their interest and excitement in life, they are able to maintain a false sense of omnipotence as if they retained some power over life and death.

In elucidating these dynamics underlying people's gradual retreat from life, Ernest Becker (1973/1997) wrote: "The irony of man's condition is that the deepest need is to be free of the anxiety of death and annihilation; but it is life itself which awakens it, and so we must shrink from being fully alive" (p. 66). The authors believe that insight into this seeming paradox is essential to the process of change when dealing with toxic personality traits.

Modifying toxic personality traits

From the discussions within the friendship circle, a process for altering objectionable personality characteristics evolved involving four distinct, yet interrelated, components: (1) Direct confrontation; (2) Expanding the capacity for feeling; (3) Identifying destructive voices that govern toxic personality traits; and (4) Collaboratively planning and applying corrective experiences that counter the negative prescriptions of the voice.

Direct confrontation

As noted, the ongoing group process allowed members to express their feelings toward each other, both positive and negative. This was often a difficult and painful situation, but it occurred in a compassionate setting of affection and concern for everyone's well-being. People recognized that the feedback they received came from people who were their friends and therefore had their best interests at heart. Those who were tolerant of this close scrutiny made significant progress in their development.

The authors found that the group setting itself facilitated the honest exchange of feelings and perceptions. Within this setting, everyone received a fair hearing; each person was listened to openly and responded to honestly. Individuals discovered that it was often more productive to talk with each other in the group situation than to try to convey the same feelings, perceptions, or criticisms on a one-to-one basis. Those who wished to express an angry feeling or negative perception to someone in the group felt freer to do so because they trusted the responses of the other participants.

The participants learned to communicate their anger or hurt feelings appropriately, that is, in "I" statements, which allowed each person to take responsibility for how he/she handled feelings of anger or disappointment. Statements such as "I was angry when you did thus-and-so," delivered in a matter-of-fact tone of voice were typical, rather than angry, name-calling statements that categorized or defined the other person as undesirable or "bad."

As the discussions progressed, people discovered that the constructive criticism they received was in general more helpful than positive feedback. It helped them identify and change traits and behaviors that they disliked in themselves. Despite the fact that feedback was generally conveyed with sensitivity and compassion, there were occasions when some people reacted angrily and defensively. Angry rebuttals, stonewalling, changing the subject, diverting attention by pointing out another's faults, refusing to talk, emotional outbursts, and intensified self-destructive behaviors were among the reactions. Because people had extensive knowledge of each other's life history and present-day circumstances, they continued to try to respond with kindness in the face of the other person's defensive reaction. This is not to say that people's defensiveness had no adverse effect. At times, struggling with these angry reactions threatened to disrupt the group process altogether, and considerable effort was expended to further understand this form of resistance. Subsequently, it became apparent that people tend to react defensively when the negative feedback they receive corresponds to their own self-attacks or destructive thoughts.

Expanding the capacity for feeling

Recovering and regaining feelings that had been suppressed, often since childhood, became an important goal for people in the friendship circle. They were dedicated to understanding their innermost emotions and desired to explore new techniques that might facilitate the process. They understood the ethical implications of being cut off from or refractory to one's feelings, noting that those individuals who were able to remain in contact with themselves on a feeling level generally had a positive rather than a negative effect on others.

As noted in Chapter 1, within the supportive atmosphere of the weekend encounter groups, people's emotions often reached a primal level of intensity which led to important insights. In looking for new methods to access these feelings, the participants found effective techniques in the work of Arthur Janov (1970), *The Primal Scream*. While not subscribing entirely to Janov's theory and methodology, the authors utilized his technique of deep breathing with the simultaneous release of sounds. When people followed the suggestion, breathing deeply and repeatedly making noises to express their emotions, virtually everyone exhibited the same intense release of affect that Janov had described.

As a result of our experience with this form of deep feeling release, there were meaningful insights and personal progress. People were able to advance beyond previous barriers in their psychological development. Three important effects have persisted to the present, thirty years later: (a) people became comfortable with the expression of intense emotions by themselves and others; (b) they became less defensive when confronted with negative information or feedback and, consequently, experienced better reality-testing; and (c) they became more tolerant of others and more compassionate when offering feedback or when confronting toxic traits and destructive behaviors in their friends. All three effects have led to better mental health in general.[11]

People were able to identify specific defenses that had functioned to cut off their painful feelings. They recognized that when they suppressed their feelings, they would become removed emotionally from people close to them and that those people would suffer as a result. They realized that if they did not remain vulnerable in spite of the possibility of being hurt in a relationship, they would be indifferent to or react adversely to love that was directed toward them. They knew that if they tried to avoid sadness, they would become irritable or even depressed. They learned that being open to feelings had a positive effect on their children; for example, they were more tolerant when their children were frightened, troubled, or insecure. They understood, too, that if they did not feel about the existential issues of life and death, they would distance themselves from their loved ones and, on some level, continue to act out negative traits they were trying to change.

Identifying destructive thoughts that control toxic traits

Early in our investigations, we found that many people were unaware that they were not acting from their own point of view, but from a negative point of view that was internalized or introjected during their developmental years. The voice process, which is comprised of a pattern of destructive thoughts that are malevolent in nature will be explained in greater detail in Chapter 6 (R. Firestone, 1988).

People found that verbalizing their negative thoughts toward themselves in the second person often elicited strong emotions and led to spontaneous insights. In switching their mode of expression of negative thoughts about themselves from "I" to "you" (e.g. "I'm no good" to "You're no good"), they were able to distinguish their own point of view from the incorporated one. With this same technique, they were able to identify the hostile, cynical voice statements they were experiencing about others (e.g. "What am I doing with this guy? He's probably just leading me on" to "What are you doing with this guy? He's probably just leading you on!"). Even when there was an element of truth in these negative statements, people recognized that the snide, degrading tone associated with them reflected a level of malice that was inappropriate to the real or current situation. In general, learning to separate exaggerated, malicious attitudes toward self and others from more rational or objective perceptions facilitated the process of change.

In the process of identifying the negative thoughts that supported their unpleasant and undesirable traits, and in releasing the accompanying feelings of anger and sadness, people in the friendship circle recalled family interactions in which they had internalized their parents' offensive attitudes towards them. They developed insight into the connection between their parents' views and the negative point of view they had incorporated as their own. In coming to understand why they acted out certain toxic traits in everyday interactions, they were able to regain feelings of compassion for themselves, which in turn, provided much of the impetus for altering their negative traits on an action level.

Corrective suggestions to modify toxic traits

The collaborative planning of corrective experiences was important in the overall process of change for people in the friendship circle. Individuals cooperated in thinking of practical suggestions for each other and for themselves that directly altered the toxic traits and maladaptive behaviors that were being influenced by their negative thoughts and attitudes. The corrective suggestions for change fell into two categories: (a) suggestions that challenged and decreased behavioral manifestations of negative, toxic personality traits, and (b) suggestions for exploring a new identity, overcoming fears, and enhancing positive traits and behaviors.

In challenging individuals' negative traits and behavior, these corrective suggestions led to corrective emotional experiences. For example, when a person stops provoking distance in a relationship by acting sarcastic, critical, or hostile, he or she creates a new set of circumstances, which generates a different and warmer emotional climate. Subsequently, there is a period of adjustment as the person learns to tolerate the anxiety that accompanies positive change and gradually adapts to a new environment that is warmer, richer, and more emotionally fulfilling than the environment he or she experienced in the past.[12]

> Someone made a suggestion to another participant, a computer programmer who was highly intellectual and who spoke rapidly, to try to slow down so that he could feel something about what he was saying. His communication style bothered other participants in group discussions primarily because it cut them off from their feelings. As he attempted to follow this recommendation, people found themselves feeling deeply for him as he spoke. He gained feeling for himself and began revealing details of his life that held special meaning for him and resonated with others. People responded positively to this change and came to know him on a different level than before. This man's long-standing appraisal of himself as an "unfeeling computer geek" was modified by the simple suggestion.

Like this man, most people tend to categorize themselves in a negative way. They see their traits and behaviors as being an essential part of their identity, which they conceptualize as fixed rather than flexible or amenable to change. In contrast, as a result of their experiences, the participants in the discussion groups no longer subscribe to this incorrect assumption about "identity." They recognize that they have the potential to challenge and overcome any long-standing behavior pattern or well-established character trait.

Within the group process, there were also suggestions to help people expand their boundaries, overcome fears related to pursuing goals, and develop a more positive view of self.

One young woman spent most of her time immersed in her studies and involved in taking care of several young children. She was helpful to a fault and rarely said no when asked to work additional hours. Her life was completely out of balance—she seldom dated or enjoyed an evening out with friends. As a result, she was becoming increasingly depressed and lonely.

In the group discussions, she spoke about this problem and about her growing awareness of how her compulsive patterns of overworking and self-denial were affecting her overall mood. While talking, it occurred to her that her mother had no social life to speak of. She described feeling rejected by both parents, but receiving praise for being "a good girl" when she cleaned the house or took care of her little brother. She realized that she felt worthwhile only when studying or helping others. At this point, she asked for any suggestions her friends might have to help her break out of this pattern.

Someone suggested that for the next week she should try an experiment. Every morning she should plan to do something social that day: for example, going out to dinner or to a movie with friends. The choice of social activity was up to her. In effect, this suggestion provided the permission she seemed to need to stop denying herself a personal life. It circumvented some of the guilt she would have felt in leading a more social life and in having more friends than her mother. Complying with this suggestion ameliorated her depression and she found herself eagerly looking forward to what each new day would bring. In this manner, she gradually expanded her life to include more gratification.

Resistance to altering toxic traits

There is a fundamental resistance to planning corrective experiences and following through with actual changes that alter one's self-concept in a positive direction. It would seem that people would welcome this change, understand that these traits are not really a part of their basic identity, and be happy to modify negative views of themselves. However, changing a toxic trait is always accompanied by anxiety. Modifying character traits that reflect one's negative identity formed in the family inadvertently interferes with the idealization of one's parents. This idealization is essential for maintaining the defense of self-parenting and thus disrupting it threatens one's sense of security. Because there is usually considerable anxiety in affirming one's belief in oneself, many individuals prefer to hold on to and preserve a static, albeit negative, view of themselves and continue to act out manifestations of the toxic personality traits that support that view.

> A woman who was disliked because of her defensiveness and argumentativeness was given the suggestion by someone in her psychotherapy group to respond to feedback by simply saying, "Thank you for the information." She had few friends and was constantly in conflict with her husband. In the group sessions, she had provoked so much anger and animosity from other participants that this suggestion was their last ditch effort to establish a rapport with her.
>
> The woman managed to follow the suggestion for several weeks. The other participants began to like her and to respond positively to her. Unfortunately, this profound change in her interpersonal world completely unnerved her; she suffered a series of panic attacks. Her dramatic reaction to being liked underscored the powerful stake that this woman had in maintaining this toxic defensive behavior. Her defensiveness, which provoked hostility and rejection from others, had served the function of preserving the negative self-image she had formed in her family-of-origin. In pushing others away, she had been able to maintain an inner psychological equilibrium, even though the cost to her personally was considerable.

Many people are also reluctant to conceptualize definitive goals and take specific actions to move in a direction that brings out their positive attributes and traits. They are plagued by strong voice attacks and guilt reactions when they manifest positive behaviors and characteristics that differ from those of their parents. This differentiation from parental figures and the symbolic separation from the family frequently precipitate a setback in one's progress toward change.

In a sense, individuals must give up their protective armor, their negative traits and behaviors, before they learn, on an emotional level, that there is no actual threat. They need to hold on to the new territory and learn to tolerate anxiety states and the increased voice attacks that inevitably come with any positive change. If they persist in the new behavior, sweat through the anxiety, and refuse to give in to their destructive thoughts, they can make substantial progress.

Conclusion

Negative character traits that individuals develop as part of a defensive process early in life have a pervasive destructive impact on relationships and on society as a whole. These toxic characteristics and aversive behaviors reflect an inward, self-protective state of mind and lead to a deadened lifestyle in which emotional transactions with other people are seriously restricted, causing corresponding harm to relationships.

These undesirable traits can be identified, assessed, modified, and replaced by more positive ways of being and behaving. Although most people have resistance to becoming aware of objectionable traits in themselves, they can approach the problem with more compassion through understanding that these traits evolved as a natural response to childhood pain. They can come to realize that they are actively, yet unconsciously, utilizing these negative ways of acting in order to push others away and maintain their defenses and psychological equilibrium.

It is possible to modify even well-established negative character traits. When one has the courage to face certain truths about oneself, challenge undesirable personal qualities that provoke other people, and ultimately make the adjustment to a new and unfamiliar interpersonal world, one will find that no trait is so entrenched that it cannot be altered.

In this chapter, we elucidated a number of methods for accomplishing this goal: confronting negative traits in the context of a compassionate group setting; expanding the capacity for feeling; identifying destructive thought processes that support the maintenance of offensive traits and behaviors; and planning corrective experiences that are diametrically opposed to the dictates of the critical inner voice (R. Firestone, et al, 2003).[13]

The authors have found that corrective suggestions, when put into action, act as catalysts to move individuals toward new situations and experiences where they will be unprotected by their customary defenses (R. Firestone, 1985). After learning to tolerate the anxiety that comes with any positive change, people discover that they can live without the negative behaviors and traits that previously kept others at a "safe" distance. As a result, they feel better about themselves, experience a sense of relief from the guilt they felt for hurting others, and enjoy closer relationships. The process of modifying the toxic traits and destructive behaviors described here generally leads to a better overall adjustment and the opportunity for a more successful, fulfilling, and ethical life.

Notes

1. Susan Forward (1989) in her book *Toxic Parents*, popularized the term "toxic" in describing parents who "like a chemical toxin" inflict emotional damage that "spreads throughout a child's being, and as the child grows, so does the pain" (p. 6). With respect to the term "personality traits," J. Singer (2005) defined traits as "'dimensions of individual differences' in thoughts, feelings, and behaviors that show reasonably consistent patterns across situations, time, and role" (p. 7). See Hampson and Goldberg's (2006) 40-year longitudinal study of 799 subjects during childhood and at midlife, which showed considerable stability in the traits Conscientiousness and Extraversion.

2. For an extreme example of toxic personality traits in a destructive leader, see Henry A. Murray's (1943) classic study, *Analysis of the Personality of Adolph Hitler*.

3. Robert Vogel (2007) found that:

   In the 16-year follow-up of the Multiple Risk Factor Intervention Trial (MRFIT), men with high hostility … were 1.6 times more likely to be victim of cardiovascular disease than men with low hostility and were more than 5 times more likely to die if they experienced a nonfatal event during the study (p. 401)

   Also see Birks and Roger's (2000) study differentiating type-A behaviors that were "toxic" from "nontoxic" behaviors in terms of subjects' motives to achieve and their correlations with deterioration in health status.

4. Reis and Gable (2003) cited research on relationships and interpersonal events (Rook, 1998) supporting "the same conclusion that Taylor (1991) drew in her review of the extensive literature on adaptation to life events: "Negative events appear to elicit more physiological, affective, cognitive, and behavioral activity and prompt more cognitive analysis than neutral or positive events" (cited by Reis & Gable, p. 134). However, Rook (1998) added a note of caution when analyzing these studies: "The inference that negative exchanges generally matter more for emotional health than do positive exchanges appears to require stronger empirical support" (p. 388).

5. Forward (1989, 2001) described numerous examples of invalidating techniques and their effects on family members. Herb Goldberg (1983, 2001) explored the dynamics of relationships in which partners' toxic traits, gender biases, and invalidating behaviors played a significant part in the couple's distress.

6. In many borderline disorders, this ego-syntonicity can be a prominent feature. Meissner (1995) noted that the patient's acceptance of destructive behaviors and traits often characterizes the more primitive or lower-functioning borderline personality disorders. In fact, "the degree of ego syntonicity of symptoms" (p. 68) is an important prognostic sign.

7. See Leary and Springer's (2001) description of situational variables that influence the effects of various aversive behaviors including teasing, gossip, disrespect, and betrayal on partners in their relationships.

8. Kowalski (2001b) described situations in which both victim and perpetrator suffer from the aversive interaction. "Perpetrators who tease, hurt the feelings of others, or engage in other aversive behaviors may experience any of a number of negative emotions, including shame, guilt, and remorse" (p. 303).

9. Personality researchers have developed a number of such instruments, among them the Revised NEO-PI-R (Costa and McCrae, 1992) which contains the 5 major factors of Neuroticism (N), Extraversion (E), Openness (O), Agreeableness (A) and Conscientiousness (C) in self-report questionnaires using adjective lists. The majority of items on the Neuroticism (N) subscale and a few on the Agreeableness (A) subscale contain adjectives depicting the toxic personality traits discussed throughout this chapter. Also see Wiggins and Pincus (2002) for a description of the Personality Adjective Check List (PACL). Nettle (2006) pointed out that even traits subsumed under the Neuroticism domain have certain benefits in terms of selective fitness in the evolutionary sense.

10. The term "inwardness" is not to be confused with introspection or time spent alone for self-reflection and/or creative endeavors. Rather it refers to a defended, depersonalized state of mind manifested in self-protective, self-defeating, and hostile behaviors (R. Firestone, 1997a).

11. During the entire investigation of primal phenomena, there were no cases that resulted in an alarming or negative outcome. Not one person among the more than two hundred individuals who participated in the program had a psychotic break or suicidal reaction. In all fairness, this was probably influenced by the process of selection. The people were screened and those who posed a threat of psychosis or indicated a serious suicidal inclination were not accepted (Firestone, 1985).

12. The term "corrective experience" was coined by Franz Alexander (cited in Arlow, 1989) who proposed that "most patients had been traumatized by parental mismanagement during childhood" and that "it was necessary for the analyst to arrange 'a corrective emotional experience' to counteract the effects of the original trauma" (p. 35).

13. See *Conquer Your Critical Inner Voice: A Revolutionary Program to Counter Negative Thoughts and Live Free from Imagined Limitations* (R. Firestone, Firestone, & Catlett, 2002) for additional guidelines and exercises designed to help challenge and overcome internal barriers to ethical living.

PART III
DYNAMICS UNDERLYING
UNETHICAL BEHAVIOR

CHAPTER SIX

The source of unethical behavior

Human beings must seek to uphold their sense of integrity, their oneness, in the face of division both within themselves and without.

Eugene V. Torisky (2005, p. 3).

In general, a consideration of ethics involves contemplating the relationship between an individual's conscious value system and his/her behavior. Ethical behaviors refer to those verbal and physical actions which are based, in part, on thoughtful consideration of their effect on other people (see Hauser, 2006).[1] Yet, most of the behaviors that have a significant negative or unethical impact on interpersonal relationships are the outgrowth of unconscious motivations and defensive machinations and are predisposed by alien, hostile attitudes toward the self.

Most people consciously want to behave ethically in their relationships but many find it difficult to live consistently by their values and ideals. To understand better why individuals unintentionally harm others, it is necessary to examine environmental, social, and cultural factors that contribute to the propensity to act against one's best interests as well as those of others.[2]

129

Separation theory

The first author's theoretical approach, separation theory, integrates psychoanalytic and existential systems of thought to show how early trauma and separation experiences lead to defense formation. It explains how these defenses are reinforced or crystallized in the personality as children gradually become aware of the concept of death (R. Firestone, 1985, 1994b, 1997a).

The primary defense against the pain of childhood deprivation, separation anxiety, and the fear of death is the fantasy bond,[3] an imaginary fusion or illusion of connection with one's parents, family, ethnic group, nation, or religious or ideological cause (R. Firestone, 1984, 1985).[4] Maintaining this fantasy bond offers short-term relief from anxiety and fear, but diminishes long-term vitality and predisposes negative responses in interpersonal relationships.

Separation theory explains how the voice process—the secondary defense—supports the fantasy bond and illusions of self-sufficiency and regulates self-destructive and aggressive behaviors. Within each individual there exists an essential dualism, a primary split between forces that represent the self and those that oppose the self. These elements can be conceptualized as the "self system" and the "antiself system" (R. Firestone, 1997a). The two systems develop independently and continually evolve over time.[5] In other words, people possess conflicting points of view and beliefs about themselves and others, their relationships, and events in the world, depending on which aspect of the personality, self or antiself, is dominant at any given time. The former point of view is rational, objective, and life-affirming. The latter is made up of a destructive thought process, the "voice," an overlay on the personality that is opposed to one's self-interests and to the ongoing development of the self, and that is hostile toward other people.

A fundamental philosophical assumption underlying this approach reflects the authors' view of people as innocent rather than inherently bad or corrupt. Children are born with the potential for good or bad; the extent to which they need to protect themselves against stress early in life largely determines which path they will follow throughout life (D. May & Solomon, 1984). In other words, human beings are not innately destructive or self-destructive; they become aggressive or harmful to themselves and others only in response to the anxiety, frustration, and emotional pain they experience in the process of growing up (A. Miller, 1980/1984, 1998; Shengold, 1989; Stettbacher, 1990/1991).[6]

Life may be conceptualized as a series of separation experiences—birth, separation from the breast, from the mother, from parents, the first day at school, the first sexual experience, moving away from home, moving in with a romantic partner, getting married, pregnancy, becoming a parent, becoming a grandparent. Each event or milestone creates new situations that are potentially traumatic because they signify a loss of parental support and arouse separation anxiety. As Otto Rank (1936/1972) observed:

> The problem of the neurosis itself is a separation problem and as such a blocking of the human life principle, the conscious ability to endure release and separation, first from the biological power represented by parents, and finally from the lived out parts of the self which this power represents, and which obstruct the development of the individual personality (p. 73).

The "biological power represented by parents" that Rank referred to is the transcendental solution that parents unknowingly offer their children, that is, the possibility of alleviating the terror of aloneness and triumphing over death by merging with them. This illusion of fusion is costly, however, because both children and adults then become afraid of separation and a separate identity and, as Rank emphasized in his work, too guilty to individuate and live their own lives.

Separation theory provides a cogent explanation of why children's defensive reactions to early environmental distress restrict their lives as adults and incidentally hurt other people. An understanding of the voice offers insight into why these psychological adaptations to early life circumstances are primarily responsible for people's harmful behaviors rather than a lack of will-power or resolve to live up to their ethical principles.

An introduction to the concept of the fantasy bond

The fantasy bond is the primary defense against separation anxiety and psychological pain. It is an illusion of connection to one's parent or primary caregivers that is formed early in childhood as an attempt to compensate for frustration and hurt in the family constellation. The degree of reliance on fantasy processes is proportional to the degree of damage experienced. Furthermore, the fantasy bond is an attempt to heal the fracture of separation and aloneness that is an inevitable part of the human condition. The fantasy bond predisposes the idealization of the family at the child's expense, the projection of the negative parental qualities on to the world at large, and the incorporation into the child's personality of the critical, hostile attitudes that were directed toward him/her (R. Firestone, 1984, 1985). The introjection of these destructive attitudes becomes a well-integrated, albeit alien, aspect of the child's personality. In the process, children develop a pseudoindependent attitude and tend to parent themselves throughout their lives in a manner similar to the way they were treated. They react emotionally to themselves and regulate their responses to others based on these introjects, to the detriment of both themselves and others (Benjamin, 2003b).[7]

To maintain emotional distance, the fantasy bond promotes a core withholding of positive, loving, and supportive personality traits. Once defenses are formed and soothing fantasy processes are in place, people are reluctant to relinquish the apparent comfort and safety they offer. Once hurt, they are reluctant to become vulnerable again. Challenging the primary defense predisposes experiencing considerable anxiety. When faced with the choice of relinquishing defenses or hurting another person, there is usually no contest. Maintaining one's defensive posture, whether conscious or unconscious, is almost always the choice.

The paradox is that, as vulnerable children, people need defenses to survive psychologically, yet these same defenses lead to emotional suffering, maladaptive responses, and alienation in their adult lives. A great deal of people's inhumanity toward others springs from this source. There is no way to be innocently defended because the fantasy bond and the defenses it predisposes lead to inappropriate, maladaptive behaviors that interfere with the formation of loving and intimate attachments. It is a destructive legacy that is handed down through generations of family life (R. Firestone, 1990b).

A developmental perspective

From birth to six months, an infant's denial of separateness from the mother (or primary caregiver) is achieved through the subjective feeling or illusion of being at one with the mother. This is the primary fantasy bond. As such, the fantasy bond helps alleviate separation anxiety and the fear of being alone. Winnicott (1958) has portrayed the ability of the infant to fantasize an image of the mother's breast: "A subjective phenomenon develops in the baby which we call the mother's breast" (pp. 238–239).

At the next stage (six months to two years), the child gradually accommodates to reality, that is, to an awareness of being separate from the mother (Mahler, Pine, & Bergman, 1975). However, under stress, children still tend to regress to the earlier phase where they imagine that they and their mother are one. Louise Kaplan (1978) described the infant's first months of life as follows:

> From the infant's point of view there are no boundaries between himself and mother. They are one. This is how we first discovered merging bliss and inner harmony. This is how our psychological birth began. Yet all was not harmony during these early months (p. 28).

There is a primitive anxiety that an infant experiences during the inevitable separations that occur in any childhood. Lacking any sense of time, the baby feels abandoned for all time; it is alone, hungry, and desperate. It screams in frustration, fear, and protest. To cope with this overwhelming feeling, the infant builds a fantasy of omnipotence, imagining that it has a permanent connection to its all-powerful mother.

Sometime between the ages of three and seven, children become aware that people die, that their parents are vulnerable to death and that they themselves cannot sustain their own lives (S. Anthony, 1971/1973; Kastenbaum, 1974, 1995; Nagy, 1948/1959). Their evolving knowledge of death turns their world upside down and they realize that everything they previously had experienced as permanent is temporary. In general, children try to alleviate this powerful blow to their security by regressing to an earlier stage of development before they were aware of death. They attempt to reinstate and reinforce the original imagined connection with their parents (R. Firestone, 1985; Piven, 2004). On a behavioral level, these children appear to be more preoccupied with fantasy, become distant from their parents, and have nightmares filled with themes of death.

In a previous work (R. Firestone, 1997a), the first author described the impact of death anxiety on the defense system:

> Dating from this time, most people to varying degrees accommodate to the fear of death by withdrawing energy and emotional investment in life-affirming activity and close, personal relationships. The thought of losing one's life, losing all consciousness, losing all ego through death is so intolerable that the process of giving up offers relief from the anguish (pp. 82–83).[8]

Circumstances that intensify separation anxiety
Every child needs warmth, affection, direction, and guidance from adults who ideally would possess both the desire and ability to provide satisfaction of these basic needs.[9] However, no parental environment is perfect or ideal, and many parents lack the ability to offer the nurturing and socialization experiences necessary for the emotional development of their children. At times, a parent's inadequacies lead to insensitive treatment that intensifies the child's feelings of separation anxiety. Morrant and Catlett (2008) explained how the infant copes with the situation:

> When love-food is scanty, or the mother is mostly emotionally absent, the infant experiences "separation anxiety," a euphemism for being overcome by rage and the terror of annihilation. Then imagination, as Healer, steps into the breach. To cope with this anxiety, the infant imagines a make-believe mother, a *fantasy*, to comfort loneliness and dread. He or she incorporates all the experiences of the mother, transforming the woman of flesh and blood into a cognitive image. The infant develops a relationship with this inner fantasy of the mother. Firestone calls this relationship the *fantasy bond* …. It is the primary and greatest defense against separation anxiety and gives a counterfeit comfort in the place of insufficient love, sensitivity, tenderness, and control (pp. 357–358).

Infants are highly reactive to environmental inputs and respond with their whole body to painful intrusions from the outside world. Furthermore, these early impingements have a negative effect on the baby's developing mind (Cozolino, 2002, 2006; Perry, 1996, 2001; Schore, 1994, 2003; D. Siegel 1999; D. Siegel & Hartzell, 2003; van der Kolk, McFarlane, & Weisaeth, 1996). Parents' fears, depression, or hostility are conveyed, largely nonverbally, through physical interactions with the child.[10]

According to D. Siegel (1999), the development of the infant's mind is almost completely dependent on stimuli from people in its immediate environment, especially during its first two years of life. Cozolino (2002) asserted that "the building of the social brain between 18 and 24 months is driven by the attunement between the right hemisphere of the parent and the right hemisphere of the child" (p. 192). Drawing on findings from neuroscience and attachment theory, Schore (2002a) described the impact on the development of the infant's and the toddler's social brain resulting from stress caused by excessive misattunements and a caretaker's failure to repair breaks in attunement: "Instead of modulating she [the caregiver] induces extreme levels of stimulation and arousal, very high in abuse, and very low in neglect ... . Traumatized infants forfeit potential opportunities for socio-emotional learning during critical periods of right brain development" (pp. 449–450).

Thus, the prolonged dependency of the infant, its desperate need for its parents, and faulty or abusive parenting make the formation of the primary defense imperative.

The self-parenting process
The imagined fusion with the parent is highly effective as a defense because a human being's capacity for imagination provides partial gratification of needs and reduces tension (Keys, Brozek, Henschel, Mickelsen & Taylor, 1950; Silverman, Lachmann, & Milich, 1982).[11] The fantasy bond originates from the child's attempt to parent him or herself and involves self-nourishing habit patterns as well as self-punishing attitudes and behaviors. Self-nourishing behaviors begin with thumb-sucking, compulsively fingering or holding onto a blanket, or stroking oneself, and can develop into eating disorders, alcoholism, drug abuse, excessive masturbation, routine or compulsive activities that reduce pain, and/or an impersonal, repetitive style of sexual relating. Self-critical thoughts, guilt reactions, attacks on self,

and self-limiting, self-destructive actions are examples of the self-punishing component.

The fantasy bond is essentially a way of parenting oneself both internally through fantasy and externally through the use of objects and persons in one's environment (R. Firestone, 1997a; Guntrip, 1961).[12] As noted, the infant employs a variety of rudimentary self-nourishing behaviors to calm itself. These behaviors tend to support an illusion of pseudoindependence in the child—a feeling of being able to completely gratify him or herself and needing nothing from the outside world. The child experiences this false sense of self-sufficiency because he or she has introjected an image of the "good and powerful" parent into the self. At the same time, unfortunately, the child must necessarily incorporate the parent's covert or overt rejecting attitudes toward him/her. These incorporated parental attitudes form the basis of the child's negative self-concept (R. Firestone, 1985). In this way, children develop an illusion of being at once the good, strong parent and the bad, weak child, and tend to conceptualize themselves as a complete, self-sufficient system.

Although the self-parenting process allays the anxiety of feeling separate and alone and helps stave off feelings of emotional starvation and emptiness, it creates numerous distortions, e.g. the idealization of the parents at the child's own expense. For the fantasy bond to work, children must conceptualize themselves as bad or unlovable to protect themselves against the awareness that their parents are inadequate, rejecting, or destructive (Arieti, 1974; Kempe & Kempe, 1978; Oaklander, 1978, 2006). The parents' negative traits and inadequacies are projected on to the outside world, fostering a suspicious, cynical, or paranoid view of other people.

Children who have experienced excessive stress, rejection, or deprivation often come to prefer self-gratifying habit patterns and fantasy over deep feeling and associations with others. These self-parenting behaviors eventually become part of an addictive process that persists into adult life.

The fantasy bond is a maladaptive solution that occurs not only in seriously disturbed individuals but also, to a lesser degree, in "normal" people. "No child has an ideal environment; thus all people depend to varying degrees on internal gratification through self-parenting mechanisms and illusions of connection" (R. Firestone, 1985, p. 42).

In adults, the fantasy bond is manifested externally through the use of another person or people in the interpersonal environment. People tend to utilize new relationships and their partners to externalize their particular mode of self-parenting (R. Firestone, 1987a).

By the time they reach adulthood, most people have solidified their defenses and exist in a psychological equilibrium that they do not wish to disturb. However, in the first stages of a relationship, they relinquish their defenses to a certain extent and are more open and vulnerable. Although the state of being in love is exciting, it can also be frightening. Fears of loss, rejection, or abandonment and a poignant sadness aroused by positive emotions may become difficult to tolerate. At the point where they begin to feel anxious or frightened, many people retreat from feeling close and form an imaginary connection with each other, gradually giving up the most valued aspects of their relationships. They may also begin to act out of a sense of obligation rather than a genuine desire to be together. Many people progressively relinquish their independence, move away from special interests, reject meaningful friendships, and isolate themselves in an exclusive relationship (R. Firestone & Catlett, 1999). In one couple, these symptoms began to appear early in the relationship:

> Linda met Mark at a business conference. They were immediately drawn to one another and felt a strong compatibility and sexual attraction. They maintained a long distance relationship until Mark moved to Linda's city to live with her. Linda's friends had noticed how happy and alive Linda had become since meeting Mark, and when they met him, they were struck by how tender and affectionate the couple was with each other. However, after the couple began living together, her friends saw less and less of Linda. When they did see her, she was always with Mark; people found themselves thinking of Linda and Mark as a single person.
>
> Her friends began noticing behaviors in Linda that disturbed them. For example, she was no longer interested or involved in the activities they had known her to enjoy. Instead, she became involved in activities that Mark enjoyed, even some that she had previously expressed disinterest in. Even more alarming

was Linda's rejection of her teenage daughter, Sara. Linda had developed a close relationship with Sara, whom she had been distant from during the girl's early childhood. The renewed relationship was meaningful to both mother and daughter. But since meeting Mark, Linda rarely spent time with Sara, yet when Mark's children visited, she doted on them.

Linda no longer looked attractive and radiant; instead she appeared dumpy and her facial expression was without affect. She revealed to a close friend that Mark was jealous when he observed the ease and familiarity between her and her friends. His possessive reactions caused tension in their relationship. As time passed, these problems intensified: Mark became more exacting, parental, fatherly, and Linda became more timid, submissive, and childlike. Both partners were less considerate and respectful to each other. There was less physical affection between them and a decrease in their sexual activity. Although the couple still spent much time together, it seemed that Linda had lost her sense of identity.

As is true of most people in a fantasy bond, Mark and Linda resisted recognizing these negative trends in their relationship and claimed to still love each other.

When one or both partners sacrifice their individuality to become one-half of a couple, their basic attraction to each other can be jeopardized. As this process of deterioration continues, the couple's emotional responses become progressively less appropriate, friendly, or kind. Often all that exists after years together is a fantasy bond that both partners protect by maintaining the form of love while giving up the substance; that is, they have substituted role-determined behaviors, ritual, and routine habitual activities for the genuine affection, friendship, and attraction that originally characterized the relationship. In this way, they are able to preserve the fantasy that they love each other long after they have stopped behaving in a loving, respectful manner.

The voice process

The distinguishing characteristic of selfhood ... is not rationality but the critical awareness of man's divided nature (Lasch, 1984, p. 258).

Unconsciously ... people inflict punishments on themselves to which an inner court has sentenced them. A hidden authority within the ego takes over the judgment originally expected of the parents (Reik, 1941, p. 10).

The voice is the language of the defensive process. It refers to a systematized pattern of thoughts, attitudes, and beliefs, antithetical to the self and cynical toward others that is associated with varying degrees of anger and sadness and is at the core of all forms of maladaptive and aversive behaviors. Our operational definition excludes those thought processes that are concerned with constructive planning, creative thinking, self-appraisal, fantasy, value judgments, and moral considerations (R. Firestone, 1988). There is also a distinction between the voice and a conscience. Although the negative self-statements of the voice may at times seem to parallel one's value system, they often have a distinctly judgmental, harsh, or malicious tone. The voice tends to increase one's self-hatred rather than motivate one to alter behavior in a constructive manner.

The voice is not an actual hallucination but an identifiable system of thoughts. It is a form of intrapsychic communication that ranges from minor self-criticisms to major self-attacks and fosters self-nurturing habit patterns, isolation, and a self-limiting, self-destructive lifestyle. The first author adopted the term the "voice" to describe the hostile, alien point of view that people have incorporated toward themselves and others.[13]

Voice attacks are sometimes experienced consciously as an internal running commentary that is belittling or sarcastic in tone. More often than not, these destructive thoughts are only partially conscious or entirely unconscious. Most people are aware of calling themselves "a fool" or "clumsy" or "stupid" after making a mistake; however these minor critical thoughts are merely the tip of the iceberg. The average person is largely unaware of the extent to which negative thoughts influence or control behavioral responses, interfere with the pursuit of personal and career goals, and contribute to a depressed, antagonistic mood.

Origins of the voice

In situations of unusual stress, the child assumes the characteristics and attitudes of the angry, punishing parent in an attempt to escape overwhelming anxiety and psychological pain (R. Firestone, 1994b). The child's tendency to split off from the identity of the powerless "victim" and to identify with the powerful parent partly relieves his or her fear (Ferenczi, 1933/1955; A. Freud, 1966). Describing the long-term effects of this defensive identification in adult individuals, Morrant and Catlett (2008) noted: "Our parents' attitudes, behaviors, and sayings become incarnate in us, that is, they haunt us and direct almost every aspect of our lives. When we defy these 'parents in our heads,' we feel frightened, guilty, and alone" (pp. 356–357).

Children assimilate or incorporate parental attitudes when their parents are at their worst, i.e, at those times when they are the most defended, the most aggressive, and the most feared. The child internalizes the anger, fear, self-hatred, in fact, the whole complex of emotions the parent is experiencing. Children ascribe their own meaning and content to the parental hostility. They tend to develop an antagonistic point of view toward themselves that can go beyond a representation of what their parents' negative attitudes toward them may have been.

Investigations into the voice process

Early in my clinical group therapy practice, the first author became aware that people seemed overly sensitive to certain kinds of feedback. I concluded that it was not the truth per se that hurt; it was the fact that these descriptions validated the person's own distorted view of self and aroused a self-hating thought process. Therefore, any external evaluation or criticism, whether mild or harsh, was capable of activating self-critical associations. I thought it would be valuable to understand the types of events and feedback that arouse self-attacks. Therefore, the authors began to investigate this phenomenon in a discussion group composed of our professional associates and several participants from the friendship circle. It became apparent that people's defensive reactions were strongest when the feedback corresponded with their own negative self-attitudes.

A technique of verbalizing self-attacks evolved within this group process. Initially, participants expressed their negative thoughts and attitudes in a rational, cognitive, or analytic style. They discovered that these thoughts were easily accessible when articulated in the second person (e.g. "You're no good". "You're a failure") as though there was another person addressing them. In these first sessions, we were surprised by the intensity of the emotions aroused when participants verbalized their self-attacks (their distorted views of self), in this second person format. The degree of self-hatred and anger toward self that emerged indicated the depth and pervasiveness of the internalized destructive thought process.

Findings

As various dimensions of this negative thought process were brought to the foreground in this new group and in work with patients, we became aware of the powerful impact of this destructive force in people's lives. Since 1976, we have conducted more structured investigations of the voice process. We expanded the first author's study of this phenomenon and began to systematically examine a variety of actions that could be taken to elicit, understand, and challenge the voice. (1) First, as described, we recognized that people's destructive propensities toward self and others could be accessed by using the methodology of putting voice attacks in the second person. (2) Second, we discovered that formulating harsh judgmental thoughts in the second person led to valuable insights regarding the sources of the voice and its effects on one's behavior and lifestyle. (3) Third, we found that verbalizing the voice in this format not only brought out deep feeling but it also helped people separate these alien attitudes from their own point of view. Once articulated through this mode of expression, the specific attacks could be more effectively evaluated and countered by establishing new behavior patterns.[14]

We were able to delineate three levels of intensity of the voice in terms of affect: (1) At the first or mildest level of voice attack, we found that each person could identify an internal running commentary that criticized and derided him or her, one that was capable of producing a mild state of agitation or a depressed mood. (2) When participants verbalized these self-attacks in the second person, they frequently launched into an angry diatribe against themselves that was startling in its intensity. At this second level of voice intensity, these expressions were accompanied by strong affect, anger, and sadness that had previously been repressed. (3) At the third and highest level of voice intensity, people experienced a strong rage toward the self, manifested by suicidal urges or by injunctions to cause injury.[15]

In observing both the participants in the longitudinal study and clients in psychotherapy, we became aware of a more subtle aspect of the voice process. In addition to the obviously malicious or hostile voices that issue injunctions to destroy the self emotionally and/or physically, we identified seemingly protective, parental voices that act to stifle one's enthusiasm, spontaneity, and sense of adventure. These voices have overtones similar to those of an overprotective parent, cautioning, directing, controlling, and advising people in a manner that seems at first to be in their best interest. These apparently self-protective voices function to block people's desires before they can be translated into positive action.

The dual focus of the voice process
As noted, individuals have hostile thoughts toward themselves as well as cynical, suspicious thoughts toward others. Our findings indicate that hateful, judgmental views of other people result from the same internal voice process that promotes self-attacks. When people believe and accept the contents of their voice attacks as statements of fact, they tend to retreat to a defended, pseudoindependent stance. Whether attacking oneself, *"You're so unattractive. Who would want to be involved with you?"* or attacking another, *"He(She) is so cold and rejecting,"* the result is the same. One is tempted to withdraw one's emotional investment in the other person and become inward, thereby avoiding give-and-take emotional interactions. There is a tendency to retreat to self-parenting defenses and back away from seeking external gratification. In this way, the voice process supports and reinforces the fantasy bond.

The role of the voice in the intergenerational transmission of negative parental behaviors
Our investigations into the voice process included three generations of individuals and allowed us to document the similarity between children's expressions of the voice and their parents' voice attacks. A close correspondence was demonstrated between parents' self-critical thoughts and those expressed by their children in terms of negative core beliefs. This was especially true in regard to the parent of the same sex.[16] For example, a father who was perfectionistic and

who had unrealistically high expectations for his son, revealed the following self-attacks:

> W: I have a voice telling me things like: *"You'd better get this right, buddy, if you don't say it right, just shut up! Don't say a goddamn thing, just say it right! You'd better be right!"* That's an attack that I've got all the time. *"Say it right! Or don't say anything!"* It all comes down to this fury that I feel against myself, strong anger, and I feel it against my son (tearful) I don't want to.

Some time later, in a separate group discussion, W's 16-year-old son said:

> When I was in elementary school, I was terrified to get bad grades. I made all A's but if I got just one B, I felt terrible. And in sports, I have to be either the greatest or the worst, I can't just be normal, I have to live up to something. In baseball, if I make an error, it's like I just tear into myself, I think I'm such an idiot. I just sit there and call myself an idiot a hundred times. It's like I'm screaming at myself inside my head.

The voice functions to tie individuals to their parents in the sense that, even though physically separate or geographically distant from the family, adults still possess an internal parent that directs, controls, and punishes them. These voices, albeit unpleasant and malicious, function to maintain the fantasy bond and shield the individual from experiencing his or her aloneness, sense of separateness, and death anxiety.

The ethical consequences of leading a defended life

> By understanding how pain and neurosis are passed down from generation to generation, people might decide to break the chain. They could choose to live by an implicit code of morality that ... doesn't fracture their feelings and experiences or those of others, a morality that enhances their well-being and personal development ... creating a society that is sensitive to the emotional and psychological fulfillment of all its members (R. Firestone & Catlett, 1989, p. 14).

From our discussion of the ethics of interpersonal relationships, it has become apparent that people cannot be innocently defended. When individuals protect themselves from anxiety, pain, and sadness—emotions that are inherent in all personal relationships—they push away, hurt, and punish the people who care for them the most. The majority of people are unaware that they are living out a negative destiny according to their past programming, preserving their negative identity formed in the family and, in the process, pushing love away and hurting other people. Punishing one's partner to preserve a negative fantasy of who one is represents a basic dynamic in personal relationships and is more common than most people would like to believe (R. Firestone & Catlett, 1999).

Similarly, to the extent that parents are defended, they necessarily hurt their children. Because children tend to imitate their parents' toxic traits and negative behaviors, when they become parents themselves they are compelled to act out on their children the same abuses they endured during childhood (R. Firestone, 1990b). Most people are not cognizant of this compulsion because the defensive apparatus is triggered without conscious awareness. When people begin to feel a minimal level of anxiety, they start to make the defensive adaptation before they are fully conscious of what they are adapting to.

There are other ethical implications related to the voice. People tend to be trustworthy only to the degree that they are operating from their own point of view instead of from the dictates of the critical inner voice. Many are unaware of the power of the influence of the voice underlying their self-destructive or harmful behaviors toward others, particularly when unconscious negative thoughts take precedence over conscious, rational thinking.

In addition, self-destructive behaviors exert a powerful social pressure on other people to behave in similar self-defeating or self-destructive ways. As noted, self-destructive behavior is manipulative in that it is capable of eliciting fear, anger, guilt, or alarm in other people (R. Firestone & Seiden, 1987). There is a fear of losing the self-destructive person as well as the guilt inherent in feeling that one is responsible for another person's life or death. Considerable stress and emotional turmoil are experienced by a friend or family member who is closely involved with a person persistently engaged in self-destructive behavior. People who refuse to give up self-destructive or addictive behaviors that possibly endanger their physical health cause much ongoing dissension in couples and families.

The voice also supports self-denial and the renunciation of natural wants and desires through a distortion of conventional values and mores. These distortions arise originally because many people have been taught as children to conform to unnecessary prohibitions at the expense of self; they have learned to be selfless and to feel guilty for having wants and needs. There is a strong social pressure exerted by people who are selfless or self-denying that has a negative influence on others.

Individuals who are withholding, incompetent, or fail to perform to the level of their abilities provoke anger, guilt, and demoralization in coworkers and employers. People who regress to childish modes of relating and withhold adult responses, whether in the workplace or in their personal life, are able to manipulate other people into taking care of them. In this way, they preserve the imagined security of the original fantasy bond with their parents. The process of eliciting or provoking negative parental reactions—worry, fear, anger, and even punishment—causes considerable damage to the person who is manipulated into playing the parental role. In all of the situations described above, the individuals who acted out aversive, hurtful behavior constituted a serious drain on the energy of others and on the families and communities in which they lived.

Conclusion

People come by their defenses honestly. Painful experiences early in life make it necessary for them to form fantasy bonds and self-protective defenses in order to survive. In their present-day lives, people are limited by the same defensive behaviors or harm others by maintaining these defenses. To whatever degree individuals have incorporated their parents' punitive attitudes, they will tend to hate and punish themselves, their loved ones, and eventually their children.

From an ethical perspective, there is a considerable difference between judging behavior from a moral standpoint and attributing blame, and developing a compassionate understanding of the pain inherent in human relationships. Moral condemnation merely increases guilt, which leads to more self-hatred and further disharmony in interpersonal relationships. The guilt or blame for the unnecessary pain and trauma of childhood cannot be assigned to one person or group of persons. Because parents were themselves once the neglected, mistreated children about whom we are writing, it is counterproductive to dwell on blame rather than accountability. In contrast, understanding the sources of aversive behaviors opens up the possibility for personal development.

Separation theory provides an understanding of why most people have difficulty living a principled existence and suggests methods for overcoming these difficulties. The methodology of voice therapy helps people identify and separate from destructive thought processes or voices that control aversive behaviors and predispose destructive lifestyles. Working through these problems facilitates movement toward individuation, autonomy, and integrity. The therapeutic process involves disrupting imagined connections or fantasy bonds and moving toward a life of personal responsibility and independence. Challenging an inward, defensive posture is essential to living a truly ethical life.

Notes

1. Hauser (2006) proposed that rational thinking or conscious deliberation alone does not determine human beings' sense of right and wrong. "When people give explanations for their moral behavior, they may have little or nothing to do with the underlying principles. Their sense of conscious reasoning from specific principles is illusory" (p. 67).

2. See Bandura's (1999) discussion of "moral disengagement," a concept similar to the concept of cognitive dissonance. In moral disengagement, people are able to harm others through restructuring their thoughts to rationalize harmful actions. Bandura argued that, "People do not ordinarily engage in harmful conduct until they have justified to themselves the morality of their actions ... . People then can act on a moral imperative and preserve their view of themselves as moral agents while inflicting harm on others" (p. 194). Also see Moore's (2007) paper "Moral Disengagement in Processes of Organizational Corruption." She noted that "Two cognitive mechanisms (displacement of responsibility and diffusion of responsibility) *minimize the role of the individual* in the harm that is caused by an individual's actions" (p. 130). The present authors

suggest that these cognitions, as well as thoughts that attribute blame to others, are part of the destructive voice process described in this chapter.

3. We are not referring to a bond of loyalty, love, and affection within a couple or family. We are describing a destructive way of relating to another person based on an imagined connection or merged identity, a fantasy of love that is a substitute for real love and closeness.

4. Hellmuth Kaiser (Fierman, 1965) identified people's strong tendencies to form imagined connections with another person, both in the therapeutic setting and in everyday life. He proposed that these attempts "to create in real life by behavior or communication the illusion of fusion" could be conceptualized as the "universal psychopathology" (pp. 208–209).

5. The antiself system is made up of the primary defense, the fantasy bond, and the secondary defense, the voice process. The extent to which the antiself system may prevail over the self system is proportional to the amount of damage sustained by the individual while growing up. The self system is made up of the unique physical, temperamental, and genetic predispositions of the individual, tendencies and behavior based on the harmonious identification with parents' positive attitudes and traits, and the effects of experience and education on the individual (see R. Firestone, 1997a).

The concept of a self and antiself system is similar in some respects to the notion of a divided consciousness, described initially by Hilgard (1977) in *Divided Consciousness: Multiple Controls in Human Thought and Action*. Elements of the antiself system can be compared to certain components in the "Experiential Mind" as described by Seymour Epstein (1998). Although the "experiential mind" is not conceptualized as necessarily destructive by Epstein, he does encourage readers to identify their "automatic thoughts" and to use their "rational mind to train [their] experiential mind" (p. 222).

6. Stettbacher (1990/1991) described the effects on the child and later the adult individual of emotional abuse and neglect as well as physical and sexual maltreatment in childhood as follows: "The latent, destructive power we harbor within us is strong and dangerous in proportion to the severity of the primal injuries inflicted on us. Old destructive powers work on in us like a ticking bomb. They were created in the victim: the abused child" (p. 37). Similarly, Shengold (1989) asserted that when the traumatic crises are chronic, ordinary defenses will not suffice and regression to early, massive, "'analnarcissistic defenses' (which used to blank out primal feelings)

will also become chronic .... As Ferenczi (1933) put it, 'The [abused] child changes into a mechanical obedient automaton' (p. 163) ... . But the automaton has murder within" (p. 25).

7. See Benjamin (2003b) who wrote: "Problem patterns are linked to learning with important early loved ones via one or more of three copy processes: (1) Be like him or her; (2) Act as if he or she is still there and in control; and (3) Treat yourself as he or she treated you" (p. vii).

8. Robert Langs (2004) postulated three forms of death anxiety: (1) predatory death anxiety (responsiveness to a threat of harm); (2) predation death anxiety, when an individual causes physical and/ or psychological harm to others; and (3) existential death anxiety, "the dread of the inevitability of death for all living humans; especially oneself" (p. 91).

9. Greenspan (1997), in *The Growth of the Mind*, emphasized the importance of both parental affection and direction for facilitating children's moral development: "Limit setting without nurturing breeds fear and an amoral desire to beat the system. Nurturing without limits breeds self-absorption and irresponsibility" (p. 195).

10. Re: how parents' emotional states are conveyed to the child, see especially Schore's (2003) chapter "Clinical Implications of a Psychoneurobiological Model of Projective Identification" (pp. 58–101). See also "Advances in Neuropsychoanalysis, Attachment Theory, and Trauma Research: Implications for Self Psychology" (Schore, 2002a) and "The Effects of Early Relational Trauma on Right Brain Development, Affect Regulation, and Infant Mental Health" (Schore, 2001a).

11. Silverman, et al (1982) conducted research on the ameliorative effects of the subliminal message "Mommy and I are One" when presented subliminally on the tachistoscope. P. Siegel and Weinberger (1998) reported findings of more recent studies in "Capturing the 'Mommy and I Are One' Merger Fantasy: The Oneness Motive." Re: oneness fantasies, see Mahler's (1974) clinical description of toddlers whom she observed following the departure of the mother from the room.

12. Describing individuals with schizoid tendencies, Guntrip (1961) depicted "self-parenting" and the resultant pseudoindependent posture as follows: "One patient remembers thinking at the age of nine: 'I can manage by myself. I don't need to trouble mother.' ... This secret inner burden of responsibility for self, beginning at far too early an age when the child still needs the closest parental care, is gravely undermining" (pp. 440–441). Bollas (1987) expanded the

concept of self-parenting and generalized it to all his patients: "It is my view that each person transfers elements of the parents' child care to his own handling of himself as an object" (p. 59). Frances Tustin (cited in Koenigsberg, 2003) also described the infant's illusion that he and the mother are fused ("a continuum of bodily stuff"), noting that early in life, defensive reactions "set in to block our awareness of bodily separateness" (para. 4–5).

13. In terms of psychoanalytic/object relations theories, the concept of the voice is similar in some respects to the antilibidinal ego described by Fairbairn (1952) and Guntrip (1961, 1969). According to Guntrip (1961), "The Anti-Libidinal Ego (Anti-L.E.) [is] an accurate term that has the advantage of making clear the fact that this part of the personality plays a persecutory role in relationship to the L.E. [Libidinal Ego]" (p. 329).

    The concept also has elements in common with the concept of internal working models described originally by Bowlby (1980) and elaborated by Ainsworth (1989), Main (1996), Bretherton (1996), and other attachment theorists. These theorists and researchers proposed that internal working models represent children's beliefs about self and relationships and regulate their attachment behavior throughout life. According to attachment theorists Bakermans-Kranenburg and van IJzendoorn (1993), internal working models or "current 'state of mind' with respect to attachment relationships determines parents' sensitivity to their infants' attachment behavior, and, in turn, shapes the infants' own internal working models of attachment" (p. 870). Maternal insensitivity or lack of attunement predisposes the formation of negative internal working models or destructive cognitions. Therefore, one can hypothesize that "internal working models" or destructive thought processes are responsible for the repetition of abnormal or maladaptive attachment patterns over the life span (R. Firestone & Catlett, 1999).

14. Re: establishing new behavior patterns, in terms of psychotherapy, brain neuroplasticity and the potential for repairing or rewiring damaged neuronal connections, Tancredi (2005), in *Hardwired Behavior: What Neuroscience Reveals about Morality*, cited studies showing that both interpersonal therapy (ITP) and cognitive-behavioral therapy (CBT) bring about "significant positive changes not only in the clinical condition of the patient but also in neural pathways" (p. 44).

15. In research using voice therapy techniques, we learned that the exposure of unconscious or partly conscious aggression had profound implications for advancing our knowledge of psychopathology (R. Firestone, 1997b). Subsequently, R. Firestone and L. Firestone

developed two assessment instruments, The *Firestone Assessment of Destructive Thoughts* (FAST)/*Firestone Assessment of Suicidal Intent* (FASI) (R. Firestone & Firestone, 2006). Reliability and validity studies found that the FAST and FASI discriminated previous suicide attempters from nonattempters more accurately than the Suicide Probability Scale (SPS, Cull & Gill, 1988) and the Beck Hopelessness Scale (BHS, Beck, 1988).

16. Participants in the three-generational longitudinal study included approximately 23 mothers and 24 fathers, who participated in specialized parenting groups over a ten-year period. For a description of these groups, see "Parenting Groups Based on Voice Therapy" (R. Firestone, 1989). In a separate group, 14 of their offspring participated in a group discussion where they verbalized critical thoughts and attitudes toward themselves and toward others.

CHAPTER SEVEN

The fantasy bond in couple and family relationships

It is always the inability to stand the aloneness of one's individual self that leads to the drive to enter into a symbiotic relationship with someone else.

Erich Fromm (1941, p. 180)

The paradox of the human condition is that the fantasies and illusions that spare us from the core anxiety of facing separation issues and death, the ultimate separation, distance us from our real lives, our mates, our children, our sexuality, and even ourselves. Core defenses and fantasies of safety and security alienate us from our essential humanness and turn us against other people. The fantasy bond, which originates within the family, promotes a false sense of superiority in relation to other people, leading to a sense of alienation and suspiciousness toward those who look or live differently. The process of separating ourselves from others and elevating ourselves above them spreads to aggrandized feelings about our neighborhoods, our cities, and eventually our nations. This identification offers an illusion of safety and a feeling of being special but its outcome results in distrust, division, prejudice, and

151

aggression. Thus, the fantasy bond is not only harmful to close personal relationships but has a negative impact on cultures and societies as well.

Although other issues in life cause us concern—crime, war, terrorism, poverty, and existential issues of aloneness and death—we seem to experience the most hurt, distress, and turmoil in our interpersonal relationships. In fact, dissatisfaction or rejection in a relationship or marriage is perhaps the most common reason people enter psychotherapy. Fincham (2000), in an article appropriately titled "Kiss of the Porcupines," emphasizes the painful and aversive dimensions of personal relationships:

> Humans harm each other and humans are social animals .... How to maintain relatedness with fellow humans in the face of being harmed by them [is the challenge]. This challenge is most acute, and most important, in close relationships. In a seeming paradox, fulfillment of our deepest affiliative needs as social animals occurs in close relationships where it appears to be accompanied by injury; it is a rare person who has never felt "wronged," "let down," "betrayed," or "hurt" by a relationship partner (p. 2).

The instability and problematic nature of intimate relationships and marriage have been well-documented. Approximately 40% of marriages will eventually end in divorce while 50% of individuals who stay married report feeling emotionally and/or physically dissatisfied and unfulfilled. Recent surveys indicate that there are "more than 40 million Americans stuck in a low-sex or no-sex marriage" (McCarthy & McCarthy, 2003, p. 4).[1]

Many parents today, too busy with their own lives, fail to offer their children guidance, affection, or love. Their adolescent offspring, who suffer from this lack of direction, spend much of their time partying, drinking, and using drugs. Many children are left to seek guidance, solace, peer-support, and friendship in inappropriate places. For example, they may seek out personal communication on the internet, visiting sites regularly used by sex predators to make inappropriate contact with young people. "The National Center for Missing and Exploited Children says on its Web site that one in five children who use the Internet have been solicited sexually" (J. Myers, 2006, para. 1) (Pierce, 2006).[2] At the other extreme, there is a phenomenon currently referred to as "helicopter parenting," where parents "hover" over their children, structuring their lives and directing their every move.[3] When the young person leaves for college, the hovering often continues via the cell phone or e-mail (Indiana University, 2007).

What factors are responsible for these negative trends in family life? Why do so many couples have nonsexual relationships? Why do so many marriages end in divorce? It is the authors' contention that defenses formed in childhood are responsible for much of the distress and disharmony in intimate relationships and family life. The major reasons for conflict within couples and the subsequent breakdown of relationships and marriages are not the factors listed in typical explanations of the problem: economic hardship, religious differences, wrong choice of partner, decline of family values, breakdown of religious affiliation, or sexual incompatibility. Rather, difficulties in close relationships are due primarily to a fear of vulnerability, a lack of real personal communication between partners, and the formation of a fantasy bond in place of genuine closeness. Understanding the manifestations and defensive functions of the fantasy bond also helps explain why many marriages that remain intact do so at great expense to the individuality of the participants, why sexual relationships often deteriorate or become routine, and why so many couples distance themselves from one another and become, in effect, intimate enemies (R. Firestone & Catlett, 1999).

The fantasy bond in couple relationships

> Perhaps the problem begins ... with the gloomy fact that adult love doesn't ever completely quell that constitutional human sense of lack and separation trauma that sets its quest in motion. Anxiety is not just endemic to the enterprise, it's also incurable .... Nevertheless, there we are, chasing tantalizing glimpses of some lost imaginary wholeness in a lover's adoring gaze ... . There we are, hoping that the flimsy social safety nets we've committed ourselves to—monogamy, domesticity, maturity—resolve our anxieties (Kipnis, 2003, pp. 57–58).

An essential component in resistance to closeness in couple and family relationships is the concept of the fantasy bond as a primary defense. As described in the previous chapter, the imagined connection to the mother or primary caretaker is the earliest manifestation of this fantasy process. Later this compensatory self-parenting process is elaborated in the family context. Eventually, the illusion of self-sufficiency and associated self-protective mechanisms act as barriers to fulfilling, satisfying adult relationships.

The fantasy bond, or merged identity, provides an individual with a false sense of safety, security, and permanence. It is a core defense that partially allays the fear of aloneness, separateness, and death.[4] It allows people to maintain an unconscious sense of omnipotence and immortality. The original fantasized connection to one's parents and family of origin is transferred to new associations: friends, husbands, wives, and children. The fantasy process goes beyond interpersonal relationships and extends to affiliations with hometown, state, country, and religious orientation (R. Firestone, 1994b). It relates to the identification with being Catholic or Protestant, Republican or Democrat, capitalist or communist, Israeli or Palestinian, and a variety of other isms. It is the true "opiate of the people."

The fantasy bond represents a desperate attempt to deny or negate the existential truth of human existence, the fact that people are essentially alone and must eventually die. In trying to digest the full importance of this core defense, one must understand the depth of fear attendant to separation experiences, human beings' incredible dread of abandonment, and the anxiety and torment associated with their awareness of mortality (Becker, 1973/1997). The illusion of connectedness attempts to heal this fracture and assuage the painful wounds to one's omnipotence. For this reason, it has an irresistible appeal.

As noted earlier, most people are largely unaware of experiencing existential dread or death anxiety in their everyday lives. If questioned, many would say that they spend very little time consciously thinking of or worrying about death. Nevertheless, people tend to respond to reminders of death by adopting defensive behaviors and giving up broad areas of life experience before their anxiety reaches consciousness. In an intimate relationship, the threat of rejection, fear of potential loss, a separation and, paradoxically, genuine love and closeness often arouse existential fears. When these feelings surface, they set into motion well-established core defenses that have a negative impact on a person's adjustment and his or her relationships.

This phenomenon fits the conceptual model proposed by terror management (TMT) theorists that has been validated through extensive research (Greenberg, et al, 1990; Pyszczynski, Solomon, & Greenberg, 2003; Rosenblatt, Greenberg, Solomon, Pyszczynski, & Lyon, 1989). These researchers hypothesize that defenses against death anxiety (elevated self-esteem and bias toward one's cultural worldview) exist on an unconscious level. Reminders of death, even when presented on a subliminal level, are capable of arousing these defenses (Arndt, et al, 1997; Greenberg, Arndt, Simon, Pyszczynski, & Solomon, 2000; Greenberg, Pyszczynski, Solomon, Simon, & Breus, 1994).[5]

If being exposed to the word "death" presented subliminally in an experiment is capable of arousing a defensive reaction, one can well imagine the impact on people's defenses resulting from every-day reminders of death. People are constantly bombarded by news broadcasts, stories about family members and friends dying, accidents, war, and crime.

Fantasies of imagined protection against one's fears of separation, abandonment, and death are achieved at considerable expense to a person's well-being and potential adjustment. As with all painkilling addictions, people who rely on a fantasy bond are progressively debilitated in their capacity to function effectively in their daily lives. The fantasy process drains a person's energy and vitality, reduces one's ability to cope effectively, and takes a heavy toll on personal relationships.

The need for assurances of security and the attempt to fill the emotional void of past experiences and existential aloneness cause people to place great demands on those they love.[6] The desperation for this type of connection with loved ones places an incomparable burden on couple and family relationships and often leads to serious problems of relating.

Couples in a fantasy bond often engage in habitual routines, family rituals, and superficial conversation to preserve the fantasy that they are still in love. In so doing, they come to rely on form over substance. Gradually a fantasy of closeness replaces expressions of sensitivity, affection, and mutual respect. The human capacity for self-deception makes it possible for partners to collude in their illusions of closeness and connection while acting out aversive behaviors that contradict any recognizable operational definition of love. As R. D. Laing (1961) noted:

> Collusion has resonances of playing at and of deception. It is
> a 'game' played by two or more people whereby they deceive

themselves. The game *is* the game of mutual self-deception ... . Both [partners] settle for counterfeit acts of confirmation on the basis of pretence (pp. 108–109).

For reasons pertaining to their developmental history, it is usually difficult for partners to trust in one another and tolerate real closeness, yet they fear being alone even more. A fantasy bond is the ideal solution.

People easily mistake a fantasy of love for a genuine loving relationship because they confuse their internal fantasized feelings with external manifestations of love. They expect that their feelings of love and caring can be sensed by another when, in reality, only outward expressions of affection, kindness, and respect can be experienced. How many parents have told a child, "Mommy (Daddy) really loves you. She (he) just has trouble showing it"? How often have husbands and wives claimed to love each other while treating one another poorly, consciously being deceptive about monetary issues, for example, or about other sexual relationships?

Even when members of a couple seem satisfied, maintaining a fantasy bond can hurt their relationship and limit the personal development of each individual. In giving up their autonomy in an attempt to assure themselves that they are safe and secure, they substitute habit for choice, lose vitality and feeling, and generally suffer from a decline in their sexual relating. They make less eye contact, limit or restrain their communications, and gradually distance themselves from each other. All the while, they desperately attempt to retain an illusion of closeness and demand that their mates do the same. When one member of a couple fails to offer the proper assurances, the other generally becomes harsh and punitive.

Ethical implications: Destructive effects of the fantasy bond on couple relationships

Falling in love ... doesn't just mean committing to another person, it means committing to certain emotional bargains and trade-offs also, some of which prove more workable than others. It's generally understood that falling in love means committing to *commitment* ... . Falling in love also commits us to *merging*. Meaning that unmerging, when this proves necessary, is ego-shattering and generally traumatic (Kipnis, 2003, p. 56–57).

From an ethical standpoint, it is damaging to make use of another person in the service of a defensive process. The fantasy bond not only masks negative behaviors but also supports a couple's tendency to collude in a shared distortion of reality that hurts both individuals (Dicks, 1967; R. Firestone & Catlett, 1999).[7] It is destructive to respond to another by recreating circumstances from one's past that have little or nothing to do with the new person or the present life circumstances. These transference distortions and the primal feelings that they are based on cause considerable problems in marital and family life. Furthermore it is hurtful to establish inequality in a relationship, playing either half of an unequal polarization by acting the role of the child or the parent.

Selection, distortion and provocation within couple relationships

Circumstances that are more positive than those experienced in one's formative years can cause painful feelings of sadness and anxiety to emerge. To avoid feelings of anxiety, people must modify the loving responses of their partner to maintain their psychological equilibrium. There are three basic ways that people maintain this equilibrium in their primary relationships.

First, people tend to select partners who are similar to significant figures in their early lives because these are the people who fit in with their defenses and who they feel most comfortable with (Pines, 2005). As Sam Keen (1997) observed:

> Many people wake up in middle age with the realization that in their youthful romances and early marriages, they were drawn to precisely the kinds of partners they were trying to avoid. All too often we marry stand-ins for our alcoholic fathers, shadowy replacements for our angry mothers (p. 55).

Secondly, people distort their mates and see them more like the people in their past than they really are. This primarily negative transference phenomenon does an injustice to one's partner and causes friction. All misperceptions or projections, both positive and negative, will generate problems. People want to be seen and acknowledged for themselves, and distortions cause pain and misunderstanding as well as predisposing angry reactions.

One or both partners may disown certain negative traits in themselves and perceive them in the other person. This type of projection creates a feeling in the other person that he or she actually possesses these traits. Serious distortions also occur when people externalize their self-critical thoughts or voices in their closest relationships. Through the process of defensive projective identification, they induce the same negative thoughts and disturbing emotions in their partners that they are experiencing within themselves (Firestone & Catlett, 1999; Grotstein, 2007; Ogden, 1982; Schore, 2003).[8]

This type of distortion is particularly hurtful and upsetting to the recipient, because on an unconscious level people tend to accept negative projections as real, even though on a conscious or intellectual level, they may reject them. For example, soon after she was married, a woman began to perceive her husband as mean, judgmental, and demanding. As a child, she had incorporated her mother's punitive, perfectionistic attitudes in relation to her as part of a negative self-image and had many self-depreciating thoughts. Her husband, easy-going and accepting, soon came to believe that he was, in fact, a harsh, critical autocrat who demanded perfection.

Thirdly, if these first two defenses fail to recreate the past, people will elicit familiar responses by provoking a loved one to respond like one of their parents or family members. By inducing their partners to criticize and attack them, they are evoking their own self-attacks from the other person. This serves to further externalize one's inner enemy.

Often the closest, most tender moments in relationships are followed by provocations which create distance between the partners. Men and women provoke anger and rage in each other with thoughtlessness, moodiness, forgetfulness, and other withholding responses. The result is that each partner withdraws to a less vulnerable position and reestablishes psychological equilibrium. Many marriages ultimately fail as each partner incites angry responses in the other in order to maintain a "safe" distance.

Provoking behaviors evoke painful emotions of guilt, shame, rage, and hatred as well as self-destructive thinking in the person who is their target. The person who is consistently provoked into feeling angry suffers because the loving feelings that he or she once felt are being systematically transformed into negative emotions. Eventually they are manipulated to the point where they are no longer able to love or even like the person closest to them (Tavris & Aronson, 2007).[9]

Deprived of love and, more important, of loving, the provoked person finds him/herself overly focused on the other. There is a desperate attempt to recapture the lost, longed-for loving feelings. One man, in trying to explain his reactions to his wife, said: "If I could remain objective when I'm provoked, which is impossible, and if I were free to say what I really felt, I'd say to her: 'I'm really furious with you, but I love you so much that I will overlook anything you do and I'll even believe that I'm at fault.'" This man's latter statement, his conviction that he was at fault, was the result of being distorted and provoked by his wife. In most cases, distortion and provocation are occurring simultaneously within a disturbed couple relationship.

Polarization

Many people find themselves attracted to specific qualities in a potential partner that are very different from, or the opposite of, their own personality characteristics. This phenomenon is expressed in the old adage "opposites attract." The opposing characteristics that draw people to each other also play a significant part in their sexual attraction (Mikulincer & Shaver, 2007; Pines, 2005).[10] Shy individuals seek those who are outgoing, submissive people seek those who are dominating, and aggressive people seek those who are passive. This process is gradually debilitating in that it reinforces the weaknesses of the individuals. At first each person feels a sense of wholeness or completeness. However, as these couples come to rely on each other's complementary qualities, they become progressively more dependent on each other. They often come to hate the very qualities that originally drew them together.

> In one couple, the man tended to be passive and reserved while his wife was assertive and outgoing. As the years went by, he depended more and more on her for direction, to the point where he was no longer aware of what he wanted. Although he resented her for taking over the decision-making, he was too held back and reticent to express his anger. His wife gradually assumed more and more control over the couple's activities and exerted considerable influence on her husband's career, his choice of friends, and other interests. At the same time, she came to hate him for being so passive and indecisive.

After the couple separated, the wife sought counseling and developed insight into the issues she believed had contributed to the breakup: "During those years, I remember feeling so attached, so connected to him. It almost felt like I was an extension of him, a part of his arm. It's sad, but I had no feeling for him as a person, separate from me, or any feeling for him at all. Even though I hated him for letting me control him, I couldn't stop doing it because I felt so insecure. I felt compelled to control him, but my control took over our relationship."

By acting out the aggressive, controlling role in the relationship, the woman had been able to disown and submerge her feelings of fear and insecurity. Both partners were insecure and felt inadequate and deficient in certain areas of their functioning. Both lacked a sense of being a whole person within themselves. By using each other as a compensation for their perceived deficiencies, they attained an illusion of wholeness or integration within themselves, at great cost, however, to both the relationship and themselves.

Loss of independence and individuality in couple relationships

A significant indication that a fantasy bond has been formed is when one or both partners give up a sense of separate identity—important areas of personal interest, unique points of view and opinions—in order to become one half of an imagined unit. The attempt to find security in an illusion of merging with another leads to a gradual loss of identity in each person. The individuals involved tend to have habitual contact, which leads to a subsequent decline in personal feeling for one another.

Furthermore, the tendency for each person in the couple to relinquish independence, autonomy, important interests and goals, and even long-standing friendships is supported by conventional attitudes about the exclusivity of couple relationships. These include mistaken beliefs about togetherness and the myth of unconditional love.

Leonard and Janet were college students when they first met. Leonard was immediately impressed by Janet's intelligence, her views about politics and life in general, and her plans for the future. Janet was drawn to Leonard's enthusiasm and ambition, his sense of responsibility, and his extensive knowledge about a wide range of subjects. The couple spent hours talking about themselves and their interests and enjoyed lively debates about politics and religion as they got to know each other. Several months after they became engaged, Janet found out she was pregnant and they were married.

Soon afterward, Janet dropped out of college, pulled away from her friends, and stopped pursuing interests that had once excited her. She even stopped driving, claiming it was hard on her back. Instead she prevailed upon Leonard to take her to doctors' appointments. She became depressed and increasingly dependent on him. As time went on, Leonard came to resent Janet's demands on his time. He missed the conversations they once had and longed for the equality they had shared. In an attempt to improve the situation, he found himself offering his wife advice about her health and emotional state. His approach became increasingly parental, and she responded by becoming more childish.

Years later, in therapy, Janet realized that she had become less independent after her marriage. She became aware that she had made a serious mistake in dropping out of college and giving up the close friendships and activities she had enjoyed.

Janet: "Looking back, one of the most painful things is that I gave up my opinions and my point of view. I actually was afraid to disagree with Leonard for some reason, whereas before that, I never thought twice about contradicting his views and opinions when I felt he was wrong. I think I became terrified that he would reject me. I even imagined that he felt resentful because he felt trapped into marrying me.

"When I think back to that time period, I feel appalled at the way I acted. And it didn't get any better until Leonard confronted me recently and asked for a separation. The anxiety and panic attacks I experienced at that point motivated me to enter therapy, where I began to think clearly about myself and my situation. I realized I had been using Leonard as a critical parent throughout our marriage. I distorted him and saw him as being very much like my mother, who was extremely critical and punishing toward me as a child. It's sad to think about what happened to our relationship now, because it was all so unnecessary."

The authoritarian role that Leonard gradually adopted made him appear to be a strong and confident man; however, it had serious consequences for him. It gave him a false sense of superiority, while in reality he felt insecure at work and in relation to his sexual performance. The resulting marital discord led to tension and anxiety and a reliance on alcohol. He felt disconnected from his own wants, desires, and goals in life. After the separation from Janet and the resultant breakdown in the fantasy bond, Leonard felt a renewed sense of himself.

Leonard: "Even though I felt relieved and had a feeling of my own freedom for the first time in years, I also felt strange, fearful, disoriented, as though I didn't know exactly who I was or what I was going to do with my life. I realized then that I had forgotten completely about my own goals in focusing so much on Janet's well-being. Basically I had lost track of my life. But the worst part of those years with Janet was the torture of watching her fade into oblivion from the bright, intelligent, energetic woman she had been when we first met. It's difficult for anybody to understand how painful that process was, how much it hurt me."

Decline in sexual relating in couple relationships

When one or both partners in a fantasy bond sacrifices independence and individuality in the process of merging their identities, the original attraction between them tends to decrease. In contrast to how they felt during the early phases of the relationship, both partners usually become more distant, more routine and habitual in their love-making. Many people pull away from their mates in subtle ways even before their fears of intimacy, rejection, or loss reach the level of conscious awareness. They begin to unconsciously hold back their affection and sexual responses, substituting a more inward, impersonal style of sexual relating. Consequently, their love-making tends to be more mechanical and focused on performance, which often leaves them feeling emotionally unsatisfied and empty.

There is often a decrease in sexual desire and frequency in making love or an overall deterioration in the quality of sexual relating after the birth of a child. The stress of an added dependent, the woman's guilt about being sexual after becoming a mother, and the existential anxiety aroused by becoming a parent lead to a deterioration in the quality of relating and to an increased reliance on the fantasy bond.[11]

Studies by family researchers Cowan and Cowan (2000) indicate that when one or both partners perceived their families-of-origin as having considerable conflict, there was a decline in each partner's marital satisfaction during the transition to parenthood. In another investigation, only two of the 38 couples studied showed improvement in their relationship during pregnancy and following the birth of their first child (Lewis, Owen, & Cox, 1988).

Duplicity and dishonesty in couple relationships

Although people may be aware of the deceptions and manipulations manifested by other couples, most are not aware of the extent to which they are dishonest or abusive in their own relationships. Duplicity in a relationship often exists in regard to sexuality, finances, preferences, opinions, and/or feelings.

People are reluctant to reveal their lies and manipulations to their mates for fear of losing the relationship. In addition, a good deal of self-deception is necessary to alleviate feelings of guilt about being dishonest. Self-deception facilitates deception of the other.[12] The probability of successfully deceiving one's partner is dependent on the extent to which one truly believes one's own lies.

As an example, the authors remember seeing an afternoon talk show about deception in marriage where several participants revealed how they lied to each other (faking orgasms, hiding sexual affairs, getting pregnant surreptitiously, sneaking money from a mate's wallet, and other secrets and hidden agendas). The level of dishonesty was shocking yet those revealing the secrets claimed to be loving. Worse yet, the talk show host and audience were amused, while the guest psychologists (a husband and wife team) actually implied that deception was necessary for maintaining marital harmony. One man in the audience protested, saying that he thought that lies and deceit invalidated any sense of meaning in a relationship. He was booed by the audience and his opinion was summarily dismissed by the psychologists. The authors were surprised and pained that the dishonesty in couple interactions manifested on the TV show was dealt with as commonplace and there was little or no concern for integrity.

The destructive effect of society's expectations regarding marriage

Societal institutions and social mores reinforce the formation of the fantasy bond in couples and families. For example, the state of being married is not simply perceived as a tradition, but as an indication of normalcy in our culture. If one is not married or living with someone by a certain age, one runs the risk of being categorized as eccentric, peculiar or deviant (Betchen, 2005).[13] Society's expectations about what men and women are "supposed to do" support people's self-attacks that they are deficient, worthless, and unlovable if they choose to live differently.

The ability to find and keep a partner offers people a sense of security, status, and a feeling of belonging. On the other hand, the state of being single, separated, or divorced is a conventional indication of failure. Feelings of failure are validated when people experience difficulties in finding a partner, when a mate has an affair, or when a relationship is dissolved through separation or divorce.

Longevity in a relationship does not necessarily imply that it is a fulfilling or satisfying relationship. Unions based on a fantasy bond may endure for years but usually manifest a gradual depletion in the spirit, individuality, and emotional health of the partners. In relationships, it is the individuals who should matter, not the couple or family unit. "Couples" and "families" are merely abstract concepts, not real entities; however, each individual is real and matters a great deal.

To summarize, each of us is essentially alone and there is no way to effectively become one-half of a couple by merging with another person. When we attempt to connect to another and give up our individuality, we are of little or no value to ourselves or our partners. In becoming selfless, immersing or losing ourselves in relating to the other, we gradually disappear and have little to offer in the way of emotional sustenance.

Ethical implications: The destructive effects of the fantasy bond on the family

The emotional climate into which a child is born is largely determined by the nature of the parents' relationship (Cowan & Cowan,

2000; J. Lewis, et al, 1988; Mikulincer & Shaver, 2007; Simpson, Rholes, Campbell, Wilson, & Tran, 2002). By the time a child is born, the couple's fantasy bond is generally well-established. The partners have allowed their love to erode and each has been diminished in his or her sense of self. In this state, parents have little energy to offer love or to care for others, especially for their children.

Although close family interactions encourage family members to grow psychologically and develop their individuality and independence, this pattern is the exception rather than the rule. To the degree that parents have formed a destructive fantasy bond in their coupling, they pass on to their children their illusions and inward behavior patterns. Through the process of imitation, children adopt the parents' defenses, while attempting to cover up any indication that family members are not close. Children learn to distort their real perceptions and deny the destructive reality of their circumstances.

Murray Bowen (Bowen, 1978; Kerr & Bowen, 1988) has written extensively about parents with low levels of self-differentiation, i.e. parents with little or no sense of personal identity who grew up "as dependent appendages of their parents, following which they seek other equally dependent relationships" (Bowen, 1978, p. 367). He contended that children of "undifferentiated" parents are expected to meet their parents' emotional needs. In the resulting dysfunctional family, the child is either excluded from the parents' bond with each other or, at other times, is merged with one or the other parent.

In addition, children must unquestioningly accept the identity handed to them in the family system: for example, the smart one, the bad one, the pretty one, the hard worker, the slacker, or the troublemaker. To maintain the imagined connection with the family, many people stubbornly hold on to this assigned identity throughout their lives. They distrust people who see them differently than they were seen in their families. A more positive relationship would disrupt the fantasy bond with one's family of origin, fostering an anxious state of disequilibrium.

Restrictions on communication

Because of the dishonesty and pretense involved in maintaining the fantasy bond, communication within most families is customarily duplicitous and manipulative. Freedom of speech is curtailed because certain topics are forbidden. In general, any communication that threatens to disturb the fantasy bond or interrupt the illusion of enduring love between family members is not permitted. Any hint that a parent might be inadequate or weak, or that maternal love is not an inherent feminine quality, any indication that a husband is not preferred at all times by his wife, any sign of sexual infidelity in either partner threatens the illusion being protected in the family.

Realistic perceptions of children or parents are not discussed. Parents often maintain an idealistic view of their children as good and innocent long after they have developed undesirable and toxic personality traits. Having a more accurate view of children, that is, seeing their positive and negative qualities rather than a fantasized family image of them, would tend to disrupt the fantasy bond within the family. Similarly, any indication or statement that one's family is not superior to those of one's friends and neighbors is censored because it would jeopardize the image of the family as special. Family members are encouraged to maintain superior attitudes about their family: "We eat the right food, wear the right clothes, drive the right car, practice the right religion, and raise our children the right way."

Within many families, children are afraid to speak honestly for fear of upsetting their parents, causing them pain, arousing their anger, or eliciting a punishing response. Children also fear the loss of the parents' love. When communication is limited or restricted, the resulting hostility and resentment create a toxic environment for the developing child.[14] However, the child must not show his or her pain or unhappiness, because this would betray the destructiveness of the family and break the fantasy bond. Perceptions and feeling responses that would disrupt the illusion of closeness are suppressed, which increases the child's tendency toward inwardness and cynicism.

Intergenerational transmission of childhood abuses

The paradox of the family in conventional society is that it serves the function of nurturing and protecting the physical lives of its members, while at the same time distorting their sense of reality and stifling all but socially role-determined feelings. As noted, a discouraging fact about family life is that parents who have suffered abuse and deprivation in their own childhoods more often than not pass on this damage to their offspring despite their best intentions. It is common knowledge that many of the children who were beaten tend to physically abuse their children when they become parents. It is less obvious but equally true that other emotional abuses are passed on, such as rejection, lack of affection, irritability, criticality, and overly severe disciplinary action (Rohner, 2004).

When parents are defended, they necessarily, albeit unconsciously, suppress the aliveness and spontaneity of their offspring. Accepting the genuine love that their children feel for them will often revive sad feelings from their own childhoods. To avoid these painful primal feelings, they often fail to respond appropriately, inadvertently hurting their children and damaging them in their capacity to love. In addition, primal pain is triggered in parents when their children reach ages or developmental stages that correspond to those in the parent's developmental history that were traumatic (Gerson, 1995). In failing to resolve their own early trauma and then recreating similar circumstances for their offspring, parents precipitate the intergenerational transmission of abusive child-rearing practices (Briere, 1992; Garbarino, Guttman, & Seeley, 1986; Kerr & Bowen, 1988; A. Miller, 1980/1984; Shengold, 1989, 1991; Straus, 2001).

> Tony's father was short and felt inferior to other men. He had been severely criticized and humiliated by his own father who compared him unfavorably with his peers. Tony's father went on to criticize Tony in a similar fashion. He criticized his performance in sports and school. When he came upon Tony joking around with his sisters and their girlfriends, he accused him of being like a girl. Tony began compensating by involving himself in various self-improvement projects. He took lessons in flying, tennis, boxing, horseback riding and he exercised aggressively.
>
> Even before the birth of his son, Steve, Tony anticipated that his son would be short and was determined to not make him self-conscious about his height. He did not want to pass on to his own son the insecurity that he identified as coming from his father.
>
> However, when Steve was born, instead of simply spending time with the boy and enjoying him, Tony constantly taught him. He extended his exaggerated self-improvement approach to Steve. During the times that Steve was being "instructed" by

his father, he was able to sense his father's underlying insecurity about him and felt inadequate. He began to feel that he really did need to be improved. Steve became an angry child, was defensive about his size, and mean toward other children.

The truth is that rather than compensate for perceived inadequacies, people can face the reality of their childhood, understand and work through their emotional pain, and move on to more constructive and healthy forms of interaction in their intimate associations. By understanding the dynamics of the fantasy bond and relinquishing the behavioral manifestations that interfere with intimacy, they can achieve a better life with mates and family members.

Ethical implications: Destructive effects of the fantasy bond on careers

People who have been damaged in their earliest relationships tend to spend a large part of their waking lives in a fantasy state. This state is far more extensive and inclusive than simple daydreams. Shyness, unsociability, and introspective qualities are customarily associated with symptoms of a preoccupation with fantasy (Person, 1995). However, these qualities are not the only signs that a person is focused on fantasy to the detriment of real concerns. People who appear extroverted or outgoing on the surface can in fact be acting out roles while investing little real feeling in their personal relationships or in their careers. Both introverted and extroverted individuals often utilize fantasy as part of a self-parenting process, as a means of gratifying themselves internally, while rejecting real relationships and avoiding actions that would help them fulfill their goals in reality.

When a prized fantasy or lifelong dream becomes a reality, the real situation is no longer under the person's total control. Rather than satisfying one's wants in fantasy, one is then forced to depend on outside gratification. Real accomplishments disrupt fantasies that people may have used since early childhood as a means of psychological survival. As a result, people often avoid or sabotage real successes and cling to fantasy solutions.

Melissa had always dreamed of being a fashion designer. The youngest child in an abusive family, she sustained herself by retreating into an elaborate fantasy world in which she was a famous New York designer. After working for years in the design business, Melissa was offered her dream job. She was hired as the lead designer for a growing luxury fashion design company. Six months later, Melissa and her two business partners headed for New York City to prepare their line for the fall runway shows.

Initially, Melissa felt challenged and excited; she thoroughly enjoyed the rapid pace required to complete the line. However, when the showroom carrying the line offered some minor criticism, Melissa fell apart, leaving the studio in tears. From that point on, she became increasingly incompetent. She began to defer to her business partners, inappropriately asking for feedback on her sketches and guidance in choosing fabrics. This seemed strange to them since they had no expertise in this area. The partners offered Melissa encouragement and support, but her childish behavior persisted. They were reluctantly forced to replace Melissa.

Melissa's regression after her fantasy became reality is not unusual in the business world. Serious, long-term regressions often occur in individuals when they are promoted to a coveted position or achieve in reality a cherished fantasy that they had been utilizing as an internal source of self-gratification. In these situations, people tend to withhold the skills that led to the achievement.

Furthermore, increased reliance on fantasy processes tends to be progressively incapacitating because it interferes with real planning, creativity, and tangible actions directed toward the actual accomplishment of one's goals. When faced with failure, a negative spiral is set into motion, leading to more frustration, increased dependence on fantasy, and often other addictive behaviors. People usually mistakenly believe that their regressions date from these failures rather than from the fact that real success threatened the fantasy process.

Friendship and love relationships

We all live on the hope that authentic meeting between human beings can still occur (Laing, 1967, p. 46).

In contrast to the fantasy bond, real friendship and loving relationships are characterized by freedom and genuine relating. In a friendship, a person acts out of choice, whereas in a fantasy bond he or she acts out of obligation or attempts to manipulate the other. People cannot be coerced into feeling the right or correct emotion; when they attempt to make their emotions conform to an image or a certain standard, their affect becomes shallow and inappropriate and they lose energy. Therefore, friendship can be considered to have therapeutic value whereas, by definition, a fantasy bond is anti-therapeutic in nature.

Men and women can remain close friends if manifestations of the fantasy bond are understood and relinquished. Healthy relationships are characterized by each partner's independent striving for personal development and self-realization. In a loving relationship, open expressions of physical and verbal affection are evident. Acting out of choice leads to feelings of joy and happiness while, at the same time, diminishing one's self-hatred. In good relationships, hostility and anger are not acted out but disclosed in the couple's ongoing dialogue. Negative perceptions, disappointments, and hurt feelings can be dealt with, without holding grudges (Tavris & Aronson, 2007).[15] In the type of relationship that is growth-enhancing, partners refrain from exerting proprietary rights over one another. Each is respectful of the other's boundaries, separate points of view, goals, and aspirations.

In an updated Preface to his book, *Love in the Western World*, Denis De Rougemont (1983) observed a style of relating among many young people that seemed to reflect a lack of possessiveness, proprietary rights, and control:

> A new idea of marriage, of fidelity, conceived as a free creation between *equals*, rather than constraint, seems to be quietly emerging in replies of young people to polls and surveys and in their social behaviour. A more convivial vision of community may be emerging, one with a new ethic of love, having as a goal the full authentic freedom of a real person: *The control, not of others, but of oneself* (p. 7).

In the "ideal" couple relationship, each person would feel congenial toward the other's aspirations and would try not to interfere, intrude, or manipulate to control the relationship. Both partners would recognize that the motives, desires, and goals of the other were as important as their own and would conceptualize their own personal freedom and the freedom of the other as a congruent, not contradictory, value (R. Firestone & Catlett, 1999).

In a personal story recounted in a previous work (R. Firestone, et al, 2006), a man described how he felt, after 25 years of marriage, about the importance of respect, equality, and personal freedom in his relationship with his wife:

> In our relationship there has always been a sense of equality and mutual respect. We fully believe in the personal freedom of each other and pose no limits on each other's development. This has been a guiding principle for us even when it caused us inconvenience or pain. I think that's why our relationship is still fresh and exciting. In that respect, we feel different from what we see in so many other couples. They appear to be so much more possessive and intrusive on each other and act different in each other's company than otherwise. I find the company of most couples to be boring. They seem to cancel out each other's sexuality and appear deadened in each other's presence … .
>
> To this day, we are lovers and the best of friends, rely on each other for support and companionship, and are a vital part of each other's lives. I know that she knows me and loves me and that I make her happy. She says that her life would be impossibly dull without me. I can barely imagine the horror of living life without her (p. 33).

The fact that many people prefer to pursue relationships in fantasy and reject genuine friendship and love accounts for a great deal of their seemingly perverse or irrational behavior. An individual's fantasy source of gratification is threatened by genuinely satisfying experiences. For this reason, people's actions are often directly contrary to their own best interests. Understanding the dynamics of the fantasy bond helps explain self-limiting and self-destructive behaviors that interrupt the flow of goal-directed activity and that incidentally hurt other people.

Conclusion

The fantasy bond represents a maladaptive solution because individuals come to depend on inner fantasy for gratification and progressively give up actual gratification from interactions with others. In their style of coupling, many people surrender their individuality and unique points of view for the sense of safety and eternal love they experience in merging with another person in their imagination. The illusion of being connected to another person imbues individuals with a sense of immortality, a feeling of living forever, but robs them of their everyday life experience. In contrast, living in a less defended, nonfused state brings people face to face with their existential aloneness and separateness. The addictive and compelling nature of the fantasy bond lies in the fact that it helps to deny death and relieves people's anxiety about an uncertain future (R. Firestone, 1997a). The disadvantage is that it generates a powerful resistance to living a free, independent existence, and acts to limit genuine closeness and harmony with our loved ones.

From an ethical standpoint, the fantasy bond and the resulting inward lifestyle predispose critical and harmful behaviors, potential failure in couple relationships, and conflict in family life. Furthermore, the illusion of fusion or merged identity plays an active role in the transmission of abusive parenting practices from one generation to the next. In order to hold on to and connect to their families-of-origin, many individuals maintain a negative image of themselves and cynical, hostile attitudes toward others throughout their lives. Distorting a loved one and misunderstanding his or her motives not only hurts the other's feelings, but also precipitates self-attacks and self-destructive thinking in the person being distorted.

To break a fantasy bond and sustain genuine intimacy in one's relationships, one must go through the anxiety of giving up core defenses and remaining close to another, despite the increased sense of vulnerability. In working with couples, the authors encourage people to tolerate the anxiety of more positive treatment in their lives instead of acting out aversive behaviors that alter the positive situation. As they overcome their resistance to change and avoid destructive patterns, individuals become aware of the specific thoughts and internalized voices that have functioned to protect their imagined connection with their families and mates. They can expand their lives by challenging old attitudes and feelings that interfere with giving and receiving love. Intimacy and mutual regard can only be achieved when individuals struggle through the anxiety aroused in moving toward real closeness and individuation. Indeed, the hope for the couple, as well as the future of the family, is for people to break out of the imprisonment of their defensive self-parenting posture. By freeing themselves from destructive, imaginary connections, facing and working through childhood trauma, and moving toward independence and autonomy, individuals can restore genuine love and closeness to their relationships.

Notes

1. McCarthy and McCarthy (2003) defined "no-sex" marriages or relationships as those in which partners are sexual less than ten times a year: "Approximately 20% (one in five) of married couples have a no-sex relationship ... One in three nonmarried couples who have been together more than 2 years have a no-sex relationship" (pp. 5–6).

2. The Pew Internet and American Life Project reported that "87% of U.S. teens aged 12–17 use the internet" (Pew Internet & American Life Project, 2004, para. 2). Pierce (2006) concluded that "The computer is a sex offender's closest companion because it allows a level of anonymity that is not available in the real world" (Conclusion section, para. 2). Also see an extensive report on this topic by Clemmitt (2006).

3. See David Elkind's (2001) classic work *The Hurried Child*. Regarding some of the dangers of children's involvement in computers, see Jane Healy's (1998) *Failure to Connect*. For a critique of the thesis warning of the "dangers" of over-scheduling children and adolescents, see Mahoney, Harris, and Eccles (2006).

4. As noted in the previous chapter, other theorists have elaborated on the concept of the fantasy bond, including Hellmuth Kaiser (Fierman, 1965), Karpel (1976, 1994), Shapiro (2000), Wexler and Steidl (1978), and Willi (1975/1982). Also see "Oneness Experience: Looking through Multiple Lenses," by Chirban (2000), who made a distinction between "oneness experiences," which are progressive and transformative, and "oneness fantasies" which are based on longings for merger with figures from the past and thus are generally regressive.

5. For example, Pyszczynski, et al (2003) found that "increased worldview defense [elevating one's own worldview or cultural standards while denigrating other people with different views] is a result of heightened accessibility of death-related thoughts *outside of conscious awareness*" (italics added) (p. 64). In another experiment, judges were found to be much more severe in their penalties after death salience (Rosenblatt, et al, 1989). In the neuroscience literature, LeDoux (1996, 2002), Schore (1994, 2001a), and Siegel (1999) have shown that people often react automatically to fear stimuli. This is because impulses rapidly travel from the limbic system and amygdala via the autonomic nervous system to the motor centers of the brain, resulting in a behavioral response, without involving the centers of consciousness in the cerebral cortex.

6. In *Intrusive Partners, Elusive Mates: The Pursuer-Distancer Dynamic in Couples*, Betchen (2005) focused on the expectations that many people bring to marriage that fuel desperate feelings which in turn can lead to the formation of a fantasy bond. Betchen cited the work of Fogarty (1976, 1979) who originally called attention to this dynamic.

7. Dicks (1967), in *Marital Tensions*, introduced his theoretical model of couple interactions by stressing the ethics involved in marriage and by warning of the harm inflicted on individuals, children, and society by disturbed marital relations.

8. See Scharff & Scharff (1991) who described defensive projective identification within couples. They noted that the partner who has disowned or expelled a part of him- or herself and perceives it in the love object "so convincingly identifies the part of the self in the external object that the feeling state corresponding to that part of the self is evoked in the … spouse" (p. 58). Ogden (1982) made the point that in projective identification "the projector subjectively experiences a feeling of oneness with the recipient with regard to the expelled feeling, idea, or self-representation" (p. 34). Thus, projective identification may be conceptualized as a primitive defense that functions to reinforce the fantasy bond or illusion of connection to one's mate.

Schore (2003), in describing the etiology of projective identification, proposed that this process is correlated with right hemisphere attachment trauma and the primitive defense of dissociation: "I suggest that an infant with an early history of 'ambient' … or 'cumulative trauma' … must excessively utilize defensive projective identification in order to cope with all-too-frequent episodes of interactive stress that disorganize the developing self" (p. 68).

Schore also noted that in the therapist-patient relationship, "The patient does not project an internal critic [critical inner voice] into the therapist, but rather the therapist's internal critic, stimulated by the patient's negative affective communications, resonates with the patient's and is thereby amplified" (pp. 90–91).

In *A Beam of Intense Darkness: Wilfred Bion's Legacy to Psychoanalysis*, Grotstein (2007) quoted Freud's (1915/1957a) statement "It is a very remarkable thing that the *Ucs.* [the Unconscious mind] of one human being can react upon that of another, without passing through the *Cs.*" [the Conscious mind] (Grotstein, p. 168).

9. Re: the cycle of distortion, provocation and attribution of blame to the other person within warring couples, Tavris and Aronson (2007) observed that: "negative ways of thinking and blaming usually come first and are unrelated to the couples' frequency of anger, either party's feelings of depression, or other negative emotional states" (p. 172).

10. In *Falling in Love: Why We Choose the Lovers We Choose*, Ayala Pines (2005) commented: "It seems that we are attracted to partners to whom we are similar in general—in background, values, interests, and intelligence—but who complement us in a particular significant personality dimension" (p 59). She noted that in the selection process, these complementary traits or behavioral tendencies often serve a defensive function, particularly in individuals who have low self-esteem or low differentiation of self (Bowen, 1978). Pines cited research conducted by Z. Solomon (1986) showing that people with low self-acceptance chose partners they viewed as different from them. Re: Attachment theory and the selection process: Mikulincer and Shaver (2007) reported studies showing that "insecure people were more attracted than secure ones to insecure potential partners" (p. 289). There was also some evidence that "avoidant individuals preferred anxiously attached partners" (p. 289).

11. Another important aspect of the new baby's impact on parents' defenses is a heightened awareness of death, particularly in first-time parents. In some sense, childbirth symbolizes a turning of the wheel in the life process, so to speak, i.e. child, parent, grandparent, death. Thus, parents tend to become more aware of these existential realities as they move toward assuming the responsibilities for the care and survival of the newborn. Their increased death anxiety often leads to progressive denial and a strong need for a fantasy connection. Also see Mikulincer and Shaver's (2007) research demonstrating that "less secure spouses scored lower on two dimensions of family dynamics: *family cohesion* (the extent of emotional bonding between family

members) and *family adaptability* (the extent to which a family is able to adjust its rules in response to changes)" (p. 307).

12. See David Shapiro's (2000) elaborations on Kaiser's concept of the illusion of fusion and how it is manifested through duplicitous communication. According to Fierman (1965), Kaiser contended that duplicity or indirect communication is a symptom of the universal psychopathology, the effort to form an illusion of fusion with the therapist. In a chapter, "Search for the Locus of the Universal Symptom: Re-examination of Hellmuth Kaiser's *Duplicity*," Krakowski (2004) explored treatment of patients based on an understanding of duplicity in therapist-patient interactions: "It was his [Kaiser's] claim that therapeutic changes can take place by means of a technique of bringing patients' *duplicitous* behaviors to their attention" (p. 31).

13. Betchen (2005) pointed out that "We live in a couples-oriented society.... While couplehood is an admirable objective, the pressure to find a permanent partner can be emotionally overwhelming" (p. 167).

14. Studies have shown that being forced to suppress one's perceptions or having one's perceptions continuously invalidated in a defended family structure is a primary causative factor in psychological disturbances, both psychotic and borderline disorders (Bateson, 1972; Gibney, 2006; Sluzki & Veron, 1977; Weakland, 1977). Also see "Prometheus Double-Bound," in which Megan Mustain (2002) applies Bateson's "double-bind" theory to communication and behavioral disturbances in general. As Gibney (2006) summed it up: "the contradiction is not able to be communicated on and the unwell person is not able to leave the field of interaction" (p. 49).In other research, psychologists found that many families invade and attempt to distort each individual's sense of reality (Beavers, 1977; Tedeschi & Felson, 1994).

15. Tavris and Aronson (2007) have articulated a similar optimistic prognosis for couples who learn to drop grudges, to give up their need to be "right," and who have come to respect the other's point of view: "The couples who grow together over the years have figured out a way to live with a minimum of self-justification, which is another way of saying that they are able to put empathy for the partner ahead of defending their own territory" (p. 180).

PART IV

DESTRUCTIVE LIFESTYLES

CHAPTER EIGHT

Addiction

> Most addicts appear reluctant or unable to seek satisfaction in normal interpersonal relationships and instead remain aloof and independent and use the drug to induce a blissful, symbiotic, narcissistic state. The drug replaces interpersonal relationships as a primary source of achieving satisfaction and pleasure.
>
> Blatt, McDonald, Sugarman, and Wilber (1984, p. 168)

From an ethical perspective, addictions are perhaps more damaging to individuals and interpersonal relationships than any other aversive behavior. People who are involved in an addictive lifestyle are focused primarily on the gratification of their addiction at the expense of their personal relationships. When confronted by a friend, lover, or family member about their destructive habit patterns, they respond with anger and are punitive toward those offering help.

Alcoholism and drug abuse are widespread in our society and have profound negative consequences for millions of people. For example, a recent survey (Department of Health and Human Services, 2006) found that 23 percent of persons age 12 or older (or about 57 million people) participated in binge drinking at least once in the

30 days prior to the survey. Heavy drinking, defined as five or more drinks on the same occasion on each of 5 or more days in the past 30 days was reported by 6.9 percent of the population, or 17 million people.

The destructive impact of addictions can be measured in terms of the cost to the mental and physical health of substance abusers, their families, and others who are often innocent bystanders. As an example, in 2005 approximately 40 percent of traffic fatalities in the United States were alcohol related (National Highway Traffic Safety Administration, 2006). Undoubtedly many of the fatalities included people who were strangers to the driver who killed them. Studies also show that alcohol is a primary factor in the three leading causes of death for 15- to- 24-year-olds: automobile crashes, homicides, and suicides. Alcohol is known to have a disinhibiting effect on impulsive behavior and facilitates the acting out of suicidal and homicidal impulses in individuals of all ages. Maltsberger (1986) has reported that "about a fourth of the patients who commit suicide are in fact alcoholics" (p. 74).[1] According to a report from the National Institute on Alcohol Abuse and Alcoholism (2007), alcohol and tobacco are among the top causes of preventable deaths in the United States.

Furthermore, many drug users and dealers commit criminal acts such as petty theft, armed robbery, prostitution, and even violent crimes to support their habit. Erickson (2001) called attention to this fact in a paper titled "Drugs, Violence and Public Health:" "Not surprisingly, drug offenders (those in jail for crimes of illicit possession or sale) have the highest rates of self-reported drug use, followed by robbers and property offenders" (p. 4). "Two-thirds of youthful crack sellers admitted hurting or killing someone due to their involvement in the drug trade" (p. 10).

The psychodynamics of addiction

Internal fantasy processes are inextricably involved in the etiology of addictive behaviors and lifestyles (R. Firestone, 1993). As described in the previous chapter, when children are deprived of emotional sustenance, they gradually compensate with fantasy gratification. The fantasy bond, in conjunction with primitive self-nurturing patterns, can become a survival mechanism for those who suffer excessive deprivation in childhood. Unfortunately, the methods that people adopt to numb their pain or reduce their emotional distress become habit-forming and, to varying degrees, generalize to an addictive lifestyle. Therefore, one of the most important challenges facing individuals who are motivated to live a more ethical life is learning to give up the addictive habit patterns and fantasies that they use to avoid or relieve psychological pain.

Fantasies and addictive habit patterns act to deprive a person of the ingredients necessary for a happy life. It becomes an ethical issue when people prefer fantasy and self-gratifying behaviors to genuine relating because they necessarily hurt others close to them. Individuals who are excessively dependent on food, drugs, alcohol, or other substances have a destructive effect in that these addictions leave a person defensive and closed to feelings. When addictive patterns are acted on, they jeopardize couple and family relationships. For example, the husband who watches TV all night rather than making love to his wife, the mother who drinks in secret while neglecting her young children, the workaholic who ignores his or her family, the teenager who refuses to give up his or her drug habit—all evoke feelings of resentment, guilt, fear, and a sense of demoralization in their loved ones.

The addictive properties of fantasy

The capacity of human beings to imagine and symbolize is both a strength and a weakness. The ability to create a fantasy image of one-self and the fulfillment of one's goals in place of real goal-directed behavior can set the stage for psychological disturbances, especially those of an addictive nature. For example, research has shown that fantasy can act as a reward or substitute gratification to compensate for conditions of deprivation. In one experiment (Keys, et al, 1950), volunteers were deprived of food and kept on a minimum suste-nance diet. The subjects reported that they spent hours fantasizing about food, which partly alleviated their tension and hunger drive. Similarly, under conditions of emotional deprivation, fantasy func-tions to fill the void and "nourish" the self by partially gratifying primitive needs and emotional hunger.

The fantasy process eventually becomes addictive in its own right. It persists for long periods even after the depriva-tion has ceased and predisposes negative behavioral responses.

Individuals who primarily exist in an inward state of fantasy drastically reduce their emotional transactions with others and manifest a withholding style of relating in which both giving and taking are restricted. As Eric Hoffer (1955/2006) observed: "We do not really feel grateful to those who make our dreams come true, they ruin our dreams" (p. 97).

Healthy functioning versus addictive lifestyles

> Addiction is an emotional relationship with an object or event, through which addicts try to meet their needs for intimacy (Nakken, 1996, p. 8).

Addictive tendencies can be represented along a continuum, ranging from an outward lifestyle of pursuing goals in the real world to an inward lifestyle characterized by fantasy, passivity, and isolation.[2] A healthy, outward lifestyle is characterized by one's involvement in goal-directed behaviors that lead to self-affirmation and self-fulfillment. In contrast, an inward, addicted lifestyle is characterized by self-denial, the seeking of gratification in fantasy, and involvement in self-destructive behaviors. An increased involvement with addictive substances, habitual responses, and rituals interferes with the achievement of one's career goals and limits gratification in one's personal relationships.

Self-nourishing habits and addictive painkillers

> The culture of drink endures because it offers so many rewards: confidence for the shy, clarity for the uncertain, solace to the wounded and lonely, and above all, the elusive promise of friendship and love (Hamill, 1994, p.1).

Self-nourishing habit patterns can be categorized as "ego-syntonic" in that they are pleasurable, and originally perceived as positive. Until their use becomes obviously self-destructive or potentially dangerous, they are in consonance with the person's ego. However, well-established, self-nurturing habits become progressively self-limiting and self-destructive because they eventually interfere with a person's capacity to cope with everyday experiences. When these behaviors are associated with a more generalized retreat from the world, they no longer feel acceptable to the self and arouse considerable guilt (R. Firestone, 1985). People are highly defensive about their addictive patterns, fantasy involvement, and inwardness and react angrily when they are confronted about engaging in these behaviors.

Addictive reactions associated with a self-nourishing lifestyle can be divided into three groups: (1) addiction to physical substances; (2) addiction to ritualistic behavior and routines; and (3) addictive attachments.

Addiction to physical substances

Food often becomes a primary focus for children who are starved for emotional sustenance in the family situation. In these cases, food takes on a special meaning other than simple enjoyment and gratification of a physical need. When food is consistently used as a drug or painkiller to minimize or defend against painful emotions and experiences, it becomes part of an addictive pattern. This pattern is apparent in the repetitive cycles of overeating and dieting, as well as in binges and subsequent purges. These self-feeding patterns are inward, self-centered, and functionally maladaptive.

The health risks associated with obesity and eating disorders cause significant concern to mates and family members of the addicted individual. The steady rise of obesity over the past decades is an indication of people's tendencies to turn to food as a method of avoiding anxiety and pain. Anorexia nervosa and bulimia nervosa, conditions that affect more than 8 million individuals, can reach life-threatening proportions. These disorders represent self-feeding patterns in that the individual is exercising total control over food intake as a substitute for other outside gratifications.[3]

The same issues are central in alcoholism and drug abuse. A compulsive need for self-nourishment and control is characteristic of an individual's addiction to alcohol, cigarettes, and drugs, whether illicit or prescription. Anxiety that is allayed by these substances comes to the foreground when the addicted person stops using the drug of choice. The perceived loss of control that accompanies withdrawal leaves the individual in a disoriented state, feeling helpless and at the mercy of outside forces. Regression to childish behaviors and angry outbursts of temper are common. The compulsive overeater, the anorectic, the alcoholic, the drug-user, all attempt to deny their dependency on other persons and have pseudoindependent attitudes—"I can feed myself, I don't need anything from anyone else."

The determinants of substance addiction are varied, yet all addictions are attempts to numb both pain from the past as well as suffering due to present-day frustration and stress. However, in repeatedly turning to these habit patterns for relief and for a sense of control over their pain, individuals progressively block out important emotional reactions. For this reason, they become more incapacitated in their ability to work productively or to function adequately in social situations. Family members and friends experience considerable suffering and become increasingly alienated as this process spirals downward.

One of the most destructive processes observed in couple and family relationships is the acting out of subtle microsuicidal impulses by indulging in addictive activities and behaviors. People who urge their loved ones to stop overeating, cut down on their drinking, or abstain from drug use are essentially pleading with them to not commit a form of suicide. Interventions set up by psychotherapists or addiction counselors generally bring friends and family members' pain and anger to the surface and their efforts are met with resistances of all sorts. Nevertheless, the confrontation with the addicted person can be an important first step toward treatment and rehabilitation.

Addiction to routines and habitual responses

> Wise living consists perhaps less in acquiring good habits than in acquiring as few habits as possible (Hoffer, 1955/2006, p. 107).

Almost any repetitive behavior, routine, or ritual may be used to dull one's sensitivity to painful feelings and can be said to have addictive qualities. An individual who suffers from emotional stress in life may easily fall prey to habits that are tension-reducing. Once these patterns are established, any behavior seems preferable to the anxiety that the person would experience if these routines were to be interrupted (R. Firestone, 1985). Routines and rituals also lend an air of certainty or seeming permanence to a life of uncertainty and impermanence.

Obsessive or compulsive patterns that temporarily reduce anxiety become habitual and later foster anxiety. When these habits intensify, they can become seriously maladaptive. Even within the "normal" range of functioning, many people become addicted to routines and personal habits such as TV watching, the morning cup of coffee, video games and computer games, browsing the Internet, compulsive reading, compulsive work, compulsive shopping, among others. Family observations of holidays, birthdays, and reunions are often ritualistic in nature and are characterized by a good deal of role-playing. Religious rituals are observed to ease pain and grief. They offer structure to relieve the anxiety inherent in existential issues of aloneness and death.

Very often, routines and habitual behaviors are perceived as acceptable, or even desirable. Despite the fact that physical-fitness programs are beneficial to one's health, jogging, running, and exercising are potentially addictive because they are primarily inward, narcissistic activities. These activities are worthwhile, yet when carried to excess they can interfere with important aspects of life. In general, repetitive behaviors and lifestyles function to cut off feelings and deaden people emotionally, contributing to dissatisfaction in personal relationships.

Similarly, "workaholics" use what might otherwise be considered constructive work activities to isolate themselves, dull their feelings, and soothe their pain. They effectively retreat from relationships and significantly impair the quality of their lives while utilizing defensive rationalizations that justify hard work. Individuals working at repetitive, mechanical jobs (bookkeepers, accountants, computer programmers) are in an environment that tends to cut off feelings, causing people to become inward and impersonal, whether they intend to or not. When one's work, avocation, or hobby takes on an addictive element characterized by long hours and great difficulty pulling oneself away from the task, it has a destructive effect on the individual and his or her loved ones. Robert, a writer, recalls his father's compulsion to work:

> When we moved into the San Fernando Valley, my father set to work remodeling the house and landscaping the yard. Our house resembled every other house in the small subdivision—so new that there were no lawns, but it became an empty canvas to

my father and he set to work on elaborate patios, small gardens, attractive fences, and fine paths over well-manicured grass. He found himself obsessed with details. He pictured a family living there in harmony and that dream fueled his enthusiasm.

But in his youth my father had been robbed of the ability to feel the satisfaction of accomplishment and he worked as if his father (my grandfather) were still critically supervising his labor, moving him through the fields from one row of tobacco to the next. As each household project was completed to perfection, he would move on to the next without looking at the final product. He'd come home from his 10-hour work day and march into the backyard without changing his clothes, so that soon all of his fine suits had tattered knees and splashes of paint. He'd work endlessly into the night until a neighbor would call and ask him to please quit sawing or hammering or to turn off his work lights so their children could sleep. He'd work in downpours and the blazing sun for hours as if he were immune to the elements and his own fatigue.

The sad part was he never developed the family life he dreamed of. We were all isolated and distant from one another. He was always involved in his projects, my mother was in her own world, and the children all went their separate ways.

Behaviors or rituals that temporarily reduce anxiety can develop into an obsessive-compulsive disorder (OCD). Obsessive-compulsive patients often experience panic attacks when unable to perform their rituals (Kozak & Foa, 1997; Levenkron, 1991). The anticipatory anxiety related to the threat of a panic attack reinforces the need to engage in the ritualistic, habitual behavior. When these habits intensify, they become seriously maladaptive, consuming increasing amounts of the person's time and energy.[4]

Habitual or excessive masturbation to reduce tension is generally a symptom of emotional deprivation. The child discovers that touching his or her genitals not only leads to pleasant sensations but tends to neutralize emotional distress. This activity can develop into a self-soothing, isolated method of taking care of oneself and, in the extreme, can become preferable to sexual activity with another person.

Sexual addiction, although not categorized by the DSM-IV as a psychiatric disorder, has an obsessive, unmanageable nature. Carnes

(1992) noted that the behavior of sex addicts generally conforms to "a four-step cycle which intensifies with each repetition:

> *Preoccupation*—the trance or mood wherein the addicts' minds are completely engrossed with thoughts of sex. This mental state creates an obsessive search for sexual stimulation.
> *Ritualization*—the addicts' own special routines which lead up to the sexual behavior. The ritual intensifies the preoccupation, adding arousal and excitement.
> *Compulsive sexual behavior*—the actual sex act, which is the end goal of the preoccupation and ritualization. Sexual addicts are unable to control or stop this behavior.
> *Despair*—the feeling of utter hopelessness addicts have about their behavior and their powerlessness.
> The pain the addicts feel at the end of the cycle can be numbed obscured by sexual preoccupation which re-engages the addiction cycle (p. 9).

A recovering sex addict described this cycle as follows:

> Sex to me was, and can still be, an opiate. Addictive sexual arousal produced chemicals inside my brain so strong that alcohol and drugs pale in comparison. What an amazing effect was the "rush" of a new sexual experience! For most of my life, I welcomed the excitement and morphine-like effect of these chemicals. Until, that is, a combination of alcohol, drugs and sexual addiction tore my life apart (International Service Organization of SAA, 2005, p. 238).[5]

For many people who are not "sexually addicted," sexual relationships can also function as painkillers when they are used as a means of partially gratifying primitive longings and deeply repressed oral needs (Carnes, 1991, 1992; Carnes, Delmonico & Griffin, 2001; Kasl, 1989). In these cases, there is often an emphasis on control and fantasy to increase excitement. Couples often develop a routinized, mechanical style of lovemaking, concomitantly holding back affection and a full sexual response. Whenever sex is being used primarily for control, power plays, manipulation, security, or self-soothing, that is, for purposes other than its natural functions of pleasure, procreation, and as an emotionally rewarding exchange between two people, there is generally deterioration in the sexual relationship (R. Firestone & Catlett, 1999).

Addictive attachments

The fantasy bond is an addictive attachment because, in its attempt to answer a very human need for safety and security, it fosters an illusion of connection and oneness that provides relief for the emotional pain associated with both interpersonal problems and existential issues. Becoming excessively dependent on another person out of a desire for security is one of the most prevalent forms of addiction and plays a prominent role in the deterioration of couple and family relationships.

The fantasy bond or addictive attachment is often operating even during the early stages of a relationship when individuals seek compensatory qualities in their partners. For example, an aggressive person will be attracted to a passive, submissive person. An individual who needs to take care of others will be drawn to a person who feels the need to be taken care of. These relationships are often characterized by an initial strong sexual attraction. There is a sense of attaining wholeness from this union when, in reality, it weakens both partners as they come to depend on each other for these complementary traits. As noted in the previous chapter (7), these couples eventually come to resent and even hate these qualities in the other, and there is often a serious decline in their sexual attraction (R. Firestone & Catlett, 1999; Halpern, 1982; Mellody, 1992; Peele, 1975; Willi, 1975/1982).

Later, when either partner moves away from this type of codependent relationship toward independence or autonomy, symptoms similar to those manifested in withdrawal from chemical dependency are aroused. These symptoms include feelings of desperation, emotional hunger, disorientation, and debilitating anxiety states. The intensity of these emotional reactions indicates the powerful nature of the fantasy bond existing between the partners (Battegay, 1991).[6]

One woman, in describing her reasons for marrying, inadvertently defined the essence of addictive attachment:

> I knew I was afraid of being in a real feeling relationship with any person, man or woman, and I knew, too, that I was terrified

of being alone. Forming a fantasy connection with my husband was a solution. I could feel physically close without really feeling very much for him emotionally. And I knew I would always have somebody there for me.

The role of the voice in supporting addictive habit patterns

People who engage in addictive behaviors are acting out self-destructive tendencies promoted by the voice process. As described earlier, the destructive thoughts that control these behaviors take two contradictory forms. First they encourage the individual to engage in the behavior: *"You've done great on your diet. What's the harm in having one small piece of cake?" "You've had a hard day. Take the edge off with a drink (hit, pill)."* Once the suggestions of the voice are acted on, the destructive thoughts switch in their tone and become extremely punishing. *"Now just look at yourself in the mirror. You're a fat pig!" "You drank, (used) again. You're hopeless!"* The voice ruthlessly criticizes the individual for having engaged in the very behavior it had originally encouraged.

In attempting to alleviate the pain of these self-recriminations, an individual invariably resorts to more painkillers and the cycle continues: *"You've gone off your diet already. What difference will it make if you eat the rest of the cake?" "Go on, have another drink (take another hit)."* Feelings of demoralization aroused by the voice increase the likelihood that the person will act out the destructive, addictive behavior. The indulgence of one's addiction, followed by punishing voice attacks, increases psychological pain, which, in turn, necessitates the use of more substances. This sets into motion an insidious cycle of guilt, acting out, more perturbation, and inescapable psychological pain which, in extreme cases, can lead to suicide (R. Firestone, 1997b).

The voice also encourages habitual routines that numb emotional pain and anxiety. In relation to compulsive work patterns, the voice advises: *"Of course, you'd like to go out tonight! But how do you expect to get ahead if you don't work hard? There's no way you can't work late tonight!"* In relation to excessive masturbation or addictive sexuality, the voice suggests: *"Go ahead and masturbate. It's so much easier than having sex tonight." "You could go on a porn website tonight, or hook up with someone in a chat room. It's much less hassle than trying to find a real date."* In relation to obsessive-compulsive behaviors, the voice warns: *"Watch out! Don't touch that door knob—it's probably covered with germs! Pull down your sleeve and cover your hand first."*

Voice attacks promote the insecurity and desperation that lead to addictive attachments: *"What does he see in you? You'd better hold on to him! You're lucky to have anyone interested in you!" "Where is she going? Why didn't she ask you to go along? She is probably losing interest in you!" "Did you see the way he looked at her? I bet he is way more attracted to her than to you!"*

Overall, voices act to promote addiction and resistance to positive change. Only by identifying this destructive thought process, releasing the accompanying affect, and taking appropriate action against the voice's inducements can the individual gain full control of addictive processes.

Ethical implications of addiction and addictive attachments

Children of alcoholics (COAs) received a great deal of research attention as an at-risk population … . Concern with this population stems from the belief that parental alcoholism leads to disrupted and dysfunctional family environments that have ill effects for those who grow up in them These ill effects are driven by parental modeling of dysfunctional and destructive behaviors, corruption and deterioration of parenting behaviors, or an amalgamation of both processes (Segrin, 1998, p. 345).

Destructive effects of addictions on the family and children

There are two essential conditions that work together influencing a propensity toward addictive behavior: (1) a significant degree of emotional deprivation, and (2) parents' reinforcement of pain-killing and self-nourishing habits. Well-intentioned parents who, because of their own discomfort with strong emotions are quick to try to eliminate their child's pain and sadness, can inadvertently foster an addictive process. This leads to a generalized pattern of overprotectiveness and overindulgence which fuels a sense of omnipotence and pseudoindependence that is a fundamental part of an addictive lifestyle.

Addicted parents transmit their addictive behaviors and lifestyles to their children by teaching them by example that these are the preferred methods for coping with pain. Despite their parents' attempts to influence them otherwise, children imitate parents' defenses and addictive habit patterns. If one's mother overate to relieve her anxiety, one is likely to automatically adopt this pattern. If one's father drank when he felt stressed, one is more likely to take on this behavior. Claudia Black (1981) reported that "fifty to sixty percent of all alcoholics (a low estimate) have, or had, at least one alcoholic parent. Alcoholism is a generational disease" (p. 4).

Addiction to food, drugs, or alcohol on the part of a parent is destructive to children in other ways. In repeatedly turning to addictive habit patterns for relief and for a sense of control over their pain, parents progressively block out important emotional responses to their children, which interferes with the child's developing a core sense of self, stability, and coherent identity (Schore, 2001a, 2001b; Stern, 1985).[7] Studies have revealed that parents' alcohol use also contributes to stress, ineffective parenting, and maladaptive forms of individuation, that is, emotional distancing and separation on the part of adolescents (Getz & Bray, 2005). Research conducted by Getz and Bray showed that the mother's use of alcohol and family conflict predicted heavy drinking in her adolescent offspring. "Collectively, these findings suggest that family processes or behaviors that are indicative of ineffective parenting encourage the initiation of alcohol use as well as acceleration to heavy use through involvement with alcohol-using peers" (p. 112).

The destructive effects of living with an alcoholic or substance-abusing parent tend to persist into adulthood, limiting one's ability to develop or sustain a loving, fulfilling relationship.

> When Barbara was 13, her mother died of complications from diabetes and obesity. During the years leading up to her death, Barbara was required to take care of her mother and played the role of housekeeper for her father.
>
> Barbara: "I stood helplessly by and kept quiet while I watched my father, time and time again, bring home 'treats' for my mother: lox, bagels, doughnuts, ice cream (her favorites) against doctor's orders. I wondered, did he wish her dead? Or was he only trying to make her feel better? Recently I read

about 'enabling' behaviors on the part of spouses of alcoholics and that gave me some answers. But I hated him for how he treated my mother.

"I resented having to take care of my mother when I could have been over at a friend's house. I was furious with her for not taking care of herself. Her habit of overeating clearly brought on her diabetes. I had no respect for what I saw her doing to herself. I saw her as deliberately trying to destroy herself and wondered why. I felt confused, tormented, and guilty for hating her. Yet the thought of her dying terrified me because even though I knew that she wasn't taking care of me, I felt I would be alone in some way that scared me.

"So I think that I grew up thinking that my only worth was in taking care of people. This affects my life today because my husband now is partially incapacitated and when I assume the 'caretaking' role, which I do so easily because it feels natural to me, our love and attraction for each other completely disappear."

Destructive effects of addictive attachments on the family and children

As noted, many people who experienced rejection and deprivation early in life develop an addictive attachment in their intimate relationships. Feelings of desperation, longing, and emptiness from childhood contribute to a basic insecurity and an inner dread of never being chosen or loved. This process has a negative impact on both partners and on the relationship.

Rick: From the time I was about five or six, I fantasized what it would be like when I grew up and finally had a girlfriend and got married and had a family. All the emptiness that I experienced in my family was lumped into that fantasy, and that's what I was looking to have fulfilled every time I entered into a relationship. I feel like I've turned every relationship I've ever had into something to satisfy that emptiness in me, so that the woman that I'm involved with is no longer even a person. She's simply someone else that I've been able to plug into that slot from relationship to relationship my entire life. And that's very distressing to me because it's a highly impersonal way of treating another person. Worse yet, I become completely obsessed with the woman. I lose my concentration at work and demand attention. Then when things eventually go wrong I suffer from a long depression.

Many parents have strong tendencies to develop addictive attachments to their offspring. In our observations of families, the authors have found that parents' illusory feelings of connection to their child are often based more on the unfulfilled needs of the parent for love than on a genuine concern and affection for the child. Many parents experience increased separation anxiety as their child progresses through the various stages of development and becomes more independent. They increase their attempts to preserve the imagined connection, an effort which leads to negative consequences for both parent and child.

Edward's friends recognize that he is a devoted father, yet they also sense an extreme overinvolvement on his part with his teenage daughter, Amelia. He brags about how beautiful, intelligent, and talented she is and bores everyone with the details of her monthly visits with him. This father's overbearing interest in his daughter is manifested in intrusive behaviors that completely disregard her wants and priorities. While Amelia was still in high school, Edward applied, without her knowledge, to various Ivy League colleges that he selected for her. He boasted to friends that he had cleverly posed as Amelia by filling in her information on the applications, even forging her signature.

Eventually Amelia discovered her father's "intervention," but only after she received an acceptance letter from one of the colleges her father had contacted. She was furious but her anger quickly changed to guilt when her father insisted that he was only looking out for her best interests. Amelia felt caught in a double-bind: attend the college of her choice which would threaten to hurt and anger her father and therefore cause her anxiety, or attend the college of her father's choice which would be going against her own desires.

Society's reinforcement of addictive lifestyles

Few of us recognize how much our everyday emotional responses owe to the submerged icebergs of our cultural models, how much a particular local setting shapes what it is to be a self relating to other selves effectively and well (Luhrmann, 2000, p. 282).

The destructive effects of addictions and addictive ways of living are not limited to the individual, couple relationships, and the family; they extend to the larger society. Conventional mores and institutions tend to reinforce each person's defense system through negative social pressure. Social pressure, which is a strong pull from significant people in one's family and from society in general to imitate the behavior of others, has a profound impact because there are strong tendencies in most people toward conformity.

Many advertisers take advantage of people's conforming nature by associating their products with positive symbols and famous individuals. They pay celebrities to use their products in public. Since direct cigarette ads have been heavily restricted, tobacco companies have expended considerable sums on financing movies with the condition that characters in the films smoke. This is especially true in movies that appeal to young audiences.

Social institutions and cultural attitudes, in collusion with the family, generally tend to support addictive behaviors that help numb painful feelings. The media strongly influence people's dependence on prescription drugs through advertising a myriad of painkillers that dull one's personal experience and hold out the promise of instant relief from mental disorders and addictions. Today, perhaps even more than in the past, human beings are losing contact with feeling, embracing self-deception, seeking outlets that mask or interfere with self-realization, and gravitating toward quick fixes that are guaranteed to make them feel better.

Sluzki (1998) called attention to the increasing and pervasive influence of the "medical-industrial complex" on the general public:

Psychotherapeutic approaches (family therapy included) ... [have] been replaced in the 90s by a "brain-without-a-mind" view of mental health, characterized by a medicalization of human pain and emotional suffering in which genes and neurotransmitters are the focus of interest while the context and talking therapies have been relegated to a marginal place … . these policies have been strongly endorsed by managed care … as well as by the ever-growing pharmaceutical conglomerates and private medical-industrial complex (para 7).

The mass media, including radio and television commercials, continually bombard us with "evidence" showing that alcoholism and drug abuse are diseases caused by a biochemical imbalance in the brain and therefore can be cured by drugs that correct that imbalance. This increasing emphasis on addiction as a disease removes the individual's responsibility for his or her self-destructive behavior and avoids the painful awareness and guilt that other people have suffered as a result of the addiction. In contrast, the Alcoholics Anonymous program stresses the importance of an alcoholic individual acknowledging his/her addiction and its harmful effect on loved ones. This factor plays an influential role in AA's positive success rate.

Although the medical model tends to de-stigmatize addiction and mental illness, it is inherently damaging because it disregards the full humanity of the addicted individual. There are other limitations to the medical model. For example, Lurhman (2000) has argued that "To say that mental illness [or addiction] is nothing but disease, is like saying that an opera is nothing but musical notes. It impoverishes us. It impoverishes our sense of human possibility" (p. 266).

Conclusion

Based on more than 40 years of combined experience with clinical and nonclinical populations, the authors have come to the conclusion that all people suffer from some degree of addiction that interferes with their living fully. As described earlier, there are three major types of addiction: (1) addiction to physical substances; (2) addiction to routines and habitual behaviors; and (3) addiction to a personal attachment (the formation of a fantasy bond with another person or persons). Addictions temporarily diminish painful feelings but they have an overall deadening effect, emotionally depleting an individual's energy, vitality, and ability to cope with life.

Addictions often come to prevail over more adaptive actions and seriously limit personal relating. Giving primary importance to addictive substances or routines is the key factor that predisposes the acting out of hurtful behaviors in close relationships. People's fantasies of omnipotence and self-sufficiency, the rationalizations that they use to justify and preserve their addictions, the blame that they project onto others, and the negative role model they offer their children, all cause serious damage.

In our opinion, no depth therapy allows for the full potential growth of the individual without dealing with addictive processes. Even subtle aspects of this form of defense need to be identified and addressed. They often go unnoticed by the patient and may be neglected by the therapist as well.

Giving up one's reliance on a particular substance or compulsive routine is a challenging endeavor. It involves developing an awareness of the specific routines, habit patterns, and relationships that one uses to relieve pain and anxiety. Addictive processes once served a survival function; they originated in times of developmental stress and were the best adaptation to the interpersonal environment. Therefore, it serves no purpose to punish or attack oneself for the addiction; it is far more effective to move toward change.[8]

As people give up their addictions, they will necessarily re-experience the painful feelings and deep frustration that originally caused them to seek gratification inwardly. Because they were totally dependent as children, most people feel on a deep level that they cannot bear the pain they would have to face in coping with primitive wants and rejection; they believe they are still as vulnerable and defenseless as they once were. Yet in the reality of an adult's life, these same situations are not threatening. Unfortunately people must relinquish their defenses before they can realize that they are able to tolerate their emotions and survive even conditions of rejection and abandonment. Yet in facing their wants honestly and taking appropriate risks, they maximize their chances of finding positive gratification (R. Firestone, 1993; Halpern, 1982).[9]

Our primary goal is to help people come to terms with their painful feelings rather than spend a life of avoidance and denial. Many individuals live an escapist existence, on the run from primal feelings, and never really relax their guard. Only by giving up addictive processes, inward sources of gratification, the dependency on fantasy bonds, and by struggling with and overcoming painful demons from the past can a person fully experience life and in the process become less destructive to others.

Notes

1. The National Institute on Alcohol Abuse and Alcoholism (NIAAA) (2002) cited findings showing that from "1,400 college students between the ages of 18 and 24 die each year from alcohol-related unintentional injuries, including motor vehicle crashes" (p. 4). The NIAAA also cited findings showing that "45 percent of the people who began drinking before the age of 14 developed later alcohol dependence, compared with only 10 percent of those who waited until they were 21 or older to start drinking" (NIAAA, 2006 p. 3).

2. See Person's (1995) commentary on fantasy: "*fantasy* is hard to define because it applies to a diverse range of imagined material. Thus, most nonpsychoanalytic definitions of fantasy are largely descriptive, and little attempt is made to get beyond the phenomenology of the experience to an understanding of its major functions" (p 222).

3. According to American Heart Association (2007) "Among Americans age 20 and older, 140 million are overweight or obese" (p. 2). Mokdad, et al (2001) reported that "Each year, an estimated 300,000 US adults die of causes related to obesity" (Introduction, para. 1). At the opposite end of the spectrum, "the National Eating Disorders Association indicates that an estimated 5–20% of those who have anorexia nervosa will not survive complications associated with it" (Tiemeyer, 2007, Mortality section, para. 1). See Battegay's (1991) description of the dynamics operating in bulimia. "Women who suffer from bulimia and binge eat desire not only fusion with the objects in their fantasy, they also desire to incorporate and to take possession of these objects" (p. 22).

4. In an outline of his four-step treatment strategy of obsessive-compulsive disorders (OCD), Schwartz (1996) recommended: first relabeling the "intrusive thought or urge to do a troublesome compulsive behavior" (p. xxi); second, reattributing the origin of the symptom, saying "'I have a medical condition called OCD'" (p. xxi). The third step is refocusing "attention on another behavior and doing something useful and positive" (p. xxi); and fourth, revaluing—learning "to devalue unwanted obsessive thoughts and compulsive urges as soon as they intrude" (p. xxii).

5. See Step Eight in the Twelve Step Program of Sex Addicts Anonymous (International Service Organization of SAA, 2005): "We start by writing a list of all the persons we have harmed .... We also list those who have been harmed by our dishonesty, self-centered attitudes, or other behaviors that arose from our character defects" (p. 46).

6. For a discussion of the aggression (including homicidal and suicidal tendencies) aroused by the disruption of a fantasy of fusion with a couple, see Battegay's (1991) chapter titled "The Insoluble, Destructive Tendency toward Total Fusion with an Object and its Subsequent Destruction" in *Hunger Disease*.

7. Addicted parents have considerable difficulty resonating with their children, and more often than not they fail to repair the misattunements that inevitably occur during parent-child interactions. According to Schore (2001b) studies have shown that "the intimate contact [positive attunement] between the mother and her infant is mutually regulated by the reciprocal activation of their opiate systems—elevated levels of beta endorphins increase pleasure in both brains. It is established that opioids enhance play behavior" (p. 25).

8. With respect to the nonjudgmental approach, recovering addicts who are in therapy are encouraged to "accept themselves just as they are in the moment" (Linehan 1993, p. 208). However, at the same time, there is a strong belief in people's desire to grow and progress, and in their "inherent capability to change" (p. 20). The first author's therapeutic attitude is similar in many respects to Dialectic Behavioral Therapy (DBT) developed by Marsha Linehan.

9. See a discussion of steps in the psychotherapeutic process with addicted clients in "Prescription for Psychotherapy" (R. Firestone, 1990c); 'The Psychodynamics of Fantasy, Addiction, and Addictive Attachments" (R. Firestone, 1993); and "Voice Therapy: Interventions for Addicted Clients" (L. Firestone & Catlett, 2004). With respect to breaking addictive attachments, see "Addiction-Breaking Techniques: Other Useful Approaches" in Halpern's (1982) *How to Break Your Addiction to a Person.*

CHAPTER NINE

Withholding and self-denial

As connoted by the phrase, "We only hurt the ones we love," the more intimate the relationship, the higher the likelihood that aversive interpersonal behaviors occur.

Robin Kowalski (2001a, p. 12)

Withholding is one of the major secondary defenses that supports the fantasy bond and maintains defensive equilibrium. The defense involves holding back positive feelings, actions, and personal competence that are a natural expression of self. These patterns profoundly limit a person's fulfillment in life and restrict productivity in the workplace. All forms of withholding represent a retreat from life that usually arouse painful feelings of regret, remorse, and existential guilt (R. Firestone, 1987b; R. Firestone & Seiden, 1987).[1]

Withholding is a complex phenomenon that encompasses a wide range of interrelated behaviors that are both inner-directed against one's self-interests and outer-directed against others. There are four major aspects of withholding that can be differentiated. All aspects of the mechanism have a negative valence, tend to provoke anger in others, and are hurtful. Although these categories overlap at times, clarification of the primary forms of withholding is helpful:

1. Withholding as a manifestation of passive aggression, an indirect way of manifesting anger;
2. Withholding as an attempt to maintain distance and insulate one-self from being vulnerable;
3. Withholding as a form of self-denial;
4. Withholding in relation to death anxiety and existential con-cerns, a fearful reaction to individuation, independence, and self-realization.

Examples of these diversΔe patterns of withholding can be observed in every sphere of human endeavor. In the workplace, people sabo-tage their careers with their passive-aggressive behavior; in couple relationships, partners self-protectively take back the love they once expressed (Love & Shulkin, 1997); and in families, children are dam-aged unintentionally by parents' holding back love and affection (R. Firestone, 1990b).

Passive-aggressive withholding

Passive aggression due to suppressed anger is a type of withhold-ing behavior that is characterized by the presence of oppositional, negativistic traits and actions and subtle controlling behaviors. Pas-sive aggression, an indirect way of expressing hostility, may appear to be innocent but it is often as damaging or more destructive than manifestations of direct aggression (Cavaiola & Lavender, 2000).[2] It also has a destructive effect on the perpetrator.

Control through weakness is perhaps the most insidious form of passive-aggressive withholding. It is a subtle form of terrorism that induces guilt in one's partner and supports destructive voices and self-attacks. Whole families may be controlled by a weak, self-destructive person to the detriment of all concerned.

> Susan was an only child who had been doted on and catered to by her mother. When she married, she expected similar treat-ment from her husband, Ben. Ben and Susan were relatively happy in their marriage until they had their first child. Susan was overwhelmed by the responsibility of taking care of a baby,

and she was jealous of Ben's attentiveness to their daughter. She became increasingly moody and temperamental. Ben and Susan had two more children and the situation worsened. Susan became more and more controlling, irritable, and demanding—falling apart and making scenes whenever anything went against her wishes. Ben catered to her moods and the children came to treat her in the same way. The entire family was intimidated and dominated by Susan's acting out behavior; they lived in fear of her emotional reactions. Ben had no outlet for his pent-up feelings of frustration and hurt. He loved his children and he saw no solution but to remain trapped in a barely tolerable situation.

Passivity and indirect hostility are maladaptive attempts on the part of the child to cope with damaging aspects of the early environment. In most families, children have limited outlets for expressing their pain, frustration, or anger. Considering the power differential, they find it safer and more acceptable to express their anger indirectly by holding back behaviors and responses that their parents request or demand of them. This use of negative power can be more effective than a direct power play against a stronger, more powerful opponent (R. Firestone, 1985).

There are a number of parental traits that can predispose anger in the child and contribute to him or her developing hostile, self-defeating patterns of behavior. They include: parental immaturity, emotional hunger, intrusiveness, domineering attitudes, restrictiveness in relation to the child's negative emotions (Wenzlaff & Eisenberg, 1998), lack of respect for the child's boundaries, and attempts to live vicariously through the child's accomplishments (R. Firestone, 1990b). These conditions have a devastating effect on the child's capacity to respond spontaneously and positively (Barber, 2002; A. Miller, 1980/1984; Shengold, 1989).[3]

The child feels appropriately angry when intruded upon or drained by an emotionally hungry parent. The intensity of this anger is often overwhelming and terrifying because its object is the very person on whom the child is dependent for survival. Therefore, it is suppressed or even repressed, leading to a hostile attitude that is often expressed through patterns of passive-aggressive withholding. These behaviors include whining, fussing, and screaming (often in public places) and are later manifested as noncompliance, incompetence, or dawdling. Children soon discover that by not performing, by not doing what is asked of them, they have a certain leverage over their parents. Furthermore, there is some measure of release from the anger and frustration.

When children or adolescents restrict or give up their special talents and abilities as an indirect expression of anger, they eventually adopt an overall style of holding back that operates even in areas where they themselves want to excel. In a sense, these individuals have learned to say "no" to everything, including their own wants and aspirations. As such, passive-aggressive withholding is a learned response that is difficult to alter once it has become well-established.

> After two years as top salesman for a large computer manufacturing firm, Bill's sales began to diminish, which was puzzling to his coworkers as well as to himself. Although he seemed to be working as hard as ever, a certain spark was missing, specifically the energy and drive he once showed in pursuing and closing deals. He was overheard complaining about training new members of the sales force, an activity he once especially enjoyed.
>
> Bill's pattern of success, followed by a slowdown in sales, paralleled his performance as a tennis player. A fierce and accomplished player, he would typically win his first set. Then halfway through the second set, he would repeatedly double-fault, miss relatively easy shots, and end up losing. Puzzled and frustrated, Bill investigated what was beneath his inhibited performance at work and in tennis—withholding behaviors that seemed beyond his control.
>
> Bill: One thing I remember is that my mother felt there were absolutely no boundaries between herself and me while I was growing up. She acted as though everything I did was somehow related to her. Any time I brought something home from school, a drawing I did, a story I wrote, you would have thought I'd won the Pulitzer Prize. She would go on and on: "This is great! You're so talented!"
>
> When I was really young, I was happy to get her praise. But she kept raving about me, and she would hang my pictures

in the front hall for everybody to see, and read my stories out loud to relatives and her friends in my presence. It was totally embarrassing, especially as I got older. She even went so far as to tell my teacher that I should be placed in advanced art and writing classes. After a while I stopped bringing anything home to her from school. In the seventh grade, I dropped out of art class, I guess just to avoid that whole scene. But truthfully, I wasn't interested in art or writing after that. I had lost any feeling that the things I had produced were mine. It's like they had become hers.

I know this has a lot to do with the way I am today at work. I don't allow myself to really go after sales because there's a feeling that my sense of accomplishment will be taken from me. It won't really be mine. I will be left with nothing. It sounds like an exaggeration but I feel like I'll lose my own being as a person. It will be snatched away from me. I try hard to fight against it. When I'm playing tennis, I'll be determined ahead of time that I'm going to play to win but at the very point where I see that I'm winning, I sabotage the game.

Because withholding is largely an unconscious process and is manifested primarily in passive behaviors, it is complicated to confront this defense directly. It is difficult to distinguish whether failures are due to emotional withholding or practical or realistic causes. The tendency is to rationalize and explain away withholding responses and put the blame elsewhere. Often a person accused of holding back will tend to act wounded and misunderstood and become defensive when passive-aggressive techniques are exposed.

In the business arena, perhaps the most costly behavior in terms of loss of productivity can be found in employees' withholding behaviors, wherein they hold back or inhibit their positive qualities and talents. Withholding is generally directed toward authority figures or parental substitutes whose power and superior positions cause resentment. This particular type of withholding tends to be resorted to when there is no other outlet for anger or hostility. In business situations, at school, and in most formal situations, anger is rarely tolerated or accepted; therefore, angry feelings must be manifested in passive ways: procrastination, fatigue, incompetence, lack of concentration, disorganized or nonproductive working styles, complaining and acting overwhelmed, forgetfulness, and errors that could otherwise be easily avoided. The costs attributable to employee withholding in business are immense.

Double messages

In a research study by Gottman and Krokoff (1989) double messages, combined with withdrawal and withholding, were observed in videotaped interactions between partners. They found that when there is a preponderance of negative nonverbal behavioral cues, partners try to cover them up with positive verbal messages. This dynamic often predicts the eventual dissolution of the relationship.

From an ethical perspective, the way positive messages mask passive-aggressive withholding behaviors is "crazy-making" and as such is hurtful to the person being withheld from. According to Bach and Deutsch (1979), "From thousands of stress reports during individual and group psychotherapy sessions, a linkage emerged between pathogenic communication patterns and indirect, so-called passive aggression" (p. v). Bach and Deutsch applied Gregory Bateson's (1972) concept of the double-bind to explore the ways that people use positive verbal communications (the manifest message) in everyday life to portray passive-aggressive behaviors (the latent message) as simple mistakes, errors of judgment, carelessness, or innocent forgetfulness. While emphasizing the fact that "people are not usually aware that they are sending two conflicting messages" (p. 17), these authors cited hundreds of examples of double messages that confuse, mystify, and drive the recipient crazy, such as the following:

> "Wouldn't you think, after a year of living together, that Mary could remember how it bugs me when she doesn't put the car keys back on the hook by the door?" (p. 19). Why does Mary forget to put the car keys on the hook? Because her live-together partner convinced her that they could save money by selling her car and both using his. But now he still hogs the car as his own. He makes her feel that she must ask permission before using it, and he hesitates before granting it … . So she bites her tongue. But the resentment is still there. And somehow she can never remember where she put the car keys. In this way he must come

to her before he can use the car (p. 21) Such convenient and well-aimed lapses make it possible for crazymaking to madden those close to us while the crazymaker remains innocent and unaware (p. 19).

The authors have found countless examples of this type of "crazy-making." A woman enjoyed working side by side with her fiancé on projects but later, although verbally expressing the same desire, she found endless excuses for avoiding those activities. A man told his girlfriend that he was beginning to take her seriously but then made no contact with her for a week with no explanation. These mixed messages play with a person's sense of reality, confusing, disconcerting, and provoking in a manner that is disturbing and destructive to relationships (Chovil, 1994).[4]

Passive-aggressive behavior plays a significant role in personal distress but it is difficult to assess. There is considerable resistance on the part of the withholding person to acknowledge this defense and to develop an understanding of the dynamics involved. However, it is clear that because of its far-reaching effects, this type of behavior has consequences in terms of human rights issues and ethical principles.

Withholding to maintain distance

As noted in the chapter on the friendship circle, the authors observed an interesting and significant phenomenon: simply stated, most people don't want what they say they want. Everybody says that they want love, respect, positive acknowledgment, and success in their career yet relatively few can fully tolerate the realization of their goals. Many people react adversely to successes in these endeavors and often lash out at those who are supportive. Often they can only tolerate these successes in fantasy, causing them to hold back positive efforts and accomplishments when they conflict with and threaten their negative self-image.

Nowhere is this phenomenon more apparent than in the arena of personal relationships. Admiration and love can arouse anxiety and revive sad and painful emotions from the past. Because of this people who have been hurt emotionally tend to perceive love as threatening and refuse to take love in from the outside or to offer love and affection outwardly (R. Firestone & Catlett, 1999). The generalized reduction of emotional and interpersonal relating can be characterized by the reluctance or outright refusal to exchange psychonutritional products.[5] In this regard, withholding responses act to maintain a safe distance in an attempt to restore psychological equilibrium. They thereby protect the fantasy bond and the illusion of self-sufficiency from outside intrusion.

Withholding behavior, usually unconscious, tends to reduce anxiety but the retreat is costly and ultimately self-defeating. In therapy, we encourage people to "hang in there" until the anxiety has subsided and they are comfortable with the new level of closeness or success.

The effects of withholding on parent/child relationships

An environmental factor closely related to the child's developing withholding patterns of behavior is the parents' inability to accept expressions of love and affection from them. Many well-meaning parents unconsciously discourage loving responses from their children because these responses threaten their own defenses (R. Firestone, 1990b). When parents find it difficult to accept expressions of love from their offspring, their children gradually learn to disengage from themselves and to suppress their positive feelings. Many children come to believe that there is something wrong with their loving feelings and that their affection or physical nature is somehow unacceptable. They experience considerable shame regarding this personal rejection and often resolve to hold back their warmth, tenderness, and affection in future interactions. One woman, in describing her relationship with her parents, said:

> I remember when I was really young spontaneously running up to my mother and my father, wanting to jump into their arms or their lap, and each one of them having such a negative reaction. I remember my father just kind of pulling away, and my mother being tense and stiff with my affection. I remember feeling so hurt and angry and I said to myself, "Forget it, I'm never going to do that again."
>
> After that, when I was older, I would see TV shows or movies about families, where the children would run up to their

parents and the parents would scoop them up in their arms, but that wasn't me when I was growing up. That wasn't what I was. I was quiet and held back, very shy, terrified of physical contact. That is the way that I became. I would have died a thousand deaths before I would run up into somebody's arms and I still feel that way.

Other parents may vacillate between being emotionally responsive and being self-protective or inward. After a close interaction with a child, parents often revert to a more defended state and an impersonal mode of relating. Many men and women are blocked in their sensitivity and concern for their child and their withdrawal causes considerable hurt. The experience of first being loved and cared for, and then not being responded to, confuses the child. To protect themselves from this type of inconsistency, children become inward and withdrawn, and begin to hold back their feelings.

The effects of withholding on intimate relationships

Withholding is a defense that has a limiting effect on an individual's ability to sustain closeness in his or her intimate relationships. Patterns of withholding practiced by one partner can effectively change the other's positive feelings of love to those of hostility and anger (Betchen, 2005; Love & Shulkin, 1997; L. Rubin 1983).

Holding back personal qualities and behaviors that are especially loved and admired fosters confusion and frustration and predisposes anger and distancing responses in the other. For example, individuals often hold back qualities that originally attracted their mates. A woman told her fiancée that she loved his friendly, congenial nature and the fact that he enjoyed her friends and family. After they were married, she was hurt and disappointed when he became increasingly quiet and aloof at social gatherings and pulled away from the people who were important to her.

In their book, *How to Ruin a Perfectly Good Relationship*, Love and Shulkin (1997) describe a wide range of withholding manipulations. They list hundreds of directives designed to alert readers to these unconsciously motivated destructive behaviors that destroy marriages and relationships. They introduce their tongue-in-cheek injunctions to couples as follows:

> Research indicates that the following behaviors, no matter how insignificant they seem, can over time erode the love between two people. The most common reason people give for separation is "growing apart." Our goal is to show you what growing apart looks like (p. ii).
>   Make it a practice to be late (p. 2).
>   Withhold information. Let your partner find out the details from someone else (p. 3).
>   Pay more attention to the TV than your partner (p. 49).
>   Make sure your partner knows how unhappy you are so he or she will feel guilty and responsible (p. 17).
>   Refuse to follow your dreams, then blame your partner (p. 56).
>   Take pleasure in withholding pleasure (p. 56).
>   Give up on sex. Decide you're just not sexual (p. 68).
>   Reject your partner's affection.
>   Use your weight as an excuse not to be sexual (p. 72).

Essentially one or both partners may attempt to regulate the flow of love and affection, that is, the amount of gratification they will accept or give. The partner who is being withheld from is left feeling emotionally hungry. The awareness that feelings and responses are being withheld provokes longing and desperation, leading to an exaggerated focus on the partner who has become distant.

Sexual withholding

This form of withholding refers to holding back or inhibiting natural sexual desire and its expressions: physical affection, touching, physical attractiveness, and all other aspects of one's natural healthy sexuality. Although these withholding behaviors take place "in the bedroom," their damaging effects are not contained there. They are widespread and affect every aspect of family life.

  Most people encounter difficulties in trying to achieve and sustain sexual satisfaction in ongoing relationships because early in life they turned away from external sources of emotional gratification to gratify themselves internally. In some cases, sexual withholding or inhibition can be motivated by a fear of competing that has its roots in covert or overt sexual rivalry that existed within the family. Individuals who as children felt threatened by retribution from their parent of the same sex tend to retreat from expressions of mature sexuality and hold back their natural responses of affection, love, and sex when they find themselves in a competitive situation. Another influential factor is mothers and fathers who hold back affection from each other and serve as poor role models for their daughters and sons. Children observe, and later imitate in their adult relationships, the withholding behaviors that are acted out between their parents.

Habitual patterns of withholding have a progressively deadening effect on the feelings of excitement, passion, and attraction usually present at the beginning of a relationship. Adults who have become inward and self-protective experience spontaneous sexual contact as threatening to their defended state. Consequently they try to regulate or direct various aspects of the sex act, such as the frequency of lovemaking, the time, the place, the conditions, movements, positions, and manner of expressing affection (R. Firestone, et al, 2006).

Because withholding is a defense that is based on an intolerance of intimacy, it plays an important role in the development of sexual problems in a relationship, particularly problems of low sexual desire (Carnes, 1997; Weeks & Gambesia, 2002).[6] Sex therapists McCarthy and McCarthy (2003) noted that "Research studies ... find that 1 in 3 women and 1 in 7 men report inhibited sexual desire. Sometime in marriage more than 50 percent of couples experience inhibited sexual desire or desire discrepancy" (p. 5).

Typical symptoms that develop in this type of sexual relationship have been observed to follow this sequence: (1) one partner or the other generally becomes less responsive sexually. (2) The partner being withheld from reacts to this withholding in a manner similar to the way he or she initially responded to a parent's rejection, that is, with feelings of emotional hunger, anger, and/or self-hatred. (3) A pattern of immature sexual relating develops, and the sex act itself takes on a more impersonal, mechanical quality. The focus turns more to self-gratification and dependence on fantasy in order to intensify excitement; at the same time, there is a decrease in genuine emotional contact.

Generally speaking, people do not intentionally or consciously withhold affection or sexual responses as a calculated manipulation that is meant to be hurtful. As noted, for most people, withholding is largely unconscious and causes both partners pain and distress. The authors have found that much of the suffering and conflict within relationships is due to one or both partners taking back the love, affection, and sexual responses they once felt and expressed.

Jealousy and withholding

Jealousy and competitive feelings arise naturally in interpersonal relationships. One major reason people seek therapy is because of the extreme distress they experience upon discovering that their mate is sexually involved with another person (S. Glass, 2003). Jealousy is a profoundly disturbing emotion. Many people suffer with fears of abandonment and rejection. Just the suspicion alone that one's partner is sexually involved with someone else disrupts the illusion of being exclusively chosen and preferred above all others.

Sexual withholding inevitably exacerbates people's feelings of jealousy and possessiveness (R. Firestone, et al, 2006). When individuals unconsciously inhibit their sexual desires or hold back their sexual responses, they sense that they are at a disadvantage as competitors. People who are withholding are generally passive and fearful in relation to competing for a partner, which leaves them feeling insecure, possessive, and especially jealous. These men and women imagine that their rivals are more attractive, interesting, powerful, or generally better than them and thus feel that they cannot compete. People who are sexually withholding are inclined toward jealous brooding over imagined losses and tend to attack themselves rather than compete effectively. Many people choose to withdraw and give up a love object rather than cope with the anxiety and other strong emotions involved in competing. In competitive situations, actual losses are often due to an individual's withholding patterns, jealous reactions, and vindictive behaviors rather than to a rival's appeal.

Self-denial

Self-denial involves an avoidance and holding back of happiness and pleasurable experiences from oneself that is only incidentally damaging to other people. Self-denying responses must be distinguished from altruistic behaviors that are self-fulfilling and generally motivated by feelings of empathy toward others, usually toward those people who are suffering or in need. In contrast, despite rationalizations to the contrary, self-denial is a form of microsuicide.[7] It represents a giving up of interest in and excitement about life and a retreat from life-affirming activities and relationships. This tendency is built into an individual's defensive posture and often manifests itself early in life. In effect, self-denial is a destructive form of self-parenting and generally represents the internalization of excessive or even hostile parental prohibitions.

Many people make a virtue of self-denial and take pride in their asceticism, seeing it as moral and constructive (Banks, 1996; Fromm, 1939).[8] As Hoffer (1951) pointed out, "The act of self-denial seems to confer on us the right to be harsh and merciless toward others" (p. 99). However, their self-righteous attitudes and self-denial are seriously damaging to others, particularly their children. Rationalizations, which are promoted by the voice, allow individuals to casually give up activities and friendships they especially enjoy. For example, many people use seemingly reasonable excuses to postpone vacations and the pursuit of a special interest until they retire, only to find themselves limited by ill health and monetary worries when the allotted time arrives. This disengagement from life can be found in every area of human endeavor: a premature giving up of participation in sports and physical activities, a diminished interest in sex and reduction in sexual activity, a loss of contact with old friends, and a decline in social life. At the same time, there may be an increase in sedentary or self-nourishing activities, and people frequently become plagued with a sense of boredom and stagnation.

Progressive self-denial, when extreme, is a major sign of potential suicide. When people give up their special desires and their excitement about life, it supports a self-destructive spiral downward that can end with actual suicide.

> Michelle's parents exemplified self-denial. They wanted little for themselves, spending long hours working in their small shop in New York City. Growing up, Michelle saw no indication of an intimate relationship between her parents. They extended their self-denying attitudes to Michelle by consistently denying her requests and telling her she was selfish and

demanding whenever she even hesitantly expressed a desire for something.

In addition, Michelle's parents were possessive and over-protective of her. They regulated her social life and kept her close by having her work in their shop after school. When she was 16, Michelle fell in love. She hid her relationship and kept the seriousness of her involvement secret. She was guilty about her independence and about creating a life of her own. When her parents discovered the relationship, they expressed extreme disapproval and exerted pressure on Michelle to end the relationship. Unable to bear the guilt, Michelle broke up with her boyfriend. She withdrew into herself and became seriously depressed.

Michelle left home to attend college and during her second year fell in love again. Free from her parents' interference, she developed a long-lasting relationship and eventually married her college sweetheart. The couple settled down in California, pursued their careers, bought a home and had two children. Michelle reported that during this time, she felt very happy and fulfilled, both personally and in her career. However, not long after her second child was born, Michelle became absorbed in work, and she spent less and less time socializing with people she loved or participating in activities she enjoyed. When Michelle's husband and friends voiced their concern, Michelle was defensive and used work as a rationalization for giving up activities and friendships that had been genuinely rewarding to her.

As the years went by, Michelle became more and more isolated. She separated from her husband and rejected meaningful friendships. She refused to accept kindness and love from the people who were concerned about her. Both of her children were seriously impacted by their mother's retreat. During her teens, Michelle's daughter was furious at her mother but she suppressed her rage and became guilty and depressed. As an adult, she imitated her mother's behavior by working compulsively and she struggled to allow herself to have close personal relationships. Michelle's son went away to college, saying that he did not want to stay at home and witness his mother's deterioration.

People who are self-denying sense on some level that they are hurting other people. However unintentional, the damage to personal relationships increases one's self-hatred and guilt, leading progressively to still more self-denial. Many of the disputes in couples and families are provoked by self-denying behaviors. Withdrawal from favored activities by a friend or family member alarms those closest to him or her. Sensing that the person is being self-destructive, loved ones often encourage that individual to pursue his or her natural wants and desires. In response, the self-denying person tends to become oppositional to someone else taking up his or her cause. In more extreme instances, fear and worry aroused by a self-denying person can lead to intrusive behavior and aggressive interference on the part of others, which further damages the adjustment of that individual.

A family with a self-denying parent is often dysfunctional because other family members are manipulated into feeling guilty, fearful, or angry in relation to the martyred individual. The intimidating effect of this dynamic manipulates and restricts the flow of honest communication in the family. Growing up in this type of family often limits an individual's development of independence and self-reliance. People find it difficult to fulfill themselves because of their guilt about "leaving their parent behind." The self-denying behavior and attitudes induced in children by a self-sacrificing parent are then repeated in the next generation, perpetuating a defensive cycle of self-denial.

> Ray Butler, a childhood friend of Stan Dodge, was sailing up the east coast of the United States with his family. On the way, Ray anchored in the marina near Stan's home so he could visit Stan and his family. That evening, Stan's wife prepared dinner for the Butlers who were planning to depart on the next leg of their voyage at dawn the next day. After dinner, Ray, his wife, and children entertained the Dodges with exciting accounts of their sailing adventures. Ali, the Dodge's 11-year-old daughter, listened intently, becoming more and more animated with each succeeding story.
>
> Later, as the Butlers prepared to return to the marina, they invited Ali to come along to see their boat, and Ray offered to drive her home afterward. Ali was thrilled, jumping up and

down, she begged her father to let her to go for a brief tour of the boat she had just heard so much about. Stan frowned and reminded Ali that it was nearly 9 o'clock and she had to be in class by 8:30 the next morning. Ali persisted, arguing that this was a very special occasion. She promised that she wouldn't stay long and reminded her father that she was an honors student. Stan remained unconvinced, restating his position and adding that she needed a full eight hours of sleep. Ali's face fell; the enthusiasm and sparkle she had shown earlier were gone.

In Stan's mind, his caution was part of being a good father. Ever since he had married and started his family in his mid-twenties, he had led a structured, controlled life. He carefully planned his time and activities according to a strict schedule. He sincerely believed that by helping Ali approach her life in the same way, he was, in effect, teaching her good values and ideals. However, in unwittingly suppressing her spontaneity, joy, and excitement, he was having an overall adverse effect on her spirit. Like so many defended parents, he was encouraging his daughter to unconsciously stifle her enthusiasm for life.

Attitudes of asceticism and self-denial are prevalent throughout the culture and are reflected in its social or religious influences. Some radical religious groups place restrictions on dancing, public contact between young people of the opposite sex, and oppose outward signs of physical affection. Puritanical attitudes toward nudity and sexuality foster shame about the body and support the denial of one's sexual nature. These negative cultural influences support self-denying lifestyles that act as a form of social pressure on others that is contagious.

Consensually validated attitudes about age-appropriate roles and behaviors are widespread in our society and support people's tendencies to become progressively more self-denying as they grow older (R. Firestone, 2000). Manifestations of a romantic attachment are acceptable in teenagers and young adults, but incidences of older adults kissing and hugging stand out and are sometimes ridiculed. Engaging in sport activities such as baseball and football is also less acceptable as people age.

Withholding as a defense against death anxiety

> We fear our highest possibilities (as well as our lowest ones).
> We are generally afraid to become that which we can glimpse
> in our most perfect moments ... . We enjoy and even thrill
> to the godlike possibilities we see in ourselves in such peak
> moments. And yet we simultaneously shiver with weakness,
> awe, and fear before these very same possibilities (Maslow,
> 1971, p. 34).

People feel the best when they are fulfilling their potential as unique, autonomous individuals, enjoying success in their careers, or experiencing happiness in their personal and sexual relationships. Although these occasions enhance the feeling of being alive, of being fully present, or as Heidegger said, of "being-in-the world," they are often threatening at the same time. Becoming more conscious of being leads to increased awareness that life is terminal. Life seems more precious and the thought of nonexistence feels unbearable. At this point, powerful defenses come into play to relieve the pain and anxiety. There is a tendency to withdraw, deny the positive reality, and cut off feeling for the person or situation that precipitated the stress. After all, who wants to invest in a life they must certainly lose? The more we are admired, respected, or loved, the more we realize and appreciate our uniqueness, the more we are conscious of our personal mortality. Withholding our special gifts, affection, or lovability serves the purpose of reducing or eliminating the impact of this existential awareness. There is a certain logic to the withholding defense despite the heavy price paid in terms of deteriorating relationships, declining sexuality, failures in the workplace, and general malaise.

Philosophers and existential psychologists have long been aware of the existential dilemma. Rollo May (1983), in depicting the emotions that people experience during "peak" moments in life, wrote:

> Nonbeing is an inseparable part of being. To grasp what it
> means to exist, one needs to grasp the fact that he might not ex-
> ist, that he treads at every moment on the sharp edge of possible
> annihilation and can never escape the fact that death will arrive
> at some unknown moment in the future (p. 105).

The inhibition or withholding of positive responses and capabilities represents a form of microsuicide—a way of accommodating to the anxiety and dread surrounding the existential awareness of death (R. Firestone & Seiden, 1987). By withholding, many people effectively commit a partial suicide, systematically ridding themselves of all that was most valued until, in a sense, they have nothing left to lose. They are able to maintain a false sense of omnipotence, as if they retained some power over life and death (R. Firestone, 1988). Perversely, actual suicide is the ultimate defense against death anxiety. As Joseph Rheingold (1967) proposed:

> The common denominator of all negative ways of dealing with anxiety is a shrinking of the area of awareness and of activity . …
> We are afraid to die, and therefore we are afraid to live, or, as Tillich puts it, we avoid nonbeing by avoiding being. The avoidance of anxiety then means a kind of death in life (pp. 204–205).

A number of theorists (Hinton, 1975; Searles, 1961; Yalom, 1980) have proposed that death anxiety masks a lack of fulfillment and satisfaction with one's life. Their point of view is that increased death anxiety correlates with the degree of emptiness in people's lives. Our clinical experience supports the converse proposition. The authors and several other theorists, including Ernest Becker (1973/1997), feel that this point of view results from confusing existential guilt with death anxiety. Existential guilt stems from regret about denying life's satisfactions to oneself and from withholding actions that would have led to the fulfillment of one's desired goals.

We contend that consciousness of death anxiety is proportional to the degree one feels especially successful, valued, and admired. It is heightened when one prizes life, experiences significant recognition, and achieves self-realization.

> I visited a close friend of mine who lay on his death-bed in the hospital. My wife and I were especially dear to this older man. When he saw us he moaned and said: "Why did you two have to come?" Our visit tortured him because he felt so terribly sad to be losing us. His impending death caused him increased pain because we reminded him of our affection for him, his affection for us, and how precious life was.

On the other hand, we observed that when people feel wretched, demoralized, or emotionally deadened, there is a decrease in the amount of conscious thought about death. For those individuals who are suffering emotionally, the idea of death and dying often becomes acceptable or even desirable.

Withholding precipitated by positive events

Whenever an individual withholds behaviors or qualities that were once an important expression of his or her desires, he or she is no longer goal-directed and becomes more oriented toward failure. In the work arena and in their personal lives, many people tend to hold back desirable qualities that receive unusual recognition. Serious, long-term regressions can occur in reasonably well-adjusted individuals when they experience an atypical success or achievement (Clance & Imes, 1978).[9]

The authors have noted several stages in people's retreat to self-sabotaging, withholding patterns:

1. Initial Reaction: After a significant accomplishment, an individual usually experiences positive feelings of excitement and a sense of personal achievement.
2. Self-Consciousness: A Precursor to Guilt Reactions: The achievement or success precipitates reactions of admiration, envy, or resentment in other people. These responses elicit feelings of self-consciousness in the achiever regarding differences between his/her peers and him/herself. The self-consciousness is exacerbated by the public acknowledgment of success, and after such recognition, individuals often experience guilt reactions.
3. Anxiety and Fear of Loss: Separation anxiety is intensified because the individual, gaining power, recognition, or prestige, is symbolically moving away from sources of dependency. Some people have reported a feeling that life was "too good to be true" in enjoying the excitement of a significant success. They have a superstition that now that everything is so good, something terrible is going to happen.
4. Actual Retreat to Withholding Behavior: An almost imperceptible retreat into dependent, immature functioning and withholding behavior commences as the person gradually withdraws from the favorable recognition.

In addition to becoming incompetent, individuals who withhold their performance after enjoying successes frequently act out other aversive behaviors that provoke angry reactions in coworkers or colleagues. They tend to become irritable, self-centered, vain, overly concerned with their image, and contemptuous toward the very people who acknowledged or supported them. They often feel victimized by the same work situation that they previously enjoyed.

> Nicholas was a struggling director who suddenly achieved fame and recognition when the leading lady in his first feature film was nominated for an Academy Award. He received critical acclaim for the dramatic performance he brought out of an actress who had been thought to have only mediocre talent. Actresses bombarded him with requests to direct them. Studios sent him films to direct. Agencies sought to represent him. He attended the Oscars with the actress and although she did not win the Best Actress award, he was the center of attention through the evening.
>
> Nicholas signed with the most prestigious agency in Hollywood. But to their frustration, he proceeded to turn down all of the projects that they offered him. In every case, he found a reason to reject the screenplay or actor/actress involved. Time after time, the project, after having gone to another director, would become a hit movie. He finally chose a project and even though casting was complete, production never began because he kept demanding changes to the screenplay. The studio was forced to fire him and hire another director to make the film.
>
> Eventually actors stopped calling, studios stopped sending screenplays, and his agent became fed up and dropped him. Nicholas repeated this pattern through his career. He directed a music video that received recognition for its originality. Many musicians were eager to work with him but he never made another music video. He directed a made-for-television movie and received recognition for his ability to work with a famously temperamental and difficult actor. Television studios wanted him to direct their projects but he never made another movie for television.

Positive events may be even more important than negative ones in bringing out withholding tendencies. In general, any positive event that indicates a change in a person's identity, that emphasizes one's difference from one's family (especially from the parent of the same sex), or that fulfills a significant personal goal disturbs one's psychological equilibrium and has the potential for precipitating a long-term retreat from goal-directed behavior (R. Firestone, 1990a).

Regressions to defensive withholding behaviors are frequently misinterpreted as being caused by adverse reactions to negative events. This error is understandable when one considers the fact that a person's retreat after success provokes rejection from significant figures in the interpersonal environment. For example, as a result of acting out childish, incompetent, or withholding behaviors, an individual may actually lose his or her position of power, or job, or a personal relationship. These defeats in themselves lead to an emotional low characterized by feelings of failure and unhappiness.

As noted, unusual joy and fulfillment in a love relationship can cause repressed pain to surface, which in turn can lead to anger and withholding responses. The seemingly perverse, hostile, or provoking behaviors that are directed toward those who love, befriend, or choose us are also understandable in relation to death anxiety. Love and closeness make us especially value our lives, and this awareness tends to revive conscious death concerns.

> Trish: I really like our sexual relationship and I love being sexual with you. But I notice that after we make love, we'll be lying together and talking and you'll be expressing loving feelings toward me and for a while it feels really good. But then, I start to feel agitated. Like I want to get up, get away. Then I start to feel trapped and I pull back.
>
> Alan: I'm relieved to hear you say this. I always feel like there's such a wall that goes up after we make love. Then I start feeling that you're not really attracted to me, you don't love me or even like me. I start feeling insecure.
>
> Trish: It hasn't always been like this. We used to be affectionate all the time, especially after making love. I know that it has to do with something I'm doing and I want to stop. In thinking about the other night, I remember a quick thought that flitted through my mind right after we were sexual, while we were

lying there. It was: "Well, that was nice, but so what? It's not going to last. Things can't go on forever. There is no forever. Life is short!" I feel sad right now, saying that thought out loud. I think I have those kinds of thoughts a lot when we are close. I am so afraid of losing you.

Whenever there is progression toward individuation, a person becomes acutely aware of his or her aloneness and fragile existence. When people react to this awareness by inhibiting or holding back responses that have previously been part of their behavioral repertoire, they are, in a sense, negating their basic nature. Withholding these responses and turning to fantasy for security and partial satisfaction, they feel a sense of self-betrayal and incidentally a betrayal of those who love them. People who restrict their lives in this way experience a sense of emptiness and feelings of existential guilt; nevertheless, they are able to minimize or avoid some of the painful feelings associated with death anxiety that would follow from fully investing in life.

Neurotic and existential guilt

Neurotic guilt can be distinguished from existential guilt. Neurotic guilt involves feelings of remorse, shame, or self-attack that are precipitated by seeking gratification, moving toward one's goals, and pursuing one's wants. Existential guilt is precipitated by holding back or withholding one's natural inclinations. It is generally experienced by individuals when they turn away from their goals, retreat from life, or seek gratification in fantasy. Rollo May (1958) described this form of guilt as:

> rooted in the fact of self-awareness. Ontological guilt does not consist of I-am-guilty-because-I-violate-parental-prohibitions, but arises from the fact that I can see myself as the one who can choose or fail to choose (p. 55) When the person denies these potentialities, fails to fulfill them, his condition is guilt (p. 52).

If individuals achieve more than their parents did, if they seek gratification of wants denied them in their families, they experience painful feelings of self-recrimination or neurotic guilt. However, if they submit to this guilt and retreat to an inward posture of passivity, fantasy, and withholding patterns, they become progressively demoralized and self-hating and experience existential guilt. In a sense, all people are suspended between these polarities of guilt, which form the boundaries of their life experience. The process of withholding, which is essentially suicidal in nature, diminishes the guilt about pursuing a self-affirming existence, yet it inevitably leads to existential guilt, of which Ernest Becker (1973/1997) has written: "Guilt results from unused life, from 'the unlived in us'" (p. 180).

The role of the voice in withholding and self-denial

Both withholding and self-denial are regulated by the voice process (Cramerus, 1989; R. Firestone, et al, 2003).[10] Genuine behavioral responses that would otherwise be a natural part of personal interactions are held back because of an individual's critical attacks on the self. For example, voices that accuse people of being "selfish" tend to surface when they pursue their lives or surpass their parents in terms of accomplishment or satisfaction in their relationships. Guilt about moving in a direction that is more fulfilling than one experienced in one's family is often expressed by the voice in the following terms: *"Who do you think you are?" "You always want your own way." "You only think of yourself."*

Destructive thought processes are also involved in the withholding of competent and productive work habits especially following significant acknowledgement: *"Now they're going to expect more work from you. You'll have to generate more sales. You'll never be able to keep up the pace. They sure made a mistake. Just watch how you're going to fail. You can never live up to this!"*

If people feel motivated to be generous and giving, they may think that: *"He or she doesn't want anything from you!"* If the generosity takes the form of wanting to give a gift to a loved one, they may have voices, such as: *"It's not good enough"* or *"He or she won't like it"* or *"What did he or she ever do for you?"* The resulting posture is one of insulation and self-deprivation whereby the individual, in denying him or herself loving responses, pleasure, and happiness also deprives others of warmth and acts of kindness.

The ethical implications of withholding

As noted, although patterns of withholding and self-denial may be indirect and subtle, they can have the same destructive impact as more direct and obvious manifestations of aggression. Passive aggression and withholding behaviors promote personal discomfort and bad feelings, provoke emotional distance, and act as a manipulation, inducing guilt and exerting an emotional pull on other people. They cause anger and confusion and tend to increase voice attacks in recipients, who tend to blame themselves for the changing emotional condition.

As a consequence of being hurt by parents who could not accept his or her love, the withholding person now inflicts considerable harm on his or her partner and children on a daily basis by not accepting their love and affection. On a simple level, even dismissing or rejecting a genuine compliment is destructive. On a more fundamental level, altering our loved ones' positive responses by being withholding or self-denying is immoral in the sense that it damages their feelings about themselves, causes them to distrust their own motives, and bends them out of shape in numerous ways.

One particularly damaging effect of withholding is that it causes a special focus on the individual who holds back. For example, when a person cuts off his or her feelings of affection after a close moment, it inspires emotional hunger, an exaggerated need for the feeling that is missing. The recipient, whether consciously or unconsciously, looks for the response that is missing and this creates an unnatural and increasingly intense focus on the other. Often this focus is misunderstood by the withholding person as clinginess and entrapment, and he or she tends to criticize or punish the other thereby creating additional problems. This negative spiral causes pain to both people, strains their relationship, and increases their self-attacks.

When people are withholding or self-denying, it is especially damaging to their children. Children who are withheld from tend to blame themselves for the lack of love that they receive and feel that they are bad or inadequate. These children develop a sense of desperation in relation to their parents and suffer from serious attachment problems.

Harry and Alicia's son, Jeff, was a bright boy but somewhat emotionally fragile. His parents were concerned because Jeff would become frustrated and overreact to seemingly minor events. He would lose himself in crying fits during which the people who cared about him were unable to reach him.

Harry had a history of depression. He had a habit of burying himself in work and then becoming depressed under the load of self-imposed demands and deadlines. During these times, he would withdraw from both Alicia and Jeff, and become passive and quiet. Usually physically fit and athletic, Harry would become sedentary and inactive. He would eat and drink too much and put on weight, which would aggravate a chronic back problem. His back pain would then exacerbate his depression.

One summer, Harry took off a month to go on a camping vacation with his family and some of their friends. Harry came to life; he enjoyed being physically active, his back stopped hurting, he joked around with his friends, and his relationship with Alicia became romantic and sexually exciting again. Harry enjoyed spending time with Jeff. He included Jeff in his activities and interests, and because Harry was lively and energetic, his interactions with his son were lively. Jeff thrived. Everyone noticed that he was relaxed and easy-going. He was emotionally resilient and "rolling with the punches" like the other kids.

When Harry returned to work he felt like a different man. He felt happy and alive. But after a few months, he was clearly less energetic and sociable. He was not joking as much, he was not as physically active, and his relationship with Alicia had become dull. But the most noticeable difference was in Jeff; he was emotionally fragile again. When Alicia and Harry discussed the problem, Harry realized that his depression was having a direct effect on his son. When Harry recognized the impact he was having on Jeff, he was motivated to challenge his negative, withholding behaviors and strive to be the way he had been on vacation.

People who are self-denying not only limit their own lives but they also exert a negative social pressure on others. These effects are especially subtle and hurtful. They make others feel guilty for enjoying life and pursuing their goals. Ethically it is as destructive to limit or hurt oneself as it is to cause pain to the other. In addition, it often leads to playing the victim and a paranoid orientation toward life.

Conclusion

Withholding and self denial are major dimensions of a self-protective, inward process that profoundly impacts people's lives both in their personal relationships and in the workplace. The withdrawal of capabilities, affection, sexual responses, and positive personal qualities especially valued by others relieves the anxiety and fear associated with contemplating the possibility of rejection, separation, and ultimately death. However, withholding and self-denial cause considerable suffering both to one's self and others. The everyday manifestations of withholding described throughout this chapter are so commonplace that they tend to be accepted by many as "normal;" nevertheless, they have a powerful undermining effect on individuals and their relationships.

Generosity is the most powerful antidote to withholding and self-denial. Being generous in situations where one would normally withhold counters inward, self-protective defenses established early in childhood. Breaking patterns of withholding and self-denial generally leads to a freer, more energetic feeling and a happier state of mind. Changing habitual responses that have functioned to alienate others significantly expands one's emotional life and social experience. Maintaining transcendent goals and acting on the desire to contribute to the well-being of other people brings one pleasure and imbues life with meaning (Dovidio, et al, 2006; Kitwood, 1990; Oliner & Oliner, 1988).[11] The goal of becoming more generous and giving is based on sound mental health principles rather than on moral imperatives.

Not only is learning to give important, it is also important to learn how to receive. It is an offering to accept kindness and affection rather than pretending to be self-sufficient or pseudoindependent. Being receptive brings pleasure to the giver and is a key element in an interaction that is mutually rewarding. Learning how to accept love, friendship, and kindness counters self-denying tendencies, shifting the balance toward the pursuit of more satisfaction in life.

People can learn to value themselves and stop denying themselves pleasure and enjoyment. They can overcome destructive voices that limit them and realize that it is moral and ethical to pursue one's goals in life.

Notes

1. Existential guilt is described in an article "The 'Voice': The Dual Nature of Guilt Reactions" (R. Firestone, 1987b).
2. Cavaiola and Lavender (2000) discussed this type of hostile withholding, as exemplified by people who may be diagnosed with Passive-Aggressive Personality Disorder.
3. According to Wenzlaff and Eisenberg (1998), parents' restrictiveness of negative emotions can predispose thought suppression in the child, which in turn causes the child and later the adult to "be especially prone to stress-triggered, intrusive thinking and its accompanying emotional problems" (p. 311).
4. See Chovil's (1994) chapter "Equivocation as an Interactional Event" which describes disconfirmation as another disturbance of communication besides double messages that is present in some families of schizophrenic patients:

   As Cissna and Sieburg (1981) noted, examples of disconfirmation include instances of misinterpretation of the other's point of view, denial of self-attributes or self-experience, and even total unawareness of the other person. Disqualification, indifference, and imperviousness have been identified as the three general types of responses that may lead to interpersonal disconfirmation (p. 112).

5. Psychonutritional products include expressions of affection and sexuality; acts of kindness, generosity, and empathy; communication; eye contact; humor; and other positive behaviors.
6. Patrick Carnes (1997) in his book *Sexual Anorexia*, described this form of self-denial as being at the opposite extreme from sexual addiction.
7. "Microsuicide" refers to those behaviors, communications, attitudes, or lifestyles that are threatening, limiting, or antithetical to an individual's physical health, emotional well-being, or personal goals. Examples of microsuicidal behavior include patterns of progressive self-denial, inwardness, withholding, dependency bonds,

and physically harmful actions and lifestyles (R. Firestone, 2000; R. Firestone & Seiden, 1987).

8. In a paper titled "Selfishness and Self-Love," Erich Fromm (1939) noted the social and historical sources of modern (early 20th century) views of selflessness and self-denial. Referring to the work of Max Weber, Fromm noted that:

> The tremendous economic achievements of modern society would not have been possible if this kind of asceticism had not absorbed all energy to the purpose of thrift and relentless work. [but] man became the slave of a master inside himself instead of one outside (para. 17-para. 18).

For a discussion of the relationship between self-denial and eating disorders, see "There is No Fat in Heaven": Religious Asceticism and the Meaning of Anorexia Nervosa," by Banks (1996).

9. The usual explanations for the "Peter Principle" phenomenon, i.e. that people become incompetent when they are promoted to a position beyond their level of competency, may be only a partial or superficial explanation for this phenomenon.

10. See Cramerus' (1989) paper, "Self-Derogation: Inner Conflict and Anxious Vigilance" in which the author noted: "The self-derogator's continual focus on his or her weaknesses and shameful inadequacies is debilitating in task performance, hinders skill acquisition, and fosters social isolation" (p. 66).

11. See Sober and Wilson's (1998) discussion of altruism in their book *Do Unto Others: The Evolution and Psychology of Unselfish Behavior*, in which they refute many earlier explanations of the evolutional basis of altruism, notably the concepts of reciprocal altruism, and the "selfish gene" (Dawkins, 1989). Also see Dovidio, et al (2006) who commented that facing death often makes one more willing to help others. As an example, these researchers tracked the rates of volunteering before and after September 11, 2001 and reported "a two to threefold increase in volunteering following 9/11" (p. 151).

CHAPTER TEN

A victimized orientation toward life

The poor me paranoid is other-focused rather than self-focused ...
and finally blames the other as the cause of his demise—a form of the
self-serving bias seen in ordinary people except more so. The outcome
will be a set of other-blaming beliefs and demands—he should not
treat me this way! He is a worthless rat! He should be condemned!
etc. So long as the poor me paranoid can maintain his strategy, he will
retain a *high* self-esteem.

Chadwick, Birchwood & Trower (1996, pp. 159–160)

One of the most insidious and destructive ways to relate to
other people is to play the victim, judging and blaming others
for any misery and dissatisfaction in life. Behaving in a victimized manner is not only unpleasant, but provokes both guilt and
hostility. This style of thinking and complaining takes its toll on the victimized individual as well as on others and is generally maladaptive.

In her session one day, a woman complained to me (the first
author) that her husband never helped care for their three children
even though she had repeatedly asked for help. He would promise
to come home early from work so that she could have a break, but

invariably he arrived after the children were in bed, without calling to let her know that he would be late. She asked me, "Is that right?" in a tone implying that she was the victim of wrongdoing.

I responded by pointing out that her approach was ineffective and indicated that the key question was not whether the husband's behavior was right or not, fair or unfair, or morally unacceptable. Although she had a valid complaint, it was irrelevant. What was relevant was that she was viewing the situation as a passive victim, which was neither productive nor adaptive. This woman would have fared better to actively face the reality of her frustration and feel her emotional reactions cleanly rather than to distance herself by judging it and feeling victimized. She was angry and frustrated but putting the situation in a judgmental context merely led to internal brooding with no acceptable outlet or active solution.

If one is being robbed, one does not sit around thinking, "This shouldn't be happening to me. It isn't right." Instead, one reacts by calling the police, defending oneself or trying to flee. Constructive action is the opposite of victimized ruminating. Even in the worst circumstances imaginable, such as confinement in a concentration camp, it is not functional to feel victimized even though an obvious case could be made for feeling that way. One would be better off planning tactics of survival or escape rather than focusing on injustice and wrongdoing. Frankl (1954/1967) asserted that many survivors of German concentration camps maintained one vital aspect of personal freedom—the freedom to choose what position to take in relation to the deprivation and horror they faced. Frankl emphasized the importance of an attitude diametrically opposed to the posture of victimization:

> This attitude was a free one! And though on entering the camp everything might be taken away from the prisoner, even his glasses and his belt, this freedom remained to him; and it remained to him literally to the last moment, to the last breath. It was the freedom to bear oneself "this way or that way," and there *was* a "this or that." (p. 98).

People's attitudes in relation to frustration and pain are a vital factor in determining how they live and whether they will succeed or fail. The woman whose husband did not honor his promise to help her with the children had every right to feel angry and to consider constructive action, but to simply justify feeling victimized was maladaptive and ultimately meaningless.

A victimized orientation toward life is an outgrowth of the truly dependent position that the child is faced with early in life. Children are helpless recipients of whatever circumstances exist in their immediate environment. They lack any real power and are at the mercy of their parents. The events that impact children are not only outside their control but beyond their understanding.

Adults who continue to operate from a victimized point of view have failed to separate from the child ego state. They retain the child's perception of the world and project the circumstances of their early childhood onto present-day situations and relationships. They fail to recognize that, as adults, they have far more power than they had as children. Instead of engaging in mature, coping behavior, they often feel frustrated, ineffective, and overwhelmed by external situations.

In politics or business, people often prefer to play the victim in relation to their leaders and their government. They maintain a child role, feeling helpless and complaining rather than taking appropriate action. To be effective, true democracy depends on an intelligent, informed, action-oriented public; it begins to fail when its citizens function as passive, unresponsive victims.

Playing the victim has ethical implications. It creates a negative social atmosphere, prevails upon others, and supports a passive, paranoid attitude that is personally maladaptive and dysfunctional. It leads to a dependent style of relating that alleges that others are responsible for one's troubles, makes associates feel guilty or angry, and tends to drain the energy from positive enterprises. Victimized, self-righteous, judgmental individuals are generally unlikable, make others feel inferior, and when they achieve power they may castigate or actively persecute people whose ideas or ways of life differ from their own.

Characteristics of an individual with a victimized point of view

Inability to accept anger in oneself

The tendency to develop a victimized orientation represents a conversion of normal anger into feelings of being hurt or victimized, a chronic maladaptive response that is not suitable for coping with events in one's life. The inability to accept one's angry feelings or to appropriately express them increases an individual's sense of powerlessness. This posture fosters attitudes of blame and righteous indignation that progressively incapacitate the individual. It gives rise to a chronic low-grade, internalized anger that feeds on itself and has no outlet.

The victimized person believes that feelings of anger require moral justification, but anger is an automatic response to unfavorable events. Unlike actions, feelings require no justification. Individuals who feel victimized deal in judgments and "shoulds" in their interactions with others. "After all that I've done for her, the least she could do ..." These preoccupations with "rights" and "shoulds" are irrelevant to the real issues in interpersonal relationships.

People who assume a self-righteous stance are acting out a sophisticated version of the child-victim or martyr role. They experience various degrees of anger and rage because things are not going their way and the world is not the way they would like it to be. They disguise these childish feelings by issuing judgments and evaluations of others, by insisting on authoritarian methods of punishment for those who make mistakes, and by disclaiming any personal responsibility for negative events.

Passivity

The victimized person finds it especially difficult to cope with adversity. He or she generally succumbs to and is overwhelmed by negative events and circumstances. As noted, there is a tendency to complain and dwell on frustrating situations instead of experiencing anger and taking appropriate action (Kowalski, 1996; Kowalski & Erickson 1997). In the case of the woman whose husband would not help with the children, the clue that she preferred to maintain the child-victim role was that she never made a substantial effort to change her circumstances. Instead, like many people, she chose to continuously complain and passively register her dissatisfaction.

Sense of entitlement

People who play out the victim role feel that they have an inherent right to have their needs met. They think they are entitled to fair and proper treatment. They often focus on the issue of the fairness or unfairness of events and operate on the basic assumption that the world should be fair: "I should have been loved by my parents." "My children should call me or write to me." For example, they feel that they *deserve* to be loved by their families, friends, and mates. Regardless of the philosophical rightness or wrongness of this point of view, an exaggerated sense of entitlement has a negative impact on a person's adjustment. Facing situations for what they are and reacting accordingly is far more adaptive than judging whether or not they should be happening.

Psychodynamics of a victimized orientation

Parental attributes and behavior that predispose a victimized orientation

There are several environmental factors that contribute to the development of a victimized stance in children. The ways that parents relate to each other, to their children, and to others in their interpersonal world have cumulative effects on the child's personality and orientation toward life.

Emotional deprivation

Parental indifference or neglect sets the stage for the child's developing a victimized, helpless orientation in relation to other people and the world. In an environment where children's needs are not met and parents are emotionally unavailable, children are dealt with more as objects (Laing, 1969/1972; Lasch, 1984; Meissner, 1986). As described in Chapter 6, the hurt child forms a fantasy bond in an attempt to partially relieve the pain and anxiety of emotional deprivation and rejection. He/she tends to negate unpleasant realities and instead fantasizes an image of the parent or parents as being good and loving (R. Firestone, 1985). The child consciously retains an idealized image of the parents while unconsciously displacing the parents' negative characteristics onto others. This distorted sense of reality is especially transferred to important figures in one's adult life as well as projected onto the world at large. As a result, these people continue to live as victims in a threatening and dangerous interpersonal environment of their own making.

Seligman (1975) has suggested that learned helplessness, passivity, and a pessimistic world view are linked to early stimulus deprivation. He has also asserted that children who are psychologically mistreated form "the expectation that events are uncontrollable" (p. 60). According to Seligman, maternal deprivation "results in a particularly crucial lack of control" (p. 146). "An infant deprived of stimulation is an infant thereby deprived of *control* over stimulation" (p. 144). His analysis included experimental and natural settings where the infant or child was deprived of opportunities to learn how to deal with frustrating, but resolvable, conflicts.

Children tend to depersonalize and cut off feeling for themselves when they are treated as objects or possessions by parents who are emotionally unavailable. They begin to view themselves as objects; their eyes turn inward on themselves rather than outward toward the world, and they become excessively self-conscious and often distort situations. As adults, people who have detached from themselves in this way often view themselves as a poor, misunderstood child, valiantly contending with a hostile world (R. Firestone, 1990b).

Parents who have unresolved trauma from abuse or neglect in their childhoods are at times compelled to act out hostility, neglect, cruelty, or outright sadistic treatment in relation to their children. Children who are the victims of such abuse or who witness incidents of domestic violence learn early in life that anger is always dangerous and later find it difficult to counter this overgeneralization (Augustyn & Groves, 2005; Dodge, Pettit, Bates & Valente, 1995; Gewirtz & Edleson, 2004; Groves, 1997; Hornor, 2005). According to Hornor (2005) "Witnessing domestic violence may invoke in children feelings of helplessness and they may come to see the world as unpredictable, hostile, and threatening" (p. 209). Research studies have shown that as these children mature, they tend to "become hypersensitive to negative social cues" (Garbarino, 1999, p. 81). Lewis-O'Connor, Sharps, Humphreys, Gary & Campbell (2006) reported that children whose parents are involved in interpersonal violence "become sensitized to inter-adult conflicts and that rather than habituate to such conflicts, [they] ... become increasingly reactive to inter-adult anger" (p. 8).[1]

Parental prohibitions against anger
Many parents encounter considerable difficulty in relation to their feelings of anger. Some believe that anger is the opposite of love and that expressions of anger have no place in close, enduring relationships or in family life. They find it difficult to deal with the essential ambivalence of real-life situations. Many individuals have certain misconceptions about anger, viewing it as "bad" and seeing a person who feels angry as a "bad" person. Another inaccurate belief is that being angry at someone implies accusing him or her of wrong-doing. As noted earlier, the process of denying and suppressing anger contributes to the acting out of uncontrollable rage under stressful conditions.

When children's angry reactions are met with disapproval and counter-hostility, they have no outlet for their anger. These children become passive and inward, either internalizing their hostility or projecting it onto others. When they project it outward, they distort other people by perceiving them as being more angry or hostile than they really are. Even when they experience a minimal amount of hostility directed toward them, they exaggerate its intensity. In addition, by acting on expectations of anger from others, the victimized or passive individual actually provokes angry reactions and rejection in new associations (M. Solomon, 1989).

Parents who are intolerant of anger in themselves tend to discourage or stifle its expression in their children. The child readily learns to deny or subvert natural feelings of anger and, as an adult, is likely to develop a victimized orientation toward life. Most children are taught to be reasonable and rational and learn to negate their anger when it seems unreasonable or irrational, whereas in actuality, people feel angry in proportion to the degree of frustration they suffer, regardless of whether their wants are acceptable or unreasonable.

Parents' failure to provide direction, guidance, and control
Parental control and guidance are as vital to a child's healthy development as love, affection, and warmth. When children fail to receive affection and regulation, both of which are basic needs, they grow up feeling unloved and inadequate. If parents are overly permissive, they create a sense of entitlement in their children. Perhaps the most damaging aspect of this lack of direction is the practice of rewarding

a child for inappropriate expressions of anger. Giving into a child's crying, whining, pleading, and other manipulations by granting his or her requests is a faulty parenting practice because it teaches the child that acting the victim gets results.

Contrary to popular opinion, children are not just "going through a phase" when they display these undesirable behaviors or act "bad" or unpleasant. Unless interrupted, these habits will persist and develop into more sophisticated negative behavior patterns and character defenses. Children who fail to learn to appropriately control their aggressive impulses become adults who suffer because of their inability to manage their emotions. Rather than dealing effectively with their anger, they tend to act out irresponsibly and at times defiantly, develop a victimized point of view, and manifest considerable self-hatred (Behan & Carr, 2000; R. Firestone, 1990b; Shengold, 1999).

Parents' failure to support the child's independence and autonomy
Many parents are insensitive to the appropriate amount of care necessary at each successive stage of their child's development. They tend to be unaware of the functioning level of their children at different developmental phases and discourage age-appropriate activities and behaviors. Others discourage their children's initiative and fail to support them in taking steps that lead to individuation. These parents tend to be over-solicitous and baby their children, talking down to them and providing more care than is necessary. This type of infantilization deprives a child of a feeling that he or she is capable and responsible. This programmed helplessness and dependency tend to foster a victimized orientation. In contrast, if parents encourage children to do as much as possible for themselves as they grow and mature, they are more likely to be independent and strong and less likely to act the victim as adults.

In addition, over-protective attitudes that are restrictive and therefore limiting and destructive may conceal hostile or malicious attitudes toward children. A number of clinicians have emphasized the point that anxious, immature parents who are overconcerned about potential danger to their children may have hidden aggression toward them (Barber, 2002; Levy, 1943; G. Parker, 1983).

Many parents intrude on their offspring's right to develop as an individual. They fail to "let their children be," to allow their personalities and unique qualities to emerge. Others push their children in a direction that they feel is right for the child regardless of the child's specific interests. The child's spirit, vitality, initiative, and tendency to strive to fulfill his or her potentialities are damaged by such intrusions.

It is crucial for parents to "let go" of their children and not impede their independence. In general, optimal parenting practices are free of intrusive behavior, unnecessary prohibitions and surplus authority. Parents would reward children for speaking up, for saying what they see, for asking questions about so-called taboo subjects Excessive rules and regulations influence children to stifle their curiosity and to become passive observers rather than active participants in life.

Children's imitation of parents' victimized point of view

Toxic personality traits in parents not only have a destructive effect on children directly, but these negative qualities are passed on to succeeding generations through the processes of identification and imitation. Children imitate the immaturity and passivity of victimized parents and assimilate their point of view in relation to other people and the world. By the time children are 2 or 3 years old, they have begun to act out their own passive-aggressive tendencies, to be resistant or defiant, to whine and complain, and to manipulate their parents through "learned helplessness." Parents who are themselves immature and manipulative fail to challenge these expressions which then become firmly entrenched in the child.

> Anita and Dean had been married for four years when they had a baby daughter, Cindy. They looked forward to raising their child in a way that was different from how they had grown up. Anita's mother, a withdrawn, passive woman, had been emotionally distant throughout Anita's childhood and adolescence. Her father, on the other hand, had tried to make up for his wife's neglect by indulging Anita's many demands for food, toys, or other tangible indications of love and attention. Dean had been raised by an absentee father and a mother who expected him to take over as the "man of the house" and play the "father" role to his five younger siblings. Although resentful, he had complied with his mother's wishes.

After Cindy was born, things went well for almost a year. Anita was pleased to discover that Dean was a devoted father who willingly assumed most of the child-care functions for Cindy as an infant. However, because Anita herself was infantile and needy, she was jealous of the loving and caring responses that Cindy elicited from Dean, and as a result, she gradually withdrew her attention and affection from the child.

When Cindy was a year old, Dean experienced a serious setback in his business, became depressed and morose, and pulled away from his daughter. Anita responded by complaining endlessly to Dean about his growing neglect of both her and their daughter. Dean reacted to Anita's nagging with brief, perfunctory bouts of helping her take care of Cindy. He rarely, if ever, confronted Anita about her childishness and her lack of support of him during his crisis.

By age three, Cindy had developed a pattern of sulking, whining and crying, similar to that of her mother, in an effort to get the things she wanted and the attention she needed. Ever the devoted father, Dean invariably gave in to his daughter's demands as he did to his wife's. Whenever he tried to say "no" to his daughter, she dissolved into tears and often threw violent tantrums. For the most part, Anita sided with Cindy, telling Dean that he should not frustrate the child, but should give her what she wanted in order to stop her tantrums. In effect, she colluded with her daughter and in so doing, reinforced a destructive pattern of victimization and passive complaining in the child that would be difficult to reverse later on.

Feelings of victimization and the awareness of death

When children first become aware of their personal death, this knowledge contributes to a basic distrust or paranoia that may later be projected onto real-life situations that have nothing to do with the original cause. Paranoia is an understandable response to the existential dilemma. In reality, powerful forces beyond one's control, i.e. aging, physical deterioration, and death, conspire to eliminate any possibility of ultimate survival. Because of the transference effect of these phenomena, many individuals overreact with rage, fear, and panic to events far removed from these realities, events that in no way justify intense reactions of helplessness or powerlessness. For example, Meyer (1975) suggested that a displacement of problems connected with the fear of death is apparent in agoraphobia, fear of cardiac arrest, animal phobias, and claustrophobia. Lifton (1998) asserted that, in some cases, paranoia is closely associated with death anxiety or a fear of annihilation.[2]

The dynamics of passivity and a victimized orientation have been studied in the laboratory with both animals and humans. Seligman (1975), when developing his "learned helplessness" model of human motivation, defined this condition as "the state of affairs in which nothing you choose to do affects what happens to you" (Seligman, 1990, p. 5). In a series of experiments, he found that when aversive events were unpredictable, uncontrollable, and inescapable, an individual's emotional, cognitive, and behavioral responses were disrupted, leading to extreme passivity or paralysis.

The paranoid process

Paranoid thought processes and behavior represent a perversion of normal reactions to anger. Paranoid thinking is a disorder of focus and perspective whereby the subjective world of the individual (including his sensations, feelings, thoughts, and reactions) is experienced as happening to him/her rather than originating in or being caused by him/herself. As such, it is a severe form of victimization. Anger that would be felt outwardly in reaction to not getting what one wants is perverted into a feeling of being hurt or wounded. This often leads to a condition of chronic passivity in relation to events and to the expectation of harm from the outside. With this expectation and an abnormally high sensitivity to aggression in others, there is a tendency to distort and even to invent malice in other people. The anger and aggression that paranoid people expect from others is a magnified version of feelings that they are denying in themselves (R. Firestone & Catlett, 1989).

Paranoia is a self-confirming system which precludes the awareness of conflicting views or perceptions of reality. The thinking of a paranoid person is analogous to the work of a scientist who rigs the data to fit his preconceptions. Paranoid individuals are unconscious of this process and feel genuinely threatened from without. The paranoid state of feeling unfairly treated arouses punitive attitudes that are debilitating and inevitably lead to more rage and retaliatory feelings, thereby creating a downward spiral that is increasingly dysfunctional. Paranoid people cannot see that their distorted perception of danger causes them to act hostile which then precipitates hostile responses in others (Meissner, 1986, 1995).[3] Maintaining a victimized posture precludes emotional growth and causes untold damage to other people and to oneself.

In describing how the child's introjection and imitation of certain parental traits contribute to more severe forms of paranoia, Meissner (1986) conceptualized the patient's "self-organization" as including an amalgamation of "introjections of the sadistic, harsh, punitive, hostilely destructive, and rigidly demanding father on the one hand, and of the depressive, masochistic, and victimized image of the mother on the other" (p. 256). Meissner went on to argue: "Consequently, the interlocking of the parental projection with the child's internalization provides the matrix out of which the paranoid process derives" (pp. 256–257).

Paranoid psychosis is a condition in which disturbed individuals maintain a delusional system and feel victimized and persecuted. It is often combined with schizophrenic symptoms and is characterized by delusions of reference, a sense that one is the focal point of concerted action or attention. Paranoid schizophrenics are primarily narcissistic in their approach to life. They feel that people are talking about them, plotting against them, and planning to cause them humiliation or harm. Although these psychotic reactions are both extreme and distorted, there are countless examples of less severe paranoid manifestations in everyday life (Berke, Pierides, Sabbadini & Schneider, 1998).

When I (the first author) was working my way through school as an assistant at an animal hospital, I worked with Bill. He gradually developed the paranoid idea that a particular doctor had it in for him. He became increasingly nervous, angry, and sullen around this doctor. He started to make mistakes, such as sterilizing two left-handed gloves and giving wrong information to the clients who called in on the phone. Finally, it got to the point where he was in danger of losing his job. I warned him about the situation and advised him to be careful or he was going to be fired. Instead of feeling my concern for him and heeding my warning, he was angry at me and accused me of also having it in for him. He became even more careless and sullen on the job, and finally was fired. He had made his prediction about the doctor come true. Through it all, he maintained the feeling that he was the victim, including me in his sense of being persecuted.

A person who attempts to help a paranoid individual by offering a realistic picture of the situation will tend to become included in the paranoid system. If it is pointed out that it is the individual's own actions and not some outside cause that is bringing on his or her problems, the paranoid person will react with anger.

Paranoid feelings can surface in an intimate relationship, particularly when it is significantly better than one's past experiences. In the beginning, the person feels good about the positive situation, but then anxieties and distrust arise because the circumstances differ from what he or she was used to. His/her focus may shift from feeling affection for the other to worrying about what the other person feels in return. Fears of rejection and abandonment tend to be aroused. These thoughts lead to defensive reactions and anger, cause problems that disrupt the relationship, and lead to increased feelings of paranoia.

> When they were first married, Brad felt secure in his relationship with Lucille. He felt happy when they were together and loved her very much. At first, he didn't worry about how she felt toward him; he simply enjoyed the easy flow of positive feelings between them.
>
> When Lucille took a job in a law firm, Brad began to worry that his wife would be attracted to someone at work. He began to question Lucille: "Who did you eat lunch with today?" "Why can't you make arrangements to come home earlier?" "How long do you want to keep working before we start to try to have a baby?" Brad became increasingly insecure. Soon he was asking "Do you still love me as much as you used to?" and complaining that things didn't seem the same since she began working. The questioning confused and irritated Lucille, who had no interest in anyone else and whose feelings for Brad had not changed.

However, Brad's anxiety and insecurity overshadowed Lucille's reassurances. He actually accused her of being attracted to her boss and suspected that they were having an affair. Brad began withholding his own feelings of affection and love in anticipation of being rejected by Lucille. He continued to believe that she did not love him any more, while ignoring the truth that it was he who had cut off his feelings for her.

Brad's paranoia began to provoke Lucille, and they began fighting. Eventually she thought of leaving. Brad's paranoid attitudes had acted as a self-fulfilling prophecy.

The disordered focus of paranoid thinking is also evident in the business world. Many people distort everyday work situations by manifesting suspicious, distrustful, inappropriate attitudes and behaviors. It is true that some business practices are unfair, that some people in business are unethical, and that one can get "taken" in a bad business deal. However, focusing on the negative possibilities instead of being open-minded and simply checking things out is a paranoid approach and is not conducive to successful business. In fact, paranoid individuals are more likely to be deceived or cheated despite their suspiciousness because being deceived and cheated enables them to maintain their paranoid view of the world.

From an ethical perspective, people who have a victimized point of view evoke strong feelings of guilt, anger, and self-hatred in others. Paranoid individuals disturb the reality of the people who are the target of their distortions. Their accusations and/or innuendos often correspond to the worst self-attacks of the person who is the focus of their paranoia. In this way, being the focal point of paranoid attitudes can be detrimental to a person's adjustment and sense of worth.

The paranoid thought process can be treated in a positive psychotherapy situation. However, borderline, paranoid clients who are allowed to vent their grievances without being responded to often mistake attentive listening for agreement with their victimized point of view. Unless their feelings of being used, exploited, or slighted are challenged, these clients often become worse. In a therapy where there is a strong therapeutic alliance, the victimized or paranoid client's recounting of victimizations can be interrupted through direct confrontation. Exposure and understanding of paranoid projections and distortions, combined with objective inquiry, reality-testing, and good humor, along with the therapist's genuine caring, empathy, and concern, are most effective in facilitating change (R. Firestone, et al, 2003; Meissner, 1986).[4]

The role of the voice in maintaining a victimized point of view

Attitudes of victimization and paranoia are regulated by the voice. Cynical, suspicious attitudes toward others tend to occur in conjunction with the self-attacking voice process. Feelings of anger and distrust are aroused when people "listen" to voices telling them that others dislike them or do not care about them or their interests. *"They never take your feelings into consideration. Who do they think they are?"* Or more generally, *"People just don't give a damn."*

This destructive thought process promotes a state of feeling hurt or wounded that contributes to feeling victimized and paranoid. The individual then tends to project angry or self-critical thoughts onto other people who are then perceived as critical or hostile. The voice interferes with a person taking action to change an unhappy situation by focusing on "the injustice of it all." It reinforces the passive posture of the victimized person by reiterating: *"It's not fair. This shouldn't be happening to you. What did you ever do to deserve such treatment?"*

In the workplace, many people manifest angry hostile attitudes based on voices telling them that they are being exploited: *"Your boss is a real jerk! Nobody sees how much you contribute." "No one appreciates you." "Why do they always get all the breaks?" "Why work hard, they get all the money anyway."*

When people feel victimized and are hostile toward others based on irrational, negative beliefs, they tend to distance themselves and avoid close involvement. The voice process encourages isolation to protect the defense system with thoughts that predict rejection or other negative outcomes: *"Don't get too attached. You'll just be disappointed. If you show that you care too much, you'll be taken advantage of or rejected."* The voice persuades people to avoid the risk of being vulnerable and tells them never to trust anyone.

When the victimized person becomes isolated, self-protectively distancing him or herself from others, his or her voices and thoughts become increasingly negative and distrustful. The resultant acute paranoia leads to a buildup of internal hostility with a corresponding decrease in one's ability to cope effectively with negative circumstances. The accumulation of aggression can precipitate angry outbursts that are inappropriate to the reality of the situation.

In some instances, the buildup of anger can become serious enough to erupt into violent, explosive behavior. Extreme negative voices toward and about others are at the core of all forms of criminal and antisocial behavior. People who act out violent impulses justify their actions as being rightfully deserved by their victims. A mode of thinking that rationalizes revengeful action is also characteristic of perpetrators of domestic violence: "*She had it coming to her.*" "*She knew what buttons to push to make me explode.*" "*You should get even with that bastard.*" Our research (Doucete-Gates, Firestone & Firestone, 1999) and other studies (J. Gilligan, 1996b, 2001; Toch, 1992) demonstrate that a paranoid, victimized orientation increases an individual's propensity to act violently and to feel justified in doing so.[5]

In recent studies of learned optimism, Seligman (1990) found that "a pessimistic explanatory style [the reasons people give for failure] changes learned helplessness from brief and local to long-lasting and general. Learned helplessness becomes full-blown depression when the person who fails is a pessimist" (p. 76). In other words, according to Seligman, an individual's explanatory style or attitude of victimization or nonvictimization is crucial: "Changing the destructive things you say to yourself when you experience the setbacks that life deals all of us is the central skill of optimism" (p. 15). Pessimistic victimized attitudes based on destructive voices can be challenged through voice therapy and the planning of corrective suggestions that counter the behaviors they control.

Modifying the victimized orientation

"Reject your sense of injury and the injury itself disappears" (Marcus Aurelius, Meditations).

Learning to deal with anger

As noted, anger is an appropriate response to frustration and stress. When people can accept angry emotions they are less likely to act them out destructively. Ideally, rather than suppress the emotion of anger, one would acknowledge angry responses while clearly distinguishing between feelings and actions. In a healthy response to anger, one does not attempt to justify these emotions by becoming self-righteous.

It would be constructive for people who express their anger through passive-aggressive behavior, righteous indignation, or victimized brooding to relinquish the basic assumption that they are innocent victims of fate. However, people who are afraid of their anger prefer to believe that they have no recourse other than to express their anger indirectly. Refusing to challenge victimized attitudes and voices perpetuates this mode of thinking.

When people explore the emotions underlying their anger, including their feelings of hurt, emotional pain, and fear, they become more objective and noncritical in their attitudes toward others. They are able to identify the destructive thoughts that are underlying their projections onto their loved ones. As people become sensitive to the damage and pain they are inflicting on others, they can become aware of the specific ways this process is hurtful.

Hostile, cynical, and condescending attitudes usually reflect an alien point of view represented by the voice. In this regard, it is important that partners learn how to give away their angry thoughts rather than act them out with each other. This process involves talking about anger in a nondramatic tone and admitting any irrationality or feelings of being victimized. This type of communication is less likely to arouse counter-hostility and enables people to deal with their anger in a way that causes the least amount of pain to one another.

Giving up one's sense of entitlement

It is adaptive for people to realize that they do not inherently deserve to receive anything in the way of good treatment from others. It is functional to accept the idea that the world does not owe them anything—neither a living nor happiness nor pleasant surroundings. When people take the victimized position that they deserve to be loved, or that they are entitled to something better, they tend to feel cheated or deprived and become more angry, helpless, and despairing in their outlook. Unfortunately, this maladaptive orientation is often supported by the sympathizing of well-meaning friends and family.

As noted in Chapter 2, there is a distinction between sympathy and empathy. Both giving sympathy and arousing sympathy in another person are damaging to self and others in that they reinforce victimized thinking. This type of commiserating with a friend as contrasted with having empathy or compassion for his or her misfortune can be counterproductive and unhealthy for both people. Responding with sympathy to people's complaints and their tales of woe can be harmful. The same can be said for soliciting sympathy for oneself. It is possible to share another's sorrow and pain and to listen with empathy in a way that enables that person to have a compassionate, objective view of him or herself. A friend who is sensitive and compassionate without being overprotective or excessively sentimental empowers a person. For this reason, an individual's choice of friends can be crucial at the time he or she is giving up a victimized role.

Giving up complaining

It is also constructive for people to avoid complaining about their problems to others in a style that "dumps" the problem on the listener. A specific action that people can take is to drop certain words from their vocabulary, words like "fair," "should," "right," and "wrong." Relating to another person in terms of "shoulds" or obligations rather than free choice sets the stage for paranoid, victimized thinking. By challenging their habitual victimized thinking and way of speaking, people can discover a different form of communicating that involves taking full responsibility for their feelings and actions and yet leaves then free to explore alternatives.

Absolutism, feelings of superiority, rigidity, and defensiveness are barriers to good relationships. Therefore, it is advantageous for partners to relinquish their stubbornness about being "right" and to adopt a more flexible posture. Nothing has more power in changing a relationship for the better than "unilateral disarmament." As described earlier, this occurs when one or another partner puts the goal of maintaining loving feelings ahead of proving he or she is "right" and becomes more open and vulnerable in the heat of an argument. Honestly exposing and giving away cynical, hostile thoughts toward the other as well as toward oneself often has the positive effect of ending one's need to be right.

The same issue applies to nations with conflicting views and priorities. In this case, attempts at diplomacy and conciliation take ethical precedence over self-righteousness, aggressive maneuvers or indifference.

Becoming proactive

Many individuals, especially those from abusive or violent families, react as though the person who provokes or frustrates them is responsible for their angry reactions. They mistake the stimulus for the cause. "You make me angry" is a statement that reflects the assumption that they conceptualize anger as a passive process in which someone else is always to blame for their aggressive feelings. They refuse to accept active responsibility for their own emotions.

In interpersonal relationships, allowing oneself to be manipulated or mistreated by another person is damaging to both parties. In fact, when the person playing the victim does not intercede and try to stop the abuse, he or she encourages more anger and rage in the other.

Taking action to change situations with which one is unhappy directly challenges a victimized orientation. In one's relationships, one has every right to ask for what one wants, and the other person has every right to refuse. If individuals tie their feelings of frustration to an expectation that someone is obliged to satisfy them, then paranoid feelings are inevitable. Instead of chronic complaining, the wife in the original example had a variety of options. She could have asked her husband to talk about the problem, confronted him and told him that she was angry directly, asked him to change the behavior, suggested counseling, offered an ultimatum, or threatened to leave him as a last resort.

Individuals can become active agents in determining the direction of their lives. If the same unfortunate events seem to keep happening to them, they can examine themselves closely to determine if they are choosing situations and people that are destructive. A passive attitude on their part may have had more to do with these events than they previously thought. The changes that occur when a person becomes proactive and stops complaining and accusing others of causing his/her unhappiness can significantly alter people's lives.

Conclusion

Maintaining a victimized point of view precludes emotional growth and causes untold damage to other people and to oneself. Giving up a victimized point of view is therefore vital to personal development. The destructive urge to play the victim can be understood and controlled. People can learn to acknowledge that the world does in fact contain many inequities, that things are not fair and equal, and that it serves no purpose to passively complain and feel victimized. Adaptation, responding with appropriate emotion, changing one's situation or relationship, and/or taking social and political action are constructive alternatives.

There are innumerable social injustices that are discriminatory and unfair to individuals or groups of people. But even in circumstances where there are no apparent solutions for unfair conditions, people can still change and develop themselves. Individuals who give up a victimized orientation have been able to envision solutions they previously overlooked. It is far more productive to view life from this action-oriented, optimistic perspective than to remain mired in blaming failures on other people or circumstances. In reacting to injustices in a powerful, nonvictimized manner, one can facilitate changes in society as well.

Notes

1. Research cited by Gewirtz and Edleson (2004) showed that: "repeated victimization by parents may alter children's representations of relationships in a way that makes them hypervigilant to signs of threat in other social contexts" (Dodge, et al, 1995, p. 6). In other words, the previously victimized child's expectations of anger or threat become a self-fulfilling prophecy and his or her demeanor and/or behavior elicits the very anger and harm he/she fears. Also see *Children Exposed to Violence* (Feerick & Silverman, 2006).
2. See Robert Jay Lifton's (1998) chapter, "The 'End-of-the-World' Vision and the Psychotic Experience." In this chapter, Lifton cited Lionel Ovesey's (1955) suggestion that:

> The power (aggression) motivation is the constant feature in paranoid phenomenon and the essential related anxiety is, therefore, a survival anxiety. What Ovesey means by survival anxiety is close to what we mean by death

anxiety or fear of annihilation; and he understands this anxiety to result from a sequence of frustrated dependency, extreme aggression, and symbolic distortion, until the feeling 'I want to kill him' becomes converted to 'He wants to kill me.' (Lifton, p. 63).

3. See Meissner's descriptive accounts of the paranoid process in *Psychotherapy and the Paranoid Process* (1986) and *Treatment of Patients in the Borderline Spectrum* (1995). Shengold (1989), in *Soul Murder: The Effects of Childhood Abuse and Deprivation*, also described the important link between paranoia and actual experiences of child abuse.

4. The process of challenging clients' paranoid delusions and distorted perceptions requires considerable expertise. See Meissner's (1986) analysis of adolescent alienation: "If the therapist loses objectivity by accepting or endorsing the patient's presuppositions, he runs the risk of undermining therapeutic effectiveness and eliminating the possibility of testing the patients' perceptions and attitudes in reality terms" (p. 299).

5. A number of core beliefs and attitudes held by the victimized or paranoid person are similar in content to items on the *Firestone Assessment of Violent Thoughts* (FAVT) (R. Firestone & Firestone, 2008).

CHAPTER ELEVEN

Vanity and narcissism

What makes the vanity of others insufferable to us is that it wounds our own.

Francois de La Rochefoucauld (1613–1680, Maxim 389)

The man who is predominantly erotic will give first preference to his emotional relationships to other people; the narcissistic man, who inclines to be self-sufficient, will seek his main satisfactions in his internal mental processes.

Sigmund Freud (1930/1961, pp. 83–84)

*V*anity can be defined as a fantasized positive image of the self that an individual uses to compensate for deep-seated feelings of inadequacy and inferiority. It represents remnants of the child's imagined omnipotence and invulnerability that live on in the psyche. Vanity also acts as a mechanism that attempts to cope with the feelings of vulnerability and stress associated with one's consciousness of the fragility and impermanence of life.

Vanity originates in early childhood and is exacerbated when parents offer empty praise and a false buildup as compensation

249

for the lack of genuine affection, love, or acknowledgment of the child's real self (R. Firestone, 1985; Hotchkiss, 2002; Lowen, 1985; A. Miller, 1997). As Lowen (1985) asserted "If … [a boy] believes himself to be a prince, it is because he was raised in that belief" (p. 21). For children deprived of acceptance and real recognition, this inflated self-image becomes a form of self-gratification. As adults, they continue to gravitate toward people who will approve of them without question or praise and flatter them. Feeling special or superior can be considered a core defense against death anxiety. Vanity expresses itself in the secret fantasy that death happens to someone else, never to oneself (Becker, 1973/1997; R. Firestone, et al, 2003; Zilboorg, 1943).

Vanity leads to a variety of unethical behaviors because individuals who have an inflated self-image tend to demean other people. Vain, self-important people express attitudes of superiority through condescension and contempt in their everyday interactions. As noted, researchers have found contempt to be a significantly corrosive mode of communication. In his book, *Blink*, Gladwell (2005) cited John Gottman's definition of contempt as manifested in marital relationships: "Contempt is any statement made from a higher level. A lot of the time it's an insult: 'You are a bitch. You're scum.' It's trying to put that person on a lower plane than you. It's hierarchical" (p. 33). As Benjamin Franklin metaphorically stated: "Pride that dines on vanity sups on contempt."

In addition to making other people feel inferior, thus incidentally provoking their anger, vain people are often directly punitive toward those who fail to offer their approval or respect. When vain people occupy positions of power, punishment may include censure, termination of employment, incarceration, exile, physical mistreatment, or death.

Narcissism can be defined as a self-centered orientation, a fascination with the self—more specifically, with an image of self—and a corresponding lack of interest in and concern for other people. According to Lowen (1985) "Narcissism denotes an investment in one's image as opposed to one's self. Narcissists love their image, not their real self" (p. ix).[1] Like Narcissus in the myth, the narcissistic person is unable to "draw his attention away from his reflection. Narcissus was ignorant not only of Echo [who loved him], but also of his own possibilities. It is this total absorption of the self that causes a distorted world view" (M. Solomon, 1989, p. 46).

Narcissistic behavior is unethical because it leads to insensitivity toward other people. As the attention of narcissists is focused on themselves, they are preoccupied almost exclusively with their own thoughts, feelings, troubles and triumphs. They usually select as partners those persons who they recognize as potential sources of "narcissistic supplies;" that is, people who will mirror or support their grandiose image of themselves. Narcissists often engage in subtle forms of control or "emotional blackmail" in interpersonal relationships when their partners fail to meet their demands for attention, approval and admiration (Forward, 1997).

Narcissistic, self-absorbed parents inadvertently have a devastating effect on their children because their preoccupation with themselves precludes real contact with their child. Their lack of empathy and inability to attune their responses to their baby's behavioral cues interfere with their infant's forming a stable coherent "core" self at a crucial point in the developmental sequence—during the separation/individuation phase (Masterson, 1981; Stern, 1985). This harmful behavior leaves the infant or young child essentially "starved" for love-food, that is, the affection, warmth, direction, and guidance as well as the mirroring experiences necessary for healthy emotional development.

In commenting on the prevalence of narcissism in modern society, Hotchkiss (2002) asserted: "While a narcissistic personality that meets the full criteria for a clinical diagnosis may be relatively rare ... there is plenty of evidence that toxic levels of narcissism are pandemic in American society and have been for some time" (p. 31).[2]

The terms "vanity" and "narcissism" are often used interchangeably in the literature and in popular discourse (S. Freud, 1935; Kernberg, 1998).[3] There is some overlap in descriptions of the two disturbances, although narcissism typically refers to a disorder listed in the DSM-IV (American Psychiatric Association, 1994), which implies a more serious or more pathological disturbance than vanity (Jacoby, 1985/1990). According to the DSM-IV, vanity is one of the criteria required for a diagnosis of Narcissistic Personality Disorder: "Narcissists routinely overestimate their abilities and inflate their accomplishments, often appearing boastful and pretentious .... They may be surprised when the praise they expect and feel they deserve is not forthcoming" (p. 661). In other words, narcissists tend to be vain; whereas a vain individual may not necessarily be classified as a narcissistic personality (Morey & Jones, 1998).[4] However, both share a concern with the image of how they are perceived rather than the reality of who they are. In addition, both have problems with self-esteem regulation (Kernberg (1995).

Characteristics of the vain individual

> Among the things that may be hardest to understand for a noble human being is vanity... . The problem is for him to imagine people who seek to create a good opinion of themselves which they do not have of themselves—and thus also do not "deserve"—and who nevertheless end up *believing* this good opinion themselves. (Nietzsche, 1886/1966, p. 208).

Exaggerated positive image of self

As noted, people who are vain have an inflated image of themselves that they use to compensate for feelings of inferiority, powerlessness, and self-hatred. People can become addicted to the temporary "high" that flattery and exaggerated praise often produce. Efforts to maintain an inflated self-image progressively debilitate the real self and interfere with the pursuit of real goals. The vain individual must always defend against acknowledging his or her real or imagined deficiencies. In individuals who rely on fantasies of omnipotence and superiority to maintain their self-esteem, criticism threatens the fragile sense of self. In the minds of vain individuals, they are either the greatest or the worst—there is no middle ground. Therefore, when realistic appraisal, criticism or negative feedback disturbs one's image of being the greatest, there is a downward spiral either into intense feelings of self-hatred, inferiority and powerlessness or into narcissistic rage (Baumeister, 1997; Kernberg, 1975; Kohut, 1971).

Perfectionism

People who have an inflated image of self are under tremendous pressure to live up to the high standards they have imposed on themselves. Many have fantasies about being exceptionally talented and competent and imagine themselves capable of performing at unrealistically high levels (Kernberg, 1980; Young & Flanagan, 1998). When their performance falls short of perfection, or when they receive negative or even objective feedback regarding their performance, severe self-castigation and demoralization can result. There can also be anger and retaliation toward people whom they perceive as responsible for their failure, loss of self-esteem, or humiliation. Others turn their anger against themselves, which intensifies their self-hating feelings and often leads to depression and, in extreme cases, to suicidal thoughts and behaviors.

A feeling of being special

Often people who are vain were treated as "special" by parents who overprotected and indulged them. As adults, they continue to expect this kind of treatment. Their attention is focused on nurturing and caring for themselves. They tend to involve other people in their self-nurturing and require numerous services, implicitly and explicitly demanding preferential treatment from relationship partners, family members, and coworkers.

Vain people believe that because they are special, they are not subject to death as other people are. Zilboorg (1943) described this defense of "specialness" as setting one apart from one's neighbors and giving one a feeling of immunity from death: "We must maintain within us the conviction that ... we, each one of us who speaks of himself in the first person singular, are exceptions whom death will not strike at all" (p. 468). For example, soldiers going into battle are familiar with the deep-seated conviction that the bullet will not hit them—their comrades may fall to the left and right, yet their life is charmed. In his novel, The Right Stuff, Thomas Wolfe (1983) described this defense as superstition accepted as fact: Test pilots who crashed obviously didn't have "the right stuff," that special combination of masculine strength, courage, and competence that guaranteed survival (R. Firestone, 1994b).[5]

Sense of entitlement

Attitudes of superiority and a sense of entitlement are a natural outgrowth of imagining that one is extraordinary (Raskin & Novacek, 1991). When people believe they are superior because of an unusual talent, good looks, high intelligence, or other singular traits, they anticipate deferential treatment from others. In their communications, these individuals state their opinions with absolute conviction, and make known their superior status and prestige through condescending, contemptuous remarks and a patronizing tone of voice. They make others feel belittled, disregarded, and disrespected. When their expectations of being catered to are not met, such people become angry and self-righteous and freely act out their irritability and aggression on others.

Characteristics of the narcissistic individual

Self-centered orientation

Narcissistic people have an exaggerated focus on their self-image with considerable cost to their relationships. The narcissist is exemplified by a popular joke regarding a conversation at a cocktail party. The narcissist says: "Well, that's enough talk about me, tell me something about yourself. What did you think of my latest book?" Narcissistic individuals tend to talk exclusively about their problems as well as their accomplishments and insist on having everything their own way. They are deeply involved in an inward process of self-consciously viewing themselves as objects, seeing themselves through the eyes of others. They have turned their eyes in on themselves rather than focusing their vision outward toward the world and others. This internal scrutiny or self-centeredness (different from self-love or genuine self-interest) leads to distortions of reality because narcissistic people are removed from themselves and their everyday experiences. Operating from a self-centered orientation, they give themselves approval and praise or reward themselves for success, while denigrating and castigating themselves for errors or failures. In a sense, they pat themselves on the head when they are "good" and punish themselves when they are "bad" as if they were their own parents (R. Firestone, 1997a).

In her book *Why Is It Always About You?*, Hotchkiss (2002) succinctly described the noxious characteristics of self-centered, narcissistic individuals:

> Their needs are more important than anyone else's, and they expect to be accommodated in all things. They can't

seem to see the bigger picture, or to comprehend why they might not always come first. Their expectations have an almost childlike quality, yet they can be tyrannically outraged or pitifully depressed when thwarted. Often, we give in to them because it seems safer not to rock their boat (p. xiv) The Narcissist we recognize as unhealthy is someone who, no matter what age, has not yet fully developed emotionally or morally (p. xvii).

Other writers (Lowen, 1985; Masterson, 1981; Morrison, 1989) have conjectured that narcissists long to be absolutely unique and strive to be of "sole importance to someone else, a 'significant other'" (Morrison, 1989, p. 48). This demand for uniqueness "is expressed directly, as assertions of entitlement; defensively, as haughty aloofness and grandiosity; or affectively, through dejected or rageful responses to its absence or failure. Inevitably, *shame* follows narcissistic defeat" (p. 49).

Social psychologists Exline, Baumeister, Bushman, Campbell, and Finkel (2004) have called attention to the fact that self-centeredness and the sense of entitlement that characterize narcissists are correlated with an inability to forgive, which is important for maintaining a fulfilling relationship. "Forgiveness is one response that can help restore interpersonal harmony after transgression" (p. 894). Studies have shown that forgiveness may be of benefit to the forgiver's mental and physical health. Exline, et al, found that "Entitled narcissists believe that their superiority entitles them to special treatment, and they are highly invested in asserting their rights and collecting on the debts owed to them" (p. 895).[6]

Lack of awareness of others

Narcissists are people who have a diminished ability to feel empathy for other people because of the specific damage they suffered as young children (N. Brown, 2001; Lowen, 1985; Ronningstam, 2005). They are unable to put themselves in another person's shoes, so to speak, and therefore are insensitive to the wants and needs of others. They find it difficult to read social cues and behavioral signals even of the people closest to them. They fail to notice that they are continually interrupting others, talking over them, and dominating conversations. For example, narcissists give advice, make unsolicited comments on a friend's appearance, speak for the other person, or argue with a partner about how the partner feels. According to Ronningstam (2005), the narcissist's "biased self-perception, egocentricity, and self-preoccupation interfere with the ability for perspective taking and emotional resonance. By nature, entitlement and the readiness for self-serving expectations in others are incompatible with empathy" (p. 95).[7]

Often, their violations of another person's boundaries are blatant. They may open their partner's mail, view his or her e-mail, or go through his or her wallet or purse without permission. Narcissists commit these and other more egregious boundary violations thoughtlessly and with a feeling of total entitlement. As Hotchkiss (2002) noted, "In a world without fences, why should they have to knock on doors?" (p. 30).

Charming, seductive and exploitive behaviors

Narcissists can be charming, charismatic and entertaining, yet they have little interest in other people except when a person can do something for them. Their families and associates suffer, not only from the narcissist's lack of feeling and interest but also from being exploited. Narcissists often seduce and manipulate an intimate partner through pronouncements of love, gifts, support, admiration, etc. Forward (1997) has described narcissistic individuals who use fear, guilt, and obligation to emotionally blackmail their loved ones. She contended that "tantalizers" are the "most subtle blackmailers. They encourage us and promise love or money or career advancement—the proverbial carrot at the end of the stick—and then make it clear that unless we behave as they want us to, we don't get the prize" (p. 34).

Hotchkiss (2002) pointed out that "exploitation can take many forms but always involves the using of others without regard for their feelings or interests" (p. 25). In family life, parents who are self-absorbed and inward are generally unaware that they are exploiting their offspring, yet many mothers and fathers attempt to live vicariously through their children, feed off their accomplishments or exploit them in other ways for their own purposes (A. Miller, 1997; Shengold, 1989). Forward (1989) has rightfully referred to these parents as "robbers of childhood."

In the workplace, narcissistic managers tend to be typically single-minded in the pursuit of power and recognition and misuse their subordinates' talents, skills and loyalty to the company. Hotchkiss (2002) described this as shameless exploitation, noting that "The practice of stretching employees until they break and then getting rid of them has become so common that it even has a name: 'rubber band management'" (p. 147).

Ethical implications—The aversive effects of vanity and narcissism

Effect on couple relationships

In everyday interactions, one can observe the disregard and disrespect with which vain or narcissistic individuals treat an intimate partner. In their relationships, which are often unequal, partners become polarized into parental/childish or superior/inferior roles. The vain partner acts out contemptuous, degrading attitudes on the other with little or no awareness.

> Recently, returning home from vacation, I (the first author) was disembarking from the plane and observed a couple walking in front of me. I recognized the man as a well-respected physician in my community and was appalled at the scene being acted out in front of me and the other passengers. The doctor's wife was loudly berating her husband for his "stupidity" in forgetting something or other that she "needed." Meanwhile he was struggling along, carrying all of their suitcases while she walked unencumbered. The pained expression on his face reflected the humiliation he must have felt at being belittled in front of strangers, yet he had no recourse. It was clear that silently suffering his narcissistic wife's abusive diatribes was a routine occurrence in this man's life. Although extreme, this example clearly points out the status differential acted out by narcissistic individuals as well as their unconscious self-centeredness and intrusiveness.

The character traits and behaviors exemplified by this narcissistic woman have long been recognized in the clinical and research literature. According to Campbell, Reeder, Sedikides, and Elliot (2000) who have conducted empirical studies in relation to narcissism:

> The present research is ... consistent with ... the assumption long-held in the clinical literature that narcissists have impaired interpersonal relationships as a result of their self-enhancement strategies ... . Self-enhancement is associated with a host of potentially destructive interpersonal behaviors, including bragging, competitiveness and hostility. Arguably, taking credit repeatedly from another will impede the maintenance and formation of relational closeness and satisfaction (p. 343).

In other relationship constellations, a partner's vanity works in concert with the other's build-up and praise, contributing to deterioration in the quality of relating, and often leading to the dissolution of the relationship. Male vanity and superiority, generally associated with "macho" attitudes and behavior, are common examples of this form of relating. These men ask for a build-up from women; they may implicitly demand that the women in their lives look up to them and defer to them. Whether the men deserve it or not, the women are expected to laugh at their jokes, praise their masculinity and acquiesce to their superior intelligence and practical wisdom. When men are dependent on women for this build-up, women can manipulate them by playing the other half of this game, to the detriment of both (Kernberg, 1995).[8]

The myth of male superiority is still prevalent in our culture despite advances toward equality due in large part to the women's movement (Bigler, 1999; C. Gilligan, 1996; L. Silverstein, Auerbach & Levant, 2002). Stereotypic views of male superiority in practical matters and strength, and female inferiority and weakness support these dynamics in marital relationships (Glick & Fiske, 2001; Reid & Bing, 2000).

Men sometimes reveal how their actions reflect attitudes of superiority and a corresponding belief in the inferiority of women. For example, in one of the group discussions we have mentioned, a man described how he routinely expected his wife to do his laundry, pack his lunch, and pick him up at the airport on his return from business trips. While talking about these habitual behaviors, he began to realize that he had shown little regard for his wife's interests or the importance of her time spent caring for the children and their home.

Another man disclosed the anger and irritability he acted out in relation to his wife when she contradicted him or took decisive action without fully consulting him.

Women have revealed how they sometimes play on their partner's need to preserve an image of exaggerated importance. A divorced woman admitted that during her marriage, she had built up her husband as part of an unconscious contract to ensure that he would take care of her.

> I knew how to make Bill feel like he was the most brilliant, creative person in the world. He had a huge amount of vanity about being a great businessman. I remember thinking to myself, "I can treat him like he's clever, resourceful, a real leader and he'll need me for that." I also knew that he would give me anything I wanted as long as I built him up, especially in the areas where he felt weak and that were really important to him. If I played my cards right, he would take me on business trips with him, register us in high-class hotels, and buy me expensive clothes and jewelry.
>
> I was aware of all the areas where he was weak and I knew that these were inroads. I knew I could create dependency in him. As the relationship went on, I hated him when he would say stupid, embarrassing things, when he would tell inane jokes, drop names of important people as though they were his best friends, or recite baseball statistics to show off his knowledge of sports when we were out with friends. Looking back on our marriage, I realize that I never once treated him like a person. I never gave him a chance to correct these irritating habits. I was completely involved in this manipulation and hated myself for it.

As Germaine Greer (1970/ 1971) commented:

> Every wife who slaves to ... build up his [her husband's] pride and confidence in himself at the expense of his sense of reality ... to encourage him to reject the consensus of opinion and find reassurance only in her arms is binding her mate to her with hoops of steel that will strangle them both. Every time a woman makes herself laugh at her husband's often-told

jokes she betrays him. The man who looks at his woman and says, "What would I do without you?" is already destroyed (p. 157).

Whenever an insecure man's ego is threatened—by the hint of infidelity, by his wife's attention being diverted to career, school, or child-rearing, or by a break in the flow of flattery or catering—he tends to feel rejected or abandoned and his underlying feelings of inferiority and self-hatred are exposed (Kernberg, 1995).

> As a child, Rick had been continuously praised by his mother for his musical ability. By scrimping and saving, his mother had managed to set aside money for piano lessons for him. As an adult, Rick started a band and became involved in the music business. However, his income was insufficient for his growing family. When his wife suggested that he try to find a second job to supplement his sparse income from his infrequent gigs and dwindling record sales, he went into a deep depression.
>
> For years Rick had imagined a bright future, telling himself that his next album would be a smash hit. He had convinced himself that he would soon receive wide recognition as well as financial success. His wife's implication that he wasn't adequately supporting his family completely demolished his image of himself as a great musician and destroyed his dreams of the future. Rick turned his rage against himself and unconsciously punished his wife by becoming sullen, depressed, and even less productive.

Withdrawing unrealistic support or indirectly attacking a man's inflated self-image can have far-reaching consequences (R. Firestone, 1985). For example; a woman's interest or lack of interest in sex exerts considerable leverage in a relationship especially when the man's overall sense of well-being is dependent on his partner's buildup. If the woman holds back her sexual response, her mate is confused, frustrated, and threatened in his basic feelings about himself as a man. If he is vain, his image of himself as a lover is weakened considerably by this unconscious manipulation on the part of his partner. In this way, many women are able to effectively control the couple's emotional life. The woman's fidelity is essential to safe-guarding male vanity. Any possibility of a comparison sexually or any hint of an attraction on the part of "his woman" to another man can arouse deep feelings of insecurity and self-hatred in a man.

Although some research (Foster, Campbell, & Twenge, 2003) has demonstrated that more men than women show narcissistic trends, vanity and narcissism are obviously not restricted to the masculine gender; both women and men can and do manipulate to control relationships. Many women are self-centered, with an exaggerated sense of self-importance and function in a manner that is insensitive to their husbands and children. Nevertheless, the pattern described above of male vanity and female manipulations through indirect means are cultural patterns to be noted.

According to Kernberg (1980, 1995), so-called "closet narcissists" (of either gender) who compensate for feelings of inferiority and low self-worth are drawn to the superficial charm and charisma of the "true" narcissist. They tend to gratify or "feed" their underdeveloped self by immersing themselves in the reflected glow of a narcissistic, self-important partner. The strategies and manipulations required to maintain this collusive arrangement damage each partner's sense of self as well as the relationship. Campbell, et al (2000) emphasized the "dearth of genuine love" (p. 330) in such relationships. In her book, *Narcissism and Intimacy*, M. Solomon (1989) described the dynamics underlying "narcissistic" relationships:

> When there is a history of narcissistic vulnerability, partners join together to protect themselves and each other from conflict. A collusive contract maintains the consistency of each person's perceptions. In that way, neither is forced to deal with overwhelming negative feelings about oneself. By masking pathology and blending it with the present intimate other, narcissistic collusion often creates merely a joyless semblance of safety and security, not a haven of comfort and love ... . Any change in the system reactivates defensive rather than adaptive mechanisms (p. 95).

As noted, individuals who are vain or narcissistic tend to act out compensatory behaviors designed to conceal an underlying sense of inferiority or their perceived negative qualities. However, utilizing the defense of vanity as a means of compensation perpetuates feelings of inferiority and a negative self-image.

Both men and women believe that being specially chosen or preferred over all other rivals somehow guarantees them immortality through being special. Many of society's conventions, mores and institutions support this myth of exclusive and enduring love. If this illusion is destroyed, there are dire consequences, and feelings of rage and depression surface. Couples who vow to "forsake all others" as a way of promising fidelity often also renounce old friends and systematically exclude new friends—potential rivals—to preserve this illusion that they are preferred.

Aversive effects of vanity and narcissism on the family

> All the blackmailers we've seen are focused almost totally on *their* needs, *their* desires; they don't seem to be the least bit interested in *our* needs or how their pressure is affecting us ... At the heart of any kind of blackmail is one basic threat, which can be expressed in many different ways: *If you don't behave the way I want you to, you will suffer* (Forward, 1997, p. 88).

Vanity or narcissism in one or more family members tends to reverberate throughout the entire family, affecting everyone. Within the family as in the couple, the narcissist needs another person or persons to mirror his or her image of goodness, omnipotence and superiority.

M. Solomon (1989) has explained why the self-centered person exploits his or her mate and/or children to fulfill this function: "There is ... the need of the narcissistically vulnerable to sustain a precarious self that is constantly in danger of fragmentation by having another present at all times to serve certain self-enhancing functions" (p. 43).

To varying degrees, most people are susceptible to emotional blackmail, manipulation, and exploitation on the part of narcissistic or vain family members who blatantly or subtly blackmail the others to get what they want. Forward (1997) has described narcissistic "emotional blackmailers" as fearful of being deprived of the attention, praise, and special treatment they desperately need. She asserted, "Often blackmailers' self-centeredness springs from a belief that the supply of attention and affection available to them is finite—and shrinking fast" (p. 89).

In general, the narcissist is detrimental to family life because he or she drains the emotional resources of other family members. The vain individual makes everyone feel inferior, small, useless and dispensable. Whether surrendering personal wants and needs to meet the demands of the narcissistic family member, or accepting the inferior status imposed on them, they lose a sense of integrity, and on some level, feel guilty for betraying themselves.

In one family, everyone's attention and emotions revolved around the mother, Amy, who completely controlled her husband and children in the service of her narcissism. Amy and Kirk had been married for twenty-two years and had two teenagers. Amy had been raised in Italy by a physically and emotionally abusive mother. Amy's vitality, natural attractiveness and liveliness were overshadowed by her insensitivity, self-centeredness and intrusiveness in relation to her husband and children.

In conversations, Amy was compelled to assert her view of reality and could tolerate no differences of opinion. She was "right" and everyone else was either wrong or ignorant. She tended to interrupt or stone-wall her husband at the first sign of disagreement from him. She made all the major family decisions and refused to even consider her husband's input. For his part, Kirk had long since given up venturing any of his opinions and had retreated into his own world of art and intellectual pursuits.

Over the years, Amy had succeeded in alienating her children with insensitive, intrusive behaviors that were blatant violations of their personal boundaries. For example, she could not resist constantly touching and stroking her 18-year-old daughter, Mary, even in public situations, despite the fact that Mary had repeatedly asked her to refrain from this behavior, had pointed out its inappropriateness, and had told her mother how "creepy" it made her feel. It seemed that Amy was unable to see her daughter as separate from herself nor could she accept that her daughter's feelings or opinions might be different from hers.

Finally, Kirk entered psychotherapy because of a worsening depression. After several months, feeling better and more self-confident, he began to speak up in conversations with Amy and express his point of view. His new strength threatened his wife and she rapidly deteriorated into a regressed state, reverting to crying and falling apart emotionally, in an attempt to regain her control. Kirk was not silenced by his wife's outbursts. This sent Amy into a downward spiral. She became increasingly possessive, jealous, and paranoid and eventually left her husband, returning to Italy, where she commiserated with her friends about her ordeal.

The dissolution of this family can be directly attributed to the pathological narcissism that became increasingly prominent in Amy's personality as family members refused to surrender to her control or failed to support her distorted view of reality. Amy's reactions to this break in the "loyalty" shown her by her family are similar to those described by M. Solomon (1989).

> When there is a prior history of narcissistic vulnerability and failure of the other to provide necessary emotional supplies, the result is that small arguments may cause an experience of fragmentation or emotional destruction—loss of ability to think clearly and a reaction of rage or total withdrawal (p. 47).

Manifestations of vanity and narcissism in child-rearing practices and their effects

Children suffer considerable psychological damage in early interactions with narcissistic, vain parents who tend to be emotionally unavailable or neglectful, and who therefore fail to meet the child's basic needs. Alice Miller (1997) wrote:

> In the first weeks and months of life he [the child] needs to have the mother at his disposal, must be able to avail himself of her and be mirrored by her. This is beautifully illustrated in one of Donald Winnicott's images: the mother gazes at the baby in her arms, and the baby gazes at his mother's face and finds himself therein ... provided that the mother is really looking at the unique, small, helpless being and not projecting her own expectations, fears, and plans for the child. In that case, the child would find not himself in his mother's face, but rather the

mother's own projections. This child would remain without a mirror, and for the rest of his life would be seeking this mirror in vain (p. 27).

In a similar vein, Masterson (1985) has emphasized that parental "mirroring" is necessary for the healthy emotional development of the self. The lack of parental mirroring can lead to a deficient self, feelings of emptiness and a compensatory narcissistic self-structure:

> This mirroring or matching process seems vital to the development of the real self ... . Failures in this parental function make an important contribution to the failure of the self's development and, therefore, to the production of a narcissistic or borderline personality disorder (p. 29).

Lowen (1985) has described vanity and narcissism as a compensation for parental rejection. He explained that these traits are part of the child's strong identification with the rejecting parent and an illusion of fusion that develops between the self-image of the child and the powerful parental image:

> Rejection is an intolerable situation for a child. In itself, the frustrated sense of being unlovable and the conclusion that it must be due to some fault or failure in oneself is devastating. The child sees no way out of this impossible position other than to accept the offer of specialness and intimacy. Acceptance amounts to almost total identification with the rejecting parent—an identification that represents the fusion of the self-image with the parental image ... . Its effect raises the child's ego to super-normal heights, inflating it to such a degree that it seems superhuman. Since the parent is god-like to a young child, this fusion of images endows the child's ego with a similar quality (p. 108).

A number of theorists have proposed that narcissism functions as a defense against the self-hatred and shame that arise when the child is not accepted for who he or she is (Bursten, 1973; Chasseguet-Smirgel, 1985; H. Lewis, 1987; Morrison, 1989). Shame is a primitive emotion that arises early in childhood, perhaps even before the child becomes verbal. It is a deep-seated sense that one is inherently deficient, "bad" or unlovable and is unable to change. Many people grow up feeling ashamed of their desire for affection, for wanting to be touched, loved, and really seen and understood by their parents. When they fail to have these basic needs fulfilled, they feel ashamed or humiliated. Later, they are desperate to cover up any signs they perceive in themselves that might indicate to other people that they are basically unacceptable.

Parental praise and other compensatory behaviors
To compensate for withholding loving responses or a lack of love and concern, parents often build up their children and exaggerate their importance. They teach their children to rely on strokes to their vanity; consequently, children learn to seek out special treatment and dishonest buildup in preference to real acknowledgment and positive regard. In addition, many parents also build themselves up in the child's eyes by demanding unearned respect and hero worship (R. Firestone, 1988).

Many parents are disappointed in their children for diverse reasons; for example, some feel disappointed when their newborn infant is not the gender they wanted or when the child has a temperament different from siblings or the parents. Consequently, they do not accept the child for the person he or she is. On some level, they feel guilty for this and substitute praise and flattery for the lack of loving, acknowledging responses.

If a child is not an outstanding scholar, the parents may offer reassurances implying untapped potential, or they may offer a buildup in other areas to compensate. If a narcissistic mother is dissatisfied with the looks of her daughter, she may constantly reassure the child that she is beautiful or exaggerate and overly praise other traits or talents in her daughter.

In general, the process of offering false praise and reassurances leads to increased efforts on the child's part to compensate for perceived inadequacies or weaknesses. This type of destructive or indulgent parenting sets the child up for subsequent disappointment and self-attacks. Individuals who have been treated in this manner tend to become overexcited by positive events but later become easily demoralized and self-critical. They are particularly sensitive to negative feedback or expressions of disapproval because it threatens their aggrandized self-image.

Attempts to build up a child's vanity often act as manipulations to maintain control and to limit independence. The child is left feeling inadequate and comes to need the false support, eventually becoming addicted to seeking admiration instead of love. Alice Miller (1997) has described the difficulties that the child encounters as an adult:

> Without therapy, it is impossible for the grandiose person to cut the tragic link between admiration and love. He seeks insatiably for admiration, of which he never gets enough because admiration is not the same thing as love. It is only a substitute gratification of the primary needs for respect, understanding, and being taken seriously—needs that have remained unconscious since early childhood. Often a whole life is devoted to this substitute (pp. 35–36).

Parental exploitation of the child

> The promise of specialness is the seductive lure put forward in the parent's effort to mold the child into his or her image of what the child should be (Lowen, 1985, p. 195).

In many cases, parents' exaggerated buildup of their child reflects their underlying desire or need to live vicariously through the child's accomplishments. Because many parents regard their offspring as an extension of themselves, they boast about their children's accomplishments as though they were their own. Vanity and the exaggerated sense of self-importance that is extended to children act to connect them to their parents. The child is not only left feeling dependent on the parental buildup, but also feels pressure to achieve in order to support the parents' vanity.

> Edith's father was completely captivated by his daughter and constantly doted on her. She was Daddy's precious girl, belonging only to him. At an early age, she became her father's special companion and routinely accompanied him to his office on the weekends he had to work. He boasted of her intelligence and beauty, and delighted in showing off his little protégé at piano performances he arranged, first for relatives and then for public recitals.

Unlike some children who are embarrassed by being exhibited in such an obvious manner, Edith loved the praise her father
lavished on her. To defend against her mother's critical, rejecting attitudes, Edith adopted her father's aggrandized attitudes
toward her.

As an adult, Edith constructed her world to protect her narcissistic position in life. She married a man who put her on a
pedestal and doted on her much as her father had. She became
a musical performer and teacher in her community. She dominated conversations with boastful accounts of her talents as a
musician and her contributions to her community. Her children
were well-indoctrinated and served as an in-house audience
and fan club for their mother.

In this example, a child is forced to turn to the only sustenance available, the heady praise and admiration offered by a parental figure, a
conditional "love" based on the child's ability to continue fulfilling
the narcissistic needs of this parent.

Projection of negative parental traits onto the child
Many parents dispose of their self-hatred and the qualities they
dislike in themselves by projecting them onto their child. In this
process, the child is basically used as a waste receptacle or dump-
ing ground (Bowen, 1978; Brazelton & Cramer, 1990; R. Firestone,
1990b, 1997a). In particular, parents who are vain find it necessary
to disown feelings of weakness or inferiority in themselves, perceiving and punishing them in their children instead. They use a
child in the service of maintaining their own superiority by treating
him or her with disrespect and condescension. In some instances,
the parent will make a scapegoat of the child, publicly humiliating
the child through ridicule, calling attention to the child's inadequacies or insinuating that there is something basically wrong with the
child. Each of these parental power plays exacerbates the child's
feelings of inferiority, powerlessness and shame.

Jill's mother, an extremely vain woman, was desperate to
preserve her illusion of superiority and omniscience, and Jill
was the perfect object for her purposes. Shy, soft-spoken, and
longing for love, she tried hard to believe her mother's fantastic

stories about the famous people she knew and the important positions in government she had held prior to marriage. Jill's mother exuded an air of certainty and proclaimed her knowledge on a wide range of subjects. She was known to lecture friends and acquaintances on any topic, including those in which the other person was an expert. She was prideful and shameless in her efforts to control conversations and the world around her.

At the same time, she continually dismissed Jill's feelings and thoughts as inconsequential or inane. She focused her attention on problems Jill encountered in learning to read, and informed her daughter, in her usual contemptuous, condescending tone of voice, that she probably had a learning disability and would never go to college as she had. For years afterward, Jill believed that she was stupid, even retarded.

As an adult, Jill had very little self-confidence and often second-guessed herself. She doubted her opinions, thoughts and feelings and found it difficult to make decisions. In therapy, Jill gained self-assurance and realized that she had been protecting her mother's image of superiority by never raising questions about what she considered to be somewhat delusional accounts of her mother's life. She knew that she was still idealizing her mother at her own expense by implicitly supporting the glorified, superior persona her mother projected.

Lawson (2000) in her book, *Understanding the Borderline Mother*, described "Queen Mothers" who "seek special treatment because they felt emotionally deprived as children" (p. 102). Like Jill's mother, "The Queen devalues those who do not provide gratification or special treatment" (p. 107). Concerning the delusional quality of the stories related by Jill's mother, Lowen (1985) has noted that many narcissistic parents have a precarious adjustment to reality:

> In my opinion, the underlying insanity of a narcissistic parent is more difficult for a child to handle than a parent's outright nervous breakdown. Of course, dealing with a breakdown is not easy, but in that situation the child knows who is crazy. With the narcissistic parent, the facade of sanity disturbs the child. As a child, how can one be sure of oneself, one's feelings, and

one's sensing in the face of a parent's arrogance and seeming certainty? (p. 144).

The effects of vanity and narcissism on the self

As noted, vain or narcissistic individuals are not only destructive to others, but hurtful to themselves as well. According to Kernberg (1975):

> Narcissistic patients not only seem to love themselves excessively, but do so in a rather poor, often self-demeaning way so that one concludes that these patients do not treat themselves better than the other people with whom they have relationships (p. 272).

For example, there is strong pressure to be perfect, to be beyond criticism and to maintain an idealized self-image. This sets the stage for feelings of failure, rejection and disillusionment. The feelings of powerlessness and inferiority that often follow must be defended against by redoubling efforts to bolster self-esteem and repair one's positive image of self.

When children are led to believe that great things are expected of them and are indulged or pampered by overpermissive parents, they eventually come to exaggerate their abilities and/or talents.

> Strangers often stopped Angela on the street and asked if she was a movie star. She often said that she had been cursed with being born beautiful. Angela suffered from severe anxiety attacks. When she entered therapy, she had an affected manner of speaking and was almost completely cut off from her feelings; at the same time, she was extremely anxious, often physically ill, and frightened. Her doctor had advised that she breathe into a paper bag when she was hyperventilating during a panic attack. She had paper bags in every room of her house, and never went anywhere without them. In her first session, she said, "I'm scared all the time and I think that I'm really going crazy. I don't even know who I am. I can't seem to feel anything, only afraid. I can't stand this."

As a child, Angela had been envied and hated by her female peers. She said, "The other girls just stopped speaking to me somewhere in junior high school, and I felt miserable and unpopular. I couldn't wait to get out of high school. My mother's explanation was 'You're a very special person because of the way that you look. People just have to treat you differently. Men will always want you and women will always hate you—you're a very pretty girl.'"

"I really resent everybody's focus on me. My husband has always been very attentive to me. Now with my anxiety attacks, he won't leave me alone; he keeps crowding me even more. Lately I'm scared all of the time and even though I feel bugged by him, I don't want to be alone any more. I don't know what I feel. I can't seem to feel the things other people do. But I used to a long time ago. If only I could cry or even feel sad. I just get very afraid and feel very cold like I'm cut off from everyone."

Angela had never been responded to as a real person. Her beauty was real and unusual, but her interactions with the people in her interpersonal world were unreal and exploitive. As a result, she had come to believe that her beauty was her only valuable quality. She existed as an empty, beautiful shell covering an inner world of fear and weakness. Until she sought professional help, she had only received the kind of exaggerated attention and special treatment that caused her to feel empty and depressed.

In therapy she was responded to for herself for the first time in her life. Because this was in contrast to her past and current experiences, her therapy was a long and stormy process. Over time, she was able to confront the underlying feelings of sadness her vanity had been masking.

A. Miller (1997) has described the sadness and grief often experienced by depressed, grandiose patients as they improve in psychotherapy. "Because grandiosity is the counterpart of depression *within* the narcissistic disturbance, the achievement of the freedom from *both* forms of disturbance is hardly possible without deeply felt mourning about the situation of the former child" (p. 60).

The effects of vanity and narcissism on the business world

> Among the personalities that present problems for society in
> general and for the corporate world in particular are *narcissism,*
> *Machiavellianiam,* and *psychopathy* ... sometimes referred to col-
> lectively as the *dark triad* (Babiak and Hare, 2006, p. 124).

Perhaps the most common personality types to be found in the
world of business are those that could be categorized as vain
and/or narcissistic. The ambition and driving need to excel and
achieve more than competitors are typical of many high-powered
sales people and executives, and these traits are sometimes advantageous in achieving the bottom line. However, as Collins (2001)
stressed in *Good to Great: Why Some Companies Make the Leap ... and
Others Don't,* vanity and narcissism, self-centeredness, superiority, condescension, a focus on image, and the demand for special
treatment did not characterize the leaders of the exceptional companies that made the leap from being good companies to being
great.

Collins analyzed factors that enabled a select few, only eleven,
large "good" companies to transform themselves into extraordinarily successful "great" companies. He was impressed that the CEO's
of these companies were noticeably lacking in vanity and egotism:

> We were struck by how the good-to-great leaders *didn't* talk
> about themselves ... . [They] never wanted to become larger-
> than-life heroes. They never aspired to be put on a pedestal or
> become unreachable icons. They were seemingly ordinary peo-
> ple quietly producing extraordinary results (pp. 27–28).

In his study, Collins also interviewed leaders of the comparison companies, mediocre firms and those that were failing. He discovered
that "In over two-thirds of the comparison cases, we noted the presence of a gargantuan personal ego that contributed to the demise or
continued mediocrity of the company" (p. 29).

The first author (R. W. Firestone) feels that the lack of vanity
in these powerful leaders played a significant part in their unusual success because they were single-minded in their focus on
their work projects rather than on seeking acclaim. In fact, vanity

and narcissism are toxic personality traits that contribute to low productivity and business reversals.

I was personally involved in a successful business venture that became a multi-million-dollar corporation. The original entrepreneurs had a simple, respectful approach to their employees, management team, and to people in general. There was a positive concern for the sales people and staff, a lack of politicking, no hidden information and no surplus power or status on the part of management. People did their jobs and were well-paid in proportion to their contribution to the overall success of the venture. There was a sense of equality, sharing, and an extremely high morale.

Eventually the company became a public corporation. The top people were bought out or retired, and the original management was replaced by a new group of executives. The new leadership, composed of "big corporative types," was vain and superior, scoffed at the old regime and talked of bringing a new vision to the company. The CEO acted in a condescending manner toward the top salesperson in the company, a petite, energetic young woman with no formal business training. He overlooked the fact that she and her team had brought in twenty million dollars in revenues the previous year. He said that he had "important plans" and informed her that she wasn't sophisticated enough to meet with top executives from other large corporations. "There are big deals to be made," he sarcastically told her. "Don't make the mistake of thinking that you're indispensable. You've got to realize that if you were dead and gone, almost anybody else could do your job." Of course, the woman felt insulted and demeaned, and actually lost confidence in herself. She became increasingly miserable at work and finally left the company.

Similarly, the new managers were insensitive and disrespectful to the people and programs that were contributing to the bottom-line profit. They formulated a grandiose plan that never materialized or produced profit, and focused on the development of a story that would increase the stock price. The top sales people's commissions were cut, causing many of the best people to leave. Hardworking people who made the company work were denigrated and replaced by high-level middle management, creating inefficiency and unnecessarily high expenses. The original atmosphere characterized by free-flowing camaraderie was replaced by an environment which valued form, status and excessive authority. As a result, profits declined steadily from a twenty-plus-million dollar net to the present state in which millions of dollars are being lost each quarter, more than forty million in cash assets have been used up in the process, and the most productive people have resigned. The company is at present on its last legs.

Nothing is more damaging in the business world than leadership characterized by narcissism and vanity. Business success, which requires common sense, good judgment, and rationality even more than technical expertise and training, is compromised by managers whose vanity impedes this focus or ability.

This company did not fail because of a major change in the industry; many of its defectors, unsatisfied with the changes or forced out by the new policies, went on to achieve business success in the same industry. Vanity on the part of the new management, and a false sense of omnipotence blinded the leadership to the realities of what made the company successful in the first place. Furthermore, the leadership refused to recognize the futility of its master plan. They were resistant to criticism, insensitive and demeaning to people who they saw as inferior, blaming others and outside conditions for their failure. They basically lost a realistic perspective.

In this example, vanity not only sabotaged the project, but hurt people as well. The company's initial rise to success benefited many people, both practically and personally. People thrived in the positive atmosphere and developed themselves in the social milieu surrounding the business. These benefits were lost in the takeover. To varying degrees, vanity and narcissism deprived the leadership of their sensitivity, their humanness and their good judgment, while at the same time caused the employees to feel belittled, hurt and hostile.

As Christopher Lasch (1979) argued in his classic critique of modern society, *The Culture of Narcissism:*

> For the corporate manager on the make, power consists not of money and influence but of "momentum," a "winning image," a reputation as a winner. Power lies in the eye of the beholder

and thus has no objective reference at all. The manager's view of the world … is that of the narcissist, who sees the world as a mirror of himself and has no interest in external events except as they throw back a reflection of his own image (pp. 46–47).

The effects of vanity and narcissism on society-at-large

Narcissism and vanity have numerous social implications. As in the business world, their aversive effects extend into the culture and, in turn, have a destructive impact on each member of the larger society. As noted earlier, the defenses of individual members of a society combine to produce cultural attitudes, social mores, and institutions. These cultural attitudes and institutions, in turn, act back on each member of the society in the form of negative social pressure, interfering with individuals' movement toward individuation and depriving them of vital experiences necessary for pursuing personal freedom and reaching their true potential (Billig, 1987; R. Firestone, 1985; Henry, 1963; Lasch, 1979; Marcuse, 1955/1966; Mead, 1934/1967).[9]

On a simple level, one can observe manifestations of narcissism and vanity in the society-at-large. For example, the media inundates us with images of beautiful, pencil-thin women and exceptionally good-looking men designed to foster and reinforce the tendency to focus on appearance over more important personal qualities. We are encouraged to consume a meaningless series of commodities that we are conditioned to need, despite the fact that most of them are addictive, trivial, or useful only for enhancing an unreal image of ourselves. As Lasch (1979) emphasized:

> Bureaucracy, however, is only one of a number of social influences that are bringing a narcissistic type of personality organization into greater and greater prominence. Another such influence is the mechanical reproduction of culture, the proliferation of visual and audial images in the "society of the spectacle." We live in a swirl of images and echoes that arrest experience and play it back in slow motion (p. 47).

People who are vain or narcissistic tend to aggrandize their families, their neighborhood, and their nation. The sense of specialness that imbues vain individuals with a feeling of being immune to death is also manifested on a societal level. Once an individual strongly identifies with a particular religion, ethnic or cultural group and utilizes it as a defense against death anxiety, anyone who lives differently, thinks differently, or has different religious beliefs threatens his or her sense of being special and therefore exempt from death. The fear aroused can lead to an aggressive reaction, and this aggression often escalates into violence and actual warfare, nation against nation.

Conclusion

Feelings of specialness or exaggerated self-importance are symptomatic of a fragile adjustment to reality and a deficient sense of self. Maintaining vanity is stressful, drains the energy and vitality of the individual, and is harmful to others as well. When these fantasized images of self are shattered by an objective appraisal, failure, or direct competition with a rival, the underlying feelings of self-depreciation and shame invariably surface. This leads to reactions of narcissistic rage that, when acted out on other people, are extremely destructive to self and others.

From an ethical point of view, the aversive effects of a vain or narcissistic person can be readily observed in couples, families, child-rearing, business, and in the larger society where they have profound implications on the international scene. History has repeatedly demonstrated that vanity and a sense of omnipotence in charismatic, narcissistic leaders often set the stage for ethnic cleansing and warfare. Millions of innocent people are threatened by destructive actions taken by leaders and their followers when they adopt a superior, omnipotent posture and direct their animosity toward specific peoples, groups or nations.

Notes

1. See Kernberg (1975) who further clarified the meaning of "image" rather than self in this context: "Pathological narcissism does not simply reflect libidinal investments in the self in contrast to libidinal investments in objects, but libidinal investments in a *pathological self structure*" [italics added] (p. 271).
2. The personality traits that characterize the narcissistic individual range along a continuum from mild to severe in terms of the degree

of impairment of personality functioning and interference with interpersonal relating. See Kernberg's (1975) chapter, "Normal and Pathological Narcissism," in which he describes several types of pathological narcissism, ranging from the temporary decrease of libidinal investment of the self due to pathological mourning to "severe type of narcissistic pathology [which] is characterized by a more profound determination of object relations ... between a primitive, pathological, grandiose self and the temporary projection of that same grandiose self onto objects" (p. 325).

3. Raskin and Terry (1988) noted that "Narcissism was first introduced into psychological literature in 1898, when Havelock Ellis used the term *Narcissus*-like to refer to a tendency for the sexual emotions to be lost and almost entirely absorbed in self admiration" (p. 890). Freud (1935) differentiated between the concepts of narcissism and egoism: "A man may be absolutely egoistic and yet have strong libidinal attachments to objects ... [Or] A man may be egoistic and at the same time strongly narcissistic (i.e. feel very little need for objects) ... . In all these situations egoism is the self-evident, the constant element, and narcissism the variable one" (p. 361). Also see Hotchkiss (2002) who described elements of both vanity and narcissism in her description of narcissist individuals.

4. Morey and Jones (1998) listed the first criterion or Narcissistic Personality Disorder (NPD) as "1. Inflated self-esteem with marked affective reactions (such as rage or depression) to assaults on this self-esteem. The inflated self-esteem reflects a core trait of NPD and in itself reflects a distinguishing characteristic from borderline personality disorder" (p. 370). Also see Millon's (1998) typology of narcissistic subtypes arranged along a continuum, as discussed by Ronningstam (2005).

5. Ernest Becker (1973/1997) put it this way: "This narcissism is what keeps men marching into point-blank fire in wars: at heart one doesn't feel that *he* will die, he only feels sorry for the man next to him" (p. 2).

6. Re: narcissism, vanity, high self-esteem, and egotism, Baumeister (1997) defined egotism as "thinking well of yourself (regardless of whether those thoughts are justified or not)" (p. 25). In some of his earlier writing, Baumeister tended to use "egotism" (inflated self-esteem or vanity) interchangeably with "high self-esteem." More recently, he clarified the term "egotism," distinguishing it from "healthy self-esteem." Writing about egotism, he asserted: "people whose self-esteem is high but lacks a firm basis in genuine accomplishment are especially prone to be violent" (p. 25). Also see Vohs

and Heatherton's (2003) article "The Effects of Self-Esteem and Ego Threat on Interpersonal Appraisals of Men and Women: A Naturalistic Study."

7. Ronningstam (2005) cited findings from Fonagy, Gergely, Jurist, and Target (2002) that have helped uncover the "neuropsychological origins of limited empathic processing located in the amygdale and orbital frontal cortex" (p. 95). In addition, she called attention to Schore's (1994) research showing that low affect tolerance (symptomatic of many narcissists) is incompatible with empathic processing.

8. See *Love Relations* (Kernberg, 1995) for an in-depth description of the diverse patterns that can be found in couple relationships formed by narcissistic individuals: "Most frequently, the narcissistic personality enacts his or her pathological grandiose self while projecting a devalued part of the self on to the partner, whose unending admiration confirms that grandiose self" (p. 150).

9. Interestingly, studies have shown that people living in highly individualistic societies report higher levels of self-esteem (inflated self-esteem) than do people living in more collectivistic, group-oriented societies (Foster, et al, 2003).

PART V
ETHICAL AND UNETHICAL
SOCIETAL PRACTICES

CHAPTER TWELVE

The ethics of leadership

> Managements of all institutions are responsible for their by-products, that is, the impacts of their legitimate activities on people and on the physical and social environment. They are increasingly expected to anticipate and to resolve social problems ... What are the tasks? What are the opportunities? What are the limitations? And what are the ethics of leadership for the manager who is a leader but not a master?
>
> Peter F. Drucker (1985, p. 312)

Leadership is essential to any group or organization. It helps coordinate people and projects, creates efficiency, and avoids chaos and confusion. Even a small group of people with like minds and common goals needs organization and direction to make important decisions. Effective leaders are quick to make decisions and to take action, thereby facilitating the accomplishment of such goals. For example, in sailing the high seas, and especially during storm conditions or other emergencies, crew members require the leadership of a captain, one person who takes responsibility for making immediate, and, at times, life-or-death decisions. In this situation, as in many others, good leadership is prized, whereas bad leadership can be detrimental or even disastrous.

Warren Bennis (2007) stressed the importance of leadership in asserting that "In the best of times, we tend to forget how urgent the study of leadership is. But leadership always matters, and it has never mattered more than it does now" (p. 2). In light of this statement, it is disconcerting to note the dearth of literature on the topic of leadership in the field of psychology. Robert Sternberg (2007a) addressed this concern in a Foreword to a Special Issue on Leadership in the *American Psychologist*.

> Despite its importance to the United States and the world, leadership has not been a leading topic in the field of psychology. Most psychology departments have no one doing research directly bearing on leadership ... . Introductory psychology textbooks generally do not have a chapter on or even cover leadership ... . The result of this situation is that many students of psychology are relatively unfamiliar with the literature on leadership (p. 1).

Leadership is a multidimensional concept that may or may not have positive ethical implications (Adler, 2002; Galbraith, 1983; Gandz, 2007; Winston & Patterson, 2006).[1] The basic qualities that contribute to outstanding leadership potential—charisma, competence, integrity and authenticity, a creative vision or goal, high energy level, and even a sincere desire to serve people—are essentially neutral in relation to ethical considerations. Leadership and the effect that leaders have on the people they influence can be assessed from two perspectives (1) Pragmatic: Is the leader effective in achieving certain prescribed goals? (2) Ethical or moral: Does the leader meet appropriate standards of responsibility and compassion in regard to human concerns? The question of morality or ethics applies to both the means employed by the leader and to the end results (Kouzes & Posner, 2007).

When analyzed from a purely pragmatic standpoint, the characteristics which make a leader effective involve the ability to motivate others to implement one's will and move toward the successful fulfillment of specific goals in the personal, business or political arenas (Collins, 2001; Kellerman, 2004).[2] By generating profits, gratifying shareholders, or furthering the desires, needs, and political agendas of his or her constituents, an individual would meet the pragmatic requirements for being an effective leader.

Despite the fact that an individual might possess the qualities of an effective leader, his or her leadership may still be immoral or unethical (Lipman-Blumen, 2005). These qualities, which make a leader successful pragmatically, while admirable in their own right, might be used to accomplish destructive goals or might be acted upon in a manner that is autocratic, demeaning, or demoralizing to others.

The ethical or moral position of any leader can be ascertained by answering a fundamental question: Does the leader meet the needs of his or her followers without causing harm to people either inside or outside the group or organization? As an admittedly extreme example, if appraised solely from a pragmatic point of view, Hitler, Stalin, and Mao Ze-dong could be categorized as effective leaders who had idealistic visions, yet their actions led to heinous crimes against humankind. In evaluating leaders from an ethical perspective, one must consider whether their words and actions reflect a humanistic, empathic attitude toward all people, and whether the means they employ as well as the end results ultimately do no harm.

In this section, the authors discuss the components that comprise effective leadership and those that satisfy the criteria for ethical leadership. We describe the characteristics of destructive, unethical leaders and analyze their harmful effects on business enterprises, government institutions, political decision-making, and on society-at-large. In our analysis, we emphasize that the psychological make-up of the leader is crucial in determining whether the leadership is effective or ineffective, ethical or unethical. We then explore the personality traits of the members of a "good" as well as a "bad" followership and examine the dynamics of the interaction between leaders and their followers. We provide an analysis of the paradoxical reality that destructive leaders attract and retain the loyalty of so many people.

Characteristics of effective leaders

Competence

Competence is highly valued in a leader. Competence represents a combination of the necessary skill for completing the project and the ability to exercise that skill freely and powerfully. The capable leader has a positive effect on the overall project because people tend to feel more secure when led by a person they perceive as skilled and knowledgeable in his or her area of expertise.[3]

Vision

The efficient leader possesses a guiding vision of what he or she wishes to accomplish as well as a driving passion to bring that vision to fruition. Adler (2002) wrote that "vision can be defined as an inspired, long-run strategy that is not obvious to managers and executives until it is revealed by the transformational leader" (Big Leadership Section, para. 5). In *Ethics, The Heart of Leadership*, James Burns (2004) extended Adler's definition of "vision" to encompass political and social change:

> We think of vision as an overarching, evocative, energizing, moralizing force, ranging from broad, almost architectural plans for a new industry, say, to an inspirational, spiritual, per-haps morally righteous evocation of future hopes and expecta-tions for a new political movement (p. xi).

Ability to inspire others

Having a guiding vision would count for little if a leader were una-ble to inspire others to share this vision and work toward its reali-zation (Bennis, 2003; Gandz, 2000). According to Hesselbein (2002), the good leader focuses on *"how to be*—how to develop quality, character, mind-set, values, principles, and courage ... . This 'how to be' leader holds forth the vision of the organization's future in compelling ways that ignite the spark needed to build the inclusive enterprise" (p. 8).[4] Harvard Business Essentials (2005), borrowing a well-known phrase from Thomas Jefferson, pointed out that lead-ers need to speak to the head *and* to the heart of followers in order to inspire them to work toward a shared goal.[5] Margaret Wheatley (Spears, 2004b) described still another important leadership quality that is needed to motivate others to implement one's vision:

> Once you have a clear vision you have to free people up. This is where autonomy comes in. People need to be free to make sense

of the vision according to their own understandings and their own sensitivity to what's needed. If you combine the sense of great purpose and human freedom, if you can combine a vision that brings out the best of who we are and then gives us the freedom in how we're going to express that, that is how things work, in my experience (p. 256).

Authenticity and energy

Leaders who are authentic and sincere are able to inspire others to follow them because they are perceived as genuine and truthful. The absence of phoniness, superficiality, and hypocrisy in the leaders' personalities relieves people of much of the suspicion and cynicism they might otherwise feel toward an authority figure. In addition, the excitement, passion, and energy of an effective leader are contagious; these qualities tend to generate a corresponding excitement in others, inspiring them to work hard and take pride in their own contributions to the overall project (Moxley, 2000).[6]

Action-oriented approach

Effective leaders are active and highly competitive, not simply for the sake of being competitive, but in the pursuit of their goals. Rather than inspiring cut-throat competitiveness, they focus on striving for excellence. These individuals tend to be wholly committed to whatever endeavor they are involved in, with an emphasis on implementing actions to get things done (Covey, 1999). They do not waste time fantasizing about the results they hope to achieve nor do they spend too much time in detailed or elaborate planning. Instead they are eager and even impatient to translate an abstract vision into concrete action (Nohria & Berkley, 1994/1998).

A willingness to take risks and the ability to be decisive are characteristic of action-oriented individuals. When necessary, these leaders choose to take action rather than wait until all the possible information has been gathered. They have a fundamental self-confidence or trust in their ideas and their point of view that enables them to be decisive based on the amount of information that is available at the time. Moreover, the effective leader is able to judge how much information is essential before making an important decision.[7]

Foresight

The good leader has the ability to sense what lies ahead, to perceive opportunities that should be the target of action, and to see threats before they materialize (Farkas & Wetlaufer, 1996/1998).[8] Leaders must be familiar with the context—the social, political, and economic background—in which their organization is embedded. Many business leaders, although highly successful in growing and maintaining a healthy company, fall short when economic or political changes occur.

Integrity

Leaders who have integrity are those whose actions correspond to their words and are thereby able to inspire trust in others. Integrity is perhaps the most important characteristic that an effective leader needs to possess or develop (Bennis, 2003; Collins, 2001; Senge, Kleiner, Roberts, Ross & Smith, 1994). The absence of duplicity, an important aspect of integrity, is necessary for effective leadership. Integrity, as defined in broader terms, that is, as being true to oneself and one's values, including a deep respect for all human beings, is necessary for a leadership that is both ethical and effective.

Characteristics of ethical leaders

According to a majority of social theorists, political scientists, and business management experts, "great" leaders possess ethical principles, have a strong moral compass, and consistently attempt to do the "right" thing and be the "right" kind of person. Throughout her work, Hesselbein (2002) has emphasized that "It is the quality and the character of the leader that determines the performance [and] the results" (p. 3). And in his advice to potential leaders, Bennis (2004) cautioned, "The most important thing to keep in mind is this: *Never let your ambition surpass your moral compass*" (p. xiv).

Ethical leaders conduct their professional and personal lives according to an internal system of values and moral principles, and therefore function as positive role models for their employees (Bennis, 2003; Collins, 2001; Gandz, 2005). They have integrity in that their actions correspond not only to their words but also to human values that transcend the fulfillment of their own goals or the goals of their organization. Thus, integrity, in its broadest meaning, is a personality trait that must be assessed from both an ethical and a pragmatic point of view.

Emotional maturity: The ability to integrate emotions and rational thought

Ethical leaders are emotionally mature, fully adult in their orientation, and take responsibility for their own well-being. They approach problems from an independent or interdependent stance and do not rely on subordinates to solve core problems for them. They have an intuitive sense of what others need, based on their ability to remain close to their own feelings (Badaracco, 1998/2003; Goleman, Boyatzis & McKee, 2002).

The more authority and responsibility one attains in rising to a higher leadership position, the more dependent on others one is to adequately fulfill one's own functions. Similarly, the more elevated the position, the more responsible a leader is for the end results, regardless of whether others succeed or fail at their tasks. Therefore, good leaders are not only capable of trusting and relying on others; they also accept full responsibility for the outcome, without blaming others (Andrews, 1989/2003; McCoy, 1997/2003).

One indication of a mature outlook in a leader is the ability to integrate emotional responses and intellectual understanding in relation to solving problems quickly and decisively. According to Gardner (1990), "To analyze complex problems, leaders must have a capacity for rational problem solving; but they must also have a penetrating intuitive grasp of the needs and moods of followers" (p. 29). The ability of leaders to grasp the needs and moods of their followers indicates that they are aware of their own feelings, feel compassion for others, and have an empathic understanding of the dreams and desires of their followers, including their desire or need to be led (Farkas & Wetlaufer, 1996/1998). Winston and Patterson (2006) described mature leaders as having insight, that is, "the ability to grasp the true nature of a situation" (p. 12). They contended that good leaders also possess intuition, which they defined as "the act of knowing or sensing without the use of rational processes" (p. 13).

A lack of vanity and narcissism

Narcissism and vanity are characteristics that often show up in those individuals who are drawn to seeking leadership positions (Babiak & Hare, 2006; Post, 2004). As McCallum (2000) pointed out, "Egotism is one of the most counterproductive personal qualities an executive can bring to the table" (Self-Reverence section, para. 7). In contrast, the absence of egotism and narcissism in a leader is vital to the smooth operation of an organization or effective diplomacy in international relations. Leaders who are not self-centered or vain tend to inspire positive feeling and cooperation rather than anger or defiance.

As noted in the previous chapter, in an in-depth investigation of leadership in the business world, Collins (2001) found that only eleven companies of the Fortune 500 met the criteria for being "great" organizations. Collins observed a conspicuous lack of vanity in the executives in the eleven "great corporations" that he studied. His analysis revealed that "great leaders" had tremendous ambition that "was first and foremost for the company and concern for *its* success rather than for one's own riches or personal renown" (pp. 25–26). Another indication of the effective leaders' lack of vanity was that Level 5 (great) leaders:

> want to see the company even more successful in the next gen-
> eration, comfortable with the idea that most people won't even
> know that the roots of that success trace back to their efforts … .
> In contrast, the comparison leaders, concerned more with their
> own reputation for personal greatness, often failed to set the
> company up for success in the next generation (pp. 25–26).

It was apparent in Collins' study that the "great leaders," those who were not vain or egocentric, had a beneficial rather than a destructive effect on the morale, vitality, and initiative of the people within their companies.

Winston and Patterson (2006) have also described good leaders as being relatively free of egotism or vanity, and as having "a sense of confidence that removes the fear that so often prevents the leader from being humble" (p. 11). Furthermore, ethical leaders have generally developed considerable self-knowledge about their positive and negative traits and are receptive to outside criticism, using the information to improve their performance. Their lack of vanity and realistic self-appraisal contribute to their openness in relation to negative feedback, which in turn facilitates improved productivity and trust on the part of associates and employees (Goleman, et al, 2002).[9]

Appreciation of the uniqueness and humanity of each individual

In addition to possessing a compassionate understanding of one-self and others, the ethical leader would have an appreciation of the human condition, emphasize the equality of all people, and have an all-inclusive philosophical view that "We're all in the same boat." In this regard, Hesselbein (2002) has called attention to a growing trend in the business world: a movement away from "the 'tough' leaders of the past," and toward "leaders who demonstrate in language and behavior their appreciation and respect for the men and women of the enterprise" (p. 31).

Ethical leaders are respectful and tolerant of the divergent opinions and beliefs of their followers. They do not denigrate or abase others, but affirm the individuality of each person, while inspiring harmonious relationships among those they lead (Drucker, 1998). Winston and Patterson (2006) have noted that the "great" or ethical leader "recognizes the diversity of the follower(s) and achieves unity of common values and directions without destroying the uniqueness of the person" (p. 8).

The desire to serve

"Great" leaders possess a strong desire to be of service to others. However, this service orientation is not limited to the specific group, but is all-inclusive, extending to people outside of the organization (Greenleaf, 1991; Hesselbein, 2002). In contrast, many political leaders may be of service to those who elected them to office, extending them special favors, but at the same time, they may disregard the humanity and the needs of citizens or segments of the population that did not vote for them.

Valuing the means as well as the end

Good leaders take into consideration the means as well as the ends when applying their ideology to social and economic problems.

In evaluating a political system one must consider the morality of the methods by which that system attempts to accomplish its goals. For example, the underlying theory of Communism was idealistic in its goal of achieving a "workers' paradise," yet in practice it led to a fascist dictatorship, oppression, and imprisonment and death for dissenters (Radzinsky, 1996).

Teachers as ethical leaders

Inspirational teachers and educators have played important roles as ethical leaders at crucial periods throughout history. By inspiring others to think creatively about life and to develop new ideas and a fresh perspective on the world, they have generated a revolution of ideas that has had positive effects on humankind. Mahatma Gandhi, Martin Luther King, Jr., Anwar Sadat, the Dalai Lama, and numerous other teachers and gurus have made a significant difference in the lives of their students and have also provided the impetus for broad social movements that have advanced human rights issues for multitudes of people.

In summary, Gandz (2007) has described great leaders as possessing a combination of seemingly opposite personality traits. A truly great leader is "confident *and* humble, assertive *and* patient, analytical *and* intuitive, deliberate *and* decisive, principled *and* pragmatic" (Good as effective section, para. 3). "Principled and pragmatic" are two significant criteria that the authors have used to evaluate leaders along the lines of their adherence to ethical principles and their effectiveness.

Leadership in the friendship circle

As noted previously, leadership in evolutionary terms is related to competence in coping with the exigencies of life on a survival level and to planning for the future of an organization. Leaders are valued for their skills in tasks related to maintaining and protecting the survival of a particular group or community. The most highly regarded individuals in the friendship circle have become leaders for several reasons. In this group of friends, there are four major areas in which people have assumed powerful leadership roles: sailing, business, psychological insightfulness, and overall character.

Steve is an individual whose personal qualities and leadership skills embody most, if not all, of the characteristics of effective and ethical leaders described in this chapter.

When Steve was sixteen, he was already demonstrating considerable leadership potential. He was elected by his peers to be captain of a large schooner that sailed around the world, successfully completing the 17-month voyage. On his return home, Steve became involved in a fledgling business enterprise. He rapidly rose to a leadership position, became president of one of the companies, and later founded a real estate investment firm that has enjoyed significant financial success for over a decade.

Early on, Steve epitomized specific qualities that were widely admired by the young people as well as the adults. During the voyage, he was highly competent in strategizing and sailing. He had a calming influence on crew members during harrowing storm conditions. Even in competing for the captaincy, he solicited criticism regarding his leadership style and the ways he delegated the work load aboard ship. He worked alongside his fellow crew members doing maintenance on the boat and expected no special treatment or perks because of his position.

In the process of competing for the captainship, Steve expressed no degrading or belittling feelings or attitudes toward his rivals. Moreover, his openness and receptivity to constructive criticism served him well. The early years at sea and his initial experiences in the business world provided a crucible for his personal development, which was fundamental to his ultimate election as chairman of a committee of 12 men and women who were selected to address the practical concerns and the quality of life in the friendship circle. Committee meetings are open to all members of the community: adults and young people alike participate as vigorously as the elected members. Issues that must be decided by a vote are voted on by everyone.

Steve, like the other elected committee members, is among those who are most representative of the group's values and goals. He is honest, compassionate, generous, and devoted to the well-being of the overall group goals and priorities.

His service to people is unselfish and devoid of vanity, and he seeks no approval, no outside reward, or status for his contribution.

In recent years, Steve has become increasingly interested in the welfare of individuals in the friendship circle, both economically and psychologically. He is actively involved in issues related to people's financial needs. Together with the other committee members, he helps assess the common needs of the members, helps determine how much each person will contribute based on a sliding scale, and supervises the money that is jointly spent. In the area of psychology, Steve has an exceptional understanding, sensitivity, and insight into people and human behavior. He is available to talk with anyone who is experiencing difficulty at work or with personal issues.

The key to Steve's leadership is service: planning trips and schedules, settling disputes, evaluating and taking initiative in new business ventures, supervising the maintenance of the boats and captaining the vessels, generously contributing money, and guiding and inspiring members and employees in maintaining and developing the groups' assets. In all of these activities, his management style is friendly, respectful, modest, and compassionate. He works long hours at community service and the rewards are not monetary but personal: he is loved and respected by his friends and associates.

In relation to leadership, the friendship circle is constantly self-monitoring, reviewing practices and scrutinizing itself to determine any inequities or unfairness. Criticism is always welcome and there are group talks in which one can voice dissatisfactions with any of the systems politic.

Ethical leadership in business

the invention of organization as society's tool for accomplishing social purposes may well be as important to the history of man as was the invention of the specialization of labor for individuals ten thousand years ago. And the principle underlying it is … *personal strengths make social benefits* … . This is a moral principle on which authority can be based. [The manager] must accept the moral responsibility of organization, the responsibility of making individual strengths productive and achieving (Drucker, 1985, pp. 810–811).

As Peter Drucker has stressed, the personality traits of the major players, the CEOs and top managers, are reflected throughout the entire business down to the maintenance personnel who clean up the premises at the close of the business day. The leaders' vision, philosophy, and attitudes toward people and toward business permeate the entire work environment and atmosphere, affecting everyone for better or worse. Similarly, Gini (2004) in writing about "Moral Leadership and Business Ethics," argued that:

> Leadership, even when defined as a collaborative experience, is still about the influence of individual character and the impact of personal mentoring .... Although to achieve ethical behavior, an entire organization, from top to bottom, must make a commitment to it, the model for that commitment has to originate from the top (p. 41).

According to Bass and Steidlmeier (1998), the "transformational" model of leadership is ethical in that it is based on the premise that leaders of an organization guide employees to levels of higher morals: "transformational leaders set examples to be emulated by their followers .... When leaders are more morally mature, those they lead display higher moral reasoning" (Ethics, character and authentic transformational leadership section, para. 4).[10]

Traits and behaviors of ethical business leaders and their effects on employees

Respect for employees

As noted, good leaders have high regard for those who work for them. Within the ethical organization, employees are not treated impersonally or in an authoritarian manner but are made to feel that the company belongs to them (Hesselbein, 2002). The good leader sees to it that the company's profitability leads to rewards on every level. E. Sternberg (2000) pointed out that rewards to employees in the "ethical enterprise" are aligned with Rawls' principle of distributive justice. "Distributive justice is respected when business rewards are bestowed on those who actually contribute to achieving the business end, and the levels of reward are proportional to their contributions" (p. 119). In this way, the work ethic is enhanced because employees feel a strong identification with the company. They feel that they have real power and control over their working conditions, as they should.

When leaders try to exercise surplus authority or claim extra status, it is detrimental to the company and harmful to both employees and the leaders themselves. In general, the efficient leader keeps rules to a minimum, knowing that unnecessary rules are a hindrance to movement and growth. Even more important, surplus authority and unnecessary power plays are unethical because they not only stifle people's spirits, but also depress their morale. For example, a manager has the right to tell an employee what to do, but does not have the right to dominate or humiliate him or her, or to use that individual for personal services.

Honest communication between leaders and employees
Open communication between leaders and employees is crucial to any successful enterprise (Kotter, 1990/1998). An honest give-and-take of information and personal feedback that encourages trust, participation, and initiative should be the policy during every phase of the company's growth. As Bennis (2003) stressed, the good business leader has the ability to create a "culture of candor." "Nothing will sink a leader faster than surrounding him- or her self with yes-men and women" (p. xviii). When such a "culture of candor" exists within an organization, employees' complaints are listened to and responded to sensitively by management. Leaders who listen carefully to complaints instead of becoming frustrated are more effective in solving problems. Good leaders also show employees that acting victimized and passively complaining are counter-productive. They teach them to define problems objectively and to seek active solutions instead of maintaining negative attitudes.

A good leader confronts poor performance in either managers or employees. The problem is discussed openly and directly, with assistance offered to help the individual improve his or her performance.

If an employee becomes dysfunctional or nonproductive, the good leader intuitively grasps the situation and is direct and straightforward in addressing the issues with him or her.

Consideration of employees' needs and goals
Energetic, enthusiastic employees produce more and sell more. Therefore, leaders need to consider strategies and compensation plans that lead to high morale, an essential component of productivity. Hesselbein (2002) emphasized that the acknowledgment of employees' contribution to the company, both verbally and monetarily, is crucial to morale: "Part of every leader's job, whether in business, government, or the social sector is to help people see the full value of what they contribute" (p. 113). For example, one of the author's precepts is that one should never cut the commissions of highly productive salespeople or promote them to managerial positions when their talents lie in sales. Setting up a meaningful profit-sharing plan and stock options for salespersons and other employees also helps ensure high morale.

Matching employees' skills, aptitudes, and personalities to their tasks is fundamental to achieving success in business (Collins, 2002; Winston & Patterson, 2006). Ethical business leaders encourage employees to seek their own levels of achievement, moving ahead as far and as fast as they can. Each potential leader replaces him or herself as he or she moves up through the ranks (Hesselbein, 2002; Kotter, 1990/1998).[11]

In addition, in a good company, importance is placed on establishing a pleasant, aesthetically pleasing, orderly atmosphere in the company because it is conducive to a highly functioning organization. Leaders need to show equal concern for creating an emotionally supportive environment based on understanding of and concern for the individual as a person.

In recent years, an increasing number of business ventures have moved away from traditional, hierarchal models of leadership, adopting a model more aligned with the criteria for ethical business leadership described above. This model, referred to paradoxically as "servant-leadership" by its founder, Robert Greenleaf (1991), places primary importance on the well-being of employees, shareholders, and the community.[12] In describing Greenleaf's paradigm, Spears (2004a) explained:

> Since the time of the Industrial Revolution, managers have tended to view people as tools, while organizations have considered workers as cogs in a machine. In the past few decades we have witnessed a shift in that long-held view. In countless ... organizations today we are seeing traditional, autocratic, and hierarchical modes of leadership yielding to a different way of working—one based on teamwork and community, one that seeks to involve others in decision making, one strongly based in ethical and caring behavior, and one that is attempting to enhance the personal growth of people while improving the caring and quality of our many institutions (para. 2).

Ethical leadership in the political arena

The issues of political leadership differ from those of business leadership. In business, the bottom line is profitability, whereas in government or the political sphere, the ultimate goal is public service. The purpose of a government is to meet the needs of its constituency, to maintain their welfare, and to protect the country against outside threat. Ideally, serving people's basic needs, both physical and economic, would be the goal of ethical political leadership. The truly moral leader can be conceptualized as being bipartisan in the sense that he or she would ideally serve the needs of the majority while respecting the needs of the minority.

The ideal government or political system does have certain ethical concerns in common with the ideal business enterprise. In the ideal democracy, leaders would be committed to serving the populace by helping meet their basic needs as described above (in Greenleaf's model of business leadership). In this pursuit, they would oversee and support programs which would reward people appropriately for their productivity and achievements. In addition, ethical leaders would do their best to reduce inequalities among their constituents. In this regard, they could make a realistic attempt to redistribute the wealth and make economic rewards more equitable. Thomas Jefferson has been acknowledged as being in the forefront of thinkers who conceptualized methods for the redistribution of property.[13] In a letter to James Madison in 1785, Jefferson wrote:

> I am conscious that an equal distribution of property is impracticable, but the consequences of this enormous inequality producing so much misery to the bulk of mankind, legislators cannot invent too many devices for subdividing property .... It is not too soon to provide by every possible means that as few as possible shall be without a little portion of land (From Revolution to Reconstruction, 2007).

Similarly, John Rawls' (1999) concept of distributive justice proposed that, in the ideal society, the most resources would go to the least advantaged citizens. There are many people who believe that a government or society based on the concept of distributive justice is unnatural because it goes against individual self-interest. However, in our experience in the friendship circle, the authors have found that people can learn to be generous; they can share their wealth and discover the joy of giving.[14] Even in a system of distributive justice, however, the system should not reward people inappropriately nor destroy individual initiative.

Traditionally, a majority of political leaders have failed to live by or to inspire this ethical ideal of distributive justice in their constituents. R. Rorty (1998) has noted that in American society, "economic inequality and economic insecurity have steadily increased" (p. 83). He continues, "We are likely to wind up with an America divided into hereditary social castes" (p. 86). Recently, there have been signs of change on the part of several business leaders, notably Bill and Melinda Gates and Warren Buffet, who have contributed billions of dollars to education for the disadvantaged, and to the alleviation of poverty and health problems worldwide. Nevertheless, capitalistic economies are generally characterized by significant inequity, and communistic or socialistic experiments in which the leaders have tried to coerce greater equality have usually been proven ineffective.

The role of followers in relation to the leader

The dimensions of ethical leadership must be examined in a context that takes into account the nature of a follower's relationship to his or her leader. Hollander (2004) underscored this point when he wrote:

> Various streams of thought have converged on the concept of leadership as a process rather than a person or state. This process is essentially a shared experience (p. 47) But the essence of the matter is to recognize that a leader-centric focus is inadequate to understanding the interdependence of leadership and active followership (p. 49).

Leader-follower dynamics in modern society were first explored by Tarde (1890/1903), LeBon (1897), and Freud (1921/1955). "In *Group Psychology and the Analysis of the Ego* ... Freud developed his conception of the followers' identification with the leader as a shared ego-ideal" (Hollander, 2004, p. 50). Around the same time, Max Weber (1921/1946) contributed his notion of the "charismatic leader" to account for a distinct quality of the personality that inspires loyalty and devotion in followers, particularly in times of uncertainty and crisis.[15]

Many people think of the word "follower" in a negative sense. A more objective or positive understanding of the term recognizes the strong value of leadership. It is adaptive and functional for "followers" to seek help and guidance in areas where they have little or no expertise. Independent followers depend on a leader to the extent that they lack a particular skill, knowledge, or capability or the necessary traits or requirements for organizing and maintaining an effective enterprise. Because they possess dignity and a strong sense of self, they tend not to prevail on a leader in a manner that would elicit a parental response. They are not excessively dependent nor do they subordinate their personality to an authority figure. The ideal follower is neither defiant nor submissive in his or her basic orientation to others. Just as there should be no surplus power in ethical leadership, so too there should be no surplus dependency on the part of the ethical follower (Heifetz & Laurie, 1997/1998).

Ideally, followers would reject leaders who are disrespectful to them as human beings. Although economic hardship may dictate that employees keep working at a job where they are not treated respectfully, whenever possible they should seek other positions rather than accept denigration, harassment, or abuse. Good followers would hold leaders to high standards, ethically as well as practically, demanding that they fulfill their responsibilities and duties, and that they meet the physical and economic needs of their constituents.[16]

According to Hollander (2004), leaders with "an exalted sense of self-worth" tend to devalue the worth of employees and "avoid close contact with them" (p. 51). This situation generates progressively more distance between the leader and his/her followers.

> Some leaders have become so removed from followers' perceptions and needs that they can cease to be aware of how their actions affect the "team" they wish to foster. A pertinent example of this is seen in the issue of high compensation packages given to American CEOs. Such disparities may produce even more alienation of followers from their leaders (p. 53).

At the same time, however, many people continue to idealize leaders, overlook their weaknesses, and accept leaders' rationalizations for not acting on their stated goals (Lipman-Blumen, 2005). These followers do not hold leaders accountable when they become ineffectual or when they utilize unethical means to further personal power or causes. According to Kellerman (2004), there are other reasons why employees remain passive in these situations.[17] Being a "whistle-blower" in a corrupt business organization has its costs: "Nay-sayers and second guessers are frowned on in most corporate cultures" (p. 154).

> The pressure comes from inside an organization: from the hierarchical structures that characterize large enterprises, and from peers who prefer not to be personally discomforted or professionally jeopardized. And it comes from outside the organization—for example, from families of employees who rely on regular paychecks. Above all it's worth remembering that the tendency to ignore wrongdoing is natural. It's human nature ... [to protect] our basic needs for safety, simplicity, and certainty and also of our need to belong. To become a whistle-blower is to put all of these at risk (p. 154).

Ultimately people are accountable for their government's policies, for the goals that their leaders pursue, for the actions taken on their behalf, and, most important, for the means their leaders use to achieve these ends (Kellerman, 2004).

Ineffective leaders

When leaders are incompetent, inflexible, lack foresight, or are not action-oriented, it is obvious that they inevitably have a negative effect on the organizations they manage. Kellerman (2004) has delineated three major characteristics of the ineffective leader: incompetence, rigidity and intemperance. Leaders with these negative characteristics and weaknesses tend to have histories of poor performance, poor decision-making, and/or addictive, self-nurturing personalities.

In companies with ineffective leadership, both managers and employees tend to feel "helpless in making things better, not supported emotionally or professionally, unable to identify the causes of the discomfort and pain, unable to leave the situation permanently, and unable to solve problems permanently, consistently under attack," (Bacal, 2000, What Does a Toxic Organization Look Like section, para. 1). According to Bacal, another manifestation of ineffective leadership is poor internal communication. This includes complicated language and highly technical phrases employed by managers to confuse shareholders and employees, hype the organizational image, and obscure the facts (Fugere, Hardaway & Warshawsky, 2005).

Unethical or destructive leaders

In the business world, toxic leaders are sometimes effective over the short term; however, many companies who have an unethical or immoral leadership eventually encounter difficulties in sustaining a pattern of consistent growth over the long-term (Goleman, 2006).[18] Unfortunately, in the political sphere, destructive leaders appear to have considerable staying power, often inflicting suffering on multitudes of people over many decades (e.g., Mao Zedong, Pol Pot of the Khmer Rouge, Joseph Stalin Idi Amin, Robert Mugabe).

History has shown that many pathological leaders who assume positions of power early in their careers become increasingly authoritarian, paranoid, and punitive as they grow older (Post,

2004). For example, as Stalin aged, his feelings of insecurity and paranoia appeared to intensify and he embarked on a program to purge the party of suspected political heretics. According to Radzinsky (1996): "As soon as the war was over he [Stalin] had begun harping on his age" (p. 527). "In 1946, Stalin resumed his ideological bombardment" (p. 521) ... he began his purge of the country by striking first at his lieutenants" (p. 527). In 1949, "two thousand Party officials [were] arrested in Leningrad" (p. 535) in what came to be known as the Leningrad Affair. Similarly, Lipton-Blumen (2005) described Chairman Mao as "a vivid example of an initially positive leader who eventually turned toxic ... . In his later years, Mao declined into paranoia, which frequently drove him to order the elimination of his closest associates" (p.146).

Charismatic leaders often have elements of authoritarianism, paranoia and sociopathy in their personality structure (Post, 2004). Whereas most ordinary citizens feel little or no need to accumulate power by controlling or dominating others, these charismatic personality types tend to seek excess power, especially in the political sphere.

In describing the personalities of destructive leaders, Wilson-Starks (2003) noted that they "may have unresolved psychological issues (such as fear of the unknown, fear of failure, mistrust of people, feelings of inadequacy, lack of confidence, or extreme overconfidence)" (What causes a person to become a toxic leader section, para. 1).[19] She also discussed the harmful effects these individuals have on employees, "through the poisoning of enthusiasm, creativity, autonomy, and innovative expression (What is toxic leadership section, para 1).

> First, is the stifling of creativity ... . The second consequence is lack of communication ... Third, when mistrust increases, productive relationships are not likely to develop (What characteristics describe a toxic leader section, para 1) The net result of all these factors is that toxic leaders fail to appreciate the uniqueness of being human ... . The toxic leader treats people as robots, defined by whatever function the leader expects them to perform (What causes a person to become a toxic leader section, para. 2–3).

In his analysis of unethical organizations, Bacal (2000) drew an analogy between ineffective, unethical leaders and inadequate or hurtful parents:

> For every toxic organization, there is a toxic leader, a leader who, by virtue of his or her own problems, creates an environment that drives people crazy. Toxic leaders are much like poor parents, in that they exhibit certain behavior patterns that confuse and paralyze others who depend on them (The "Toxic Leader" section, para. 1).

A leadership that is negative and detrimental to individuals and institutions alike tends to go one step further than the type of mismanagement described above. In his expose of corporations such as Enron, Worldcom, Global Crossing, and others, Kilburg (2006) demonstrated that unapologetic exploitation of shareholders' and employees' salaries and life savings was the consequences of the unethical practices of destructive leaders.[20] Liechty (2005) asserted that unethical leaders are those who, "for personal gain and aggrandizement, unapologetically bilk and destroy the companies they are hired to lead … . In politics, these are the people for whom no malevolent act is out of bounds in the name of gaining and holding power" (para. 2).

Why people tend to follow destructive leaders

Unfortunately, there will always be people who will seek inappropriate, irresponsible and toxic leaders in an attempt to compensate for their own failings and dependency needs. Many individuals are so drawn to the personality of a charismatic leader that they ignore the reality of the leader's failings or remain indifferent to the immoral means by which the leader accomplishes his or her goals. In an analysis of narcissistic-charismatic leaders, Post (2004) proposed that there are "crucial aspects of the psychology of the leader that, like a key, fit and unlock certain aspects of the psychology of their followers" (p. 188).

> When these ideal-hungry followers find a mirror-hungry [vain, narcissistic] leader, we have the elements of a charismatic leader-follower relationship … . In times of social crisis these

powerful relationships can become the nuclei for powerful transforming social movements, as was the case with the reparative revolutionary leadership of Kemal Ataturk, Mahatma Gandhi, and Martin Luther King Jr., and the destructive charismatic leadership of Adolph Hitler, Ayatollah Khomeini, and Osama bin Laden (p. 199).

Wilner (1984) defined charismatic leadership as:

A relationship between a leader and a group of followers that has the following properties:
    The leader is perceived by the followers as somehow superhuman.
    The followers blindly believe the leader's statements.
    The followers unconditionally comply with the leader's directives for action.
    The followers give the leader unqualified emotional support (cited by Post, 2004, p. 188).

Other theorists have investigated the structure and functions of narcissistic, charismatic, and authoritarian personality types in an attempt to understand both sides of this complex interactive relationship (Adorno, Frenkel-Brunswik, Levinson & Sanford, 1950; Robins & Post, 1997). Adorno, et al (1950), in their classic work, *The Authoritarian Personality,* concluded:

There exists something like "the" potentially fascist character, which is by itself a "structural unit." In other words, traits such as conventionality, authoritarian submissiveness and aggressiveness, projectivity, manipulativeness, etc. regularly go together (p. 751).
    In the psychodynamics of the "authoritarian character," part of the preceding aggressiveness is absorbed and turned into masochism, while another part is left over as sadism, which seeks an outlet in those with whom the subject does not identify himself: ultimately the outgroup (p. 759).

The concept of the "authoritarian personality" has been criticized for its methodology and so fell out of favor in political and social psychology.[21] During the 90s, there was renewed interest in the subject following the publication of *The Authoritarian Specter* (Altemeyer, 1996). In this volume, Altemeyer reported findings from studies in which more stringent research methods were used:

> Both leaders and followers can be "authoritarian." Hitler, for example, believed his authority to do what he wanted superseded all human rights, laws, treaties, etc. He was an authoritarian leader. Millions of Germans in turn gladly accepted his authority over the state and everything in it. They were authoritarian followers (pp. 310–311).

Similarly, in examining the dynamics of leader-follower relationships, Lipman-Blumen (2005) emphasized that "Authoritarianism, a hallmark of toxic leaders, seeps in through the fissures created by crises. In tumultuous times, toxic leaders' predilection for authoritarianism fits neatly with their anxious followers' heightened insecurity" (p. 99).

Adorno, et al (1950) and Altemeyer (1996) analyzed characteristics of the authoritarian personality structure along psychoanalytic lines, conceptualizing them as the result of the internalization of early childhood experiences, strict parenting or parental indifference and social learning (imitation of parents' attitudes). Many destructive, charismatic leaders exhibit traits of authoritarian aggression, whereas their followers tend to be submissive. Yet the followers also tend to endorse authoritarian values and beliefs.[22]

In a previous work (R. Firestone, 1997a), the first author explained why many people are easily persuaded to align themselves with a charismatic, yet destructive, leader in support of what they perceive to be a "just cause:"

> When the parental atmosphere is immature, frightened, hostile or overly defended, the family takes on the quality of a dictatorship, wherein powerful forces operate to control other family members, fit them into a mold, "brain wash" them with a particular philosophy of life, and manipulate them through guilt and a sense of obligation. Children brought up in this manner become either defiant or compliant—mindless authoritarian personality types that are easily exploited by power-struck leaders and manipulated into a destructive mass (p. 285).

Other theorists (Kecmanovic, 1996) have explored the reasons why destructive leaders appeal to large numbers of followers and have elucidated specific family dynamics that contribute to "children's propensity to adhere to ethnocentric views" (p. 174). Lipman-Blumen (2005) has argued that these leaders:

> Offer us comfort and promise to satisfy some of our deep long-
> ings ... for authority figures to replace our parents and other
> early caretakers; for membership in the human community; for
> a conception of ourselves as significant beings engaged daily
> in noble endeavors in a meaningful world ... . [They feed our]
> hope that our existence will have served some meaningful pur-
> pose [that] allows us to live without paranoia and despair [re-
> lated to existential issues of life and death] (p. 2).

The fantasy bond—the illusion of fusion—that can result from being part of a group, a cause, or a patriotic or nationalistic movement can be exhilarating and addictive for people who see the leaders of such movements as saviors or "ultimate rescuers" (R. Firestone, 1994b). When people relinquish their autonomy early in life to form a fantasy bond in their families, they find it difficult, if not impossible, to live their adult lives with integrity according to their own values. People tend to transfer the feelings that originally characterized the imagined connection to their parents onto new figures and ideologies, thus feeling some relief from their anxiety. These individuals are especially susceptible to the influence of charismatic, authoritarian leaders who promise them certainty and safety.

It is the authors' contention that the fear of death drives individuals to support authoritarian, charismatic leaders and embrace patriotic, nationalistic movements in a search for security and immortality. Dependence on a particular group, idolization of a leader, and mindless allegiance to a cause function as defenses against death anxiety.

Hellmuth Kaiser (Fierman, 1965) proposed that the need to surrender or submit one's will to another person or group through a "delusion of fusion" represents the universal psychopathology (R. Firestone, 1997a). The fantasy of being merged with someone or something larger than oneself imbues one with feelings of omnipotence, invincibility, and immunity to death. These feelings tend to exist on a preconscious or unconscious level. Most people are aware, at least on a conscious level, that group membership and loyalty to a powerful leader do not guarantee their survival in the ultimate sense of the word. Nevertheless, they still tend to have strong reactions when their illusions of safety are threatened by reminders of death, such as the terrorist attacks of 9/11. Threats to the fantasy bond's function as a defense against death anxiety are often experienced by people on an unconscious level, and they react by strengthening their defenses before they are consciously aware of the increase in anxiety.

In circumstances of imminent threat or danger, when an awareness of death is unavoidable, people appear to prefer a charismatic, authoritarian leader whose promises of certainty and stability alleviate their fear. This hypothesis has been supported by empirical research conducted by terror management theorists (Cohen, Ogilvie, Solomon, Greenberg & Pyszczynski, 2005; Cohen, Solomon, Maxfield, Pyszczynski & Greenberg, 2004), who concluded that reminders of death, which were experimentally induced, influenced people's choice of a more dogmatic, charismatic leader over a more task-oriented leader, particularly in uncertain times and under conditions of fear such as those that prevailed following the events of 9/11.[23]

Conclusion

The effectiveness and the ethics of a particular leadership may be evaluated by examining the positive or negative impact that the leader has on the overall enterprise and on the individuals involved. In analyzing the personality traits of a leader, one needs to apply both pragmatic and ethical standards. An effective leader who utilizes harmful methods to accomplish his or her goals is still destructive and therefore unethical. An ineffective leader, even though compassionate and humanitarian, would still be likely to have a damaging effect on his/her constituents and on the overall enterprise or government.

There are many reasons why people seek leadership positions. Some wish to become leaders as a way of asserting themselves, as a method for self-transcendence, or as a means of serving others. Some seek leadership out of a defensive need to compensate for feelings of inadequacy. Toxic or unethical leaders often use their positions to bolster an inflated self-image, to defend against feelings of insecurity and inferiority, or to deny their vulnerability to death. Their charismatic, narcissistic leadership styles resonate with and exacerbate feelings of fear, inferiority, and insecurity in their followers, especially during times of crisis and uncertainty. The authors believe that insight into the dynamics operating in leadership-followership interactions is critical to understanding social and political issues in contemporary society. The role played by psychological defenses in fostering the political agendas of toxic leaders is an important and timely topic that compels our attention and concern.

Notes

1. Re: the multidimensional aspects of leadership, there are many models or paradigms of leadership that focus on one or two specific dimensions of leadership in the business and political arenas. See "Trait-Based Perspectives of Leadership" (Zaccaro, 2007); "The Role of the Situation in Leadership" (Vroom & Jago, 2007); "Promoting More Integrative Strategies for Leadership Theory-Building" (Avolio, 2007); "A Systems Model of Leadership: WICS (R. Sternberg, 2007b); and "Asking the Right Questions about Leadership" (Hackman & Wageman, 2007). Also see Winston's and Patterson's (2006) "An Integrative Definition of Leadership," and Adler (2002) who noted that "Given the importance of leadership in organizations, an attempt to integrate the many disparate concepts and constructs related to this topic is long overdue" (para. 1).

   Re: ethics and values in organizations, John Kenneth Galbraith (1983) pointed out that as is true of power, leadership "can be socially malign; [but] it is also socially essential" (p.13). Weaver (2006) acknowledged that: "Social science research into unethical behavior in organizations highlights the prominence of amoral thinking" (p. 350).

   Gandz (2007) proposed several parameters by which "good" leadership (both effective and ethical) may be appraised: "*effective* leadership—getting followers to pursue and attain goals … the *ethics* of leaders—doing the right things in the right ways, [and] ways in which leaders make followers *feel* good and, indeed, the way they feel about themselves as leaders" (para. 1).

2. In the Foreword to *Hesselbein on Leadership*, Collins (2002) commented that "Harry Truman once defined leadership as the art of getting people to do what they might not otherwise do, and to like it" (p. xi).

3. Andrews (2003) described competence as important both in relation to effective managing and making ethical decisions. "Ethical decisions therefore require of individuals three qualities that can be identified and developed. The first is competence to recognize ethical issues and to think through the consequences of alternative resolutions" (p. 72). Also see Farkas and Wetlaufer's (1996/1998) discussion of "the Expertise Approach" used by leaders who focus more on "shaping corporate policies that will strengthen their organizations' competencies" (p. 131).

4. Goleman (2006; Goleman, et al, 2002) emphasized that good leaders need to possess "emotional and social intelligence," which enables them to intuitively select individuals who share their vision and who have the enthusiasm to see the endeavor through to completion. Also see Gandz's (2000) counsel to leaders: "If you have a vision and want to see it enacted, do the following: Work on articulating that vision through carefully crafted, high-impact messages promulgated through every medium at your disposal" (p. 2).

5. See Thomas Jefferson's October 1786 letter to Maria Cosway, "The Head Heart Letter" (Junto Society, 2007).

6. In *Leadership and Spirit*, Moxley (2000) stressed the importance of authenticity and the development of self-knowledge as an important dimension of leadership: "It enables us to experience the force we call spirit; we are renewed and revitalized whenever we have the courage to be authentic. It makes leadership-as-partnership possible" (p. 127).

7. Zaleznik (1977/1998) contended that leaders must also have the patience to put off certain decisions in times of uncertainty and chaos: "Leaders tolerate chaos and lack of structure and are thus prepared to keep answers in suspense, avoiding premature closure on important issues" (p. 87).

8. Drucker (1998) and Hesselbein (2002) proposed that effective leaders need to possess the ability to reeducate managers and staff regarding the necessity for changing the status quo. According to Heifetz and Laurie (1997/1998), "Mobilizing an organization to adapt its behaviors in order to thrive in new business environments is critical" (p. 173). Farkas and Wetlauffer (1996/1998) described a specific leadership approach that they referred to as the "change approach." These leaders "spend as much as 75% of their time using speeches, meetings, and other forms of communication to motivate members of their organizations to embrace the gestalt of change" (p. 121). See Heifitz and Laurie's table "Adaptive Work Calls for Leadership" (p. 180).

9. The type of openness referred to by Goleman, et al (2002) is made up of two personal qualities: openness to feedback and a willingness to be revealing of oneself. This "transparency—an authentic openness to others about one's feelings, beliefs, and actions—allows integrity, or the sense that a leader can be trusted ... . Integrity also means that a leader lives his values" (p. 47).

10. Re: the definition of "transformational leadership," Bass and Steidlmeier (1998) delineated four components: charisma or idealized influence (attributed or behavioral), inspirational motivation, intellectual stimulation, and individualized consideration. See also Winston and Patterson's (2006) distinction between transformational and servant leadership. The implication is that "servant leaders will seek the benefit of the followers even at the expense of the organization" (p. 21). For a description of the ethics inherent in "adaptive" leadership, see *Leadership Can Be Taught* by Sharon Daloz Parks (2005) who asserted that: "acts of leadership are inevitably steeped in ethical choices and that the hunger for leadership is at its core a hunger for moral commitment—for leadership that served the common good in contrast to personal gain or aggrandizement alone" (p. 240).

11. See "The Challenge of Leadership Transition" in *Hesselbein on Leadership* (Hesselbein, 2002).

12. Greenleaf's seemingly paradoxical concept of servant-leadership has become integrated into numerous programs of leadership training and education as articulated by Stephen Covey (1999), Peter Senge (Senge, et al, 1994) and Margaret Wheatley (Spears, 2004b). See Greenleaf's (1991) original essay that set forth his ideas on the leader as servant: "The best test is: Do those served grow as persons, do they while being served, become healthier, wiser, freer, more autonomous, more likely themselves to become servants? And what is the effect on the least privileged in society? Will they benefit or at least not be further deprived?" (cited by Spears, 2004c, p. 12). Spears (1998) delineated ten characteristics as "being of critical importance, central to the development of servant-leaders" (p. 5): 1) Listening, 2) Empathy, 3) Healing, 4) Awareness, 5) Persuasion, 6) Conceptualization, 7) Foresight, 8) Stewardship, 9) Commitment to the growth of people, and 10) Building community.

13. Jefferson also proposed that:

> Another means of silently lessening the inequality of property is to exempt all from taxation below a certain point, and to tax the higher portions or property in geometrical progression as

they rise ... . The earth is given as a common stock for man to labor and live on. If for the encouragement of industry we allow it to be appropriated, we must take care that other employment be provided to those excluded from the appropriation (From Revolution to Reconstruction, 2007).

14. Cross-cultural studies have shown that in many societies, leaders, and citizens alike place a high value on generosity. At times, however, conflict arises in societies where generosity is seen as meritorious, as being closely related to accumulating power, and where the giver is perceived as having more power than the receiver. For example, see McClelland's (1975) chapter, "The Power of Giving: Traditional India."

15. Re: leader-follower interactions, see Stech's (2007) chapter "Psychodynamic Approach," in which he stated: "The primary aim of the psychodynamic approach is to raise the awareness of leaders and followers to their own personality types and the implications of those types on work and relationships" (p. 254). Stech also cited the work of Zaleznik (1977/1998), Maccoby (1981), and Berne (1961) in Transactional Analysis in relation to the psychodynamics of leaders, followers and business organizations.

16. Ideally, followers would also reject those leaders who failed to live up to their promises or to fulfill the constituents' expectations. See research conducted by Kenney, Schwartz-Kenney, and Blascovich (1996) to "identify people's expectations for a leader they label worthy of influence" (p. 1128). Being kind and being sympathetic, taking charge and being authoritative were qualities selected for leaders who would be "worthy of influence" by subjects. The authors pointed out that:

Perhaps followers, too, must meet certain leader expectations, so that the leader wants to invest the time and energy necessary for meeting follower expectations or so that the leader wants to engage in the type of influence assessed in the current research, rather than relying on coercion and arm twisting (p. 1141).

Based on their studies, these researchers concluded that when leaders fail to meet followers' expectations, it is unlikely that they will be perceived by their followers as "worthy of influence." Also see Heifetz's (1994) description of a leadership in which "a leader gets people to accept his vision, and communities address problems by looking to him" (p. 14), and a leadership in which "leaders mobilize people to face problems, and communities make progress on problems because leaders challenge and help them do so" (p. 15).

17. There are other factors underlying "poor followership" in business organizations. One significant factor may be the result of the psychological defenses of compartmentalization and moral disengagement discussed by Bandura, Barbaranelli, Caprara, and Pastorelli (1996), Bandura (2002), and C. Moore (2007). Also see social cognitive theorist Weaver's (2006) description of how various situations and roles in the workplace can trigger psychological defenses of compartmentalization and moral disengagement.

18. In *Social Intelligence*, Goleman (2006) noted that "Today Machiavellian types like the kiss-up-kick-down manager may well gain some personal success. But in the long run Machs run the risk that their poisoned relationships and resulting bad reputation may one day derail them ... while their head knows what to do, their heart remains clueless" (pp. 126-127).

19. In a book appropriately titled *Snakes in Suites*, Babiak and Hare (2006) cited research by Hogan and his associates showing that charisma can hide a multitude of problems: " more executives are fired for personality problems than for incompetence. Most problematic are 'narcissistic, psychopathic managers who exploit subordinates while currying favor with superiors'" (p. 195).

20. In *Executive Wisdom*, Kilburg (2006) analyzed the demise of these companies and their accounting firm, Arthur Anderson, in a chapter titled "Wisdom Mapping III: Situation Awareness, Values and Moral Compasses, and the Challenge of Creating Virtuous Leaders" (see pages 189-222).

21. Re: critique of Adorno, et al (1950) study, J. Martin (2001) argued that " A more fundamental bias arose from the attempt to empirically verify the existence of a 'type' of person whom the researchers thought dangerous and with whom they did not emphasize ... These subtler problems have haunted contemporary work in political psychology that avoids the methodological problems of Adorno et al; Altemeyer's work on authoritarianism ... is similarly distorted by asymmetries" (p. 1).

22. See Altemeyer's (1996) *The Authoritarian Specter* and *Conservatives Without Conscience* by John Dean (2006) in which Dean quotes Altermeyer (1996) regarding findings from recent research that used the Right Wing Authoritarianism (RWA) scale to assess authoritarian attitudes.

23. See Cohen, et al (2004) and Cohen, et al (2005). Both studies supported the hypothesis that "people would show increased preference

for a charismatic political candidate and decreased preference for a relationship-oriented political candidate in response to subtle reminders of death" (Cohen, et al, 2004, p. 846). The 2005 (Cohen, et al, 2005) study showed specifically that more registered voters who were reminded of death (experimental condition) said they intended to vote for George Bush, whereas more voters who were not reminded of death (control condition) said they intended to vote for John Kerry.

CHAPTER THIRTEEN

Power and the corruption of power

> Power is the capacity to ensure the outcomes one wishes and to prevent those one does not wish.
>
> John Gardner (1990, p. 55)

In analyzing power and influence, it is important to understand how a power structure arises, how it develops, and how it functions. For centuries, philosophers, social scientists, and psychologists have struggled to answer ethical questions regarding the use and misuse of power. They have described both the positive and the negative effects that powerful individuals have had on historical events, current world affairs, religious movements, politics and government, the business world, and individual members of society as a whole.[1]

According to R. Martin (1971), "In the most general sense power may refer to any kind of influence exercised by objects, individuals, or groups upon each other" (p. 241). "Power is one of the most central and yet problematic concepts in sociological theory. It forms the cornerstone of the conflict model of ... society, one of the two major models in sociological theory" (p. 240).

313

The sociologist Max Weber (cited by Middlesex University, 2007) defined power as follows: "By power is meant that opportunity existing within a social relationship which permits one to carry out one's own will even against resistance and regardless of the basis on which this opportunity rests" (Section 1.16, Power, authority, and imperative control). Weber believed that power is a "zero-sum game" and emphasized that for one individual to gain power, someone else must lose an equal amount of power.

Other sociologists have disagreed with Weber's analysis, notably Talbot Parsons (1967), who claimed that conflict was *not* inevitable in power relations. Parsons perceived power in terms of individuals working together to achieve a collective goal, arguing that this endeavor required "the acceptance of the [power] relation by both sides because of its function in achieving social system goals" (Martin, 1971, p. 244).

In general, sociologists have analyzed power both in terms of an individual's attributes and a "system resource" or an inherent "property of a relation." Martin (1971) explained this distinction as follows: "To revert to the analogical language which has perhaps plagued the analysis of the concept of power, it is the electric current rather than the electric generator" (p. 243). Weber (Middlesex University, 2007) also made an important distinction between *authority* and *power*, emphasizing that authority exists only when there is a belief in the "legitimacy" of the power structure or leader.[2]

Historically, power has often been viewed with suspicion or given a negative, even evil, connotation. Pejorative terms such as "harsh," "exploitive," "fascist," "sadistic," and "Machiavellian" have been used to describe the ways in which power and influence have been exercised. According to McClelland (1975): "In American society in general, individuals ... dislike being told they have a high need for Power" (p. 255). "Power must have a positive face too. After all, people cannot help influencing one another; organizations cannot function without some kind of authority relationships" (p. 257).

Power per se, like leadership, is neither positive nor negative; it is neutral or amoral. However, the specific types of power that people tend to develop over time and the methods whereby they utilize the power they have accumulated, to either inspire or to dominate other people, can be evaluated from an ethical point of view.

Sources of power

Strength of character, integrity, charisma, athletic ability, and positive physical attributes such as beauty or good looks are all potential sources of power. People accrue power though wealth, popularity, by being competent and knowledgeable in a given field, and by living according to a certain belief system or set of ethical principles. They can also accumulate power by being dominating, intimidating, coercive, aggressive, or violent.

The sources of power available to individuals vary across cultures, subcultures, and interest groups. Every society or mini-culture places high value on specific personality traits or achievements of its members; thus, individuals with these traits have considerable influence or power within that group. For example, in the political arena, the orator who is charismatic and convincing or the former general who succeeded in battle can rise to a prominent position; in a motorcycle gang, the most daring and fastest rider becomes the leader; in the business world, the executive whose company generates high earnings possesses considerable prestige; in sports, the player who is named "most valuable player" will be more popular than his teammates.

People have the tendency to deify their heroes and leaders. This idealization holds true even when leaders do not exhibit positive ethical qualities and have a negative influence on their supporters and society at large. The halo effect based of the desirable characteristics that originally earned a leader power enables people to follow inadequate or even potentially destructive leaders (Lipman-Blumen, 2005).[3]

Types of power

> Our problem, then, is to try to understand two faces of power. When is power bad and when is it good? Why is it often perceived as dangerous? Which aspects of power are viewed favorably, and which unfavorably? (McClelland, 1975, p. 257).

There is a clear distinction between the accumulation of power as part of one's self-development, self-assertion, and a natural, healthy striving for love, satisfaction and meaning in one's interpersonal world, and the amassing of power as part of a defensive process.

Viewing the exercise of power from this perspective, there are three basic types of power:

Personal power is based on strength, confidence, and competence that individuals gradually acquire in the course of their development. This type of power represents a movement toward self-realization and transcendent goals in life; its primary aim is mastery of self, not others.

Covert negative power is based on passive aggression and is manifested in behaviors indicating weakness, incompetence and self-destructive tendencies that manipulate others in the interpersonal world by arousing their feelings of fear, guilt and anger. This type of indirect power differs from aggression, force, domination, or an oppressive authority. The exercise of covert negative power through subtle manipulations may be even more destructive in interpersonal relationships than direct force as a means of controlling others.

Overt negative power is characterized by aggressive tendencies and is exercised through the use of force and/or coercion to control others. It can be manifested within a relationship or become a significant part of a political or social movement. Totalitarian governments and tyrannical leaders are examples of this type of destructive power.

Personal power

Personal power represents a positive, natural striving for satisfaction and meaning in life that is exercised in the honest attempt to realize one's unique potentialities. In a previous work (R. Firestone & Catlett, 1989), the authors defined personal power as "direct, goal-oriented behavior using all of one's resources. It is persuasive and logical rather than manipulative in relation to other people. It is strong rather than oppressive or hostile" (pp. 184–185) in relation to upholding one's values.

The process of seeking to fully develop one's potential while being sensitive to others who are pursuing their goals is a worthwhile, mentally healthy and ethical endeavor. People who have a great deal of personal power tend to be competent and knowledgeable, and possess many of the qualities that are prerequisites for becoming an outstanding leader. Personal power is more an attitude or state of mind than an attempt to maneuver or control others. When externalized it is likely to be more service-oriented and humane than other forms of power.

People who have personal power have succeeded in relinquishing the role of a child and have assumed full adult responsibility for their lives. They are creative and dynamic individuals who are active rather than passive. They tend to be inner-directed rather than outer-directed, developing and maintaining their own set of values. They strive to live honestly and with integrity, according to their principles. These individuals are comfortable with and accepting of their angry emotions. Their ability to tolerate anger in themselves enables them to control its expression and/or to manifest it appropriately. Conversely, as noted earlier, when people are unable to accept or consciously face their anger and instead try to deny or suppress it, they are more likely to act out their aggression in inappropriate or destructive behaviors. The capacity to accept and effectively deal with angry emotions contributes to an individual's strength and confidence and the ability to influence others.

People who possess personal power are independent rather than pseudoindependent or overly dependent on others. They are more likely to be ethical and direct in their interactions, have standards that make them unwilling to accept abuse, and are not afraid to compete for what they want.

From an ethical point of view, honest competition and behavior directed toward acquiring satisfaction in life are both natural and acceptable. People have a right to pursue their lives, even when their strivings incidentally conflict with or hurt others. For example, when one person is hired for a specific position, the other applicants are necessarily deprived of that opportunity. If one decides to leave a destructive or unfulfilling relationship, he or she has the right to move on in spite of the fact that another person might be hurt. Exercising these rights does not mean that one is insensitive, irresponsible, manipulative, ruthless or conniving.

From a developmental perspective, the processes of separation, individuation, and personal growth can be seen as providing opportunities for accumulating personal power. As children move from a position of dependence to one of independence and develop increased assertiveness, autonomy, and confidence in their abilities, they accrue more personal power. Those who continue to develop themselves throughout the life span tend to be creative, nonconformist, and autonomous. For example, Diego Rivera, who used his power and influence as an artist to promote revolutionary concepts so as to "bring order and strength to the people" (McClelland, 1975, p. 201) is an example of an individual who evolved to a high level of maturity with respect to attaining and exercising positive, personal power in his life.

As Castaneda (1975) asserted in *Tales of Power,* his allegorical treatise on the process of self-realization, in which the emotionally mature individual ultimately becomes a "warrior:"

> "It depends on your personal power," he [Don Juan] said. "As is always the case in the doings and not-doings of warriors, personal power is the only thing that matters .... The basic difference between an ordinary man and a warrior is that a warrior takes everything as a challenge ... while an ordinary man takes everything either as a blessing or a curse." (pp. 105–106) "A warrior cannot complain or regret anything. His life is an endless challenge, and challenges cannot possibly be good or bad. Challenges are simply challenges." (p. 105)

There are three major reasons why people who possess personal power are rare in our culture. First, many people retreat from pursuing personal power because of a learned social pressure which views power as exploitive, corrupt, and selfish. Second, some people relinquish power because, on an unconscious level, they do not really want to be responsible adults. They anticipate the anxiety that would be aroused if they were to become fully individuated and autonomous. They prefer to depend on more familiar, indirect or manipulative forms of power that they utilized as children to get what they wanted without risking self-assertion. Third, some people fear retaliation for competing. In this regard, many people fear competition, particularly with members of the same sex. The anxiety regarding all forms of competition results from inappropriate and sometimes punitive reactions to competition experienced within the original family (R. Firestone, 1994a).[4]

Attitudes toward competition, both positive and negative, are learned in the family through the process of imitation. As a result, self-realization of the part of children is either enhanced or retarded. Many children not only fear retaliation for feeling and acting competitively, but they also observe and later imitate how their parents respond in rivalrous situations.

The authors believe that each person has the right to pursue personal power—to choose a specific direction in life and to engage in actions directed toward fulfilling his or her particular goals. One has the right to challenge conventions, social mores and systems of conformity and to work toward changing attitudes, prejudices, or laws that are unjust.

Personal power is essentially strength of character and integrity. Strong individuals are neither defiant nor submissive because these negative traits are reactions to outside influences rather than being motivated from within. Neither position is independent and autonomous. Contrary to much conventional thinking, the pursuit of personal power is essentially respectful and need not intrude on the rights of others.

Covert negative power

Covert negative power is any behavior that controls or elicits a response from others through the manipulation of their feelings of fear, guilt, anger, pity, sympathy, or remorse (R. Firestone & Catlett, 1989). In contrast to personal power, covert negative power is based on maintaining an immature or childish orientation toward life. Whereas personal power is a significant indication of being an adult, covert negative power is indicative of remaining a child. By definition, the two positions or ego-states are mutually exclusive because a person has to necessarily sacrifice personal power to manipulate or control another through weakness.

People who exercise this form of destructive power are passive rather than action-oriented, have difficulty dealing with direct anger, feel victimized and self-righteous, and, to varying degrees, are suspicious or paranoid. They act weak, powerless and have a complaining attitude. They are fearful of competitive situations and tend to retreat from goal-directed behavior when there are indications of opposition, contention, or rivalry. Instead of recognizing competitive feelings, they censor these emotions, turn on themselves, and become demoralized, thereby giving up personal power. When they back away from competing for what they want, they lack integrity and are unable to honestly communicate their wants and desires. A university student who claims to want good grades and become a doctor, yet fails to study and feels victimized by the educational system is an example of this lack of integrity. A man or woman who claims to want an intimate relationship but who rejects opportunities to meet people is another example of this duplicity.

While the exercise of covert negative power or control through weakness might not appear to be immoral or unethical, this subtle type of power contributes to distress in relationships and instability in organizations. For example, the worker who acts more incompetent than he or she really is exerts a strong social pressure that drains others of energy and vitality. Cavaiola and Lavender (2000) have underscored the fact that employees with passive-aggressive personalities "are quite difficult to work with, given their negativity and resentful moods and attitudes" (p. 126). The passive-aggressive personality "can be insidious, wiping out your hard drive 'by mistake' or losing the twenty-page proposal that you've been spending months working on" (p. 128). Similarly, people who act weak or powerless in their personal lives solicit caretaking responses, thereby draining energy from those around them.

The use of covert negative power is quite common within relationships and families. It is a type of terrorism in which one person is made "accountable" for the misery and unhappiness of another. As noted, people who lead chronically addictive lifestyles, or are self-destructive or threaten suicide are especially effective in eliciting fear responses in their loved ones.

Even though covert negative power may bring about the desired results or attention, the cost to the perpetrator is immense. Therapists often point out to clients that this mode of seeking power is never worth the trouble or the limitations it necessitates. Adults who persist in using this childish form of control not only damage others but harm their own development as well. This type of unconscious manipulation requires that a person remain in an unhappy, miserable state and, at times, even suffer genuine physical pain.

> Janice was bed-ridden for more than a year with chronic, intractable back pain. Her doctors could find nothing physically wrong; nonetheless, she continued to complain of "horrible pain." Her husband, David, catered to her: shopping, cooking,

taking care of their five-year-old son, and serving as her personal masseuse. Each night, David brought her dinner in bed and spent an hour or more massaging her back.

The couple entered therapy because both partners felt distant from one another and were concerned that their sexual relationship had become virtually nonexistent. After a number of sessions, the therapist challenged Janice's disability. He suggested that her chronic pain was based on an unconscious manipulation to elicit care and attention from her husband. He pointed out to her that it was not worth continuing to play this destructive game, because in order to control David and keep him close to her, she necessarily had to experience the painful symptoms. Her condition also precluded the active sex life that she had once enjoyed with her husband, which she wished to recover.

Initially Janice was angry and insulted, and responded defensively. When she had time to reflect on the therapist's interpretation, however, she gained insight into her stake in being an invalid. Her back pain began to dissipate. When the therapist challenged Janice, David was even more angry at the therapist than his wife was. He felt protective of Janice despite the fact that the interpretation favored his best interests. It became apparent that on some level, he too had a stake in this collusive arrangement. His role as a source of strength in her helpless state fulfilled his frustrated need for power and dominance.

Overt negative power

When people exercise overt negative power through force, military might, or coercion and, in doing so, inflict harm on other people or infringe on their human rights, it is clearly unethical. Leaders who use force or threats of punishment to accomplish their goals eventually upset the stability of the larger society, depress its economy, and oppress its citizens. Totalitarian leaders and dictators tend to play on the fears of their constituents in order to establish, maintain, and increase their power base.

Most people lack the desire to change the world or to influence the masses. McClelland (1975) and his associates reported that most people have a strong need for achievement, which is different than the need for power itself. They desire only to have some element of control over their personal lives, families, finances and economic situation, and their health and work environment.

Yet there are certain types of people who actively and persistently seek out and obtain power through destructive means. In many cases, the personality structure of these individuals reflects underlying psychological disturbance, including problems with anger, narcissism, vanity, and sociopathic tendencies (Kellerman, 2004).[5] People who utilize overt negative power are generally compensating for inferiority feelings and for real or perceived inadequacies (R. Firestone & Catlett, 1989; Lowen, 1985). They tend to be cut off from feeling for themselves and others. In terms of the parent-child dichotomy described earlier, they lean toward the parental side, acting superior and judgmental while denying their child selves.

These people also attempt to deny feelings of helplessness and powerlessness in relation to death by achieving power over other people (Lipman-Blumen, 2005). Their vanity offers them a sense of being special and, as such, exempt from natural forces. This fantasy operates along with their success in dominating others to defend against death anxiety. Because this process never succeeds in completely eliminating the fear of death, the need for power becomes increasingly compelling, often leading to disastrous outcomes in a business enterprise or to serious crimes against humanity in the political scene.

Research has shown that individuals who become powerful political figures tend to be intensely ambitious, somewhat paranoid, and driven to seize power (Robins & Post, 1997). The exhilaration of having complete control over others can become addictive in that it produces feelings of elation and diminishes feelings of insecurity and inferiority.

The average person is unlikely to promote or engage in widespread aggressive acting-out behavior or warfare, but can be led into this behavior by individuals exercising overt negative power. It is not necessarily because ordinary citizens are free of destructive propensities that they would not be driven to seize power; rather, it is because they tend to lean more toward the childish side of the parent-child dichotomy, and are more afraid of and intimidated by authority than those who become leaders. In *Nuremberg Diary*, Gustave Gilbert (1947) quoted the words of Herman Goering, who tersely described this dynamic as follows:

> Naturally, the common people don't want war; neither in Russia nor in England nor in America, nor for that matter in Germany. That is understood. But, after all, it is the leaders of the country who determine the policy and it is always a simple matter to drag the people along, whether it is a democracy or a fascist dictatorship or a Parliament or a Communist dictatorship … .
>
> [Even in a democracy] the people can always be brought to the bidding of the leaders. That is easy. All you have to do is tell them they are being attacked and denounce the pacifists for lack of patriotism and exposing the country to danger. It works the same way in any country (pp. 278–279).

Even when the goals of a government and its leaders appear to be benevolent and concerned with the welfare of people, the means through which they try to achieve these ends can be cruel and destructive. The ideology underlying most political movements is usually idealistic and motivated by the desire for reform, the need to create a more egalitarian society, and the wish to help the poor and disadvantaged. Most, if not all, democratic, socialistic, and communistic ideologies have these optimistic and humanitarian underpinnings. However, the individuals who take over the power with a mandate to accomplish these positive ends generally fail because they are motivated by narcissistic power needs and become willing to use any means for attaining their goals.

Overt negative power through the control of knowledge

The control of information through the omission of certain facts, the distortion of information, and the suppression of knowledge is a subtle form of overt negative power operating in the sociopolitical arena. Only an intelligent and informed citizenry can potentially achieve a true form of democracy through the elective process.[6] A well-informed electorate has the ability to reform a corrupt government and remove a toxic leader. However, people are often limited in this regard because of misinformation and propaganda promulgated by the power structure through the media and other institutionalized sources of information. Democracy becomes even more difficult to achieve in nations where the government or a select few control the media.

After exploring the historical roots of power and knowledge, Foucault (1972) concluded that "Each society has its regime of truth, its 'general politics' of truth: that is, the types of discourse which it accepts and makes function as true" (p. 131). Truth "is produced and transmitted under the control, dominant if not exclusive, of a few great political and economic apparatuses (university, army, writing, media)" (pp. 131–132). In his book *Power Shift*, Toffler (1990) acknowledged that "The control of knowledge is the crux of tomorrow's worldwide struggle for power in every human institution" (p. 20).

> Knowledge is the most democratic source of power. Which makes it a continuing threat to the powerful, even as they use it to enhance their own power. It also explains why every power-holder—from the patriarch of a family to the president of a company or the Prime Minister of a nation—wants to control the quantity, quality, and distribution of knowledge within his or her domain (p. 19).

Toffler also stressed the fact that "Knowledge is even more mal-distributed than arms or wealth" (p. 469). In fact, the asymmetrical dissemination of information and knowledge through the media provides countless opportunities for the political power structure to exert control over members of society. For example, in the print media as well as in radio and television, the repetition of emotionally charged phrases, clichés, and slogans transmitted in sound bites numbs our sensibilities, discourages serious reflection, and fractures our sense of reality much as double messages do (de Zengotita, 2002).[7] The "framing" or "reframing" of issues so that they elicit the right connotations or positive responses is still another example of how media content and language can be manipulated. In *The Political Brain*, Westen (2007) observed that "Frames influence not only what people think and feel about an issue but what they *don't* think about" (p. 264).[8] According to Marcuse (1991), the gradual erosion of intellectual discourse in modern society is the outgrowth of institutional control of information and knowledge.

> The result is the familiar Orwellian language ("peace is war" and "war is peace", etc.), which is by no means that of terroristic totalitarianism only .... Relatively new is the general acceptance of these lies by public and private opinion, the suppression of their monstrous content (pp. 88–89).

In a similar vein, Chomsky (2005) has described propaganda as one of the most effective instruments of power being utilized by governments to manipulate public opinion:

> It was well understood, long before George Orwell, that memory must be repressed. Not only memory, but consciousness of what's happening right in front of you must be repressed, because if the public comes to understand what's being done in its name, it probably won't permit it. That's the main reason for propaganda. Otherwise, there is no point in it. Why not just tell the truth?. But power systems never tell the truth if they can get away with it, because they simply don't trust the public (pp. 99–100).[9]

In recent years, a number of media reform groups have sought to enlighten the public regarding contemporary forms of "thought-control" and to stem the tide of corporate takeovers of the print and electronic media. They reported that as of 2004, five mega-corporations controlled most of the media industry in the United States (Media Reform Information Center, 2007).[10] In a speech before the 2003 National Conference on Media Reform, Bill Moyers warned of the consequences of this monopoly:

> In earlier times our governing bodies tried to squelch journalistic freedom with the blunt instruments of the law ... . But they've found new ones now, in the name of "national security." ... Add to that the censorship-by-omission of consolidated media empires digesting the bones of swallowed independents, and you've got a major shrinkage of the crucial information that thinking citizens can act upon ... . If free and independent

journalism committed to telling the truth without fear or favor is suffocated, the oxygen goes out of democracy (para. 6–7, 11).

Power dynamics in the family

Issues of power and control enter into all interpersonal relationships. An analogy can be made between power relations in a social order and those operating within families. From an ethical perspective, the functions of power in a political system, government, or society can be compared with those served by the family in terms of whether they validate or violate the rights of each individual.

The nuclear family is revered in our society and family values are acknowledged as being ethical and good. However, some families are obviously dysfunctional and many "normal" families function in a manner that exerts excessive control over children through severe rules and prohibitions that demand obligation, blind obedience, and conformity. In these families, absolute, unquestioning loyalty is required of all family members, whether it is deserved or not (Beavers, 1977; Boszormenyi-Nagy & Spark, 1984; Kerr & Bowen, 1988; Tedeschi & Felson, 1994).

Disturbances in the balance of power between the parents, which is operationally defined as how authority, power, and decision making are distributed across partners, have been found to contribute to problematic parent-child relationships:

> One specific way in which marital power struggles have been hypothesized to perturb the coherence of the larger system is through disturbances in parent-child alliances, especially the establishment of cross-generational coalitions and the triangulation of the child into the marital conflict (Lindahl, Malik, Kaczynski & Simons, 2004, p. 625).

In a large cross-cultural study conducted by Lindahl, et al (2004), it was found that "couple power dynamics accounted for more than a third of the variance in systemic family functioning" (p. 625). "Cross-generational subsystem alliances were associated with externalizing problems for both European American and Hispanic American children" (p. 626). The researchers reported that the children who had "the most behavior problems (rising to the borderline clinical range in European American children)" were those in which the "family level functioning was observed to be most disrupted, disengaged, and affectively disorganized" (p. 627), that is, in those families manifesting disturbed power dynamics including triangulation with one or more children.

Many parents exhibit the characteristics of an authoritarian personality and exercise destructive power in the process of socializing their offspring. They establish rigid standards regarding appropriate and inappropriate behavior and often use physical punishment, humiliation, coercion, emotional blackmail, and other manipulations to keep their children in line (Barber, 2002).[11] These families tend to be autocratic and cult-like in how they operate, in that they demand submission to an irrational authority and conformity to arbitrary and unreasonable rules.

One woman, who had been the youngest of five girls, recalled the illogical, capricious rules that her parents had set up to socialize their offspring. Meals were to be eaten in silence, the chores, which were extensive because the family lived on a farm, were to be completed by 7 p.m., and the girls were to be in bed and asleep by 8 p.m., even though they were of widely differing ages.

In a group talk, the woman talked about the regimen that the parents had established for discipline. For example, if the mother felt that one child had disobeyed her or had neglected a chore during the day, she reported the incident to her husband on his return from the fields. The five girls were immediately lined up against a wall in the basement, and each one, in turn, was whipped by the father with a belt, wooden paddle, or willow tree "switch." The woman remembered how guilty she felt when she was the one whom her mother accused of being "disobedient" or "defiant." Looking back, she was unable to recall any specific acts of misbehavior on her part, but she still felt guilty because whatever she had done had given her parents an excuse to take out their sadism on all the children. She said that her feelings of guilt were even more excruciating than the physical pain that she and her siblings endured whenever the five girls were punished in this manner.

The parenting practices of the family described above illustrate a pattern of coercion and control observed by Tedeshi and Felson (1994) in their studies of family life:

> Coercion, or *power-assertion*, as it is often referred to in the literature, is one of several methods that parents use to influence their children (p. 292) Studies of parent-child interactions in American families reveal high levels of coercive behavior, including bodily force, verbal and physical punishment, physical isolation, and deprivation of resources (pp. 290–291) In the case of younger children, parents have superior size and strength as well. Parental use of coercion is supported normatively and legally by the larger society (p. 292).

In other families, the exercise of power is more covert or subtle. Control is communicated implicitly through parental attitudes manifested in behaviors that seem to have little or nothing to do with the exercise of power per se. For example, in families where any movement toward independence or autonomy on the part of a child or adolescent is perceived as rebellion or defiance, parents react to the threat to the family structure. In a desperate attempt to maintain the fantasy bond or illusion of connection with the child, a parent may exert covert negative power by becoming ill or developing symptoms of mental illness. On the other hand, the parent may wield overt negative power by directly rejecting and ostracizing the child (Richman, 1986).[12] These manipulations, power plays, and double-bind communications are aimed at reestablishing the symbiotic tie with the young person, thereby alleviating the anxiety of the impending separation.

> In one case, a father who was a physicist and mathematician became enraged when his college-age daughter informed him of her decision to change her major from math to art history and design. When she told him the news in a conversation that took place when the family was dining out, he could not restrain his anger and raised his voice so that everyone in the restaurant could hear: "So, what are you planning to become? A whore!" As a form of punishment or perhaps in a last ditch effort to control her future, the father refused to pay for the remainder of her

college education, although he continued to support his other two teenagers in college.

The coercive, punishing behavior on the part of this father alienated his daughter and she grew even more distant from him as the years passed. Yet as an adult, she found herself inadvertently imitating many of her father's behaviors, in particular his pattern of working compulsively. In her position as president of a graphic arts company, she often intimidated employees by being cool and aloof. She would often exclude from important meetings certain people who had fallen from her good graces, and at times she humiliated employees by chastising them in front of their coworkers. Thus, she came to treat people in the work situation in much the same way her father had treated her.

When children are deeply hurt, rejected, or are the receptacles for negative parental projections, they often assume the identity of the parent who has hurt, rejected and depreciated them. In an effort to maintain some semblance of ego-integrity, they identify with the powerful, punishing parent. Later, as adults, they act out destructive forms of power in their relationships or seek out positions in society where they are able to recapitulate the primal situation. They unconsciously dominate, control or mistreat other people in the same manner that they were once treated.

Finally, it is important to mention that a basic function of the family is to transmit the values, social mores, and a specific world view to the next generation. Unfortunately, the family constellation can function as a training ground in the basics of covert negative power, wherein one or both parents indirectly teach children destructive techniques of control and manipulation through role-modeling victimized, passive-aggressive behavior, as depicted in the example of Anita and Cindy in Chapter 10.

The corruption of power

Destructive power structures in the family are mirrored in a societal framework and in the political arena (Fromm, 1941; J. Gilligan, 1996a, 1996b; Lasch, 1979; A. Miller 1981/1984). On a societal level, when power is corrupted—when it is utilized to control others, to intimidate or oppress others—there is a corresponding increase in the incidence of social violence and other forms of "social evil." In this context, evil can be defined as "the inflicting of harm or suffering on another human being" (Baumeister, 1997, p. 305).[13] As Sarnoff put it, "Evil is knowing better but doing worse" (cited by Zimbardo, 2004, p. 22). In the business world and in politics, the corruption of power is facilitated when individuals become "morally disengaged" from their values and their concern for others. C. Moore's (2007) hypotheses hold promise of advancing "our understanding of how organizational corruption is initiated, facilitated, and perpetuated" (p. 137).[14]

Nowhere is "evil" more apparent than in the manifestation of prejudice, ethnic strife, the horror of ethnic cleansing, and unjust warfare. In "Thoughts for the Times on War and Death," Freud (1915/1957b) articulated his views of the inevitability of war: "So long as the conditions of existence among nations are so different and their mutual repulsion so violent, there are bound to be wars" (p. 299). Freud's pessimism concerning the future of mankind was due largely to his deterministic view of man's aggressive tendencies; yet it also reflected the stress and turmoil of the times he lived in. It is the authors' view that people's hostility and violence are responses to painful issues of childhood compounded by the awful specter of death (R. Firestone, 1994b; Morrant & Catlett, 2008).

Psychological defenses that minimize or shut out psychological pain are collectively expressed in restrictive, dehumanizing cultural patterns. The irony is that people feel these cultural patterns must be protected at all costs. The authors' conception that aggression stems from frustration and fear rather than from instinct is congenial with Becker's (1975) view: "It is one thing to say that man is not human because he is a vicious animal, and another to say that it is because he is a frightened creature who tries to secure a victory over his limitations" (p. 169).

The explanation set forth here not only provides a clear perspective concerning the underlying meaning of prejudice, racism, and war, but also an outlook that is positive, pragmatic, and action-oriented. It offers hope for the future, whereas the deterministic conception of man's essential savagery insures a self-fulfilling prophecy. Pessimistic forecasting generally precludes constructive action and people tend to feel progressively more demoralized and helpless. The authors believe that humankind has the capability to achieve peace in the world; they are, however, realistically concerned that the fight for this goal may be rejected.[15]

The origins of ethnic strife, warfare, and terrorism

The essay that follows was published originally as an article, "The Origins of Ethnic Strife" (R. Firestone, 1996) in *Mind and Human Interaction*. Portions of the essay are reproduced here without paraphrasing in order to preserve the clarity of presentation and emphasize the increased importance and timeliness of the topic.

> *You've got to be taught to hate and fear.*
> *You've got to be taught from year to year.*
> *You've got to be taught before it's too late,*
> *Before you are six or seven or eight,*
> *To hate all the people your relatives hate.*
> *You've got to be carefully taught!*

> (Lyric excerpts from "You've Got to be Carefully Taught" by Richard Rodgers and Oscar Hammerstein II).

The words of this song pertain to one aspect of a powerful defense mechanism that reifies the family, shrouding it and other forms of group identification in a fantasy bond that assures immortality in the face of the conscious and unconscious anxiety associated with death. The fantasy bond offers security at the expense of self-realization, autonomy and individuation (R. Firestone, 1984). The fantasy solution arises to counter interpersonal trauma and separation anxiety. To continue to offer a safe haven, it must be protected from all intrusion. This protection predisposes aggressiveness, hostility, and malice toward those who challenge its function.

The combined projection of individual defense mechanisms into a social framework makes up a significant aspect of culture. These consensually validated social mores and rituals in turn influence individual personality development. Members of a given social group or society have a considerable stake in how they perceive reality, and their emotional security is fractured when individuals or groups express alternative perceptions. Indeed, cultural patterns, religious belief, and mores that are different from one's own threaten the core defense that acts as a buffer against terrifying emotions. People will fight to the death to defend their customs and traditions against others who perceive and interpret reality in different terms.

The distinctive elements that support cultural integrity and loyalty in a specific group or society are at once a source of beauty and of human destructiveness. Paradoxically, the myriad cultural patterns, racial, religious and ethnic differences make for creative individuation and fascinating variations, yet they also arouse insidious hostilities. Indeed, attitudes of ethnic superiority and the resultant ethnic strife are the major problems facing humankind in the new millennium. Although issues of economics and territoriality are also stimuli for inter-group hostility, the authors support the position that religious differences and ethnic hatred constitute the more significant threat at this point in history. The rapid advance of technology and its destructive potential is out-running our rationality. Unless we understand the nature of the psychological defense mechanisms that play a major part in people's intolerance and savagery, the human race will be threatened by unending conflict, or even extinction.

Human aggression

Many scholars view human aggression as the key issue in ethnic strife and war. As noted in Chapter 6, people employ both idiosyncratic, individual defense mechanisms and social defenses to protect themselves against anxiety related to death. Much human aggression can be attributed to the fact that the individual conspires with others to create cultural imperatives, institutions, and beliefs that are designed to deny death and existential concerns. These socially constructed defenses never "work" completely as a solution to the problem of our mortality; if they did work, there would be no need for controversy and no reason to go to war over differences in religion, race, or customs. On some level, people remain insecure and unsure despite strong belief in a particular religion (Becker, 1973/1997; S. Solomon, Greenberg, & Pyszczynski, 2004). The fear of death still intrudes on their consciousness, particularly when they encounter others with different beliefs about life or religious orientations. Other cultural worldviews and systems are threatening, particularly for those individuals who are ontologically insecure.

Unfortunately, people are willing to sacrifice themselves in war to preserve their nation's or religion's particular symbols of immortality in a desperate attempt to achieve a sense of mastery over death. This same desperation can be observed in the prisoner on death row who chooses to commit suicide, thereby taking control over the time of his or her death, rather than enduring the unbearable anxiety of waiting for the hour of execution (R. Firestone & Seiden, 1987). In each case, actual death is preferable to the anticipatory anxiety and uncertainty surrounding the imagination of a death beyond our control.

Approaches to group identification

A number of theorists assert that group identification is a major causative factor in religious, racial, and international conflict. Freud's (1921/1955) work on the subject, which stressed the "mindlessness of the group mind," supports the authors' thesis that group membership offers a false sense of superiority, specialness, and omnipotence to individuals who feel helpless and powerless in an uncertain world. Freud (1921/1955) and Fromm (1941) contended that identification with the group is a significant contributing factor in religious, racial, and ethnic conflict. Freud noted that "a group is extraordinarily credulous and open to influence, it has no critical faculty, and the improbable does not exist for it ... . A group knows neither doubt nor uncertainty" (p. 78). Extending these concepts to religious groups, he went on to argue that believers naturally experience malice and animosity toward nonbelievers:

> Those people who do not belong to the community of believers ... . stand outside this tie. Therefore a religion, even if it calls itself the religion of love, must be hard and unloving to those who do not belong to it (p. 98).

Erich Fromm (1941, 1950) traced the social and psychological elements of the Nazi movement to their sources in the Age of Reformation. He explained that existential fears of aloneness and the "terrifying responsibility of freedom" compel people to take actions as a group that would be unthinkable to them as individuals:

> There is nothing inhuman, evil, or irrational which does not give some comfort provided it is shared by a group ... . Once

a doctrine, however irrational, has gained power in a society, millions of people will believe in it rather than feel ostracized and isolated (1950, p. 33).

Similarly, Piven (2006) has noted that "It just does not take that much for groups … to become lasciviously violent" (p. 234).

The members of a group may have all been uniquely humili-ated in deeply painful ways, have been shamed or abused by their family or peers, have enough rage, misogyny, or paranoia to coalesce as a group that may find common targets for their pain (p. 243).

The authors hypothesize that identification with a particular ethnic or religious group is at once a powerful defense against death anxi-ety, and a system of thought and belief that can set the stage for hatred and bloodshed. Group identification provides individuals with an illusion of immortality through imagined fusion with the membership. Conformity to the belief system of the group, that is, to its collective symbols of immortality, protects one against the horror of facing the objective loss of self. In merging his or her identity with that of a group, each person feels that although he or she may not survive as an individual entity, he or she will live on as part of something larger that *will* continue to exist after he or she is gone.

Research on prejudice and racism

In his classic work, *The Nature of Prejudice,* Allport (1954) synthesized a number of perspectives on the causative factors of prejudice, including group and individual personality dynamics based on social-cognitive principles and psychoanalytic theory.[16] He asserted that *"Discrimination comes about only when we deny to individuals or groups of people equality of treatment which they may wish. It occurs when we take steps to exclude members of an out-group from our neighborhood, school, occupation, or country"* (p. 51). Allport also emphasized the fact that "Violence is always an outgrowth of milder states of mind … . It is apparent, therefore, that under cer-tain circumstances there will be stepwise progression from verbal aggression to violence, from rumor to riot, from gossip to genocide" (p. 57).

Studies conducted by Tajfel (Tajfel, Billig, Bundy & Flament, 1971) have shown that "social categorization *per se* is sufficient as well as necessary to induce forms of in-group favoritism and discrimination against the out-group" (Turner, 1978, p. 101). Similarly, Baumeister (2005) has stressed the fact that "Groups may be formed on the basis of seemingly minimal, even trivial criteria, but people will cleave together and square off against others" (p. 377).[17] Current research into the causes of prejudice and discrimination have investigated the emotions underlying stereotyping and discrimination, including envy, pity, admiration, anger, disgust, and pride (DeSteno, Dasgupta, Bartlett & Cajdric, 2004; Fiske, Cuddy, Glick & Xu, 2002). Others have studied situational variables (Haney & Zimbardo, 1998) and the cognitive/affective underpinnings of implicit or subtle racial prejudice (Amodio & Devine, 2006).

A number of theorists, among them Parens (2007), Scharff and Scharff (2007), and Wirth (2007) have investigated negative family influences and childhood trauma that they hypothesized as contributing to the formation of "malignant prejudice." Attachment theorists Fonagy and Higgitt (2007) explained that malignant prejudice "is associated with disorganization of the attachment system" (p. 71). Disorganized attachment, as noted, has been found to be correlated with a parent's unresolved trauma and loss.

Wirth (2007) employed the example of Slobodan Milosevic to show how personal trauma and loss in his family-of-origin (his father, mother, and an uncle committed suicide) were reflected in his fellow countrymen's "chosen trauma" (the 14th century defeat of the Serbs by the Ottoman Turks). Through propaganda, Milosevic reactivated stories of the defeat, rekindling old prejudices, and executed his destructive wars in Slovenia and Bosnia, and "the beginnings of ethnic cleansing in Kosovo" (p. 119).[18]

Studies concerning people's need to maintain self-esteem within a given cultural framework are relevant to our discussion of prejudice. Ernest Becker (1971) and S. Solomon, Greenberg, and Pyszczynski (1991) have proposed that self-esteem functions as a buffer against death anxiety: "A substantial portion of our social behavior is directed toward sustaining faith in a shared cultural worldview (which provides the basis for self-esteem) and maintaining a sense of value within that cultural context" (p. 118). In another article, S. Solomon, Greenberg, and Pyszczynski (2000) stated:

> Mortality concerns contribute to prejudice because people who are different challenge the absolute validity of one's cultural worldview. Psychological equanimity is restored by bolstering self-worth and faith in the cultural worldview, typically by engaging in culturally valued behaviors and by venerating people who are similar to oneself, and berating, converting, or annihilating those who are different (p. 203).

In previous works, (R. Firestone, 1994b, 1997a), the authors have described a number of defensive maneuvers that people use to bolster their self-esteem and feelings of self-importance. The defenses of disowning one's own negative or despised characteristics and projecting these traits onto others help one maintain self-esteem, albeit falsely, and provide the basis for prejudice and racism. People of one ethnic group tend to dispose of their self-hatred by projecting it onto their enemies, perceiving them as subhuman, dirty, impure, and inherently evil (Erikson 1969; Holt & Silverstein, 1989; Keen, 1986; Newman, Duff & Baumeister, 1997; B. Silverstein, 1989). Subsequently they behave as though they can achieve perfection and immortality only through the removal of this imperfection, impurity, and evil from the world.[19]

Institutional defenses against death anxiety

Two major forms of defenses against death anxiety that have evolved into unique cultural systems are: (1) religious dogma, including belief in an afterlife, reincarnation, or union with a universal unconscious (Toynbee, 1968); and (2) group identification and nationalism, idolization of leadership, and mindless allegiance to the group cause.

    Over the millennia, people have created increasingly complex institutions, conventions, belief systems, and sanctions in their attempt to adapt to death anxiety. Each succeeding generation has added its own incremental building blocks to the system of denial and accommodation. Societies are largely moving toward more elaborate and effective defenses that act to cut off emotion or dull the highs and lows of life, thereby numbing individuals to basic existential issues. This suppression of feelings and emotions has led to an increase in aggression, violence, and criminality, accompanied by a heightened indifference to the suffering of human beings.

Religious doctrine
For the most part, religious doctrine consists of consensually validated concepts of existential truth. Traditional religious beliefs of both Western and Eastern cultures can be thought to contribute to a collective neurosis whereby defenses against death anxiety reinforce people's tendencies to deny the body (Western) or transcend or devalue the self (Eastern).[20]

Misinterpretations of teachings originally meant to enhance the spiritual and humane aspects of life have led to these self-denying, self-sacrificing orientations. Pagels (1988) noted that theologians since St. Augustine have postulated that the punishment for Adam's act of disobedience in the Garden of Eden was death. Their interpretation offers the promise that by denying sexual desire and bodily pleasures, one's soul can triumph over the body and survive death. Similarly, many people have misunderstood the teachings of Taoism and Buddhism and assumed that all desire, striving, "ego" must be given up in order to attain enlightenment (Dalai Lama, 1999; Suzuki, Fromm & DeMartino, 1960; Watts, 1961).[21]

The question arises as to why millions of people blindly follow religious dogma based on serious distortions of original teachings. Transcendence over the body which must die, the postulation of a soul or spirit, and the union with a powerful being are the principal motivations. Religious dogmatism generally supports a process of self-limitation and self-abrogation, yet restricting or suppressing people's natural desires and feelings unwittingly contributes to an increase in the incidence of violence and immoral acting-out behavior (Prescott 1975; Vergote, 1978/1988).

There are variations in the warlike tendencies of religious groups: some have an aggressive desperation attached to their beliefs, while others are peace-loving and generate far less animosity toward people of different persuasions. Religious dogma that is rigid, restrictive, and inflexible functions to instill strong hatred and malice in believers toward non-believers. Some religious factions endorse individual sacrifice in war as a tenet of their doctrine: a heroic death in a religious war guarantees entry into the after-life.

According to many political analysts (Owen, 1993; Wirth, 2007), the Mideastern and Balkan conflicts in the early 90s were based largely on religious motives. The ethnic cleansing that took place in Yugoslavia represented yet another stage in a 600-year-old conflict that began with a religious war during the fourteenth century. Old hatreds were fueled by aggressive actions and killings that personalized the new situation. One's family members are wounded or lost, one's children experience suffering or annihilation, or one lives in everyday fear that one may be killed. In these scenarios, strong aggressive tendencies to retaliate are awakened.

Nationalism and totalitarianism

James Gilligan (2007) has defined nationalism "as a form of prejudice that privileges members of one's own nation and discredits those who belong to others:

> Once religion—the divine right of kings—lost its credibility as the source of legitimacy, another basis had to be found ... . With belief in nationalism came the belief that governments, or states, derived their legitimacy from the nation they represented and defended. The concept of nationhood and the nation-state thus replaced the now-defunct concepts of God, religion, and the divine right of kings (p. 39).[22]

Nationalism, communism, capitalism, and other "isms" function as a narcotic, a psychic painkiller that fosters a deep dependency in people who are searching for comfort, security, and relief from ontological anxiety. In any system other than a functioning democracy, the individual subordinates the self in relation to an idea or a principle and experiences a false sense of power. The illusion of fusion and connection that comes from being a part of a patriotic or nationalistic movement is exhilarating and addictive. Indeed, any cause, whether potentially good or evil, is capable of fostering a corresponding addiction in the individual.

Similarly, Falk (2004) has described nationalism as a collective illusion, a fusion of one's narcissistic, grandiose image, with the image of greatness embedded in the national group. "Nationalism can be viewed as defensive group narcissism" (p. 99). He elaborated further on this notion in asserting that nationalism, patriotism, and fascism:

> may result from an unconscious displacement of the personal narcissism of each of the individuals belonging to the group onto the national group, and of an identification with the group as a mirror image of one's own grandiose self. After the Six-Day War, when Israel suddenly quadrupled in size, some Israelis personally felt bigger and stronger (p. 99).

Totalitarian regimes are generally associated with the outcome of the vacillations of socioeconomic forces, but their roots tend to lie more in the psychological make-up of the populous. As Albert Einstein asserted, *"Nationalism is an infantile disease, the Measles of Mankind."* As noted earlier, the average person's desperate, childlike dependence on the group, idolization of the leader, and unswerving allegiance to a cause are all associated with defenses against death anxiety. When these defenses are threatened by outside influences, people are terrified of reexperiencing the pain, anticipatory grief, and dread of death. Generally, they respond to this anxiety on a preconscious or unconscious level by intensifying their defenses without true awareness. On a more conscious level, however, many individuals become highly defensive and angry at those who disagree with their solutions and may mobilize action against these enemies as did the medieval crusaders who attempted to impose their fanatic religious beliefs on heretics in bloody holy wars. According to Piven (2006):

> For many people the mere existence of alternative ways of thinking arouses terror, horror, rage, and sanctimonious fervor (p. 237) An ideology that defends against death itself is sacred, intoxicating, and precious, and the mere existence of other competing ideologies or theologies is often enough to arouse fear, hatred, and the urge to humiliate and destroy heretics or infidels (p. 236).

Empirical research

The data supporting existential approaches to aggression were initially observational and longitudinal; however, recent findings from over 200 empirical studies based on terror management theory (TMT) tend to validate these views. According to Pyszczynski (2004):

> One of our earliest and most widely replicated findings [in TMT research] is that reminders of death increase nationalism and other forms of group identification, making people more accepting of those who are similar to themselves and more hostile toward those who are different (p. 837).

These studies, which demonstrated increased reliance on defense mechanisms to maintain self-esteem as a result of the experimentally manipulated arousal of death anxiety, have provided support for the authors' hypotheses (McGregor, et al, 1998; Mikulincer & Shaver, 2001; S. Solomon, et al, 1991). In discussing the implications of this research in terms of TMT theory, Greenberg, et al (1990) concluded:

> People's beliefs about reality [and their cultural expressions of such beliefs] provide a buffer against the anxiety that results from living in a largely uncontrollable, perilous universe, where the only certainty is death (p. 308) Enthusiasm for such conflicts [religious wars and ethnic conflict] among those who actually end up doing the killing and the dying is largely fueled by the threat implied to each group's cultural anxiety-buffer by the existence of the other group (pp. 309–310).

Conclusion

In this chapter, the authors do not attempt to offer a simple solution in the struggle for peace, nor do we feel there can be one. However, the lack of an immediate, obvious course of action or definitive pragmatic program should not be interpreted as cause for pessimism or devalued on those grounds (Volkan, 1997). We offer guidelines explaining the part played by human aggression in the corruption of power that, if properly understood, could lead to an effective program of education that would foster the development of personal power and social responsibility in individuals rather than overt and covert forms of negative power. It is possible that with such education, people would come to know themselves in a manner that could effectively alter destructive child-rearing practices and social processes that foster aggression. As the UNESCO Charter declares: "Since wars begin in the minds of men, it is in the minds of men that we have to erect the ramparts of peace" (cited by Keen, 1986, p. 10).

Freud (1915/1957b) shaded his own pessimistic view when he declared that people might benefit from the awareness, rather than the denial, of their mortality:

> Would it not be better to give death the place in reality and in our thoughts which is its due, and to give a little more prominence to the unconscious attitude towards death which we have hitherto so carefully suppressed? (p. 299)

In a similar vein, Becker (1971) concluded *The Birth and Death of Meaning* with the following affirmation:

> As the immortal Plato lamented in words that haunt us today more than ever: "Human affairs are hardly worth considering in earnest and yet we must be in earnest about them—a sad necessity constrains us." (p. 197) It seems clear that comfortable illusion is now a danger to human survival ... . Man now seems to have to move ahead with his own strength to the frontiers of anxiety. And who knows what would come of that (pp. 198–199).

The authors propose that in order to overcome prejudice, racism, and hostilities associated with ethnic differences, we need a more inclusive, truly global, tolerant, and compassionate view of people everywhere. *Inclusion, not exclusion, is the key to our survival.*[23] In order to find peace, we must face existential issues, overcome our personal upbringings, and learn to live without soothing psychological defenses. In some sense we must continually mourn our own death in order to fully accept and value our life. There is no way to banish painful memories and feelings from consciousness without losing our sense of humanity and feeling of compassion for others. An individual *can* overcome personal limitations and embrace life in the face of death anxiety. Such a person would find no need for ethnic hatred or insidious warfare.

Notes

1. See Plato's *Republic*, and Machiavelli's *The Prince*. Machiavelli believed that a leader, "a prince," should be both loved and feared, but if both were not possible, then he should choose to be feared rather than loved.
2. See Max Weber's (Middlesex University, 2007) description of "The Three Pure Types of Legitimate Authority" (Section 2, The three pure types of legitimate authority, para. 1–4).
3. Lipman-Blumen (2005) observed that:

   Illusions are the umbilical cord linking leaders and followers. Leaders understand their followers' need for illusions. So do their entourages, who promote illusions about the leader's omnipotence and omniscience (p. 51) Many of us look to leaders who project an aura of certainty—real or imagined—that we lack within ourselves. And if they are not *actually* knowledgeable and in control, we convince ourselves that they truly are, to satisfy our own desperate need (p. 53).

   Re: The dynamics of ongoing interactions between the powerful and less powerful, see *Disturbing the Peace* by Vaclav Havel (1990) who reminded the reader that: "All power is power over someone, and it always somehow responds, usually unwittingly rather than deliberately, to the state of mind and the behavior of those it rules over. One can always find in the behavior of power a reflection of what is going on "below" (p. 182).
4. See "A New Perspective on the Oedipal Complex" (R. Firestone, 1994a) in which the author explained that: "parents' rivalrous and aggressive feelings toward their children are incorporated by their children as a destructive voice process. Later, when competitive situations and feelings arise in life, these voices are generally activated" (pp. 349–350). See Kotter (1985) who discussed the rarity of positive or personal power in business organizations, "one of the biggest problems in modern organizations is related not to an excess of power, but to the fact that too many people have too little power" (p. 136).

Leadership experts have described another reason why people may be resistant to pursuing and/or maintaining powerful positions in organizational life. According to Boyatzis and McKee (2005): *"Power stress is part of the experience that results from the exercise of influence and sense of responsibility felt in leadership positions.* In addition, leadership effectiveness requires the regular exercise of self-control: ... The exercise of self-control is also stressful" (p. 206). See Boyatzis and McKee is discussion of the effects of Chronic Power Stress on the sympathetic nervous system (SNS) in Appendix A of *Resonate Leadership*. Also see Gailliot, Schmeichel, and Baumeister's (2006) explanation of how stress can result from ego-depletion, that is, from an individual's having expended energy in a previous task requiring self-control and self-regulation.

5. However, it is important also to note Kellerman's (2004) critique of this "trait" hypothesis of bad leadership. "It is now widely argued that to overemphasize the leader's traits is to underemphasize other important variables, such as the situation, the nature of the task at hand, and of course, the followers" (p. 19).

6. See Westen's (2007) critique of the myth of the "rational" educated voter. "In one version or another, the vision of an ideally dispassionate electorate has dominated political science as well as political philosophy" (p. 26). However "the marketplace that matters most in American politics is the *marketplace of emotions*. Republicans has a keen eye for markets, and they have a near monopoly in the marketplace of emotions" (pp. 35–36). Also see *The Myth of the Rational Voter: Why Democracies Choose Bad Policies* by Bryan Caplan (2007) with respect to irrational views of contemporary economics.

7. See de Zengotita's (2002) "The Numbing of the American Mind." He pointed out that in the current "information revolution," we are becoming psychically numb and can no longer distinguish between reality and virtual reality or fabrication. The constant bombardment by all forms of media has devastating effects psychologically. De Zengotita warned: "For here, too, there is a psychological threshold. Today your brain is, as a matter of fact, full of stuff that was *designed* to affect you" (p. 37). The danger, as de Zengotita sees it, is that "The (absence of) sensation that is physical numbness is constituted by a multitude of thrills and tingles at a frequency beyond which you feel nothing" (p. 38).

8. Re: the "framing" of politically motivated messages, Westen (2007) contended that: "By framing the Iraq War as a war of liberation and

part of the broader war on terror, all the carnage and destruction in Iraq became so invisible that U.S. journalists rarely even ventured a guess about how many Iraqis had died in the initial 'liberation.'" (p. 264). Also see Lakoff's (2002) book, *Moral Politics*, in which he used a "family" metaphor for morality to analyze people's loyalty to a particular political party. Lakoff employed methods from cognitive linguistics to describe the moral systems of conservatives and liberals: "It is the common, unconscious and automatic metaphors of the Nation-as-Family that produces contemporary conservatism from Strict Father morality and contemporary liberalism from Nurturant Parent morality" (p. 13).

Amodio, Jost, Master, and Yee (2007) found differences between liberals and conservatives in the neural circuitry of the brain, the anterior cingulate cortex, when faced with a go-no-go experimental situation: "liberalism (versus conservatism) was associated with significantly greater conflict-related neural activity when response inhibition was required (that is, on No-Go trials) ... . Stronger conservatism (versus liberalism) was associated with less neurocognitive sensitivity to response conflicts" (p. 1247).Their results confirmed previous research showing that conservatives score higher on "psychological measures of personal needs for order, structure and closure. Liberals, by contrast, report higher tolerance of ambiguity and complexity, and greater openness to new experiences on psychological measures" (p. 1246).

9. In tracing the historical roots of propaganda, Noam Chomsky (2005) noted, "Propaganda became an organized and very self-conscious industry only in the last century [in Great Britain]. The Wilson administration reacted by setting up the first state propaganda agency here, the Committee on Public Information. This is already Orwellian, of course" (pp. 18–19). "They had learned you can control 'the public mind,' you can control attitudes and opinions, and, in Lippmann's phrase, 'manufacture consent'" (p. 20).

10. The Media Reform Information Center (2007) reported that in 2004, "Only 5 huge corporations—Time Warner, Disney, Murdoch's News Corporation, Bertelsmann of Germany, and Viacom (formerly CBS)—now control most of the media industry in the U.S (General Electric's NBC is a close sixth" (para. 2). (This is a reduction in number from the 50 corporations that controlled the media in 1983.)

11. See Nelson & Crick's (2002) chapter "Parental Psychological Control: Implications for Childhood Physical and Relational Aggression."

12. See *Family Therapy for Suicidal People* (Joseph Richman,1986).

13. See Baumeister's (1997) Chapter 12 "Why is There Evil?" in which he emphasized that:

> Evil does not exist in terms of solitary actions by solitary individuals. Perpetrators and victims—and in many cases, by-standers or observers, too—are necessary to the vast majority of evil acts. Evil is socially enacted and constructed. It does not reside in our genes or in our soul, but in the way we relate to other people (p. 375).

14. See Moore's (2007) elaboration of Bandura's concept of moral disengagement in relation to organizational corruption and Johnston's (2005) analysis of corruption in 98 countries, in which he defined corruption in a broad sense, including the effects of citizens' perceiving that their government is innately corrupt.

Sarnoff's quote appears in Zimbardo's (2004) reassessment of the Stanford prison experiment in which he concluded that assuming a leadership position as a defense against anxiety is never really effective, as was demonstrated in the Stanford Prison Experiment described in Chapter 4. The students who played the role of guards became increasingly punitive and sadistic as the study progressed. The authoritarian role they played not only failed to protect them from underlying feelings of inadequacy, but the students needed to up the ante, that is, become increasingly cruel, in an attempt to maintain the defense.

15. One positive change in strategy in the political sphere that could lead to a more optimistic, yet realistic, forecast has been in strategies of "soft power" used in the context of international relations. Arquilla and Ronfeldt (1999), in a Rand Corporation Monograph Report entitled "The Emergence of Noopolitik: Toward an American Information Strategy," proposed that "it would work through 'soft power' rather than 'hard power.' Noopolitik is guided more by a conviction that right makes might, than by the obverse" (p. x).

16. Dovidio, Glick, and Rudman (2005) described Allport's seemingly contradictory viewpoint on prejudice as on one hand "natural" and on the other hand, as "a fundamentally irrational hatred, born of ignorance and the ego-defensive maneuvers of people with weak personality structures" (pp. 1–2).

17. Comprehensive essays on prejudice by Elisabeth Young-Bruehl (2007) and James Gilligan (2007) can also be found in *The Future of Prejudice* (Parens, Mahfouz, Twemlow & Scharff, 2007). Re: another

manifestation of prejudice and social identity theory: A special subcase of strong inter-group prejudice or bias can be observed in various forms of identity politics (Boyle, 2000; Johnson-Roullier, 1997) prevalent in the second feminist movement, Black Civil Rights, and gay and lesbian liberation movements.

18. See Wirth's (2007) description of the interaction between Milosevic's traumatic personal life and the Serbian-Bosnian and Kosovo conflicts:

> Slobodan Milosevic's idiosyncratic disorder—his borderline personality disorder, his sadomasochism, the depression he denied, his latent suicidalism, and his inability to confront the suffering in his life—fit the Serbs' ethnic disorder as a key fits a lock. Milosevic had an intuitive sympathy for the trauma-tized feelings of his people because during his own life, he had experienced a mixture of traumatic loss, insults to his feeling of self-worth, and grandiose, wishful fantasies of his own great-ness similar to those experienced by the Serb collective (p. 125).

19. Erikson (1969) has written extensively about how group member-ship and discrimination have been used by human beings to alle-viate existential anxieties. In discussing people's propensities to categorize themselves and others into the in-group and out-group, Erikson argued: "So far in history he [man] has made every effort *not* to see that mankind is one species" (p. 431). Re: research on defensive projection, see "A New Look at Defensive Projection: Thought Suppression, Accessibility, and Biased Person Perception" (Newman, et al, 1997).

20. Re: Western and Eastern religious approaches to death, see "The Universal Fear of Death and the Cultural Response" by Moore and Williamson (2003).

21. His Holiness the 14th Dalai Lama (Dalai Lama, 1999) attempted to clarify this point. He explained that today we need a spiritual revo-lution, that is, "a radical reorientation away from our habitual pre-occupation with self [not a renunciation of self]. It is a call to turn toward the wider community of beings with whom we are con-nected and for conduct which recognizes others' interests alongside our own" (p. 23). Re: Tibetan Buddhism, the Dalai Lama (1999) dis-cussed his notion of "dependently originates reality" in which "self and others can only really be understood in terms of relationship ... self-interest and others' interest are closely interrelated" (p. 47). See "The Nature of Reality" in *Ethics for the New Millennium*.

22. In a chapter, "Terrorism, Fundamentalism and Nihilism," J. Gilligan (2007) traced the decline of morality and religion after the scientific revolution and the rise of nationalism, totalitarianism and fundamentalism: He wrote:

> For example, the ideology called nationalism, which is gener- ally considered to have come into existence definitively with the French Revolution, clearly originated as a means of filling the vacuum created by the death of God, that is, the loss of cred- ibility of traditional religious institutions (p. 53).

According to Benedict Anderson (1991), a nation is an "imagined political community—and imagined as both inherently limited and sovereign" (p. 6). Anderson made a distinction between national- ism and racism: "The fact of the matter is that nationalism thinks in terms of historical destinies, while racism dreams of eternal con- taminations, transmuted from the origins of time through an end- less sequence of loathsome copulations: outside history" (p. 149).
   Also see David Ronfeldt's (2007) Rand Working Paper "In Search of How Societies Work: Tribes—the First and Forever Form" for a history of the evolution of the nation-state, which he described as a "hierarchy" or institution "such as the monarchy, the state, the army, the court, the bank, the trading company" (p. 18).

23. Re: nationalism versus an inclusive worldview, Buddhist leader Daisaku Ikeda (Gage, 1976) asserted: "the feeling that the earth is one's homeland and a love of all man kind must take the place of the narrow patriotism of the past. When world-embracing patriotism gains precedence, national patriotism will sink to the level of loy- alty to a locality" (p. 198). Similarly, Russian political philosopher Mikhail Bakunin (Anarchy Archives, 2007), argued that the existence of nation-states precludes peaceful co-existence between peoples of the world: "So long as States exist, there will be no peace. There will be only more or less prolonged respites ... but as soon as the State feels sufficiently strong to destroy this equilibrium to its advantage, it will never fail to do so" (Perpetual War is the Price section, para 1). Also see Leon Botstein's (2007) paper "Freud and Wittgenstein: Lan- guage and Human Nature" in which he asks:

> Our question [in the year 2007] is Freud's from the 1930s: Is there any reasonable prospect that humankind can find a way to organize social economic and political life without

murderous hatred and extreme violence and do so not at the cost of freedom and human dignity? (p. 604)

On a cautiously optimistic note, Vamik Volkan (1997), in *Bloodlines: From Ethnic Pride to Ethnic Terrorism*, observed that sometimes there is a rare individual who because of his position, sense of history and compassionate understanding of human beings, can add a small building block to the pursuit of peace:

> Neither the assertion that wars are inevitable because of humankind's aggressive drive nor the theory that a state is identified with a parent or sometimes with oneself has had much practical diplomatic use. Then, in 1971, German psychoanalyst Alexander Mitscherlich urged his colleagues to participate in research into the collective behavior of groups by working with scholars from other fields .... His plea was largely ignored. Interestingly enough, six years later, it was a politician, Egyptian president Anwar el-Sadat, who indirectly issued an invitation to mental health professionals to work side by side with diplomats. This led to new psychoanalytic insight about *emotionally bonded, large-group identities and behaviors* that could have practical diplomatic implications (p. 29) (italics added)

CHAPTER FOURTEEN

The ethical society

There is no pattern of a good society that we or anyone else can simply discern and then expect people to conform to. It is central to our very notion of a good society that it is an open quest, actively involving all its members. As Dennis McCann has put it, the common good is the pursuit of the good in common.[1]

Bellah, Madsen, Sullivan, Swidler & Tipton (1991, p. 9)

Ethical considerations necessarily extend beyond interpersonal relationships and can be applied to the actions of individuals within society, and more importantly, to an examination of the impact of society on the individual. According to the sociologist George Herbert Meade (1934/1967), "Ethical ideas, within any given human society, arise in the consciousness of the individual members of that society from the fact of the common social dependence of all these individuals upon one another" (pp. 319–320). Similarly, Matt Ridley (1996) asserted that "The roots of social order are in our heads, where we possess the instinctive capacities for creating not a perfectly harmonious and virtuous society, but a better one than we have at present" (p. 264).

The tyranny, coercion, and manipulations that characterize social systems which have been corrupted by the misuse of power parallel the toxic personality traits and destructive behaviors which are acted out by many people in their interpersonal relationships. Both phenomena are unethical in that they seriously impair individuals. Authoritarian or totalitarian states that demand conformity impose numerous restrictions on their citizens. In contrast, the ideal democratic state would allow its citizens more personal freedom and would provide opportunities for upward mobility in their economic status.

The functions of an ethical society

In evaluating the functions served by a particular society from an ethical perspective, one must consider the extent to which it provides for the welfare of its constituency. The ideal ethical government or state would assure the economic security of all of its citizens and would strive to protect their freedom, liberty, and basic human rights. Its policies would be based on philosophical principles that place a greater value on the life of each person than on the survival of the system. In contrast, when protection of the society or any system becomes the primary goal of the government and its policies and supersedes the protection of the individual, the majority of its citizens are not well-served. As a result, they suffer on a personal, economic, and political level.

Moreover, as Simone Weil (1949/1952) has pointed out, citizens within this type of social structure suffer on a spiritual level as well. In her book on social ethics, *The Need for Roots: Prelude to a Declaration of Duties towards Mankind,* Weil stressed the importance of the individual over the state or "collectivities." She insisted that "it may happen that the obligation toward a collectivity which is in danger reaches the point of entailing a total sacrifice. But it does not follow from this that collectivities are superior to human beings" (p. 8).

All societies and governments necessarily entail some degree of compromise between protecting an individual's rights and working toward achieving the "common good." Rawls has discussed this quandary in his works, *A Theory of Justice* (1999) and

Justice as Fairness: A Restatement (2001), and in a 1998 interview (Prusak, 1998):

> Liberal constitutional democracy is supposed to ensure that each citizen is free and equal and protected by basic rights and liberties ... . The point I would stress is this: You hear that liberalism lacks an idea of the common good, but I think that's a mistake. For example, you might say that, if citizens are acting for the right reasons in a constitutional regime, then regardless of their comprehensive doctrines [religious or secular] they want every other citizen to have justice. So you might say they're all working together for one thing, namely to make sure every citizen has justice (Prusak, 1998).

Thus, in Rawls' view, the common good is, more often than not, synonymous with individual rights, at least in relation to his concept of justice as fairness.[2]

Becker's view of the functions of the "Good Society"

Becker (1971) delineated four major functions that the ideal society would fulfill. In criticizing the notion of "cultural relativism," he emphasized that the benevolence or malevolence of a given society or culture should be judged.[3] He contended that a society could be evaluated as being ethical or unethical according to the extent that it fulfills the following four functions:

1. The good culture provides for the physical needs of its people within limits of its technology and resources.
2. The good culture provides opportunities for as many people as possible to feel good about themselves.
3. The good culture fulfills the first two functions without damaging others, either inside the culture or outside.
4. The good culture teaches its people how to die well. It provides people with answers to cosmological questions.

According to Becker, the good culture provides stories about the origins of life—creation myths—and stories about what happens after death (Becker, 1964, 1973/1997). In this regard, religion and, to some extent, new age spiritualities provide people with literal immortality—beliefs about actual life after death in some form or another. Similarly, the prospect of living on through a group, a cause, one's business, one's children, or a creative work or accomplishment all offer some form of symbolic immortality (Becker, 1973/1997; R. Firestone, 1994b; 1996).

The authors will attempt to apply Becker's four criteria to the friendship circle, as an example of a small but ethical society. In spite of the complexity of applying these same concepts to larger social orders, the authors feel that humanity at large could embrace these same ethical values and make them work for the best interest of all people.

The friendship circle has developed as a distinct culture within the larger culture, with its own unique values, attitudes, and styles of working, traveling, and socializing. Despite the fact that members of the friendship circle are not different from other people in their physical appearance or manner of dress, passersby notice the smiling faces, overt physical affection, unusual amount of eye contact, and aliveness. Because of their free-moving style and easy affection with each other, it is often difficult to determine who are in intimate relationships and who are simply close friends or other family members. As Stuart Boyd (1982) observed in his *Analysis of the Friendship Circle:*

> The attempt to cut loose from the demoralizing influence of the larger culture by small communities of like-minded individuals has usually ended in material wretchedness or internal dissension and dissolution. It is therefore arresting to me, as a social scientist and liberal artist, to find myself among a community which seems to have solved some of the age-old problems of harmony, happiness, personal growth and fulfillment, and economic independence and power, without withdrawing from the larger destructive culture and without involvement in the political power game; and to have done so without resort to force and loss of liberty, or submission to cultism or pseudo-mystic or religious principle, without dogma or inviolable code, and committed to experiment and change .... There is undoubtedly a principle—the commitment to honesty of feeling, rational and ethical action and the appropriate expression of this.

Thirty years of talking personally in an open forum, confronting issues of how to live an ethical and fulfilling emotional life, and thinking about life and death philosophically have shaped the destiny of this small culture. The reader can trust our description of the group or suspend belief but in either case the ethical principles by which they live stand by themselves.

Becker's criteria applied to the friendship circle

1. A good society provides for the physical needs of its people
As described in Chapter 1, in the early 70s, several families became friends and shared recreational interests. Although only moderately successful, they pooled some of their savings and bought recreational equipment that they shared (small boats, an RV, motorcycles, etc.). In 1973, they bought a sailing schooner, again using combined funds and in October 1975, they formed a small co-op to help finance the rebuilding of the boat and to pay for provisions and other supplies. In 1976, with the beginning of the circumnavigation, they purchased an apartment building and thirty-five friends and family members moved in.[4]

Over the years, as the number of people grew and their financial obligations increased, participants decided to contribute roughly thirty percent of their earnings to cover expenses including rent, utilities, food, community vehicles, and childcare. In addition, they made sure that everyone had adequate health insurance coverage. A "Robin Hood" fund was created to provide members who needed help with a means to pay unusual medical bills, take vacations, get by during difficult times, and enjoy a better life. These financial arrangements existed within a general context of kindness and generosity that provided each person a maximum opportunity to achieve his or her practical needs and goals. As a typical example, when a young man wanted to go to a private college and his parents could not afford it, the group of friends contributed to his tuition.

There were numerous acts of personal generosity. For example, a close friend required a liver transplant. A liver became available on a holiday weekend when her insurance company was unable to advance the necessary funds. On Saturday afternoon, fifteen of her friends presented their credit cards to the hospital finance office, requesting that each card be used to its limit to cover the cost of the operation.

The basic philosophy of the friendship circle was "If there is a need, why not attempt to gratify it?" Utilizing one's resources in this manner became a creative aspect of self-realization as people gradually learned to both offer and receive loving gestures. As the friendship circle was evolving, other economic concerns arose: how to support the young people and the elderly, and how to equalize the wealth. Several policies were implemented. Each child born into the friendship circle receives $20,000 a year until he or she turns 21. A retirement plan of approximately $200,000 per person allows everyone to retire without financial worry. The money for these programs is contributed voluntarily and is provided on a sliding scale.

Currently four people in the friendship circle contribute 40 percent of the overall funds necessary for the group's practical existence, another nineteen people provide 30 percent, and the remaining eighty-seven members contribute the final 30 percent. In addition, each year, the more affluent members distribute substantial financial gifts to those family members and friends who are less well off.

The economics could be characterized as capitalism with a strong social conscience. People have learned that being generous is a sound mental health principle that offers great personal satisfaction and enhances one's self-esteem. People reading this material might think that it is easy to be generous when one is so successful financially. Yet these friends embraced the same principles when they were struggling financially and we believe they would maintain them to the best of their ability even if they lost their resources.

2. The good culture provides opportunities for people to feel good about themselves

The Therapeutic Value of Friendship. Friendship, in contrast to a fantasy bond, is characterized by a lack of exclusiveness or possessiveness. Because friendships are based on free choice, they provide companionship without obligation. Friendship inevitably brings out aspects of an individual's personality that he or she may not have been aware of. It increases self-awareness and self-knowledge and encourages an individual to emerge from an inward, defended posture, enhancing one's feeling of self-worth and self-esteem.

Researchers Block (1980) and D. Myers (2000) have pointed out that friendship is conducive to good physical and mental health. Block, who surveyed more than 2,000 individuals about their life-long friendships observed: "The experience of friendship ... is not a mere luxury. For optimal functioning, it is an imperative" (p. 211).

In a previous work (R. Firestone & Catlett, 1989), the authors described friendship as:

> A dynamic, honest communication with feelings of respect and compassion between people .... What makes friendship special and therapeutic is principally the quality of the communication. There is no subject that is taboo to friends in their talking with each other (p. 225).

People tend to relate as independent individuals within a friendship, with considerable give and take in terms of gratifying each other's needs. Ideally, friends refrain from playing roles or trying to apply or enforce conventional rules on each other. As a result, people feel left alone to pursue their priorities and goals. A genuine friendship involves closeness without false illusions of safety or security and thus enables an individual to experience the truth of his or her separate existence.

In the friendship circle, spontaneous expressions of warmth and affection allow for positive emotions to be mutually stimulated, which helps participants to feel better about themselves and stronger in their point of view. The physical affection that is consistently available is supportive of the individual rather than of elements of the personality that are critical, hostile, and self-destructive. As noted, acts of generosity positively affect the person extending the kindness as well as the recipient. Many people find meaning and derive self-esteem from their ability to positively affect other people's lives. This is one of the internal rewards of having a life of dedication and service to others.

In addition to positively affecting the personal development of the individual, these friends have helped one another expand their boundaries and achieve success in many areas. The process of sharing adventure, travel, and work has been essential to people's sustaining their long-term friendships. They have challenged and inspired one another to be bolder in conceiving and realizing adventuresome projects. Without their friendships, these people would not have achieved the high degree of success in their business ventures that they did.

People in the friendship circle interact in ways that would surprise an outside observer. For example, picture 50 friends on a 100-foot boat, living together in peace and harmony for weeks at sea. Typically, in the sailing world, two couples cannot get along on a weekend sail to Catalina. The people of the friendship circle transform a luxurious, well-appointed sailing yacht into a virtual campground where men, women, and children of all ages pitch in, and everyone participates as crew in the traditional four-hour watches. All of this takes place in a ship-shape, orderly, and relaxed atmosphere.

In another work, (R. Firestone, et al, 2003), the authors described personal impressions of everyday life among this group of friends:

> A crowd of happy people in a large living room, all laughing and good-natured before a serious talk … . Wild scenes at sea: huge frightening waves, violent motion, the powerful force of the wind on the sails and the heel of the boat as she rushes through the water … . Individuals working together, plotting courses, navigating through dangerous waters and struggling to take down sails during stormy conditions … . Sweating together over business problems … . Shared projects, where we revel in each other's accomplishments.
>
> The deep respect for one another and the painful disillusionment at those times when friends are stubborn, defensive, or rejecting. The anguish we all experience when a person reveals a particularly painful childhood episode … . So many faces etched in pain and so many tear-streaked faces … . The torture of losing close friends through sickness or death. The joy and exaltation we feel when we observe a person breaking out of a life-long defensive pattern … . The great moments when everyone is enlightened. The surge of energy when repressions are lifted, our minds are clear, and we feel strong and centered in ourselves … . The nostalgia and the gratitude we feel when looking back we realize how impoverished our lives would have been if we had never met (pp. 374–375).

These images depict the advantages of friendship and its therapeutic value and reflect how this unique environment offers its members a sense of meaning and purpose and an optimistic positive feeling about their lives.

The Value of an Extended Family. As an African proverb states, "It takes a village to raise a child." The friendship circle is in essence an extended family. Virtually all of the adults are concerned with the development of the children, regardless of whether they have children of their own. They attempt to create a home environment that is optimal for the realization of each person's full potential. Friendships transcend conventional boundaries based on age, blood relationship, or gender. In contrast to the traditional nuclear family, adults and children in the friendship circle are exposed to many different points of view and expertise in numerous fields, and so are less dependent on any single source of gratification. This disrupts a tendency to form exaggerated co-dependency relationships, provides for general good feeling, and offers a wider, more secure base.

Technically, an extended family may be defined as consisting of one or more adults, in addition to the child's natural parents who maintain a relationship with the child over a significant period of time (R. Firestone, 1990b). In the larger society, an older sibling, a grandparent, a favorite relative, a god parent, neighbor, teacher, counselor, or mentor often serves this function.

The advantages of an extended family in terms of enhancing children's self-esteem and overall well-being have been documented in research investigating the long-term effects of child abuse. For example, low incidence of physical child abuse has been found in cultures, primitive as well as modern, that live in small kinship groups rather than in family units (B. James, 1994; Korbin, 1981).[5] As noted, studies have shown that "resilient" children, those who grew up in extremely traumatic circumstances yet were able to survive emotionally, did so because they had a positive relationship with another adult, generally someone outside the nuclear family (E. Anthony & Cohler, 1987; Werner, 1990). Even when the contact between child and adult was of brief duration, it still had an ameliorative effect on the child's sense of self. By offering an alternative point of view and a more congenial, accepting attitude, devoid of negative projections, this type of relationship may help avert a pathological outcome.

One major effect of the extended family in the friendship circle is that child-rearing does not become an all encompassing task that deprives parents of their overall enthusiasm, sexuality, and vitality. The demands of child-rearing are considerably reduced as others share the responsibility. Because of this, parents are able to spend "quality time" with their children, those times where they are not feeling stressed, overwhelmed, or resentful.

Parents in the friendship circle realize that by taking a constructive interest in each other's children, they are providing better parenting for all the children (R. Firestone, et al, 2003). The children in the group are noticeably better behaved and tend to be more independent than their peers in the larger culture. This extended community not only helps with child-rearing but offers the adults and children more opportunities for companionship, intellectual stimulation, shared pursuits, personal growth, and the availability of wise counsel. In this type of social atmosphere, people recover more quickly from ordinary emotional setbacks.[6]

3. The good society fulfills the first two functions without harming others either inside or outside the culture
As noted, the friendship circle exists in the larger culture and is in no way isolated from outside community concerns. Attitudes are liberal and there is a conspicuous lack of racial or religious prejudice, class consciousness, or any other form of stereotyping. This includes an aversion to stereotypical attitudes towards men, women, or children that polarize people and lead to animosity. People casually share domestic and other practical tasks with little if any status differential. All people are perceived as being equal and worthy of respect regardless of their individual strengths or weaknesses.

These friends make no distinction between how they treat each other and how they treat those outside of the friendship circle. There is no claim to be superior, no proselytizing or desire to recruit new "members" nor any implication that their way is the only avenue to a better life. At the same time they are open and inclusive of anyone who does take an interest.

As noted, people pay their fair share, but no one is required to participate in the acts of generosity. Along with being financially generous within the community, these people also contribute money to outside causes and have founded a nonprofit organization, the Glendon Association, whose purpose it is to disseminate psychological information and provide local community service. This organization educates the general public about child abuse, child-rearing, couple and family relationships, self-destructive, suicidal and violent behavior.

Among this group of friends, the well-being and independence of any single individual is of primary importance even over other considerations, such as the preservation of the couple or family unit, or even the group itself. In this context, group policies or intrusions that interfere with the dignity, self-respect, and autonomy of the individual are considered inappropriate and destructive. As a result, there are a minimum of rules or obstructions to personal freedom and there is an overall atmosphere of equality.

These people's emphasis on human rights issues reaches its highest level of concern in relation to the respect for and well-being of children. It applies to adult interactions as well. Their principles involve a concern for personal freedom over destructive bondage in regard to relationships and institutions. There is a sincere concern for the psychological well-being of individuals, couples, and families, as well as a compassionate feeling of generosity and altruism. These principles embody a respectful, healthy, nonjudgmental attitude toward individual differences and life styles. The friends favor humanitarian causes in general, abhor authoritarian practices and status, are strongly opposed to guns and violence, and support a worldview over nationalistic interests. There is a love of people both at close quarters and far reaches.

4. The good culture teaches its people how to die well and provides answers to cosmological questions

> Society itself is a codified hero system, which means that society everywhere is a living myth of the significance of human life, a defiant creation of meaning (Becker, 1973/1997, p. 7).

Existential Issues in the Friendship Circle. The authors question Becker's premise that a good society provides answers to core cosmological questions. The authors believe rather that a good society teaches people to live well facing death's inevitability, with or without clear answers to cosmological questions. The ideal society would allow members to experience the pain, uncertainty, and ambiguity that are a necessary part of life, provide a meaningful ethical code, and maximize the individual's acceptance and tolerance of personal feelings. Under these conditions, people would be free to experience the full range of joy as well as the anguish of the human condition. Regarding death and dying, a good culture would provide the understanding that death is a simple natural phenomenon, not fair or unfair, involving neither punishment nor reward. There is no original sin or shame in one's vulnerability.

When human beings fear death, they attempt to divorce themselves from their animal nature. Because they know that animals die, that the physical body will eventually deteriorate and expire, they postulate a soul that will transcend the untenable situation and achieve immortality. Yet the trade-off predisposes prohibitions against bodily functions and free-flowing emotion, complicates and assures guilt about nudity and sexuality, and diminishes ones aliveness and freedom in countless ways.

In *The Denial of Death*, Ernest Becker (1973/1997) asserted that human behavior and the formation of various cultural patterns are deeply affected by man's unique consciousness of his mortality. These concerns, and the defenses erected to avoid the disturbing awareness, lead to social orders that serve the function of lending meaning to one's life, confer security on their members, and act to deny death's finality. Becker observed that, at the same time:

> Most people play it safe ... . They accept the cultural definition of heroism and try to be a 'good provider' or a 'solid citizen.' In this way they earn their species immortality as part of a social group of some kind ... . Almost everyone consents to earn his immortality in the popular ways mapped out by societies everywhere, in the beyonds of others and not their own (p. 170).

According to Becker, culture is a humanly constructed and shared set of beliefs about reality whose primary function is to reduce the anxiety surrounding the awareness of death. In his view, the good society offers respites from painful existential issues in the form of myths about creation and an afterlife that comfort the populace.

From an ethical perspective, the benevolent or malevolent effects of this particular function of culture can be evaluated. As Becker (1975) noted:

> If each historical society is in some ways a lie or a mystification, the study of society becomes *the revelation of the lie*. The comparative study of society becomes *the assessment of how high are the costs of this lie*. Or, looked at from another way, cultures are fundamentally and basically *styles of heroic death denial* ... . These costs can be tallied roughly in two ways: in terms of the tyranny practiced within the society, and in terms of the victimage practiced against aliens or "enemies" outside it (p. 125).

In concluding *The Denial of Death*, Becker (1973/1997) argued that it is impossible for individuals to find any viable solution to the anguish of the human condition, not though the "heroic" roles prescribed by society, nor through religion or psychotherapy: "Whatever is achieved must be achieved from within the subjective energies of creatures, without deadening, with the full exercise of passion, of vision, of pain, of fear, and of sorrow" (pp. 283–284).

From the authors' point of view, and the prevailing views within the friendship circle, the ideal society or culture would face up to existential realities of aloneness and death, allow for them to be a topic for open communication, and accept the full range of feelings associated with the subject. Face-to-face with these painful truths, many people despair and become cynical, cut off feeling, retreat from close affiliations in life, or form an alliance with death by giving up their lives prematurely. The authors believe there is an alternative: people could chose to place greater value on their lives, their personal freedom, and their own search for love and meaning. They could develop a philosophical approach that considers all people to be in the same predicament, that is, a humanistic, inclusive, world view rather than a sectarian view. This approach respects and reveres life, despite the limitation in time.

People in the friendship circle take this position of life-affirming death awareness. Their aim is to seek truth and love in spite of pain and anxiety, and expose and dispel hypocrisy and illusion on both a personal and societal level. Their philosophy is one of attempting to live as much as possible without illusions or psychological defenses that fracture or distort the precious experience of life. Although the environment is supportive emotionally, it is painful on many real levels and not suited for those who seek comfort at the expense of reality.

Spirituality. A critical component in pursuing the good life involves developing our sense of the sacred, enhancing the spiritual dimensions of our experience, exploring the mysteries of existence, and seeking meaning in life (R. Firestone, et al, 2003).

Harvard scientist E.O. Wilson (Petzinger, 2000) emphasized that "Man's predisposition to religious belief is the most complex and powerful force in the human mind, and in all probability an eradicable part of human nature" (p. R16). Yet presently, more that at any time in history, science has made a powerful intrusion on religious belief systems. Wilson stated that, "The more we understand from science about how the world really works, all the way from subatomic particles up to the mind and on to the cosmos, the more difficult it is to base spirituality on our ancient mythologies" (p. R16).

For example, the scientific data and understanding of evolution play havoc with creation theory and the concept that the very existence of humankind has a core sense of meaning or ultimate purpose. There have been many other blows to man's egocentric sense of self, omnipotence, and belief in rationality. Freud (1935) convinced us that much of what we call "will" is determined by unconscious motives. Menninger (1938) and others (Farberow, 1980) indicated that many of these motives were of a nature antithetical or destructive toward self. Voice Therapy theory (R. Firestone, 1988, 1997a) identifies a destructive pattern of thoughts or inner voice process that is alien to one's best interests, yet prevails in one's life. These facts, combined with an understanding of genetic predisposition and evolutionary proclivities, considerably reduce a human being's confidence in free choice.

Nevertheless, in spite of recognizing the impact on belief systems caused by scientific advances and the realization that we are not fully conscious of our motivations, one cannot rule out faith, because so much is still unknown.

In *Creating a Life of Meaning and Compassion*, the authors (R. Firestone, et al, 2003) explained that:

> Aristotelian logic and modern science not only fail to explain existence, they preclude its possibility. All that we know in the

scientific sense points to the fact that something cannot come from nothing; even if one postulates a God, one is burdened by the question of where could that essence have come from. Faced with this preposterous logical contradiction, we are left with a hypothetical problem that goes beyond human intelligence and intellect … . We are forced to accept the blow to our vanity and face the painful truth of our intellectual limitations, but there is a consolation. We are left with the fact of mystery, free to contemplate the awesome spectacle of existence of all varieties, and we are left open to form our own conclusions about life and meaning.

In spite of skepticism about extrasensory phenomena, precognition, psychokineses, auras, and the like, there is a body of generally disregarded experimental data and experiential evidence that is at the least suggestive that there is more to life than we usually consider. There is still magic in the world (p. 380).

We agree with Wilson when he emphasizes that "whatever we feel in our hearts, we need to believe that there is some ultimate measure of sacredness, whether you perceive it as secular in origin through the organic evolution of humanity, or whether you conceive of it as God directed" (p. R16). He has suggested that we must be "proactive in seeking it and defining it instead of reactive in the traditional manner of taking the sacred texts and beliefs handed down to us and trying to adapt them to an evolving culture" (p. R16).

Some seek the sacred in nature, in our natural surroundings, others in music and the arts, and some find it in love. Indeed, if death anxiety is conceptualized as the poison, then love may well be the antidote (p. 378).

The concept of spirituality usually refers to various belief systems about life after death, nirvana, religious faith, relegation to heaven or hell, reincarnation, and such. Sometimes it relates to contact and communication with the dead or with one's past lives. In an extended context it refers to a deep concern about matters of morality, how to live one's life and find meaning, and about one's essential connection to oneself, others, one's natural surroundings and the universe-at-large.

Most individuals in the friendship circle do not participate in organized religious practices as such; few attend church or involve themselves in other types of formal worship. They personally hold a wide range of beliefs about creation, and the existence or concept of God or a super being. Some believe in prayer while others are agnostics or outright atheists. In spite of their lack of organized religion, it would be a gross misconception to consider these people lacking in a sense of spirituality. Their mode of existence has a deep spiritual quality, a regard for the sacredness of life and humanity that pervades every aspect of their being. This spiritual quest is not an isolated phenomenon, practiced on designated occasions but instead is lived out every hour of every day. Their life together and its extension to the larger world around them involve a powerful existential awareness of aloneness, of life and death, and the essential dilemma and mystery of existence. They are actively concerned with moral principles and human rights issues that transcend conventional morality. They exhibit a deep and abiding respect for people's feelings, their well-being and personal freedom and these sentiments are manifested in extraordinary acts of kindness, sensitivity and compassion. In this sense, they have elevated the concept of love and loving to a high level of spirituality that plays a central role in their everyday lives.

Application of the ethical principles of the friendship circle to the larger society

I believe the basic premise of the Enlightenment which I feel we cannot abandon and continue to be working scientists—namely, that there is nothing in man or nature which would prevent us from taking some control of our destiny and making the world a saner place for our children (Becker, 1975, p. xviii).

I know of no community which is of the larger culture, works and has its economic and social meaning there, moving freely in and to all ranges of it, sustaining strengthening and enriching its members psychologically as well as physically, sharing without losing individuality, and convinced it has found a better life, a better way of being with one's fellows, with consequent increased and enduring happiness, except for the friendship circle and its environment (Boyd, 1982).

Many people are cynical and skeptical about the present and future condition of life on the planet, particularly the incidences or potential incidences of ethnic strife, warfare, poverty, crime, terrorism, and global warming. These pessimistic attitudes appear to be justifiable when one considers some of the horrors of our current civilization, and the powerful forces within societies and nations that act as a resistance to change.

Those who maintain this negative prognosis hold that people who believe in humankind's fundamental goodness, and in the possibility of a peaceful world and a fair and just society, are pathetic and naïve. But in their skepticism they assure that these negative eventualities will fulfill their dire prophecy. Others embrace a childish optimism that denies the painful realities of life that currently exist and instead hope for some miraculous outside intervention.

The authors believe that the basic ideas that were developed during the evolution of this small society may be generally valid for human behavior in the larger society. These ethical principles can be adapted to a wide range of circumstances and environments. Challenging and giving up defenses, living more socially, and learning to be more honest in communicating are all courses of action open to most people (Firestone, et al, 2003).

On a broader international scale, it is possible to change and better the world, and in that new world, as in the friends' group, there would be concern for the feeding, housing, education and medical care of the populace and a requirement for peaceful coexistence for all peoples. The new culture would provide the maximum opportunity for happiness, meaning, creativity, and fulfillment for every person. There are many factors that provide for change, social movement or formation of a new culture. One key requirement is dissatisfaction with the status quo. However, passivity, an attitude of powerlessness, or a victimized, complaining orientation preclude actions that might lead to positive change.

Characteristics of the membership of the friendship circle that led to constructive changes in the socialization process

It is impossible to conceive of a free and creative life in the humanist sense as one lived without alertness, sensitivity, and insight. This tells us what Socrates meant when he said that the best life is the considered life. To the question, 'What is good,' then, the answer can only be: 'The considered life—free, creative, informed and chosen, a life of achievement and fulfillment, of pleasure and understanding, of love and friendship; in short, the best human life is a human life in a human world, humanely lived.' (Grayling, 2003, p. 249)

The original friends and families of the friendship circle were people who desired to transform their dreams into reality. If someone had an idea that made sense, it was embraced, and before long it was translated into action. "Let's sail to Mexico." "Why not sail around the world?" "Let's start a business." "Okay, that worked out; let's start another bigger, better business." These friends believed in their ability to make things work and became more confident over time as they achieved their goals.

Early on, when some of the friends participated in psychotherapy retreats, reached deep levels of feeling for themselves and others, and achieved standards of honest communication they had never approached before, they wanted to maintain the warmth and insight of those occasions. As noted in Chapter 1, upon returning to their everyday lives and the accompanying routines, they found that much of the luster wore off, and the excitement of those weekends faded. At that point, someone said, "Why don't we share more social activities and talk openly about our lives in our group of friends just like in the marathons? Why don't we approach psychotherapy as a lifestyle?" And that was the beginning.

Ten years later, Dr. Stuart Boyd visited the friends and recorded his impressions of these people:

> Those of the friendship circle brought with them these special characteristics of high intelligence, courage, zest for life, and, perhaps most important of all, a desire to know themselves better in their deepest relationships and to change on the basis of this increased self, and other, awareness. These characteristics were powerfully reinforced within the circle of friends, and are now clearly being transmitted to the children.

The individuals who participated in the evolution of the friendship circle had strong feelings about the hypocrisy and dishonesty in couples, families, and society at large. Many of them had suffered from the prevailing mores and duplicitous communication characteristic of these institutions. In addition, they were personally troubled by the prevalence of inhumanity and destructiveness that characterized the general state of the world.

What most distinguished these people from their peers was their strong desire for a different life, based on their dissatisfaction with the ordinary and conventional. The friends disapproved of socially constructed rules, standards and roles that conferred prestige and status on certain individuals and groups while disregarding the welfare, security, and well-being of others.[7] They resented the emphasis on form over substance. They recognized the dishonesty and hypocrisy of religious "love" that sponsors murder and ethnic wars in the name of God, Allah, or other deities. They strongly objected to the myth of unconditional parental "love," to the double messages in families, and the resultant parenting practices that had hurt them as children.

Although disenchanted with modern society and its unethical practices, they were neither pessimistic nor cynical; indeed, they disapproved of such attitudes. At the same time, they understood why most people were cynical, recognizing that this view stemmed from a sense of powerlessness and helplessness. In contrast, the friends had an optimistic, enthusiastic attitude that inspired movement toward a better way of life. In this pursuit they were committed to challenge their most strongly held illusions. They were willing to face the attendant anxiety, pain, antagonism, and controversy that are inevitable whenever new ideas are proposed.

They have been able to achieve these goals by maintaining an ongoing forum for honest communication that is always operant and self-correcting. Nothing is sacred or beyond scrutiny and there are few if any secrets. Any form of dishonesty or mixed messages that fracture one's sense of reality is regarded as unprincipled and unethical. Lies and deceit, whether conscious or not, have a damaging effect on the individual's mental health. As Boyd (1982) noted: "Honesty is the only professed policy as far as I can make out. Honesty about essential feeling toward the self and to others. The commitment to truth is not to philosophical-epistomological truth but to the truth of feeling."

The friends express a respect, tolerance, and love of their fellow human beings and have faith in humankind's inherent goodness. They have intuitively challenged Freud's and Klein's ideas that people are primarily motivated by a death instinct and so are innately aggressive, violent, or evil. Instead, they have a generally favorable impression of what people would naturally be like if they were left alone, were not intruded on by an inimical socialization process, and were not damaged by a myriad of other aversive environmental inputs.

Psychological insights

> It seems that what is now stimulating, reenergizing, and moving the community is the insight into the nature of relationships as they constitute connection and dependencies and manipulations, versus equalities, freedoms, and responsibilities (Boyd, 1982).

It is impossible to conceive of the evolution of this group of people without its psychological orientation and the many insights into human behavior that have been attained. In some sense, the friendship circle could be conceptualized as an experiment in applied psychology in that the participants continually apply psychological knowledge to understanding themselves and others. Through inspired leadership and a widespread and powerful educational process, society-at-large could benefit from adopting this type of perspective. As its members came to understand the role of the unconscious and how people are essentially divided within themselves, they could become increasingly aware of their negative propensities and be better able to challenge them.

The group sessions held by the friendship circle have allowed for the release of primal emotions, and along with the catharsis, there have been powerful insights leading to a better adaptation. The participants are generally more comfortable with and accepting of feeling. More importantly, they realize that their problems are to a large extent related to primal feelings and defenses rooted in childhood experiences. As a result, they have learned that dramatic emotional reactions are rarely if ever appropriate to current situations but instead reflect irrational transference phenomena. Were the members of society at large to share this therapeutic insight, they would be able to recognize their projections and correct for their biases rather than distort their experiences. They would be less defensive and intrusive and less likely to act out irrationally or negatively toward others. They would be nonjudgmental and accepting in their attitudes toward their fellow human beings.

The different units within a society—couples, families, countries, religions, etc.—would benefit from recognizing the common tendency among all people to form a fantasy bond as an unconscious solution to feeling frightened, unloved, or insecure. People could learn to cope effectively with every aspect of the fantasy bond that divides and alienates them, one from the other. They could challenge the illusion of fusion that offers comfort and security at the expense of real relating, in which imagining and talking of love replace genuinely loving actions. Within couples, families and society, people would be intolerant of this discrepancy. They would recognize that real love is more than internal thoughts and ideation; that it is reflected in outward, observable behaviors of kindness, close companionship, physical affection, and respectful concern for the other's boundaries and well-being. Within couples, partners would not be able to delude themselves that they were loving if their behavior was insensitive, unkind, hostile, superior, or did not comply with any reasonable definition of the word "love." Partners would take back their negative projections and stop blaming one another for their personal difficulties. They would give away their hostile feelings rather than act them out on each other. In challenging the fantasy bond, they would attempt to disrupt patterns of domination or submission, as well as habitual routines and taking each other for granted.

As their talks progressed, the participants in the friendship circle discovered that a large part of their unethical behavior was based on an only partly conscious internalized voice process. The negative thoughts and attitudes of the voice predispose criticism and attacks on self and others that disrupt one's life and cause harm to others. Once they began to realize the impact of these early parental introjects, these people were able to identify and challenge the thought processes that were limiting them. People everywhere can benefit from identifying the negative voices that dictate actions that are destructive to themselves and to others.

As with the friendship circle, focusing on psychological ideas enables people to contend with difficult subjects that arise among social groups, such as competition, sexual rivalry, and jealousy. When dealing with these potentially problematic topics, all thoughts and feelings should be accepted uncritically, whereas actions should be subjected to realistic self-interest and concern and most importantly ethical and moral considerations. In every society, as in the friendship circle, there should be a particular emphasis on each member's independence, on his or her feelings of being a separate individual.

In essence, the most valuable lesson that society can learn from the friendship circle is that men and women can make essential changes in their way of being, overcome barriers to their personal evolution, and learn how to love. During their ongoing learning process, the friends have become more vulnerable and open in situations where previously they had defended themselves from the possibility of being hurt and lashed out. They discovered that the most effective way to combat destructive thought patterns was to make them available to consciousness, learn to take appropriate risks and to alter negative, defensive behaviors, rather than attacking or manipulating others to maintain distance.

Conclusion

The authors believe in humankind's capacity to alter negative personality characteristics and unethical practices. Just as the individual can create a more positive identity and new destiny for him or herself, a similar result can be achieved in society and culture. In spite of the present state of affairs and the complexity of the battleground— humankind's demonstrable selfishness, narcissism, and hatred, the powerful force of resistance and the psychopathic predilection of those who attempt to become leaders—one must not fail to maintain hope. Without cautious optimism, without giving significant value to life and experience, all that is precious about civilization will be lost. As in the hypothetical model of the friendship circle, transforming an ideal, ethical vision into a reality depends on the unique combination of an understanding of our psychological makeup, a compassionate, dedicated and courageous leadership, a desire by the populace for authenticity and personal freedom, and incredible resolve.[8]

In ending this work, the first author refers to another quote from my friend, well-known author and psychoanalyst R. D. Laing. After visiting the friendship circle, spending more than a week aboard our sailing ship, he told me that, "You should preach what you practice." In the Foreword to my book, *Compassionate Child-Rearing* (R. Firestone, 1990b), in his closing words, Laing (1990) ventured the hope that "Maybe a plague of love will break out. Why not? Are we so immune to the virus of compassion?" (p. xi).

Notes

1. The quote from Dennis McCann (1987) can be found in "The Good to Be Pursued in Common," in *The Common Good and U.S. Capitalism*.
2. In a critique of Rawls' theory, Peters (1966) argued that "Other principles must be invoked to supply content to the abstract form laid down by the principle of justice" (p. 126). "What is lacking in such a situation is not necessarily lack of equality in any distributive sense but lack of respect for persons" (p. 142).
3. Becker (1975) concluded that a scientific study of societies would: "Make public a continuing assessment of the costs of mankind's impossible aims and paradoxes ... Then men might struggle, even in anguish, to come to terms with themselves and their world" (p. 168). Becker's ideas regarding the functions of the good society were summarized in a lecture by Sheldon Solomon at Seattle University in 1998.
4. The friendship circle currently (2008) consists of 51 men, 55 women, and 28 children under the age of 14.
5. See Jill Korbin's (1981) description of Polynesian society, in which she found "a relative absence of child abuse" (p. 192). "The preconditions of a rejective pattern which Ron Rohner ... [1976] has identified cross-culturally are not present" (p. 190).

    In many Polynesian islands, until approximately 30–40 years ago, multiple parenting had been the tradition and the children were socialized by peers and siblings.
6. Re: the advantages of an extended family, Bruce Perry (2006) suggested that:

    The human brain is designed for a different world ... . Of the 250,000 years or so that our species has been on the planet, we spent 245,000 years living in small transgenerational hunter-gatherer bands of 40-50 individuals ... . For each child under the age of 6, there were four developmentally more mature persons who could protect, educate, enrich, and nurture the developing child—a ratio of 4:1. In contrast, our modern world is defining a caregiver-to-child ratio of 1:4 as a "best-practice" ratio for young children (1/16th the relational ratio the human brain is designed for) (pp. 44–45).

Fragmental, mobile nuclear families separate children from extended family members. A host of factors combine to produce hundreds of thousands of children growing up in homes and communities that are impoverished in relationships. This poverty of relationships contributes to a host of neuropsychiatric problems. The more isolated physically and socially a family becomes, the more vulnerable a child becomes ... . The primary therapeutic implication is the need to increase the number and quality of relational interactions and opportunities for the high-risk child (pp. 45–46).

Also see *Beyond Civilization: Humanity's Next Great Adventure* by Daniel Quinn (1999).

7. From the beginning, there was an emphasis on gender equality and strong women played a major role in the formation of the new society. The authors observed that women appeared to be more passionate about, and dedicated to, reform because they had been disadvantaged and disenfranchised for centuries within the traditional patriarchal society.

8. Michael Salzman (2001) in "Globalization, Culture, and Anxiety: Perspectives and Predictions from Terror Management Theory" has expressed sentiments similar to those of the authors:

TMT researchers have found that when subjects whose worldviews valued tolerance and respect for diversity are exposed to the mortality-salience condition, they bolstered that worldview and actually exhibited greater tolerance ... . This is cause for optimism (p. 350).

Becker (1975) concluded: "We have no way of knowing what gain will come out of Freudian thought when it is finally assimilated in its tragic and true meanings. Perhaps it will introduce just that minute measure of reason to balance destruction" (p. 170).

REFERENCES

Adler, T. (2002, September 22). An attempt at a consentience regarding formal leadership. *Journal of Leadership & Organizational Studies* [Electronic version]. Retrieved 10/5/07 from http://www.allbusiness. com/human-resources/employee-development-leadership/387543.1.

Adorno, T.W., Frenkel-Brunswik, E., Levinson, D.J. & Sanford, R.N. (1950). *The authoritarian personality.* Oxford, UK: Harpers.

Ainsworth, M.D.S. (1989). Attachments beyond infancy. *American Psychologist, 44*: 709–716.

Allport, G.W. (1954). *The nature of prejudice.* New York: Basic Books.

Altemeyer, B. (1996). *The authoritarian specter.* Cambridge, MA: Harvard University Press.

American Heart Association. (2007). Statistical fact sheet—Risk factors: 2007 update. Retrieved 9/16/07 from http://www.americanheart. org/downloadable/heart/.

American Psychiatric Association. (1994). *Diagnostic and statistical manual of mental disorders* (4th ed.). Washington, DC: Author.

Amodio, D.M. & Devine, P.G. (2006). Stereotyping and evaluation in implicit race bias: Evidence for independent constructs and unique effects on behavior. *Journal of Personality and Social Psychology, 91*: 652–661.

Amodio, D.M., Jost, J.T., Master, S.L. & Yee, C.M. (2007). Neurocognitive correlates of liberalism and conservatism. *Nature Neuroscience, 10*: 1246–1247.

Anarchy Archives. (2007). Bakunin archive: *The immorality of the state* by Mikhail Bakunin (1814–1876). Retrieved 10/22/07 from http://dwardmac.pitzer.edu/anarchist_archives/bakunin/bakuninimmorality.html.

Anderson, B. (1991). *Imagined communities: Reflections on the origin and spread of nationalism* (rev. ed.). London: Verso.

Anderson, C.A. & Bushman, B.J. (2002). Human aggression. *Annual Review of Psychology, 53*: 27–51.

Andrews, K.R. (2003). Ethics in practice. In *Harvard business Review on Corporate Ethics* (pp. 67–83). Boston, MA: Harvard Business School Publishing. (Original work published 1989)

Anthony, E.J. & Cohler, B.J. (Eds.). (1987). *The invulnerable child.* New York: Guilford Press.

Anthony, S. (1973). *The discovery of death in childhood and after.* Harmondsworth, UK: Penguin Education. (Original work published in 1971)

Archer, J. (2000). Sex differences in aggression between heterosexual partners. *Psychological Bulletin, 126*: 651–680.

Arieti, S. (1974). *Interpretation of schizophrenia* (2nd ed.). New York: Basic Books.

Arlow, J.A. (1989). Psychoanalysis. In: R.J. Corsini & D. Wedding (Eds.)., *Current psychotherapies* (4th ed.) (pp. 19–62). Itasca, IL: F.E. Peacock.

Arndt, J., Greenberg, J., Pyszczynski, T. & Solomon, S. (1997). Subliminal exposure to death-related stimuli increases defense of the cultural worldview. *Psychological Science, 8*: 379–385.

Arquilla, J. & Ronfeldt, D.F. (1999) *The emergence of Noopolitik: Toward an American information strategy.* Rand Corporation Monograph Report. Santa Monica, CA: Rand Corporation.

Augustyn, M. & Groves, B.M. (2005). Training clinicians to identify the hidden victims: Children and adolescents who witness violence. *American Journal of Preventive Medicine, 29*: 272–278. *American Psychologist, 62*: 25–33.

Avolio, B.J. (2007). Promoting more integrative strategies for leadership theory-building. *American Psychologist; 62*: 25–33.

Babbitt, S.E. (1996). *Impossible dreams: Rationality, integrity, and moral imagination.* New York: HarperCollins.

Babiak, P. & Hare, R.D. (2006). *Snakes in suits: When psychopaths go to work*. New York: HarperCollins.

Bacal, R. (2000). Toxic organizations—Welcome to the fire of an unhealthy workplace. Retrieved 10/16/07 from http://conflict 911.com/conflictarticles/toxicorgs.htm.

Bach, G.R. & Deutsch, R.M. (1970). *Pairing*. New York: Avon Books.

Bach, G.R. & Deutsch, R.M. (1979). *Stop! You're driving me crazy*. New York: Berkley.

Bach, G.R. & Goldberg, H. (1974). *Creative aggression*. Los Angeles, CA: Wellness Institute.

Badaracco, J.L. Jr. (2003). The discipline of building character. In *Harvard Business Review on Corporate Ethics* (pp. 139–163). Boston, MA: Harvard Business School Publishing. (Original work published 1998)

Bakermans-Kranenburg, M.J. & van IJzendoorn, M.H. (1993). A psychometric study of the Adult Attachment Interview: Reliability and discriminant validity. *Developmental Psychology, 29*: 870–879.

Bandura, A. (1973). *Aggression: A social learning analysis*. Englewood Cliffs, NJ: Prentice Hall.

Bandura, A. (1986). *Social foundations of thought and action: A social cognitive theory*. Englewood Cliffs, NJ: Prentice-Hall.

Bandura, A. (1991). The social cognitive theory of moral thought and action. In: W.M. Kurtines & J.L. Gewirtz (Eds.), *Handbook of moral behavior and development* (Vol. 1, pp. 45–103). Hillsdale, NJ: Lawrence Erlbaum.

Bandura, A. (1999). Moral disengagement in the perpetration of inhumanities. *Personality and Social Psychology Review, 3*: 193–209.

Bandura, A. (2001). Social cognitive theory: An agentic perspective. *Annual Review of Psychology, 52*: 1–26.

Bandura, A. (2002). Selective moral disengagement in the exercise of moral agency. *Journal of Moral Education, 31*: 101–119.

Bandura, A., Barbaranelli, C., Caprara, G.V. & Pastorelli, C. (1996). Mechanisms of moral disengagement in the exercise of moral agency. *Journal of Personality and Social Psychology, 71*: 364–374.

Bandura, A. & Walters, R.H. (1963). *Social learning and personality development*. New York: Holt, Rinehart, and Winston.

Banks, C.G. (1996). "There is no fat in heaven": Religious asceticism and the meaning of anorexia nervosa. *Ethos, 24*: 107–135.

Barber, B.K. (Ed.). (2002). *Intrusive parenting: How psychological control affects children and adolescents.* Washington, DC: American Psychological Association.

Bass, B.M. & Steidlmeier, P. (1998). Ethics, character, and authentic transformational leadership. Binghamton, NY: Center for Leadership Studies. Retrieved 10/27/07 from http://cls.binghamton.edu/BassSteid.html.

Bateson, G. (1972). *Steps to an ecology of mind.* New York: Ballantine.

Battegay, R. (1991). *The hunger diseases.* Toronto: Hogrefe & Huber.

Baumeister, R.F. (1997). *Evil: Inside human violence and cruelty.* New York: Henry Holt.

Baumeister, R.F. (2005). *The cultural animal: Human nature, meaning, and social life.* New York: Oxford University Press.

Baumeister, R.F., Smart, L. & Boden, J.M. (1996). Relation of threatened egotism to violence an aggression: The dark side of high self-esteem. *Psychological Review, 103:* 5–33.

Beavers, W.R. (1977). *Psychotherapy and growth: A family systems perspective.* New York: Brunner/Mazel.

Beck, A.T. (1988). *Beck Hopelessness Scale.* San Antonio, TX: Psychological Corporation.

Beck, A. (1999). *Prisoners of hate: The cognitive basis of anger, hostility, and violence.* New York: HarperCollins.

Becker, E. (1964). *The revolution in psychiatry: The new understanding of man.* New York: Free Press.

Becker, E. (1971). *The birth and death of meaning: A perspective in psychiatry and anthropology* (2nd ed.). New York: Free Press.

Becker, E. (1975). *Escape from evil.* New York: Free Press.

Becker, E. (1997). *The denial of death.* New York: Free Press. (Original work published 1973)

Beckwith, F.J. (Ed.). (2002). *Do the right thing: Readings in applied ethics and social philosophy* (2nd ed.). Belmont, CA: Wadsworth/Thomson Learning.

Behan, J. & Carr, A. (2000). Oppositional defiant disorder. In: A. Carr (Ed.), *What works for children and adolescents? A critical review of psychological interventions with children, adolescents and their families* (pp. 102–130). London: Routledge.

Bellah, R.N., Madsen, R., Sullivan, W.M., Swidler, A. & Tipton, S.M. (1991). *The good society.* New York: Vintage Books.

Benjamin, L.S. (2003a). *Interpersonal diagnosis and treatment of personality disorders* (2nd ed.). New York: Guilford Press.

Benjamin, L.S. (2003b). *Interpersonal reconstructive therapy: Promoting change in nonresponders*. New York: Guilford Press.

Bennis, W. (2003). *On becoming a leader* (rev. ed.). New York: Basic Books.

Bennis, W. (2004). Foreword: Why servant-leadership matters. In: L.C. Spears & M. Lawrence (Eds.), *Practicing servant-leadership: Succeeding through trust, bravery, and forgiveness* (pp. xi–xvi). San Francisco, CA: Jossey-Bass.

Bennis, W. (2007). The challenges of leadership in the modern world. *American Psychologist, 62*: 2–5.

Berke, J.H., Pierides, S., Sabbadini, A. & Schneider, S. (Eds.). (1998). *Even paranoids have enemies: New perspectives on paranoia and persecution*. London: Routledge.

Berkowitz, L. (1990). On the formation and regulation of anger and aggression: A cognitive-neoassociationistic analysis. *American Psychologist, 45*: 494–503.

Berkowitz, L. (1993). Pain and aggression: Some findings and implications. *Motivation and Emotion, 17*: 277–293.

Berne, E. (1961). *Transactional analysis in psychotherapy*. New York: Grove.

Betchen, S.J. (2005). *Intrusive partners, elusive mates: The pursuer-distancer dynamic in couples*. New York: Routledge.

Beyette, B. (1978, April 28). The Vltava's voyage to understanding. *Los Angeles Times*, Part IV, G1–G5.

Bigler, R.S. (1999). Psychological interventions designed to counter sexism in children: Empirical limitations and theoretical foundations. In: W.B. Swann Jr., J.H. Langlois & L.A. Gilbert (Eds.), *Sexism and stereotypes in modern society: The gender science of Janet Taylor Spence* (pp. 129–151). Washington, DC: American Psychological Association.

Billig, M. (1987). *Arguing and thinking: A rhetorical approach to social psychology*. Cambridge, England: Cambridge University Press.

Birks, Y. & Roger, D. (2000). Identifying components of type-A behaviour: "Toxic" and "non-toxic" achieving. *Personality and Individual Differences, 28*: 1093–1105.

Black, C. (1981). *It will never happen to me!* Denver, CO: M.A.C.

Blair, R.J.R. (2001). Neurocognitive models of aggression, the antisocial personality disorders, and psychopathy. *Journal of Neurological and Neurosurgical Psychiatry, 71*: 727–731.

Blair, R.J.R., Colledge, E., Murray, L. & Mitchell, D.G.V. (2001). A selective impairment in the processing of sad and fearful expressions in children with psychopathic tendencies. *Journal of Abnormal Child Psychology, 29*: 491–498.

Blatt, S.J., McDonald, C., Sugarman, A. & Wilber, C. (1984). Psychodynamic theories of opiate addiction: New directions for research. *Clinical Psychology Review, 4*: 159–189.

Block, J.D. (1980). *Friendship.* New York: Macmillan.

Bohart, A.C. & Greenberg, L.S. (Eds.). (1997). *Empathy reconsidered: New directions in psychotherapy.* Washington, DC: American Psychological Association.

Bollas, C. (1987). *The shadow of the object: Psychoanalysis of the unthought known.* New York: Columbia University Press.

Bond, E.J. (1996). *Ethics and human well-being: An introduction to moral philosophy.* Malden, MA: Blackwell.

Bonhoeffer, D. (1955). *Ethics* (N.H. Smith, Trans.). New York: Simon & Schuster. (Original work published 1949)

Borduin, C.M., Mann, B.J., Cone, L.T., Henggeler, S.W., Fucci, B.R., Blaske, D.M., et al. (1995). Multisystemic treatment of serious juvenile offenders: Long-term prevention of criminality and violence. *Journal of Consulting and Clinical Psychology, 63*: 569–578.

Boscan, D.C., Penn, N.E., Velasquez, R.J. Savingo, A.V., Maness, P., Guzman, M., et al. (2002a). MMPI-2 performance of Mexican male university students and prison inmates. *Journal of Clinical Psychology, 58*: 465–470.

Boscan, D.C., Penn, N.E., Velasquez, R.J., Reimann, J., Gomez, N., Guzman, M., et al. (2002b). MMPI-2 profiles of Colombian, Mexican, and Venezuelan university students. *Psychological Reports, 87*: 107–110.

Boss, J.A. (2004). *Ethics for life: A text with readings* (3rd ed.). New York: McGraw-Hill.

Boszormenyi-Nagy, I. & Spark, G. M. (1984). *Invisible loyalties: Reciprocity in intergenerational family therapy.* New York: Brunner/Mazel.

Botstein, L. (2007). Freud and Wittgenstein: Language and human nature. *Psychoanalytic Psychology, 24*: 603–622.

Bowen, M. (1978). *Family therapy in clinical practice.* New York: Jason Aronson.

Bowlby, J. (1980). *Attachment and loss: Vol. III. Loss: Sadness and depression.* New York: Basic Books.

Boyatzis, R. & McKee, A. (2005). *Resonant leadership: Renewing yourself and connecting with others through mindfulness, hope, and compassion.* Boston: Harvard Business School Press.

Boyd, S. (1982). *Analysis of the friendship circle.* Unpublished manuscript.

Boyle, J. (2000). Universalism, justice and identity politics: From political correctness to constitutional law. Retrieved 10/22/07 from http://www.law.duk,edu/boylesite/identity.htm

Brazelton, T.B. & Cramer, B.G. (1990). *The earliest relationship: Parents, infants, and the drama of early attachment.* Reading, MA: Addison-Wesley.

Brennan, W. (1998). Aggression and violence: Examining the theories. *Nursing Standard, 12*: 27, 36–38.

Bretherton, I. (1996). Internal working models of attachment relationships as related to resilient coping. In: G.G. Noam & K.W. Fischer (Eds.), *Development and vulnerability in close relationships* (pp. 3–27). Mahwah, NJ: Lawrence Erlbaum.

Briere, J.N. (1992). *Child abuse trauma: Theory and treatment of the lasting effects.* Newbury Park, CA: Sage. Thousand Oaks, CA: Sage Publications.

Brown, G.L., Linnoila, M. & Goodwin, F.K. (1990). Clinical assessment of human aggression and impulsivity in relationship to biochemical measures. In: H.M. van Praag, R. Plutchik & A. Apter (Eds.), *Violence and suicidality: Perspectives in clinical and psychobiological research* (pp. 184–217). New York: Brunner/Mazel.

Brown, N.W. (2001). *Children of the self-absorbed: A grownup's guide to getting over narcissistic parents.* Oakland, CA: New Harbinger Publications.

Brown, S.L., Nesse, R.M., Vinokur, A.D. & Smith, D.M. (2003). Providing social support may be more beneficial than receiving it: Results from a prospective study of mortality. *Psychological Science, 14*: 320–327.

Browning, D. (2004). An ethical analysis of Erikson's concept of generativity. In: E. de St. Aubin, D.P. McAdams & T. Kim (Eds.), *The generative society: Caring for future generations* (pp. 241–255). Washington, DC: American Psychological Association.

Burns, J.M. (2004). Foreword. In: J.B. Ciulla (Ed.), *Ethics, the heart of leadership* (2nd ed.). Westport, CT: Praeger.

Bursten, B. (1973). Some narcissistic personality types. *International Journal of Psycho-Analysis, 54*: 287–300.

Bushman, B.J. & Baumeister, R.F. (1998). Threatened egotism, narcissism, self-esteem, and direct and displaced aggression: Does self-love or self-hate lead to violence? *Journal of Personality and Social Psychology, 75*: 219–229.

Campbell, W.K., Reeder, G.D., Sedikides, C. & Elliot, A.J. (2000). Narcissism and comparative self-enhancement strategies. *Journal of Research in Personality, 34*: 329–347.

Canary, D.J., Cupach, W.R. & Messman, S.J. (1995). *Relationship conflict: Conflict in parent-child, friendship, and romantic relationships.* Thousand Oaks, CA: Sage Publications.

Caplan, B. (2007). *The myth of the rational voter: Why democracies choose bad policies.* Princeton, NJ: Princeton University Press.

Carlson, J. & Sperry, L. (Eds.). (1998). *The disordered couple.* Bristol, PA: Brunner/Mazel.

Carnes, P. (1991). *Don't call it love: Recovery from sexual addiction.* New York: Bantam Books.

Carnes, P. (1992). *Out of the shadows: Understanding sexual addiction* (2nd ed.). Center City, MN: Hazelden.

Carnes, P. (1997). *Sexual anorexia: Overcoming sexual self-hatred.* Center City, MN: Hazelden.

Carnes, P., Delmonico, D.L. & Griffin, E. (with J.M. Moriarity). (2001). *In the shadows of the net: Breaking free of compulsive online sexual behavior.* Center City, MN: Hazelden.

Carter, J. (2003). *Nasty people: How to stop being hurt by them without stooping to their level* (rev. ed.). New York: McGraw-Hill.

Castaneda, C. (1975). *Tales of power.* New York: Washington Square Press.

Cavaiola, A.A. & Lavender, N.J. (2000). *Toxic coworkers: How to deal with dysfunctional people on the job.* Oakland, CA: New Harbinger Publications.

Chadwick, P., Birchwood, M. & Trower, P. (1996). *Cognitive therapy for delusions, voices and paranoia.* Chichester, UK: John Wiley.

Channing Bete Company. (2007). PATHS (Promoting Alternative Thinking Strategies). Retrieved 11/29/07 from http://www.channingbete.com/prevention-programs/paths/facts-and-faqs.php

Chasseguet-Smirgel, J. (1985). *The ego ideal: A psychoanalytic essay on the Malady of the Ideal* (P. Barrows, Trans.). New York: W.W. Norton.

Chirban, S. (2000). Oneness experience: Looking through multiple lenses. *Journal of Applied Psychoanalytic Studies, 2*: 247–264.

Choca, J.P. (2004). *Interpretive guide to the Millon clinical Multiaxial Inventory* (3rd ed.). Washington, DC: American Psychological Association.

Chomsky, N. (2005). *Imperial ambitions: Conversations on the post-9/11 world.* New York: Henry Holt.

Chovil, N. (1994). Equivocation as an interactional event. In: W.R. Cupach & B.H. Spitzberg (Eds.), *The dark side of interpersonal communication* (pp. 105–123). Hillsdale, NJ: Lawrence Erlbaum.

Clance, P.R. & Imes, S.A. (1978). The impostor phenomenon in high achieving women: Dynamics and therapeutic intervention. *Psychotherapy: Theory, Research & Practice, 15*: 241–247.

Clemmitt, M. (2006). Cyber socializing [Electronic version]. *CQ Researcher, 16*(27): 625–648.

Cohen, F., Ogilvie, D.M., Solomon, S., Greenberg, J. & Pyszczynski, T. (2005). American roulette: The effect of reminders of death on support for George W. Bush in the 2004 presidential election. *Analyses of Social Issues and Public Policy, 5*: 177–187.

Cohen, F., Solomon, S., Maxfield, M., Pyszczynski, T. & Greenberg, J. (2004). Fatal attraction: The effects of mortality salience on evaluations of charismatic, task-oriented, and relationship-oriented leaders. *Psychological Science, 15*: 846–851.

Coie, J.D. (1996). Prevention of violence and antisocial behavior. In: R.S. Peters & R.J. McMahon (Eds.), *Preventing childhood disorders, substance abuse, and delinquency* (pp. 1–18). Thousand Oaks, CA: Sage Publications.

Coie, J.D., Watt, N.F., West, S.G., Hawkins, J.D., Asarnow, J.R., Markman, H.J., et al. (1993). The science of prevention: A conceptual framework and some directions for a national research program. *American Psychologist, 48*: 1013–1022.

Collins, J. (2001). *Good to great: Why some companies make the leap … and others don't.* New York: HarperCollins.

Collins, J. (2002). Foreword. In: F. Hesselbein, *Hesselbein on leadership* (pp. xi–xviii). San Francisco: Jossey-Bass.

Comte-Sponville, A. (2001). *A small treatise on the great virtues: The uses of philosophy in everyday life* (C. Temerson, Trans.). New York: Metropolitan Books. (Original work published 1996)

Connor, K.R., Cox, C., Duberstein, P.R., Tian, L., Nisbet, P.A. & Conwell, Y. (2001). Violence, alcohol, and completed suicide: A case-controlled study. *American Journal of Psychiatry, 158*: 1701–1705.

Costa, P.T., Jr. & McCrae, R.R. (1992). *Revised NEO Personality Inventory (NEO-PI-R) and NEO Five-Factor Inventory (NEO-FFI) professional manual.* Odessa, FL: Psychological Assessment Resources.

Covey, S.R. (1999). *Living the 7 habits: The courage to change.* New York: Simon & Schuster.

Cowan, C.P. & Cowan, P.A. (2000). *When partners become parents: The big life change for couples.* Mahwah, NJ: Lawrence Erlbaum.

Cozolino, L.J. (2002). *The neuroscience of psychotherapy: Building and rebuilding the human brain.* New York: W.W. Norton.

Cozolino, L. (2006). *The neuroscience of human relationships: Attachment and the developing social brain.* New York: W.W. Norton.

Cramerus, M. (1989). Self-derogation: Inner conflict and anxious vigilance. *Journal of Contemporary Psychotherapy, 19:* 55–69.

Cull, J.G. & Gill, W.S. (1988). *Suicide Probability Scale (SPS) manual.* Los Angeles, CA: Western Psychological Services.

Dalai Lama. (1999). *Ethics for the new millennium.* New York: Riverhead Books.

Davidson, R.J., Putnam, K.M. & Larson, C.L. (2000, July 28). Dysfunction in the neural circuitry of emotion regulation: A possible prelude to violence. *Science, 289:* 591–594.

Dawkins, R. (1989). *The selfish gene* (2nd ed.). Oxford, UK: Oxford University Press.

Dawkins, R. (2006). *The God delusion.* Boston: Houghton Mifflin.

Dean, J.W. (2006). *Conservative without conscience.* New York: Viking.

Decety, J. & Jackson, P.L. (2006). A social-neuroscience perspective on empathy. *Current Directions in Psychological Science, 15:* 54–58.

Decety, J. & Moriguchi, Y. (2007). The empathic brain and its dysfunction in psychiatric populations: Implications for intervention across different clinical conditions. *BioPsychoSocial Medicine, 1:22.* Retrieved 1/25/08 from http://www.bpsmedicine.com/content/1/1/22

De Rougemont, D. (1983). *Love in the Western world* (rev. ed.) (M. Belgion, Trans.). Princeton, NJ: Princeton University Press.

DeSteno, D., Dasgupta, N., Bartlett, M.Y. & Cajdric, A. (2004). Prejudice from thin air: The effect of emotion on automatic intergroup attitudes. *Psychological Science, 15:* 319–324.

De Waal, F. (2006). *Primates and philosophers: How morality evolved.* Princeton, NJ: Princeton University Press.

DeZengotita, T. (2002, April). The numbing of the American mind. *Harper's Magazine,* 33–40.

De Zulueta, F. (1993). *From pain to violence: The traumatic roots of destructiveness*. London: Whurr Publishers.

Dicks, H.V. (1967). *Marital tensions: Clinical studies towards a psychological theory of interaction*. London, UK: Karnac Books.

DiGiuseppe, R., Eckhardt, C., Tafrate, R. & Robin, M. (1994). The diagnosis and treatment of anger in a cross-cultural context. *Journal of Social Distress and the Homeless, 3*: 229–261.

Dodge, K.A., Pettit, G.S., Bates, J.E. & Valente, E. (1995). Social information-processing patterns partially mediate the effect of early physical abuse on later conduct problems. *Journal of Abnormal Psychology, 104*: 632–643.

Doherty, W.J. (1995). *Soul searching: Why psychotherapy must promote moral responsibility*. New York: Basic Books.

Doucette-Gates, A., Firestone, R.W. & Firestone, L.A. (1999). Assessing violent thoughts: The relationship between thought processes and violent behavior. *Psychologica Belgica, 39*: 113–134.

Dovidio, J.F., Glick, P. & Rudman, L.A. (2005). Introduction: Reflecting on *The Nature of Prejudice: Fifty years after Allport*. In: J.F. Dovidio, P. Glick & L. Rudman (Eds.), *On the nature of prejudice: Fifty years after Allport* (pp. 1–15). Malden, MA: Blackwell Publishing.

Dovidio, J.F., Piliavin, J.A., Schroeder, D.A. & Penner, L.A. (2006). *The social psychology of prosocial behavior*. Mahwah, NJ: Lawrence Erlbaum.

Drucker, P.F. (1985). *Management: Tasks, responsibilities, practices* (rev. ed.). New York: Harper Colophon.

Drucker, P.F. (1998). *On the profession of management*. Boston, MA: Harvard Business School Publishing.

Dutton, D.G. (1995a). *The batterer: A psychological profile*. New York: Basic Books.

Dutton, D.G. (1995b). *The domestic assault of women: Psychological and criminal justice perspectives* (Rev. ed.). Vancouver, BC: UBC Press.

Eaker, E.D., Sullivan, L.M., Kelly-Hayes, M., D'Agostino, R.B. & Benjamin, E.J. (2007). Marital status, marital strain, and risk of coronary heart disease or total mortality: The Framingham Offspring Study. *Psychosomatic Medicine, 69*: 509–513.

Eckhardt, C.I. & Dye, M.L. (2000). The cognitive characteristics of martially violent men: Theory and evidence. *Cognitive Therapy and Research, 24*: 139–158.

Egeland, B., Sroufe, L.A. & Erickson, M. (1983). The developmental consequences of different patterns of maltreatment. *Child Abuse and Neglect, 7*: 459–469.

El-Bassel, N., Gilbert, L., Wu, E., Go, H. & Hill, J. (2005). Relationship between drug abuse and intimate partner violence: A longitudinal study among women receiving methadone. *American Journal of Public Health, 95*: 465–470.

Elkind, D. (2001). *The hurried child: Growing up too fast too soon* (3rd ed.). Cambridge, MA: Da Capo Press.

Epstein, S. (1998). *Constructive thinking: The key to emotional intelligence.* Westport, CT: Praeger.

Erickson, P.G. (2001, April). Drugs, violence and public health: What does the harm reduction approach have to offer? [electronic version]. *Fraser Institute Digital Publication.* Vancouver, BC: Fraser Institute.

Erikson, E.H. (1963). *Childhood and society* (2nd ed.). New York: W.W. Norton.

Erikson, E.H. (1964). *Insight and responsibility.* New York: W.W. Norton.

Erikson, E.H. (1969). *Gandhi's truth: On the origins of militant nonviolence.* New York: W.W. Norton.

Eron, L.D., Gentry, J.H. & Schlegel, P. (Eds.). (1994). *Reason to hope: A psychosocial perspective on violence and youth.* Washington, DC: American Psychological Association.

Exline, J.J., Baumeister, R.F., Bushman, B.J., Campbell, W.K. & Finkel, E.J. (2004). Too proud to let go: Narcissism entitlement as a barrier to forgiveness. *Journal of Personality and Social Psychology, 87*: 894–912.

Fairbairn, W.R.D. (1952). *Psychoanalytic studies of the personality.* London, UK: Routledge & Kegan Paul.

Falk, A. (2004). *Fratricide in the Holy Land: A psychoanalytic view of the Arab-Israeli conflict.* Madison, WI: University of Wisconsin Press.

Farberow, N.L. (1980). Introduction. In: N.L. Farberow (Ed.), *The many faces of suicide: Indirect self-destructive behavior* (pp. 1–12). New York: McGraw-Hill.

Farkas, C.M. & Wetlaufer, S. (1998). The ways chief executive officers lead. In *Harvard Business Review on Leadership* (pp. 115–146). Boston, MA: Harvard Business School Publishing. (Original work published 1996)

Feerick, M.M. & Silverman, G.B. (Eds.). (2006). *Children exposed to violence.* Baltimore, MD: Paul H. Brookes Publishing.

Feingold, A. (1992). Gender differences in mate selection preferences: A test of the parental investment model. *Psychological Bulletin, 112*: 125–139.

Felitti, V.J., Anda, R.F., Nordenberg, D., Williamson, D.F., Spitz, A.M., Edwards, V., et al. (1998). Relationship of childhood abuse and household dysfunction to many of the leading causes of death in adults: The Adverse Childhood Experiences (ACE) study. *American Journal of Preventive Medicine, 14*: 245–258.

Felson, R.B. (2002). *Violence and gender reexamined.* Washington, DC: American Psychological Association.

Ferenczi, S. (1955). Confusion of tongues between adults and the child. In: M. Balint (Ed.), *Final contributions to the problems & methods of psycho-analysis* (E. Mosbacher & others, Trans., pp. 156–167). New York: Basic Books. (Original work published 1933)

Fierman, L.B. (Ed.). (1965). *Effective psychotherapy: The contribution of Hellmuth Kaiser.* New York: Free Press.

Fincham, F.D. (2000). The kiss of the porcupines: From attributing responsibility to forgiving. *Personal Relationships, 7*: 1–23.

Firestone, L. & Catlett, J. (2004). Voice therapy interventions with addicted clients. *Counselor: The Magazine for Addiction Professionals, 5*(5): 49–69.

Firestone, R.W. (1957). *A concept of the schizophrenic process.* Unpublished doctoral dissertation, University of Denver.

Firestone, R.W. (1984). A concept of the primary fantasy bond: A developmental perspective. *Psychotherapy, 21*: 218–225.

Firestone, R.W. (1985). *The fantasy bond: Structure of psychological defenses.* Santa Barbara, CA: Glendon Association.

Firestone, R.W. (1987a). Destructive effects of the fantasy bond in couple and family relationships. *Psychotherapy, 24*: 233–239.

Firestone, R.W. (1987b). The "voice": The dual nature of guilt reactions. *American Journal of Psychoanalysis, 47*: 210–229.

Firestone, R.W. (1988). *Voice therapy: A psychotherapeutic approach to self-destructive behavior.* Santa Barbara, CA: Glendon Association.

Firestone, R.W. (1989). Parenting groups based on voice therapy. *Psychotherapy, 26*: 524–529.

Firestone, R.W. (1990a). The bipolar causality of regression. *American Journal of Psychoanalysis, 50*: 121–135.

Firestone, R.W. (1990b). *Compassionate child-rearing: An in-depth approach to optimal parenting.* Santa Barbara, CA: Glendon Association.

Firestone, R.W. (1990c). Prescription for psychotherapy. *Psychotherapy, 27*: 627–635.

Firestone, R.W. (1993). The psychodynamics of fantasy, addiction, and addictive attachments. *American Journal of Psychoanalysis, 53*: 335–352.

Firestone, R.W. (1994a). A new perspective on the Oedipal complex: A voice therapy session. *Psychotherapy, 31*: 342–351.

Firestone, R.W. (1994b). Psychological defenses against death anxiety. In: R.A. Neimeyer (Ed.), *Death anxiety handbook: Research, instrumentation, and application* (pp. 217–241). Washington, DC: Taylor & Francis.

Firestone, R.W. (1996). The origins of ethnic strife. *Mind and Human Interaction, 7*: 167–180.

Firestone, R.W. (1997a). *Combating destructive thought processes: Voice therapy and separation theory*. Thousand Oaks, CA: Sage.

Firestone, R.W. (1997b). *Suicide and the inner voice: Risk assessment, treatment, and case management*. Thousand Oaks, CA: Sage.

Firestone, R.W. (2000). Microsuicide and the elderly: A basic defense against death anxiety. In: A. Tomer (Ed.), *death attitudes and the older adult: Theories, concepts, and applications* (pp. 65–84). Philadelphia: Brunner-Routledge.

Firestone, R.W. & Catlett, J. (1989). *Psychological defenses in everyday life*. Santa Barbara, CA: Glendon Association.

Firestone, R.W. & Catlett, J. (1999). *Fear of intimacy*. Washington, DC: American Psychological Association.

Firestone, R.W. & Firestone, L. (2006). *Firestone Assessment of Self-Destructive Thoughts (FAST)/Firestone Assessment of Suicidal Intent (FASI) professional manual*. Lutz, FL: Psychological Assessment Resources. (Original work published 1996)

Firestone, R.W. & Firestone, L. (2008). *Firestone Assessment of Violent Thoughts (FAVT) professional manual*. Lutz, FL: Psychological Assessment Resources.

Firestone, R.W., Firestone, L. & Catlett, J. (2002). *Conquer your critical inner voice: A revolutionary program to counter negative thoughts and live free from imagined limitations*. Oakland, CA: New Harbinger Publications.

Firestone, R.W., Firestone, L.A. & Catlett, J. (2003). *Creating a life of meaning and compassion: The wisdom of psychotherapy*. Washington, DC: American Psychological Association.

Firestone, R.W., Firestone, L.A. & Catlett, J. (2006). *Sex and love in intimate relationships*. Washington, DC: American Psychological Association.

Firestone, R.W. & Seiden, R.H. (1987). Microsuicide and suicidal threats of everyday life. *Psychotherapy, 24*: 31–39.

Fiske, S.T., Cuddy, A.J.C., Glick, P. & Xu, J. (2002). A model of (often mixed) stereotype content: Competence and warmth respectively follow from perceived status and competition. *Journal of Personality and Social Psychology, 82*: 878–902.

Flexner, S.B. (Ed.). (1998). *Random House Webster's unabridged dictionary* (2nd ed.). New York: Random House.

Flugel, J.C. (1945). *Man, morals and society.* New York: International Universities Press.

Fogarty, T. (1976). Marital crisis. In: P. Guerin (Ed.), *Family therapy: Theory and practice* (pp. 325–334). New York: Gardner Press.

Fogarty, T. (1979). The distancer and the pursuer. *The Family, 7*: 11–16.

Fonagy, P. (1999). Male perpetrators of violence against women: An attachment theory perspective. *Journal of Applied Psychoanalytic Studies, 1*: 7–27.

Fonagy, P. (2001). *Attachment theory and psychoanalysis.* New York: Other Press.

Fonagy, P. (2004a). Early-life trauma and the psychogenesis and prevention of violence. *Annals of the New York Academy of Science, 1036*: 181–200.

Fonagy, P. (2004b). The developmental roots of violence in the failure of mentalization. In: F. Pfafflin & G. Adshead (Eds.), *A matter of security: The application of attachment theory to forensic psychiatry and psychotherapy* (pp. 13–56). London: Jessica Kingsley.

Fonagy, P., Gergely, G., Jurist, E.L. & Target, M. (2002). *Affect regulation, mentalization, and the development of the self.* New York: Other Press.

Fonagy, P. & Higgitt, A. (2007). The development of prejudice: An attachment theory hypothesis explaining its ubiquity. In: H. Parens, A. Mahfouz, S.W. Twemlow & D.E. Scharff (Eds.), *The future of prejudice: Psychoanalysis and the prevention of prejudice* (pp. 63–79). Lanham, MD: Rowman & Littlefield.

Fonagy, P., Target, M., Steele, M. & Steele, H. (1997). The development of violence and crime as it relates to security of attachment. In: J.D. Osofsky (Ed.), *Children in a violent society* (pp. 150–177). New York: Guilford Press.

Forgays, D.K. & DeMilio, L. (2005). Is teen court effective for repeat offenders? A test of the restorative justice approach. *International Journal of Offender Therapy and Comparative Criminology, 49*: 107–118.

Forward, S. (with C. Buck). (1989). *Toxic parents: Overcoming their hurtful legacy and reclaiming your life.* New York: Bantam Books.

Forward, S. (with d. Frazier). (1997). *Emotional blackmail: When the people in your life use fear, obligation and guilt to manipulate you.* New York: HarperCollins.

Forward, S. (with D. Frazier). (2001). *Toxic in-laws: Loving strategies for protecting your marriage*. New York: HarperCollins.

Foster, J.D., Campbell, W.K. & Twenge, J.M. (2003). Individual differences in narcissism: Inflated self-views across the lifespan and around the world. *Journal of Research in Personality, 37*: 469–486.

Foucault, M. (1972). *Power/knowledge*. New York: Pantheon Books.

Fowers, B.J. (2005). *Virtue and psychology: Pursuing excellence in ordinary practices*. Washington, DC: American Psychological Association.

Fraiberg, S., Adelson, E. & Shapiro, V. (1980). Ghosts in the nursery: A psychoanalytic approach to the problems of impaired infant-mother relationships. In: S. Fraiberg (Ed.), *Clinical studies in infant mental health: The first year of life* (pp. 164–196). New York: Basic Books. (Original work published 1975)

Frankl, V.E. (1959). *Man's search for meaning* (Rev. ed.). New York: Washington Square Press. (Original work published 1946)

Frankl, V.E. (1967). Group psychotherapeutic experiences in a concentration camp. In: V.E. Frankl, *Psychotherapy and existentialism: Selected papers on logotherapy* (pp. 95–105). New York: Simon & Schuster. (Original work published 1954).

Freud, A. (1966). *The ego and the mechanisms of defense* (Rev. ed.). Madison, CT: International Universities Press.

Freud, S. (1935). *A general introduction to psycho-analysis* (J. Riviere, Trans.). New York: Simon & Schuster.

Freud, S. (1955). Group psychology and the analysis of the ego. In: J. Strachey (Ed. and Trans.), *The standard edition of the complete psychological works of Sigmund Freud* (Vol. 18, pp. 63–143). London: Hogarth. (Original work published 1921)

Freud, S. (1957a). The unconscious. In: J. Strachey (Ed. and Trans.), *The standard edition of the complete psychological works of Sigmund Freud* (Vol. 14, pp. 159–215). (Original work published 1915)

Freud, S. (1957b). Thoughts for the times on war and death. In: J. Strachey (Ed. and Trans.), *The standard edition of the complete psychological works of Sigmund Freud* (Vol. 14, pp. 273–302). (Original work published 1915)

Freud, S. (1959). An autobiographical study. In: J. Strachey (Ed. and Trans.), *The standard edition of the complete psychological works of Sigmund Freud* (Vol. 20, pp. 7–75). London: Hogarth. (Original work published 1925)

Freud, S. (1961). Civilization and its discontents. In: J. Strachey (Ed. and Trans.), *The standard edition of the complete psychological works of Sigmund Freud* (Vol. 21, pp. 64–145). London: Hogarth. (Original work published 1930)

From Revolution to Reconstruction. (2007). The letters of Thomas Jefferson: 1743–1826. Retrieved 10/20/07 from http://odur.let.rug.nl/-usa/P/tj3/writings/brf/jefl41.htm.

Fromm, E. (1939). Selfishness and self-love [Electronic version]. *Psychiatry: Journal for the Study of Interpersonal Process, 2*: 507–523.

Fromm, E. (1941). *Escape from freedom.* New York: Avon Books.

Fromm, E. (1950). *Psychoanalysis and religion.* New Haven: Yale University Press.

Fugere, B., Hardaway, C. & Warshawsky, J. (2005). *Why business people speak like idiots: A bullfighter's guide.* New York: Free Press.

Gage, R.L. (Ed.). (1976). *Choose life: A dialogue: Arnold Toynbee and Daisaku Ikeda.* Oxford, UK: Oxford University Press.

Gailliot, M.T., Schmeichel, B.J. & Baumeister, R.F. (2006). Self-regulatory processes defend against the threat of death: Effects of self-control depletion and trait self-control on thoughts and fears of dying. *Journal of Personality and Social Psychology, 91*: 49–62.

Galbraith, J.K. (1983). *The anatomy of power.* Boston: Houghton Mifflin.

Gandz, J. (2000). Global leadership and personal power [Electronic version]. *Ivey Business Journal Online,* May/June.

Gandz, J. (2005). The leadership role [Electronic version]. *Ivey Business Journal Online,* January/February.

Gandz, J. (2007). Great leadership is good leadership [Electronic version]. *Ivey Business Journal,* May/June.

Garbarino, J. (1995). *Raising children in a socially toxic environment.* San Francisco: Jossey-Bass.

Garbarino, J. (1999). *Lost boys: Why our sons turn violent and how we can save them.* New York: Free Press.

Garbarino, J. (2006). *See Jane hit: Why girls are growing more violent and what can be done about it.* New York: Penguin Press.

Garbarino, J. & Gilliam, G. (1980). *Understanding abusive families.* Lexington, MA: Lexington Books.

Garbarino, J., Guttmann, E. & Seeley, J.W. (1986). *The psychologically battered child.* San Francisco: Jossey-Bass.

Gardner, J.W. (1990). *On leadership.* New York: Free Press.

Geen, R.G. (1994, August 12). Human aggression: Current theories and research. Paper presented at the annual convention of the American Psychological Association, Los Angeles, CA.

Geen, R.G. (1998). Processes and personal variables in affective aggression. In: R.G. Geen & E. Donnerstein (Eds.), *Human aggression: Theories, research, and implications for social policy* (pp. 1–21). San Diego, CA: Academic Press.

Geen, R.G. (2001). *Human aggression* (2nd ed.). Buckingham, UK: Open University Press.

Geen, R.G. & Donnerstein, E. (Eds.). (1998). *Human aggression: Theories, research, and implications for social policy.* San Diego, CA: Academic Press.

Gershoff, E.T. (2002). Corporal punishment by parents and associated child behaviors and experiences: A meta-analytic and theoretical review. *Psychological Bulletin, 128*: 539–579.

Gerson, R. (1995). The family life cycle: Phases, stages, and crises. In: R.H. Mikesell, D. Lusterman & S.H. McDaniel (Eds.), *Integrating family therapy: Handbook of family psychology and systems theory* (pp. 91–111). Washington, DC: American Psychological Association.

Getz, J.G. & Bray, J.H. (2005). Predicting heavy alcohol use among adolescents. *American Journal of Orthopsychiatry, 75*: 102–116.

Gewirtz, A. & Edleson, J.L. (2004). Young children's exposure to adult domestic violence: Toward a developmental risk and resilience framework for research and intervention. Series Paper #6, *Early childhood, domestic violence, and poverty: Helping young children and their families.* Iowa City, IA: University of Iowa.

Gibbs, J.C. (2003). *Moral development and reality: Beyond the theories of Kohlberg and Hoffman.* Thousand Oaks, CA: Sage Publications.

Gibney, P. (2006). The double bind theory: Still crazy-making after all these years. *Psychotherapy in Australia, 12*(3): 48–55).

Gilbert, G.M. (1947). *Nuremberg diary.* New York: Da Capo Press.

Gilbert, P. (1989). *Human nature and suffering.* Hillsdale, NJ: Lawrence Erlbaum.

Gilbert, P. (2005). Compassion and cruelty: A biopsychosocial approach. In: P. Gilbert (Ed.), *Compassion: Conceptualisations, research and use in psychotherapy* (pp. 9–74). London: Routledge.

Gillath, O., Shaver, P.R. & Mikulincer, M. (2005). An attachment-theoretical approach to compassion and altruism. In: P. Gilbert (Ed.), *Compassion: Conceptualisations, research and use in psychotherapy* (pp. 121–147). London: Routledge.

Gilligan, C. (1982). *In a different voice: Psychological theory and women's development.* Cambridge, MA: Harvard University Press.

Gilligan, C. (1996). The centrality of relationship in human development: A puzzle, some evidence, and a theory. In: G.G. Noam & K.W. Fischer (Eds.), *Development and vulnerability in close relationships* (pp. 237–261). Mahwah, NJ: Lawrence Erlbaum.

Gilligan, J. (1996a). Epilogue: Civilization and its malcontents. In: J. Gilligan, *Violence: Reflections on a national epidemic* (pp. 241–267). New York: Vintage Books.

Gilligan, J. (1996b). *Violence: Our deadly epidemic and its causes.* New York: G.P. Putnam's Sons.

Gilligan, J. (2001). *Preventing violence.* New York: Thames & Hudson.

Gilligan, J. (2007). Terrorism, fundamentalism, and nihilism: Analyzing the dilemmas of modernity. In: H. Parens, A. Mahfouz, S.W. Twemlow & D.E. Scharff (Eds.), *The future of prejudice: Psychoanalysis and the prevention of prejudice* (pp. 37–59). Lanham, MD: Rowman & Littlefield.

Gilligan, J. & Lee, B. (2004). Beyond the prison paradigm: From provoking violence to preventing it by creating "anti-prisons" (residential colleges and therapeutic communities). *Annals of the New York Academy of Science, 1036*: 300–324.

Gini, A. (2004). Moral leadership and business ethics. In: J.B. Ciulla (Ed.), *Ethics, the heart of leadership* (4th ed.) (pp. 25–43). Westport, CT: Praeger.

Gladwell, M. (2005). *Blink: The power of thinking without thinking.*

Glass, L. (1995). *Toxic people: 10 ways of dealing with people who make your life miserable.* New York: St. Martin's Griffin.

Glass, S.P. (with J.C. Staeheli). (2003). *Not "just friends:" Protect your relationship from infidelity and heal the trauma of betrayal.* New York: Free Press.

Glick, P. & Fiske, S.T. (2001). An ambivalent alliance: Hostile and benevolent sexism as complementary justifications for gender inequality. *American Psychologist, 56*: 109–118.

Goldberg, H. (1983). *The new male female relationship.* Gretna, LA: Wellness Institute.

Goldberg, H. (2001). *The new male: From self-destruction to self-care.* Gretna, LA: Wellness Institute.

Goleman, D. (2006). *Social intelligence: The new science of human relationships.* New York: Bantam Books.

Goleman, D., Boyatzis, R. & McKee, A. (2002). *Primal leadership: Realizing the power of emotional intelligence.* Boston, MA: Harvard Business School Press.

Gostick, A. & Telford, D. (2003). *The integrity advantage.* Salt Lake City, UT: Gibbs Smith.

Gottman, J.M. (1979). *Marital interaction: Experimental investigations.* New York: Academic Press.

Gottman, J.M. & Krokoff, L.J. (1989). Marital interaction and satisfaction: A longitudinal view. *Journal of Consulting and Clinical Psychology,* 57: 47–52.

Gottman, J.M. & Silver, N. (1999). *The seven principles for making marriage work.* New York: Three Rivers Press.

Grayling, A.C. (2003). *What is good? The search for the best way to live.* London: Phoenix.

Greenberg, J., Arndt, J., Simon, L., Pyszczynski, T. & Solomon, S. (2000). Proximal and distal defenses in response to reminders of one's mortality: Evidence of a temporal sequence. *Personality and Social Psychology Bulletin, 26*: 91–99.

Greenberg, J., Pyszczynski, T., Solomon, S., Rosenblatt, A., Veeder, M., Kirkland, S., et al. (1990). Evidence for terror management theory II: The effects of mortality salience on reactions to those who threaten or bolster the cultural worldview. *Journal of Personality and Social Psychology, 58*: 309–318.

Greenberg, J., Pyszczynski, T., Solomon, S., Simon, L. & Breus, M. (1994). Role of consciousness and accessibility of death-related thoughts in mortality salience effects. *Journal of Personality and Social Psychology, 67*: 627–637.

Greenleaf, R.K. (1991). The servant as leader [essay]. Westfield, IN: The Robert K. Greenleaf Center.

Greenspan, S.I. (with B.L. Benderly). (1997). *The growth of the mind and the endangered origins of intelligence.* Reading, MA: Addison-Wesley.

Greer, G. (1971). *The female eunuch.* New York: McGraw-Hill. (Original work published 1970).

Greven, P. (1990). *Spare the child: The religious roots of punishment and the psychological impact of physical abuse.* New York: Vintage Books.

Grossman, D.C., Neckerman, H.J., Koepsell, T.D., Liu, P.Y., Asher, K.N., Beland, K., et al. (1997). Effectiveness of a violence prevention curriculum among children in elementary school: A randomized controlled trial. *Journal of the American Medical Association, 277*: 1605–1611.

Grotstein, J.S. (2007). *A beam of intense darkness: Wilfred Bion's legacy to psychoanalysis*. London: Karnac Books.

Groves, B.M. (1997). Growing up in a violent world: The impact of family and community violence on young children and their families. *Topics in Early Childhood Special Education, 17*: 74–102.

Guntrip, H. (1961). *Personality structure and human interaction: The developing synthesis of psycho-dynamic theory*. New York: International Universities Press.

Guntrip, H. (1969). *Schizoid phenomena: Object relations and the self*. New York: International Universities Press.

Hackman, J.R. & Wageman, R. (2007). Asking the right questions about leadership. *American Psychologist, 62*: 43–47.

Haggard-Grann, U., Hallqvist, J., Langstrom, N. & Moller, J. (2006). The role of alcohol and drugs in triggering criminal violence: A case crossover study. *Addictions, 101*: 100–108.

Haidt, J. (2001). The emotional dog and its rational tail: A social intuitionist approach to moral judgment. *Psychological Review, 108*: 814–834.

Halpern, H.M. (1982). *How to break your addiction to a person*. New York: Bantam Books.

Hamill, P. (1994). *A drinking life: A memoir*. Boston: Little, Brown and Company.

Hamn, D.M., Castino, R.J., Jarosinski, J. & Britton, H. (1991, April). Relating mother-toddler negotiation patterns to infant attachment and maternal depression with an adolescent mother sample. In: J. Osofsky & L. Hubbs-Tait (Chairs), *Consequences of adolescent parenting: Predicting behavior problems in toddlers and preschoolers*. Symposium conducted at the biennial meeting of the Society for Research in Child Development, Seattle, WA.

Hampson, S.E. & Goldberg, L.R. (2006). A first large cohort study of personality trait stability over the 40 years between elementary school and midlife. *Journal of Personality and Social Psychology, 91*: 763–779.

Haney, C. & Zimbardo, P. (1998). The past and future of U.S. prison policy: Twenty-five years after the Stanford Prison Experiment. *American Psychologist, 53*: 709–727.

Harvard Business Essentials Series. (2005). *Power, influence, and persuasion: Sell your ideas and make things happen*. Boston, MA: Harvard Business School Press.

Hauser, M.D. (2006). *Moral minds: How nature designed our universal sense of right and wrong*. New York: HarperCollins.

Havel, V. (1990). *Disturbing the peace: A conversation with Karel Hvizdala* (P. Wilson, Trans.). New York: Alfred A. Knopf.

Healy, J.M. (1998). *Failure to connect: How computers affect our children's minds—and what we can do about it*. New York: Simon & Schuster.

Heifetz, R.A. (1994). *Leadership without easy answers*. Cambridge, MA: Belknap Press.

Heifetz, R.A. & Laurie, D.L. (1998). The work of leadership. In *Harvard Business Review on Leadership* (pp. 171–197). Boston, MA: Harvard Business School Publishing. (Original work published 1997)

Heller, A. (1996). *The ethics of personality*. Oxford, UK: Blackwell Publishers.

Henry, J. (1963). *Culture against man*. New York: Vintage Books.

Herzog, J.M. (2001). *Father hunger: Explorations with adults and children*. Hillsdale, NJ: Analytic Press.

Hesselbein, F. (2002). *Hesselbein on leadership*. San Francisco: Jossey-Bass.

Hilgard, E.R. (1977). *Divided consciousness: Multiple controls in human thought and action*. New York: John Wiley.

Hinton, J. (1975). The influence of previous personality on reactions to having terminal cancer. *Omega, 6*: 95–111.

Hoffer, E. (1951). *The true believer: Thoughts on the nature of mass movements*. New York: HarperCollins.

Hoffer, E. (2006). *The passionate state of mind and other aphorisms*. Titusville, NJ: Hopewell Publications. (Original work published 1955)

Hollander, E.P. (2004). Ethical challenges in the leader-follower relationship. In: J.B. Ciulla (Ed.), *Ethics, the heart of leadership* (2nd ed.) (pp. 47–58). Westport, CT: Praeger.

Holmes, J. & Lindley, R. (1989). *The values of psychotherapy*. Oxford, UK: Oxford University Press.

Holt, R.R. & Silverstein, B. (1989). On the psychology of enemy images: Introduction and overview. *Journal of Social Issues, 45*: 1–11.

Hornor, G. (2005). Domestic violence and children. *Journal of Pediatric Health Care, 19*: 206–212.

Hotchkiss, S. (2002). *Why is it always about you? The seven deadly sins of narcissism*. New York: Free Press.

Indiana University, IU News Room. (2007, September 8). "Helicopter parents" stir up anxiety, depression. Retrieved 9/8/07 from http://newsinfo.iu.edu/web/page/normal/6073.html.

International Service Organization of SAA, Inc. (2005). *Sex Addicts Anonymous*. Houston, TX: Author.

Jacobvitz, D. & Hazen, N. (1999). Developmental pathways from infant disorganization to childhood peer relationships. In: J. Solomon & C. George (Eds.), *Attachment disorganization* (pp. 127–159). New York: Guilford Press.

Jacoby, M. (1990). *Individuation and narcissism: The psychology of the self in Jung and Kohut* (M. Gubitz, Trans.). New York: Brunner-Routledge. (Original work published 1985)

Jaffee, S. & Hyde, J.S. (2000). Gender differences in moral orientation: A meta-analysis. *Psychological Bulletin, 126*: 703–726.

James, B. (1994). *Handbook for treatment of attachment-trauma problems in children*. New York: Free Press.

James, W. (1948). The moral philosopher and the moral life. In: A. Castell (Ed.), *Essays in pragmatism by William James* (pp. 65–87). New York: Hafner Press. (Original work published 1891)

Janov, A. (1970). *The primal scream: Primal therapy: The cure for neurosis*. New York: Putnam.

Johnson-Roullier, C. (1997). Identity politics, feminism, and the problem of difference. *Surfaces, 7*: 108.

Johnston, M. (2005). *Syndromes of corruption: Wealth, power, and democracy*. Cambridge, UK: Cambridge University Press.

Jones, D. & Shuker, R. (2004). Concluding comments: A humane approach to working with dangerous people. In: D. Jones (Ed.), *Working with dangerous people: The psychotherapy of violence* (pp. 191–198). Oxford, UK: Radcliffe Medical Press.

Josephson, M. (2004). Weekly commentary from Michael Josephson, May 3–7, 2004. Retrieved 9/26/05 from http://www.character-counts.org/knxwk356.htm

Joyce, R. (2006). *The evolution of morality*. Cambridge, MA: MIT Press.

Junto Society. (2007). Head heart letter by Thomas Jefferson. Retrieved 10/12/07 from http://www.juntosociety.com/i_documents/tjheadheartltr.html

Kam, C., Greenberg, M.T. & Kusche, C.A. (2004). Sustained effects of the PATHS curriculum on the social and psychological adjustment of children in special education. *Journal of Emotional and Behavioral Disorders, 12*: 66–78.

Kam, C., Greenberg, M.T. & Walls, C.T. (2003). Examining the role of implementation quality in school-based prevention using the PATHS curriculum. *Prevention Science, 4*: 55–63.

Kant, I. (1959). *Foundations for a metaphysics of morals.* New York: Bobbs-Merrill.

Kaplan, L.J. (1978). *Oneness and separateness: From infant to individual.* New York: Simon & Schuster.

Karpel, M. (1976). Individuation: From fusion to dialogue. *Family Process, 15*(1): 65–82.

Karpel, M.A. (1994). *Evaluating couples: A handbook for practitioners.* New York: W.W. Norton.

Kasl, C.D. (1989). *Women, sex, and addiction: A search for love and power.* New York: Harper and Row.

Kastenbaum, R. (1974, Summer). Childhood: The kingdom where creatures die. *Journal of Clinical Child Psychology,* pp.11–14.

Kastenbaum, R. (1995). *Death, society, and human experience* (5th ed.). Boston: Allyn and Bacon.

Katz, L.D. (Ed.). (2000). *Evolutionary origins of morality: Cross-disciplinary perspectives.* Thorverton, UK: Imprint Academic.

Katzman, G.H. (2005). A bioethical analysis of a form of psychologic abuse: Teaching hatred to children. *Clinical Pediatrics, 44*: 143–150.

Kecmanovic, D. (1996). *The mass psychology of ethnonationalism.* New York: Plenum Press.

Keen, S. (1986). *Faces of the enemy: Reflections of the hostile imagination.* San Francisco: Harper & Row.

Keen, S. (1997). *To love and be loved.* New York: Bantam Books.

Kellerman, B. (2004). *Bad leadership: What it is, how it happens, why it matters.* Boston: Harvard Business School Press.

Kempe, R.S. & Kempe, C.H. (1978). *Child abuse.* Cambridge, MA: Harvard University Press.

Kenney, R.A., Schwartz-Kenney, B.M. & Blascovich, J. (1996). Implicit leadership theories: Defining leaders described as worthy of influence. *Personality and Social Psychology Bulletin, 22*: 1128–1143.

Kernberg, O.F. (1975). *Borderline conditions and pathological narcissism.* New York: Jason Aronson.

Kernberg, O.F. (1980). *Internal world and external reality: Object relations theory applied.* Northvale, NJ: Jason Aronson.

Kernberg, O.F. (1984). *Severe personality disorders: Psychotherapeutic strategies.* New Haven, CT: Yale University Press.

Kernberg, O.F. (1995). *Love relations: Normality and pathology.* New Haven, CT: Yale University Press.

Kernberg, O.F. (1998). Pathological narcissism and narcissistic personality disorder: Theoretical background and diagnostic classification. In: E.F. Ronningstam (Ed.), *Disorders of narcissism: Diagnostic, clinical, and empirical implications* (pp. 29–51). Northvale, NJ: Jason Aronson.

Kerr, M.E. & Bowen, M. (1988). *Family evaluation: An approach based on Bowen theory*. New York: W.W. Norton.

Keys, A., Brozek, J., Henschel, A., Mickelsen, O. & Taylor, H.L. (1950). *The biology of human starvation, (Vol. 2)*. Minneapolis: University of Minnesota Press.

Keyes, C.L.M. & Haidt, J. (Eds.). (2003). *Flourishing: Positive psychology and the life well-lived*. Washington, DC: American Psychological Association.

Kidder, R.M. (2007). Moral courage. Retrieved 8/24/07 from http://www.moral-couarge.org/mc_chapter_one.html.

Kiecolt-Glaser, J.K., Malarkey, W.B., Chee, M., Newton, T., Cacioppo, J.T., Mao, H.Y., et al. (1993). Negative behavior during marital conflict is associated with immunological down-regulation. *Psychosomatic Medicine, 55*: 395–409.

Kierkegaard, S. (1954). *The sickness unto death* (W. Lowrie, Trans.). New York: Anchor. (Original work published 1849)

Kilburg, R.R. (2006). *Executive wisdom: Coaching and the emergence of virtuous leaders*. Washington, DC: American Psychological Association.

Kingery, P.M., Pruitt, B.E. & Hurley, R.S. (1992). Violence and illegal drug use among adolescents: Evidence from the U.S. National Adolescent Student Health Survey. *International Journal of the Addictions, 27*: 1445–1464.

Kipnis, L. (2003). *Against love: A polemic*. New York: Pantheon Books.

Kitwood, T. (1990). *Concern for others: A new psychology of conscience and morality*. London: Routledge.

Klein, M. (1964). *Contributions to psycho-analysis 1921–1945*. New York: McGraw-Hill. (Original work published 1948)

Kluger, J. (2006, Apr. 24). Taming wild girls [electronic version]. *Time*.

Koenigs, M., Young, L., Adolphs, R., Tranel, D. Cushman, F., Hauser, M., et al. (2007). Damage to the prefrontal cortex increases utilitarian moral judgments. *Nature, 446*: 908–911.

Koenigsberg, R.A. (2003, July 15). Foucault-L discourse and unconscious fantasy. Retrieved 9/11/07 from http://www.foucault.info/Foucault-L/archive/msg08786.shtml.

Kohlberg, L. (1981). *Essays on moral development, Vol. 1, The philosophy of moral development.* New York: Harper & Row.

Kohut, H. (1971). *The analysis of the self: A systematic approach to the psychoanalytic treatment of narcissistic personality disorders.* New York: International Universities Press.

Korbin, J.E. (Ed.) (1981). *Child abuse and neglect: Cross-cultural perspectives.* Berkeley, CA: University of California Press.

Kotter, J.P. (1985). *Power and influence.* New York: Free Press.

Kotter, J.R. (1998). What leaders really do. In *Harvard Business Review on Leadership* (pp. 37–60). Boston, MA: Harvard Business School Publishing. (Original work published 1990)

Kotulak, R. (1996). *Inside the brain: Revolutionary discoveries of how the mind works.* Kansas City, MO: Andrews McMeel Publishing.

Kouzes, J.M. & Posner, B.Z. (2007). *The leadership challenge* (4th ed.). San Francisco, CA: Jossey-Bass.

Kowalski, R.M. (1996). Complaints and complaining: Functions, antecedents, and consequences. *Psychological Bulletin, 119*: 179–196.

Kowalski, R.M. (2001a). Aversive interpersonal behaviors: On being annoying, thoughtless, and mean. In: R.M. Kowalski (Ed.), *Behaving badly: Aversive behaviors in interpersonal relationships* (pp. 3–25). Washington, DC: American Psychological Association.

Kowalski, R.M. (2001b). The aversive side of social interaction revisited. In: R.M. Kowalski (Ed.), *Behaving badly: Aversive behaviors in interpersonal relationships* (pp. 297–309). Washington, DC: American Psychological Association.

Kowalski, R.M. & Erickson, J.R. (1997). Complaining: What's all the fuss about? In: R.M. Kowalski (Ed.), *Aversive interpersonal behaviors* (pp. 91–110). New York: Plenum Press.

Kozak, M.J. & Foa, E.B. (1997). *Mastery of obsessive-compulsive disorder: A cognitive-behavioral approach: Therapist guide.* San Antonio, TX: TherapyWorks.

Krakowski, J. (2004). Search for the locus of the universal symptom: Re-examination of Hellmuth Kaiser's *Duplicity.* In: D. Bower (Ed.), *Person-centered/client-centered: Discovering the self that one truly is* (pp. 30–55). Lincoln, NE: iUniverse.

Krebs, D. (2000a). As moral as we need to be. In: L.D. Katz (Ed.), *Evolutionary origins of morality: Cross-disciplinary perspectives* (pp. 139–143). Thorverton, UK: Imprint Academic.

Krebs, D. (2000b). Evolutionary games and morality. In: L.D. Katz (Ed.), *Evolutionary origins of morality: Cross-disciplinary perspectives* (pp. 313–321). Thorverton, UK: Imprint Academic.

Laing, R.D. (1961). *Self and others.* Harmondsworth, UK: Penguin Books.

Laing, R.D. (1967). *The politics of experience.* New York: Ballantine.

Laing, R.D. (1969). *The divided self.* London: Penguin Books. (Original work published 1960)

Laing, R.D. (1972). *The politics of the family and other essays.* New York: Vintage Books. (Original work published 1969)

Laing, R.D. (1976). *The facts of life: An essay in feelings, facts, and fantasy.* New York: Pantheon Books.

Laing, R.D. (1985). *Existential therapy* [Videotape]. Phoenix, AZ: Milton H. Erickson Foundation.

Laing, R.D. (1990). Foreword. In: R. W. Firestone, *Compassionate child-rearing: An in-depth approach to optimal parenting* (pp. vii–xi). Santa Barbara, CA: Glendon Association.

Lakoff, G. (2002). *Moral politics: How liberals and conservatives think* (2nd ed.). Chicago: University of Chicago Press.

Langs, R. (2004). *Fundamentals of adaptive psychotherapy and counseling.* New York: Palgrave Macmillan.

Lasch, C. (1979). *The culture of narcissism: American life in an age of diminishing expectations.* New York: W.W. Norton.

Lasch, C. (1984). *The minimal self: Psychic survival in troubled times.* New York: W.W. Norton.

Lawson, C.A. (2000). *Understanding the borderline mother: Helping her children transcend the intense, unpredictable, and volatile relationship.* Lanham, MD: Rowman & Littlefield.

Leary, M.R. & Springer, C.A. (2001). Hurt feelings: The neglected emotion. In: R.M. Kowalski (Ed.), *Behaving badly: Aversive behaviors in interpersonal relationships* (pp. 151–175). Washington, DC: American Psychological Association.

Leary, M.R., Springer, C., Negel, L., Ansell, E. & Evans, K. (1998). The causes, phenomenology, and consequences of hurt feelings. *Journal of Personality and Social Psychology, 74*: 1225–1237.

LeBon, G. (1897). *The crowd: A study of the popular mind* (2nd ed.). London: T.F. Unwin.

LeDoux, J. (1996). *The emotional brain: The mysterious underpinnings of emotional life.* New York: Simon & Schuster.

LeDoux, J. (2002). *Synaptic self: How out brains become who we are.* New York: Viking.

Leiter, L.D. (2003). From a student. In: J. Carter, *Nasty people: How to stop being hurt by them without stooping to their level* (rev. ed.) (pp. xi–xii). New York: McGraw-Hill.

Lerner, H.G. (1985). *The dance of anger: A woman's guide to changing the patterns of intimate relationships.* New York: Harper & Row.

Levenkron, S. (1991). *Obsessive-compulsive disorders: Treating & understanding crippling habits.* New York: Warner Books.

Levy, D.M. (1943). *Maternal overprotection.* New York: Columbia University Press.

Lewis, H.B. (1987). Shame and the narcissistic personality. In: D. Nathanson (Ed.), *The many faces of shame* (pp. 93–132). New York: Guilford Press.

Lewis, J.M., Owen, M.T. & Cox, M.J. (1988). The transition to parenthood: III. Incorporation of the child into the family. *Family Process, 27* 411–421.

Lewis-O'Connor, A., Sharps, P.W., Humphreys, J., Gary, F.A. & Campbell, J. (2006). Children exposed to intimate partner violence. In: M.M. Feerick & G.B. Silverman (Eds.), *Children exposed to violence* (pp. 3–28). Baltimore, MD: Paul H. Brookes Publishing.

Lieberman, A.F. & Zeanah, C.H. (1999). Contributions of attachment theory to infant-parent psychotherapy and other interventions with infants and young children. In: J. Cassidy & P.R. Shaver (Eds.), *Handbook of attachment: Theory, research, and clinical applications* (pp. 555–574). New York: Guilford Press.

Liechty, D. (2005). [Review of the book *The allure of toxic leaders: Why we follow destructive bosses and corrupt politicians—and how we can survive them*]. The Ernest Becker Foundation. Retrieved 10/27/07 from http://faculty.washington.edu/neglee/hidden/hidn_5.htm.

Lifton, R.J. (1998). The 'end-of-the-world' vision and the psychotic experience. In: J.H. Berke, S. Pierides, A. Sabbadini & S. Schneider (Eds.), *Even paranoids have enemies: New perspectives on paranoia and persecution* (pp. 59–74). London: Routledge.

Lifton, R.J. (2003). *Super power syndrome: America's apocalyptic confrontation with the world.* New York: Thunder's Mouth Press.

Lifton, R.J. (2005, February 16). American and the human future: Surviving Vietnam, 9/11, and Iraq. Lecture presented at the 4th Annual Frank K. Kelly Lecture on Humanity's Future, Santa Barbara, CA. Santa Barbara, CA: Nuclear Age Peace Foundation.

Lindahl, K.M., Malik, N.M., Kaczynski, K. & Simons, J.S. (2004). Couple power dynamics, systemic family functioning, and child adjustment: A test of a mediational model in a multiethnic sample. *Development and Psychopathology, 16*: 609–630.

Linehan, M.M. (1993). *Cognitive-behavioral treatment of borderline personality disorder.* New York: Guilford Press.

Linnoila, M., Virkkunen, M., Roy, A. & Potter, W.Z. (1990). Monoamines, glucose metabolism and impulse control. In: H.M. van Praag, R. Plutchik & A. Apter (Eds.), *Violence and suicidality: Perspectives in clinical and psychobiological research* (pp. 218–241). New York: Brunner/Mazel.

Liotti, G. (1999). Disorganization of attachment as a model for understanding dissociative psychopathology. In: J. Solomon & C. George (Eds.), *Attachment disorganization* (pp. 291–317). New York: Guilford Press.

Lipman-Blumen, J. (2005). *The allure of toxic leaders: Why we follow destructive bosses and corrupt politicians—and how we can survive them.* New York: Oxford University Press.

London, P. (1964). *The modes and morals of psychotherapy* (2nd ed.). New York: Hemisphere Publishing.

Love, P. & Shulkin, S. (1997). *How to ruin a perfectly good relationship.* Austin, TX: Authors.

Lowen, A. (1985). *Narcissism: Denial of the true self.* New York: Simon & Schuster.

Lubit, R. (2004, March/April). The tyranny of toxic managers: Applying emotional intelligence to deal with difficult personalities. *Ivey Business Journal,* 1–7.

Luhrmann, T.M. (2000). *Of two minds: The growing disorder in American psychiatry.* New York: Alfred A. Knopf.

Lyons-Ruth, K. & Jacobvitz, D. (1999). Attachment disorganization: Unresolved loss, relational violence, and lapses in behavioral and attentional strategies. In: J. Cassidy & P.R. Shaver (Eds.), *Handbook of attachment: Theory, research, and clinical applications* (pp. 520–554). New York: Guilford Press.

Lyons-Ruth, K., Yellin, C., Melnick, S. & Atwood, G. (2005). Expanding the concept of unresolved mental states: Hostile/helpless states of mind on the Adult Attachment Interview are associated with disrupted mother-infant communication and infant disorganization. *Development and Psychopathology, 17*: 1–23.

Maccoby, M. (1981). *The leader: A new face for American management.* New York: Ballantine Books.

Mahler, M.S. (1974). Symbiosis and individuation: The psychological birth of the human infant. In: R.S. Eissler, A. Freud, M. Kris & A.J. Solnit (Eds.), *The psychoanalytic study of the child* (Vol. 29, pp. 89–106). New Haven, CT: Yale University Press.

Mahler, M.S., Pine, F. & Bergman, A. (1975). *The psychological birth of the human infant: Symbiosis and individuation.* New York: Basic Books.

Mahoney, J.L., Harris, A.L. & Eccles, J.S. (2006). Organized activity participation, positive youth development, and the over-scheduling hypothesis. *Social Policy Report, XX*(IV), 3–15.

Main, M. (1996). Introduction to the special section on attachment and psychopathology: 2. Overview of the field of attachment. *Journal of consulting and Clinical Psychology, 64*: 237–243.

Main, M. & Hesse, E. (1990). Parents' unresolved traumatic experiences are related to infant disorganized attachment status: Is frightened and/or frightening parental behavior the linking mechanism? In: M.T. Greenberg, D. Cicchetti & E.M. Cummings (Eds.), *Attachment in the preschool years: Theory, research, and intervention* (pp. 161–182). Chicago: University of Chicago Press.

Maltsberger, J.T. (1986). *Suicide risk: The formulation of clinical judgment.* New York: New York University Press.

Marcuse, H. (1966). *Eros and civilization: A philosophical inquiry into Freud.* Boston: Beacon Press. (Original work published 1955)

Marcuse, H. (1991). *One-dimensional man: Studies in the ideology of advanced industrial society* (2nd ed.). Boston: Beacon Press.

Martin, J.L. (2001). *The Authoritarian Personality*, 50 years later: What lessons are there for political psychology? *Political Psychology, 22*: 1–26.

Martin, R. (1971). The concept of power: A critical defence. *British Journal of Sociology, 22*: 240–256.

Maslow, A.H. (1971). *The farther reaches of human nature.* Harmondsworth, UK: Penguin.

Masterson, J.F. (1981). *The narcissistic and borderline disorders: An integrated developmental approach.* New York: Brunner/Mazel.

Masterson, J.F. (1985). *The real self: A developmental, self, and object relations approach.* New York: Brunner/Mazel.

May, D.S. & Solomon, M. (Producers). (1984). *Theoretical aspects of attachment* [Video]. Los Angeles, CA: UCLA Neuropsychiatric Institute and Hospital.

May, R. (1958). Contributions of existential psychotherapy. In: R. May, E. Angel & H.F. Ellenberger (Eds.), *Existence: A new dimension in psychiatry and psychology* (pp. 37–91). New York: Basic Books.

May, R. (1983). *The discovery of being: Writings in existential psychology.* New York: W.W. Norton.

McCallum, J.S. (2000, May/June). Tennyson on management [Electronic version]. *Ivey Business Journal.*

McCann, D. (1987) The good to be pursued in common. In: O.F. Williams & J.W. Houck (Eds.), *The common good and U.S. capitalism* (pp. 158–178). Lanham, MD: University Press of America.

McCarthy, B. & McCarthy, E. (2003). *Rekindling desire: A step-by-step program to help low-sex and no-sex marriages.* New York: Brunner-Routledge.

McClelland, D.C. (1975). *Power: The inner experience.* New York: John Wiley.

McCoy, B.H. (2003). The parable of the sadhu. In *Harvard Business Review on Corporate Ethics* (pp. 165–181). (Original work published 1997)

McFarlane, A. & van der Kolk, B.A. (1996). Trauma and its challenge to society. In: B.A. van der Kolk, A.C. McFarlane & L. Weisaeth (Eds.), *Traumatic stress: The effects of overwhelming experience on mind, body, and society* (pp. 24–46). New York: Guilford Press.

McGregor, H.A., Lieberman, J.D., Greenberg, J., Solomon, S., Arndt, J., Simon, L., et al. (1998). Terror management and aggression: Evidence that mortality salience motivates aggression against worldview-threatening others. *Journal of Personality and Social Psychology, 74:* 590–605.

McLemore, C.W. (2003). *Toxic relationships and how to change them: Health and holiness in everyday life.* San Francisco: Jossey-Bass.

Mead, G.H. (1967). *Mind, self, and society: From the standpoint of a social behaviorist.* Chicago: University of Chicago Press. (Original work published 1934)

Media Reform Information Center. (2007, January 31). Number of corporations that control a majority of U.S. media. Retrieved 10/21/07 from http://www.corporations.org/media/

Meissner, W.W. (1984). *The borderline spectrum: Differential diagnosis and developmental issues.* New York: Jason Aronson.

Meissner, W.W. (1986). *Psychotherapy and the paranoid process.* Northvale, NJ: Jason Aronson.

Meissner, W.W. (1995). *Treatment of patients in the borderline spectrum.* Northvale, NJ: Jason Aronson.

Mellody, P. (with A.W. Miller & J.K. Miller). (1992). *Facing love addiction: Giving yourself the power to change the way you love—The love connection to codependence.* New York: HarperCollins.

Menninger, K. (1938). *Man against himself.* New York: Harcourt, Brace & World.

Messman, S.J. & Canary, D.J. (1998). Patterns of conflict in personal relationships. In: B.H. Spitzberg & W.R. Cupach (Eds.), *The dark side of close relationships* (pp. 121–152). Mahwah, NJ: Lawrence Erlbaum.

Meyer, J.E. (1975). *Death and neurosis* (M. Nunberg, Trans.). New York: International Universities Press.

Middlesex University. (2007) Extracts from Max Weber. Retrieved 4/1/2007 from http://www.mdx.ac.uk/WWW/STUDY/xweb.htm

Mikulincer, M., Florian, V., Birnbaum, G. & Malishkevich, S. (2002). The death-anxiety buffering function of close relationships: Exploring the effects of separation reminders on death-thought accessibility. *Personality & Social Psychology Bulletin,* 287–299.

Mikulincer, M., Gillath, O., Sapir-Lavid, Y. Yaakobi, E. Arias, K., Tal-Aloni, I., et al. (2003). Attachment theory and concern for others' welfare: Evidence that activation of the sense of secure base promotes endorsement of self-transcendence values. *Basic and Applied Social Psychology, 25:* 299–312.

Mikulincer, M. & Shaver, P.R. (2001). Attachment theory and intergroup bias: Evidence that priming the secure base schema attenuates negative reactions to out-groups. *Journal of Personality and Social Psychology, 81:* 97–115.

Mikulincer, M. & Shaver, P.R. (2007). *Attachment in adulthood: Structure, dynamics, and change.* New York: Guilford Press.

Milgram, S. (1974). *Obedience to authority: An experimental view.* New York: Harper & Row.

Miller, A. (1984). *Thou shalt not be aware: Society=s betrayal of the child* (H. & H. Hannum, Trans.). New York: Farrar, Straus & Giroux. (Original published 1981)

Miller, A. (1984). *For your own good: Hidden cruelty in child-rearing and the roots of violence* (H. Hannum & H. Hannum, Trans.) (2nd ed.). New York: Farrar, Straus & Giroux. (Original work published 1980)

Miller, A. (1997). *The drama of the gifted child: The search for the true self* (Rev. ed.) (R. Ward, Trans.). New York: HarperCollins.

Miller, A. (1998). The political consequences of child abuse. *Journal of Psychohistory, 26*: 573–585.

Miller, A. (2005). *The body never lies: The lingering effects of cruel parenting* (A. Jenkins, Trans.). New York: W.W. Norton.

Miller, G. (2000). *The mating mind: How sexual choice shaped the evolution of human nature.* New York: Anchor Books.

Miller, H. (1947). *Remember to remember.* New York: New Directions.

Miller, N.E. & Dollard, J. (1941). *Social learning and imitation.* New Haven, CT: Yale University Press.

Miller, W.I. (2000). *The mystery of courage.* Cambridge, MA: Harvard University Press.

Millon, T. (1998). DSM Narcissistic Personality Disorder: Historical reflections and future directions. In: E.F. Ronningstam (Ed.), *Disorders of narcissism: diagnostic, clinical, and empirical implications* (pp. 75–101). Northvale, NJ: Jason Aronson.

Millon, T. & Davis, R.D. (1996). *Disorders of personality: DSM-IV and beyond.* New York: John Wiley.

Mokdad, A.H., Bowman, B.A., Ford, E.S., Vinicor, F., Marks, J.S. & Koplan, J.P. (2001). The continuing epidemics of obesity and diabetes in the United States [Electronic version]. *Journal of the American Medical Association, 286*: 1195–1200.

Moore, C. (2007). Moral disengagement in processes of organizational corruption. *Journal of Business Ethics, 80*: 129–139.

Moore, C.C. & Williamson, J.B. (2003). The universal fear of death and the cultural response. In: C.D. Bryant (Ed.), *Handbook of death and dying* (pp. 3–13). Thousand Oaks, CA: Sage Publications.

Morey, L.C. & Jones, J.K. (1998). Empirical studies of the construct validity of narcissistic personality disorder. In: E.F. Ronningstam (Ed.), *Disorders of narcissism: Diagnostic, clinical, and empirical implications* (pp. 351–373). Northvale, NJ: Jason Aronson.

Morrant, C. & Catlett, J. (2008). Separation theory and voice therapy: Philosophical underpinnings and applications to death anxiety across the life span. In: A. Tomer, G.T. Eliason & P.T.P. Wong (Eds.), *Existential and spiritual issues in death anxiety* (pp. 345–373). New York: Lawrence Erlbaum.

Morrison, A.P. (1989). *Shame: The underside of narcissism.* Hillsdale, NJ: Analytic Press.

Motz, A. (2001). *The psychology of female violence: Crimes against the body.* New York: Brunner-Routledge.

Moxley, R.S. (2000). *Leadership and spirit: Breathing new vitality and energy into individuals and organizations.* San Francisco: Jossey-Bass.

Moyers, B. (2003, November 8). Keynote address to the National Conference on Media Reform. Retrieved 11/4/07 from http://www.commondreams.org/cgi-bin/print.cgi?file=/view03/1112-10.htm

Murray, H.A. (1943). *Analysis of the personality of Adolph Hitler.* Harvard Psychological Clinic.

Mustain, M.R. (2002). Prometheus double-bound: Educating the social individual. *Philosophical Studies in Education, 33:* 105–114.

Myers, D.G. (2000). The funds, friends, and faith of happy people. *American Psychologist, 55:* 56–57.

Myers, J.C. (2006). Teens' MySpace web site a boon for 'predators.' *Times Argus Online.* Retrieved 9/13/07.

Nagy, M.H. (1959). The child's view of death. In: H. Feifel (Ed.), *The meaning of death* (pp. 79–98). New York: McGraw-Hill. (Original work published 1948)

Nakken, C. (1996). *The addictive personality: Understanding the addictive process and compulsive behavior* (2nd ed.). Center City, MN: Hazelden.

National Highway Traffic Safety Administration (NHTSA). (2006). *Motor vehicle traffic crash fatalities and injuries: 2005 Projections.* Washington, DC: NHTSA National Center for Statistic and Analysis.

National Institute on Alcohol Abuse and Alcoholism. (2002, April). A call to action: Changing the culture of drinking at U.S. colleges. Retrieved 9/22/07 from http://www.collegedrinkingprevention.gov/NIAAACollegeMaterials/TaskForce/Reference

National Institute on Alcohol Abuse and Alcoholism. (2006, October). Alcohol alert. Retrieved 9/16/07 from http://pubs.niaaa.nih.gov/publications/AA70/AA70.htm

National Institute on Alcohol Abuse and Alcoholism. (2007, January). Alcohol alert. Retrieved 9/16/07 from http://pubs.niaaa.nih.gov/publications/AA71/AA71.htm

Nelson, D.A. & Crick, N.R. (2002). Parental psychological control: Implications for childhood physical and relational aggression. In: B.K. Barber (Ed.), *Intrusive parenting: How psychological control affects children and adolescents* (pp. 161–189). Washington, DC: American Psychological Association.

Nettle, D. (2006). The evolution of personality variation in humans and other animals. *American Psychologist, 61:* 622–631.

Newman, L.S., Duff, K.J. & Baumeister, R.F. (1997). A new look at defensive projection: Thought suppression, accessibility, and biased person perception. *Journal of Personality and Social Psychology, 72*: 980–1001.

Nicholas, M.W. (1994). *The mystery of goodness and the positive moral consequences of psychotherapy*. New York: W.W. Norton.

Nietzsche, F. (1966). *Beyond good and evil: Prelude to a philosophy of the future* (W. Kaufmann, Trans.). New York: Random House. (Original work published 1886)

Nohria, N. & Berkley, J.D. (1998). Whatever happened to the take-charge manager? In *Harvard Business Review on Leadership* (pp. 199–222). (Original work published 1994)

Oaklander, V. (1978). *Windows to our children: A gestalt therapy approach to children and adolescents*. Gouldsboro, ME: Gestalt Journal Press.

Oaklander, V. (2006). *Hidden treasure: A map to the child's inner self*. London: Karnac.

Oatley, K. (1996). Emotions: Communications to the self and others. In: R. Harre & W.G. Parrott (Eds.), *The emotions: Social, cultural and biological dimensions* (pp. 312–316). London: Sage Publications.

Ober, J. & Macedo, S. (2006). Introduction. In: F. de Waal, *Primates and philosophers: How morality evolved* (pp. ix–xix). Princeton, NJ: Princeton University Press.

Oberman, L.M., Hubbard, E.M., McCleery, J.P., Altschuler, E.L., Ramachandran, V.S. & Pineda, J.A. (2005). EEG evidence for mirror neuron dysfunction in autism spectrum disorders. *Cognitive Brain Research, 24*: 190–198.

Ogden, T.H. (1982). *Projective identification and psychotherapeutic technique*. New York: Jason Aronson.

Oliner, S.P. & Oliner, P.M. (1988). *The altruistic personality: Rescuers of Jews in Nazi Europe*. New York: Free Press.

Olson, G. (2007, October 24). Neuroscience and moral politics: Chomsky's intellectual progeny. *Dissident Voice*. Retrieved 12/9/07 from http://www.dissidentvoice.org/2007/10/neuroscience-and-moral-politics-chomskys-intellectual-progeny/.

Orbach, I. (1988). *Children who don't want to live: Understanding and treating the suicidal child*. San Francisco: Jossey-Bass.

Ovesey, L. (1955). Pseudo-homosexuality, the paranoid mechanism, and paranoia. *Psychiatry, 18*: 163–173.

Owen, D. (1993). The future of the Balkans: An interview with David Owen. *Foreign Affairs, 72*: 1–9.

Pagels, E. (1988). *Adam, Eve, and the serpent*. New York: Random House.

Parens, H. (2007). Toward understanding prejudice: Benign and malignant. In: H. Parens, A. Mahfouz, S.W. Twemlow & D.E. Scharff (Eds.), *The future of prejudice: Psychoanalysis and the prevention of prejudice* (pp. 21–36). Lanham, MD: Rowman & Littlefield.

Parens, H., Mahfouz, A., Twemlow, S.W. & Scharff, D.E. (Eds.). (2007). *The future of prejudice: Psychoanalysis and the prevention of prejudice*. Lanham, MD: Rowman & Littlefield.

Parfit, D. (1994). How both human history, and the history of ethics, may be just beginning. In: P. Singer (Ed.), *Ethics* (pp. 391–392). Oxford, UK: Oxford University Press. (Original work published 1984)

Parker, G. (1983). *Parental overprotection: A risk factor in psychosocial development*. New York: Grune and Stratton.

Parker, M. & Morris, M. (2004). Finding a secure base: Attachment in Grendon Prison. In: F. Pfafflin & G. Adshead (Eds.), *A matter of security: The application of attachment theory to forensic psychiatry and psychotherapy* (pp. 193–207). London: Jessica Kingsley.

Parks, S.D. (2005). *Leadership can be taught: A bold approach for a complex world*. Boston, MA: Harvard Business School Press.

Parr, G. (Producer and director). (1983). *Voyage to Understanding*. [Videotape/DVD]. Santa Barbara, CA: Glendon Association.

Parr, G. (Producer and director). (1985). *Teaching our children about feelings*. [Videotape]. Santa Barbara, CA: Glendon Association.

Parrott, W.G. & Harre, R. (1996). Overview. In: R. Harre & W.G. Parrott (Eds.), *The emotions: Social, cultural and biological dimensions* (pp. 1–20). London: Sage Publications.

Parsons, T. (1967). On the concept of political power. In: T. Parsons (Ed.), *Sociological theory and modern society*. New York: Free Press.

Patterson, G.R. (1982). *Coercive family processes*. Eugene, OR: Castilia Press.

Pearson, P. (1997). *When she was bad: How and why women get away with murder*. New York: Penguin Books.

Peele, S. (with A. Brodsky). (1975). *Love and addiction*. New York: Penguin.

Pepler, D.J. & Slaby, R.G. (1994). Theoretical and developmental perspectives on youth and violence. In: L.D. Eron, J.H. Gentry & P. Schlegel (Eds.), *Reason to hope: A psychosocial perspective on violence and youth* (pp. 27–58). Washington, DC: American Psychological Association.

Perry, B.D. (1996). Neurodevelopmental adaptations to violence: How children survive the intragenerational vortex of violence. Cybrary version of a chapter in *Violence and childhood trauma: Understanding and responding to the effects of violence in young children* (pp. 67–80), Gund Foundation Publishers, Cleveland, OH. Retrieved 10/4/00 from http://www.bcm.tmc.edu/cta/vortex_violence.htm.

Perry, B.D. (1997). Incubated in terror: Neurodevelopmental factors in the "cycle of violence." In: J.D. Osofsky (Ed.), *Children in a violent society* (pp. 124–149). New York: Guilford Press.

Perry, B.D. (2001). Violence and childhood: How persisting fear can alter the developing child's brain. In: D. Schetky & E. Benedek (Eds.), *Textbook of child and adolescent forensic psychiatry* (pp. 221–238). Washington, DC: American Psychiatric Press.

Perry, B.D. (2006). Applying principles of neurodevelopment to clinical work with maltreated and traumatized children: The neurosequential model of therapeutics. In: N.B. Webb (Ed.), *Working with traumatized youth in child welfare* (pp. 27–52). New York: Guilford Press.

Person, E.S. (1995). *By force of fantasy: How we make our lives.* New York: Basic Books.

Peters, R.S. (1966). *Ethics and education.* London: George Allen & Unwin.

Peterson, C. & Seligman, M.E.P. (2004). *Character strengths and virtues: A handbook and classification.* Washington, DC: American Psychological Association and New York: Oxford University Press.

Petzinger, T., Jr. (2000, January 1). Talking about tomorrow: Edward O. Wilson. *Wall Street Journal*, pp. R16, R18.

Pew Internet & American Life Project. (2004). Summary of findings. Retrieved 9/13/07 from http://www.pewinternet.org.

Pierce, T.A. (2006). Talking to strangers on MySpace: Teens' use of internet social networking sites [Electronic version]. *Journal of Media Psychology, 11*(3).

Piliavin, J.A. (2003). Doing well by doing good: Benefits for the benefactor. In: C.L.M. Keyes & J. Haidt (Eds.), *Flourishing: Positive psychology and the life well-lived* (pp. 227–247). Washington, DC: American Psychological Association.

Pines, A.M. (2005). *Falling in love: Why we choose the lovers we choose* (2nd ed.). New York: Routledge.

Pinheiro, P.S. (2006). *Study on violence against children.* Prepared for the sixty-first session of the United Nations General Assembly, 29 August 2006.

Piven, J.S. (Ed.). (2004). *The psychology of death in fantasy and history.* Westport, CT: Praeger.

Piven, J.S. (2006). Narcissism, sexuality, and psyche in terrorist theology. *Psychoanalytic Review, 93*: 231–265.

Plante, T.G. (2004). *Do the right thing: Living ethically in an unethical world.* Oakland, CA: New Harbinger Publications.

Plutchik, R. & van Praag, H.M. (1990). Psychosocial correlates of suicide and violence risk. In: H.M. van Praag, R. Plutchik & A. Apter (Eds.), *Violence and suicidality: Perspectives in clinical and psychobiological research* (pp. 37–65). New York: Brunner/Mazel.

Post, J.M. (2004). *Leaders and their followers in a dangerous world: The psychology of political behavior.* Ithaca, NY: Cornell University Press.

Potter-Efron, R. (1994). *Angry all the time: An emergency guide to anger control.* Oakland, CA: New Harbinger.

Potter-Efron, R.T. (2007). *Rage: A step-by-step guide to overcoming explosive anger.* Oakland, CA: New Harbinger.

Pratt, M.W., Skoe, E.E. & Arnold, M.L. (2004). Care reasoning development and family socialisation patterns in later adolescence: A longitudinal analysis. *International Journal of Behavioral Development, 28*: 139–147.

Prescott, J.W. (1975). Body pleasure and the origins of violence. *Bulletin of The Atomic Scientists, 10–20.* Retrieved February 27, 2004, from http://www.violence.de/prescott/bulletin/article.html.

Prescott, J.R. (1996). The origins of human love and violence. *Pre- and Perinatal Psychology Journal, 10*: 143–188.

Prusak, B.G. (1998, September 25). Politics, religion and the public good: An interview with philosopher John Rawls. *Commonweal.* Retrieved 9/17/06 from http://www.commonwealmagazine.org/print_format.pht?id_article=337.

Pyszczynski, T. (2004). What are we so afraid of? A terror management perspective on the politics of fear. *Social Research, 71*: 827–848.

Pyszczynski, T., Solomon, S. & Greenberg, J. (2003). *In the wake of 9/11: The psychology of terror.* Washington, DC: American Psychological Association.

Quinn, D. (1999). *Beyond civilization: Humanity's next great adventure.* New York: Three Rivers Press.

Radzinsky, E. (1996). *Stalin* (H.T. Willetts, Trans.). New York: Random House.

Rank, O. (1972). *Will therapy and truth and reality* (J. Taft, Trans.). New York: Alfred A. Knopf. (Original work published 1936)

Raskin, R. & Novacek, J. (1991). Narcissism and the use of fantasy. *Journal of Clinical Psychology, 47*: 490–499.

Raskin, R. & Terry, H. (1988). A principal-components analysis of the Narcissistic Personality Inventory and further evidence of its construct validity. *Journal of Personality an Social Psychology, 54*: 890–902.

Rawls, J. (1999). *A theory of justice* (rev. ed.). Cambridge, MA: Harvard University Press.

Rawls, J. (2001). *Justice as fairness: A restatement.* Cambridge, MA: Harvard University Press.

Reid, P.T. & Bing, V.M. (2000). Sexual roles of girls and women: An ethnocultural lifespan perspective. In: C.B. Travis & J.W. White (Eds.), *Sexuality, society, and feminism* (pp. 141–166). Washington, DC: American Psychological Association.

Reik, T. (1941). *Masochism in modern man* (M.H. Beigel & G.M. Kurth, Trans.). New York: Farrar, Straus.

Reis, H.T. & Gable, S.L. (2003). Toward a positive psychology of relationships. In: C.L.M. Keyes & J. Haidt (Eds.), *Flourishing: Positive psychology and the life well-lived* (pp. 129–159). Washington, DC: American Psychological Association.

Religion-online.org. (2007). The sickness unto death by Soren Kierkegaard. Retrieved 11/24/07 from http://www.religion-online.org/showchapter.asp?title=2067&C=1865.

Rennison, C.M. & Welchans, S. (2000, May). Intimate partner violence. Bureau of Justice Statistics Special Report. Washington, DC: U.S. Department of Justice.

Rheingold, J.C. (1967). *The mother, anxiety, and death: The catastrophic death complex.* Boston: Little, Brown.

Richman, J. (1986). *Family therapy for suicidal people.* New York: Springer Publishing.

Ridley, M. (1996). *The origins of virtue: Human instincts and the evolution of cooperation.* New York: Penguin.

Robins, R.S. & Post, J.M. (1997). *Political paranoia: The psychopolitics of hatred.* New Haven, CT: Yale University Press.

Rogers, C.R. (1961). *On becoming a person: A therapist's view of psychotherapy.* Boston: Houghton Mifflin.

Rohner, R.P. (1976). *They love me, they love me not.* New Haven, CT: HRAF Press.

Rohner, R.P. (2004). The parental "acceptance-rejection syndrome": Universal correlates of perceived rejection. *American Psychologist, 59,* 830–840.

Roizen, J. (1997). Epidemiological issues in alcohol-related violence. In: M. Galanter (Eds.), *Recent developments in alcoholism, Vol. 13* (pp. 7–40). New York: Plenum Press.

Ronfeldt, D. (2007). *In search of how societies work: Tribes—the first and forever form.* Rand Corporation Working Paper WR-433-RPC. Santa Monica, CA: Rand Corporation.

Ronningstam, E.F. (2005). *Identifying and understanding the narcissistic personality.* Oxford, UK: Oxford University Press.

Rook, K.S. (1998). Investigating the positive and negative sides of personal relationships: Through a lens darkly? In: B.H. Spitzberg & W.R. Cupach (Eds.), *The dark side of close relationships* (pp. 369–393). Mahwah, NJ: Lawrence Erlbaum.

Rorty, A.O. (1993). What it takes to be good. In: G.G. Noam & T.E. Wren (Eds.), *The moral self* (pp. 28–55). Cambridge, MA: MIT Press.

Rorty, R. (1998). *Achieving our country: Leftist thought in twentieth-century America.* Cambridge, MA: Harvard University Press.

Rosenblatt, A., Greeenberg, J., Solomon, S., Pyszczynski, T. & Lyon, D. (1989). Evidence for terror management theory: I. The effects of mortality salience on reactions to those who violate or uphold cultural values. *Journal of Personality and Social Psychology, 57*: 681–690.

Roth, J.A. (1994, February). Psychoactive substances and violence. Retrieved 10/24/06 from http://www.lectlaw.com/files/drg06.htm.

Rubin, L.B. (1983). *Intimate strangers: Men and women together.* New York: Harper & Row

Rubin, T.I. (1969). *The angry book.* New York: Simon & Schuster.

Ruszczynski, S. & Fisher, J. (Eds.). (1995). *Intrusiveness and intimacy in the couple.* London: Karnac Books.

Salzman, M.B (2001). Globalization, culture, and anxiety: Perspectives and predictions from terror management theory. *Journal of Social Distress and the Homeless, 10*: 337–352.

Scharff, D.E. & Scharff, J.S. (1991). *Object relations couple therapy.* Northvale, NJ: Jason Aronson.

Scharff, D.E. & Scharff, J.S. (2007). Family as the link between individual and social origins of prejudice. In: H. Parens, A. Mahfouz, S.W. Twemlow & D.E. Scharff (Eds.), *The future of prejudice: Psychoanaly-*

sis and the prevention of prejudice (pp. 97–110). Lanham, MD: Rowman & Littlefield.

Schnarch, D.M. (1991). *Constructing the sexual crucible: An integration of sexual and marital therapy.* New York: W.W. Norton.

Schore, A.N. (1994). *Affect regulation and the origin of the self: The neurobiology of emotional development.* Hillsdale, NJ: Lawrence Erlbaum.

Schore, A.N. (2001a). The effects of early relational trauma on right brain development, affect regulation, and infant mental health. *Infant Mental Health Journal, 22*: 201–269.

Schore, A.N. (2001b). The effects of a secure attachment relationship on right brain development, affect regulation, and infant mental health. *Journal of Infant Mental Health, 22*: 7–66.

Schore, A.N. (2002a). Advances in neuropsychoanalysis, attachment theory, and trauma research: Implications for self psychology. *Psychoanalytic Inquiry, 22*: 433–484.

Schore, A.N. (2002b). Dysregulation of the right brain: A fundamental mechanism of traumatic attachment and the psychopathogenesis of posttraumatic stress disorder. *Australian and New Zealand Journal of Psychiatry, 36*: 9–30. Retrieved 12/28/06 from http://www.trauma-pages.com/a/schore-2002.php.

Schore, A.N. (2003). *Affect regulation and the repair of the self.* New York: W.W. Norton.

Schwartz, J.M. (with B. Beyette). (1996). *Brain lock: Free yourself from obsessive-compulsive behavior.* New York: HarperCollins.

Searles, H.F. (1961). Schizophrenia and the inevitability of death. *Psychiatric Quarterly, 35*: 631–665.

Segrin, C. (1998). Disrupted interpersonal relationships and mental health problems. In: B.H. Spitzberg & W.R. Cupach (Eds.), *The dark side of close relationships* (pp. 327–365). Mahwah, NJ: Lawrence Erlbaum.

Seifert, K. (2003, Summer). Attachment, family violence and disorders of childhood and adolescence. *Paradigm, 14–15*, 18.

Seligman M.E.P. (1975). *Helplessness: On depression, development, and death.* New York: Freeman.

Seligman, M.E.P. (1990). *Learned optimism.* New York: Alfred A. Knopf.

Seligman, M.E.P. & Czikszentmihalyi, M. (2000). Positive psychology: An introduction. *American Psychologist, 55*: 5–14.

Senge, P.M., Kleiner, A., Roberts, C., Ross, R.B. & Smith, B.J. (1994). *The fifth discipline fieldbook: Strategies and tools for building a learning organization.* New York: Doubleday.

Shackelford, T.K., Buss, D.M. & Weekes-Shackelford, V.A. (2003). Wife killings committed in the context of a lovers triangle. *Basic and Applied Social Psychology, 25*: 137–143.

Shapiro, D. (2000). *Dynamics of character: Self-regulation in psychopathology.* New York: Basic Books.

Shengold, L. (1989). *Soul murder: The effects of childhood abuse and deprivation.* New Haven, CT: Yale University Press.

Shengold, L. (1991). A variety of narcissistic pathology stemming from parental weakness. *Psychoanalytic Quarterly, 60*: 86–92.

Shengold, L. (1999). *Soul murder revisited: Thoughts about therapy, hate, love, and memory.* New Haven, CT: Yale University Press.

Siegel, D.J. (1999). *The developing mind: Toward a neurobiology of interpersonal experience.* New York: Guilford Press.

Siegel, D.J. (2001). Toward an interpersonal neurobiology of the development mind: Attachment relationships, "mindsight," and neural integration. *Infant Mental Health Journal, 22*: 67–94.

Siegel, D.J. (2006). An interpersonal neurobiology approach to psychotherapy: Awareness, mirror neurons, and neural plasticity in the development of well-being. *Psychiatric Annals, 36*: 248–256.

Siegel, D.J. (2007). *The mindful brain: Reflection and attunement in the cultivation of well-being.* New York: W.W. Norton.

Siegel, D.J. & Hartzell, M. (2003). *Parenting from the inside out: How a deeper self-understanding can help you raise children who thrive.* New York: Jeremy P. Tarcher.

Siegel, P. & Weinberger, J. (1998). Capturing the "mommy and I are one" merger fantasy: The oneness motive. In: R.F. Bornstein & J.M. Masling (Eds.), *Empirical studies of psychoanalytic theories* (pp. 71–97). Washington, DC: American Psychological Association.

Silverman, L.H., Lachmann, F.M. & Milich, R.H. (1982). *The search for oneness.* New York: International Universities Press.

Silverstein, B. (1989). Enemy images: The psychology of U.S. attitudes and cognitions regarding the Soviet Union. *American Psychologist, 44*, 903–913.

Silverstein, L.B., Auerbach, C.F. & Levant, R.F. (2002). Contemporary fathers reconstructing masculinity: Clinical implications of gender role strain. *Professional Psychology: Research and Practice, 33*: 361–369.

Simpson, J.A., Rholes, W.S., Campbell, L., Wilson, C. & Tran, S. (2002). Adult attachment, the transition to parenthood, and marital well-being. In: P. Noller & J.A. Feeney (Eds.), *Understanding marriage: Devel-*

opments in the study of couple interaction (pp. 385–410). Cambridge, UK: Cambridge University Press.

Singer, J.A. (2005). *Personality and psychotherapy: Treating the whole person.* New York: Guilford Press.

Singer, P. (1993). *Practical ethics* (2nd ed.). New York: Cambridge University Press.

Singer, P. (Ed.). (1994). *Ethics.* Oxford, UK: Oxford University Press.

Singer, P. (1994). Introduction. In: P. Singer (Ed.), *Ethics* (pp. 3–13). Oxford, UK: Oxford University Press. (Original work published 1986)

Singer, P. (2002). *One world: The ethics of globalization* (2nd ed.). New Haven, CT: Yale University Press.

Singer, P. (2006). Morality, reason, and the rights of animals. In: F. de Waal, *Primates and philosophers: How morality evolved* (pp. 140–158). Princeton, NJ: Princeton University Press.

Skeem, J.L., Monahan, J. & Mulvey, E.P. (2002). Psychopathy, treatment involvement, and subsequent violence among civil psychiatric patients. *Law and Human Behavior, 26*: 577–603.

Sluzki, C. (1998, October). In search of the lost family: A footnote to Minuchin's essay. *Journal of Marital and Family* Therapy [Electronic version].

Sluzki, C.E. & Veron, E. (1977). The double bind as a universal pathogenic situation. In: P. Watzlawick & J.H. Weakland (Eds.), *The interactional view: Studies at the Mental Research Institute, Palo Alto, 1965–1974* (pp. 228–240). New York: W.W. Norton.

Sober, E. & Wilson, D.S. (1998). *Unto others: The evolution and psychology of unselfish behavior.* Cambridge, MA: Harvard University Press.

Solomon, M. (1989). *Narcissism and intimacy: Love and marriage in an age of confusion.* New York: W.W. Norton.

Solomon, S., Greenberg, J. & Pyszczynski, T. (1991). A terror management theory of social behavior: The psychological functions of self-esteem and cultural worldviews. *Advances in Experimental Social Psychology, 24*: 93–159.

Solomon, S., Greenberg, J. & Pyszczynski, T. (2000). Pride and prejudice: Fear of death and social behavior. *Current Directions in Psychological Science, 9*: 200–204.

Solomon, S., Greenberg, J. & Pyszczynski, T. (2004). The cultural animal: Twenty years of terror management theory and research. In: J. Greenberg, S.L. Koole & T. Pyszczynski (Eds.), *Handbook of experimental existential psychology* (pp. 13–34). New York: Guilford Press.

Solomon, Z. (1986). Self acceptance and the selection of a marital partner: An assessment of the SVR model of Murstein. *Social Behavior and Personality*, 14: 1–6.

Spears, L.C. (1998). The understanding and practice of servant-leadership. In: L.C. Spears & M. Lawrence (Eds.), *Practicing servant-leadership: Succeeding through trust, bravery, and forgiveness* (pp. 9–24). San Francisco, CA: Jossey-Bass.

Spears, L.C. (2004a, Fall). Practicing servant-leadership [Electronic version]. *Leader to Leader*, 34.

Spears, L.C. (2004b). The servant-leader: From hero to host: An interview with Margaret J. Wheatley. In: L.C. Spears & M. Lawrence (Eds.), *Practicing servant-leadership: Succeeding through trust, bravery, and forgiveness* (pp. 241–268). San Francisco, CA: Jossey-Bass.

Spears, L.C. (2004c). The understanding and practice of servant-leadership. In: L.C. Spears & M. Lawrence (Eds.), *Practicing servant-leadership: Succeeding through trust, bravery, and forgiveness* (pp. 9–24). San Francisco, CA: Jossey-Bass.

Spitzberg, B.H. & Cupach, W.R. (Eds.). (1998). *The dark side of close relationships*. Mahwah, NJ: Lawrence Erlbaum.

Staub, E. (1989). *The roots of evil: The origins of genocide and other group violence*. Cambridge, UK: Cambridge University Press.

Staub, E. (2003). *The psychology of good and evil: Why children, adults, and groups help and harm others*. Cambridge, UK: Cambridge University Press.

Stech, E.L. (2007). Psychodynamic approach. In: P.G. Northhouse, *Leadership: Theory and practice* (4th ed.) (pp. 237–264). Thousand Oaks, CA: Sage Publications.

Stern, D.N. (1985). *The interpersonal world of the infant: A view from psychoanalysis and developmental psychology*. New York: Basic Books.

Stern, D.N. (1995). *The motherhood constellation: A unified view of parent-infant psychotherapy*. New York: Basic Books.

Sternberg, E. (2000). *Just business: Business ethics in action* (2nd ed.). Oxford, UK: Oxford University Press.

Sternberg, R.J. (2007a). Foreword to the special issue on leadership. *American Psychologist*, 62: 1.

Sternberg, R.J. (2007b). A systems model of leadership: WICS. *American Psychologist*, 62: 34–42.

Stettbacher, J.K. (1991). *Making sense of suffering: The healing confrontation with your own past* (S. Worrall, Trans.). New York: Penguin. (Original work published 1990)

Stoller, R.J. (1975). *Perversion: The erotic form of hatred*. New York: Dell.

Straus, M.A. (1996). Spanking and the making of a violent society. *Pediatric, 98*: 837–842.

Straus, M.A. (2001). *Beating the devil out of them: Corporal punishment in American families and its effect on children*. New Brunswick, NJ: Transaction Publishers.

Susman, E.J. & Stoff, D. (2005). Synthesis and reconsideration of the psychobiology of aggressive behavior: A conclusion. In: D.M. Stoff & E.J. Susman (Eds.), *Developmental psychobiology of aggression* (pp. 271–289). New York: Cambridge University Press.

Suzuki, D.T., Fromm, E. & DeMartino, R. (1960). *Zen Buddhism & psychoanalysis*. New York: Harper & Brothers.

Szalai, A. (Ed.). (1972). *The use of time: Daily activities of urban and suburban populations in twelve countries*. The Hague, Netherlands: Mouton.

Tajfel, H., Billig, M.G., Bundy, R.P. & Flament, C. (1971). Social categorization and intergroup behaviour. *European Journal of Social Psychology, 1*: 149–178.

Tancredi, L.R. (2005). *Hardwired behavior: What neuroscience reveals about morality*. New York: Cambridge University Press.

Tarde, G. (1903). *The laws of imitation* (E.C. Parsons, Trans.). New York: Holt. (Original work published 1890)

Tavris, C. & Aronson, E. (2007). *Mistakes were made (but not by me): Why we justify foolish beliefs, bad decisions, and hurtful acts*. Orlando, FL: Harcourt.

Taylor, C. (1989). *Sources of the self: The making of modern identity*. Cambridge, MA: Harvard University Press.

Taylor, R. (2000). *A seven-year reconviction study of HMP Grendon therapeutic community*. Home Office Research Findings No. 115. London: Home Office Information and Publications Group.

Taylor, S.E. (1991). Asymmetrical effects of positive and negative events: The mobilization-minimization hypothesis. *Psychological Bulletin, 110*: 67–85.

Taylor, S.P. & Hulsizer, M.R. (1998). Psychoactive drugs and human aggression. In: R.G. Geen & E. Donnerstein (Eds.), *Human aggression: Theories, research, and implications for social policy* (pp. 139–165). San Diego, CA: Academic Press.

Tedeschi, J.T. & Bond, M.H. (2001). Aversive behavior and aggression in cultural perspective. In: R.M. Kowalski (Ed.), *Behaving badly: Aversive behaviors in interpersonal relationships* (pp. 257–293). Washington, DC: American Psychological Association.

Tedeschi, J.T. & Felson, R.B. (1994). *Violence, aggression & coercive actions*. Washington, DC: American Psychological Association.

Theoret, H. & Pascual-Leone, A. (2002). Language acquisition: Do as you hear. *Current Biology, 12*: R736–R737.

Tiemeyer, M. (2007). Anorexia statistics. Retrieved 9/16/07 from http:// eatingdisorders.about.com/od/anorexianervosa/p/anorexiastats.htm

Tjeltveit, A.C. (2004). The good, the bad, the obligatory, and the virtuous: The ethical contexts of psychotherapy. *Journal of Psychotherapy Integration, 14*: 149–167.

Tjeltveit, A.C. (2006). To what ends? Psychotherapy goals and outcomes, the good life, and the principle of beneficence. *Psychotherapy: Theory, Research, Practice, Training, 43*: 186–200.

Toch, H. (1992). *Violent men: An inquiry into the psychology of violence* (rev. ed.). Washington, DC: American Psychological Association.

Toffler, A. (1990). *Power shift: Knowledge, wealth, and violence at the edge of the 21st century*. New York: Bantam Books.

Torisky, E.V. (2005). Integrity and supererogation in ethical communities. Retrieved 11/15/05 from http://www.bu.edu/wcp/Papers/ soci/Socitori.htm.

Toynbee, A. (1968). Changing attitudes towards death in the modern western world. In: A. Toynbee, A.K. Mant, N. Smart, J. Hinton, S. Yudkin, E. Rhode, R. Heywood & H.H. Price (Eds.), *Man's concern with death* (pp. 122–132). London: Hodder and Stoughton.

Turner, J. (1978). Social categorization and social discrimination in the minimal group paradigm. In: H. Tajfel (Ed.), *Differentiation between social groups: Studies in the social psychology of intergroup relations* (pp. 101–140). London: Academic Press.

Tutu, D.M. (1999). *No future without forgiveness*. New York: Doubleday.

Urry, H.L., Nitschke, J.B., Dolski, I., Jackson, D.C., Dalton, K.M., Mueller, C.J., et al. (2004). Making a life worth living: Neural correlates of well-being. *Psychological Science, 15*: 367–372.

U.S. Department of Health and Human Services, Substance Abuse and Mental Health Services Administration. (2006). Results from the 2006 National Survey on Drug Use and Health: National findings. Retrieved 9/15/07 from http://www.oas.samhsa.gov/ NSDUH/2k6NSDUH/2k6results.cfm van der Kolk, B.A., McFarlane, A.C. & Weisaeth, L. (Eds.). (1996). *Traumatic stress: The effects of overwhelming experience on mind, body, and society*. New York: Guilford Press.

Vergote, A. (1988). *Guilt and desire: Religious attitudes and their pathological derivatives* (M.H. Wood, Trans.). New Haven: Yale University Press. (Original work published 1978)

Violence Prevention Coalition of Greater Los Angeles. (1991). Alcohol and violence: How alcohol abuse is linked to violence. *Injury Prevention Network Newsletter, 8*(2): 1–2.

Vogel, R. (2007). The emotional basis of coronary heart disease. In: J.H.K. Vogel & M.W. Krucoff (Eds.), *Integrative cardiology: Complementary and alternative medicine for the heart* (pp. 399–414). New York: McGraw-Hill Medical.

Vohs, K.D. & Heatherton, T.F. (2003). The effects of self-esteem and ego threat on interpersonal appraisals of men and women: A naturalistic study. *Personality and Social Psychology Bulletin, 29*: 1407–1420.

Volavka, J. (2002). *Neurobiology of violence* (2nd ed.). Washington, DC: American Psychiatric Publishing.

Volkan, V. (1997). *Blood lines: From ethnic pride to ethnic terrorism*. Boulder, CO: Westview Press.

Vroom, V.H. & Jago, A.G. (2007). The role of the situation in leadership. *American Psychologist, 62*: 17–24.

Waller, J. (2002). *Becoming evil: How ordinary people commit genocide and mass killing*. New York: Oxford University Press.

Wark, G.R. & Krebs, D.L. (1996). Gender and dilemma differences in real-life moral judgment. *Developmental Psychology, 32*: 220–230.

Watts, A. (1961). *Psychotherapy East and West*. New York: Vintage.

Weakland, J.H. (1977). "The double-bind theory" by self-reflexive hindsight. In: P. Watzlawick & J.H. Weakland (Eds.), *The interactional view: Studies at the Mental Research Institute, Palo Alto, 1965–1974* (pp. 241–248). New York: W.W. Norton.

Weaver, G.R. (2006). Virtue in organizations: Moral identity as a foundation for moral agency. *Organizational Studies, 27*: 341–368.

Weber, M. (1946). The sociology of charismatic authority. In: H.H. Gerth & C.W. Mills (Eds. & Trans.), *From Max Weber: Essays in sociology*. New York: Oxford University Press. (Original work published 1921)

Weeks, G.R. & Gambescia, N. (2002). *Hypoactive sexual desire: Integrating sex and couple therapy*. New York: W.W. Norton.

Weil, S. (1952). *The need for roots: Prelude to a declaration of duties towards mankind* (A.F. Wills, Trans.) London: Routledge. (Original work published 1949)

Welldon, E.V. (1988). *Mother, Madonna, whore: The idealization and denigration of motherhood*. London: Free Association Books.

Wenzlaff, R.M. & Eisenberg, A.R. (1998). Parental restrictiveness of negative emotions: Sowing the seeds of thought suppression. *Psychological Inquiry, 9*: 310–313.

Werner, E.E. (1990). Protective factors and individual resilience. In: S.J. Meisels and J.P. Shonkoff (Eds.), *Handbook of early childhood intervention* (pp. 97–116). Cambridge: Cambridge University Press.

Westen, D. (2007). *The political brain: The role of emotion in deciding the fate of the nation*. New York: Public Affairs.

Wexler, J. & Steidl, J. (1978). Marriage and the capacity to be alone. *Psychiatry, 41*: 72–82.

Whitfield, C.L., Anda, R.F., Dube, S.R. & Felitti, V.J. (2003). Violent childhood experiences and the risk of intimate partner violence in adults: Assessment in a large health maintenance organization. *Journal of Interpersonal Violence, 18*: 166–185.

Wiggins, J.S. & Pincus, A.L. (2002). Personality structure and the structure of personality disorders. In: P.T. Costa, Jr. & T.A. Widiger (Eds.), *Personality disorders and the five-factor model of personality* (2nd ed.) (pp. 103–124). Washington, DC: American Psychological Association.

Willi, J. (1982). *Couples in collusion: The unconscious dimension in partner relationships* (W. Inayat-Khan & M. Tchorek, Trans.). Claremont, CA: Hunter House. (Original work published 1975)

Williams, J.H.G., Whiten, A., Suddendorf, T. & Perrett, D.I. (2001). Imitation, mirror neurons and autism. *Neuroscience and Biobehavioral Reviews, 25*: 287–295.

Wilner, A.R. (1984). *The spellbinders: Charismatic political leadership*. New Haven, CT: Yale University Press.

Wilson, E.O. (1998, April). The biological basis of morality [Electronic version]. *Atlantic Monthly, 281(4)*: p. 53.

Wilson-Starks, K.Y. (2003). Toxic leadership. Retrieved 10/27/07 from www.transleadership.com

Winnicott, D.W. (1958). *Collected papers: Through pediatrics to psychoanalysis*. London: Tavistock Publications.

Winston, B.E. & Patterson, K. (2006). An integrative definition of leadership. *International Journal of Leadership Studies, 1*: 6–66.

Wirth, H. (2007). The roots of prejudice in family life and its political significance as discerned in a study of Slobodan Milosevic. In: H. Parens, A. Mahfouz, S.W. Twemlow & D.E. Scharff (Eds.), *The future of prejudice: Psychoanalysis and the prevention of prejudice* (pp. 111–127). Lanham, MD: Rowman & Littlefield.

Wolfe, T. (1983). *The right stuff.* New York: Farrar, Straus & Giroux.

Wong, Y.J. (2006). Strength-centered therapy: A social constructionist, virtues-based psychotherapy. *Psychotherapy: Theory, Research, Practice, Training, 43*: 133–146.

Woolf, H.B. (Ed.). (1981). *Webster's New Collegiate Dictionary.* Springfield, MA: G. & C. Merriam.

Yalom, I. (1980). *Existential psychotherapy.* New York: Basic Books.

Yip, K. (2005). A strengths perspective in understanding and working with clients with psychosis and records of violence. *Journal of Humanistic Psychology, 45*: 446–464.

Young, J. & Flanagan, C. (1998). Schema-focused therapy for narcissistic patients. In: E.F. Ronningstam (Ed.), *Disorders of narcissism: Diagnostic, clinical, and empirical implications* (pp. 239–268). Northvale, NJ: Jason Aronson.

Young-Bruehl, E. (2007). A brief history of prejudice studies. In: H. Parens, A. Mahfouz, S.W. Twemlow & D.E. Scharff (Eds.), *The future of prejudice: Psychoanalysis and the prevention of prejudice* (pp. 219–235). Lanham, MD: Rowman & Littlefield.

Zaccaro, S.J. (2007). Trait-based perspectives of leadership. *American Psychologist, 62*: 6–16.

Zaleznik, A. (1998). Managers and leaders: Are they different? In *Harvard Business Review on Leadership* (pp. 61–88). Boston, MA: Harvard Business School Publishing. (Original work published 1977)

Zeanah, C.H., Benoit, D., Barton, M., Regan, C., Hirshberg, L.M. & Lipsitt, L.P. (1993). Representations of attachment in mothers and their one-year-old infants. *Journal of the American Academy of Child and Adolescent Psychiatry, 32*: 278–286.

Zilboorg, G. (1943). Fear of death. *Psychoanalytic Quarterly, 12*: 465–475.

Zimbardo, P.G. (2004). A situationist perspective on the psychology of evil: Understanding how good people are transformed into perpetrators. In: A.G. Miller (Ed.), *The social psychology of good and evil* (pp. 21–50). New York: Guilford Press.

Zimbardo, P.G., Maslach, C. & Haney, C. (1999). Reflections on the Stanford Prison Experiment: Genesis, transformations, consequences. In: T. Blass (Ed.), *Obedience to authority: current perspectives on the Milgram Paradigm* (pp. 193–237). Mahwah, NJ: Lawrence Erlbaum.

Zimbardo, P.G. & White G. (1972). *Stanford Prison Experiment slide-tape show.* Stanford, CA: Stanford University.

Outline of concepts related to unethical behavior

I. Causal factors:

1. Genetic predisposition (difficult or impossible to alter)
2. Childhood emotional pain (due to separation experiences, losses, and faulty parenting)
3. Existential issues (aloneness, sickness and death)

II. These factors lead to defense formation:

1. The fantasy bond

The fantasy bond is a primary defense that is utilized in an attempt to cope with and allay emotional pain and stress, separation anxiety and death fears. The degree to which it is relied upon is proportional to the degree of frustration, emotional pain, and deprivation experienced during one's developmental years.

The fantasy bond is an illusion of connection to another person, persons or institutions—a merged identity with another individual, a family, a neighborhood, a nation, a political cause, a philosophy, or a religious belief. It supports a pseudoindependent attitude—an inward self-parenting process that precludes closeness or intimacy and fosters attitudes of superiority that lead to animosity and aggression toward other people, belief systems or entities that are different.

2. The voice process supports the fantasy bond

The "voice" is an internal thought process or dialogue involving critical, hostile attitudes toward self and others. It is a well-developed alien element of the personality that plays an active role in self-destructive behavior and violence. These destructive thoughts represent introjections of negative parental attitudes and behaviors that were directed toward the child. The voice is made up of secondary defenses that sustain the fantasy bond.

III. The negative effects of defenses and why they predispose unethical behaviors

1. The fantasy bond:

a. allows for destructive couple and family interactions that are denied, disguised or covered up by a fantasy of being loving:

b. favors isolation and insulation—predisposes a pseudoindependent attitude that is opposed to trusting and genuinely relating to others.

c. supports in-group vs. out-group attitudes—feelings of distrust or outright hostility toward different customs and peoples, and an attitude that one's family, ethnic group or religious affiliation is superior to all others.

2. The voice, the language of the defensive process:

a. supports the fantasy bond.
b. predisposes alienation from self and others.
c. distorts the world—with projection and displacement of anger, prejudice, and destructive stereotyping.
d. leads to inwardness and lack of feeling.
e. supports addictions.
f. influences a passive, victimized orientation.
g. interferes with empathy and discourages a compassionate view.
h. predisposes immaturity, dishonesty, manipulative behavior, and a lack of integrity.
i. supports self-critical attitudes and self-attacks, both verbal and physical, which are a primary factor in suicide.

    j. fosters suspicion, hostility, cynicism, and paranoid attitudes, which are a primary factor in violence.

IV. Positive effects of identifying and challenging the fantasy bond:

    a. leads to better relationships.

    b. breaks down the fantasy of merged identity, pseudoindependence and leads to real independence.

    c. influences the consideration of human rights in personal relationships.

    d. leads to an inclusive worldview over sectarian interests and helps define transcendent goals and values.

    e. challenges fantasy distortions, leads to better reality testing and more adaptive behavior.

    f. helps overcome resistances, leads to therapeutic progress for the individual and ultimately to better mental health.

V. Voice therapy challenges unethical personality traits and behaviors.

1. Utilization of voice therapy techniques:

    a. exposes negative thoughts in a second person dialogue.

    b. offers a catharsis—deep feeling release of intense emotions such as rage and sadness.

    c. helps to develop insight into the sources of an individual's destructive voices.

    d. allows for compassion toward oneself and understanding that even if one has done something unacceptable, it serves no purpose to attack oneself as that is demoralizing and actually leads to more destructive acting-out behavior. (It is far better to apologize and make restitution and change the behavior in the future.)

    e. leads to corrective suggestions to alter maladaptive, negative attitudes and behaviors.

    f. helps the individual become a more mature and compassionate person and a more valuable member of society.

2. Corrective suggestions, when followed:

    a. help develop vulnerability and trust in others.

    b. encourage appropriate risk-taking as a more constructive approach to life.

c. support honesty and discourage duplicity, encouraging direct-ness, openness, and a lack of manipulation of others.

d. teach that all feelings are acceptable but actions require both reality and moral consideration.

e. encourage non-defensiveness in relation to feedback.

f. encourage the acceptance of hostile feelings, bringing them more under one's control and less likely to be acted out destructively, leading to better anger management.

g. discourage self-destructive and impulsive acting-out behaviors, leading to better self-control.

h. challenge addictions that facilitate self-destructive behavior—i.e. substance abuse, addictive attachments, and compulsive routines.

i. although primarily made with concern for bettering the men-tal health of the individual, generally lead to more ethical behavior.

VI. Creating a better society: because society represents a pooling of individual psychological defenses that then acts back on the individual, creating a more humane society through ethical leadership can help break the chain of destructiveness.

1. Characteristics of a good leader:

a. must be competent and effective as well as ethical.

b. has integrity and lives a principled life that embodies the posi-tive values of the constituents.

c. has the courage to challenge the status quo.

d. believes in people and exhibits compassion.

e. possesses psychological insight and understanding.

f. uses ethical means to attain goals.

g. does not seek surplus power or status, but rather is service-oriented.

2. Functions of an ethical society:

a. meets the physical and emotional needs of the populace.

b. offers a context in which an individual can seek meaning and purpose.

c. deals ethically with both insiders and outsiders.

d. offers a means of dealing with existential issues of life and death.

VII. Development, implementation and application of these concepts within the friendship circle:

1. Within the friendship circle:

   a. honesty and openness are encouraged.
   b. people can speak freely (say anything, free associate, release powerful emotions, etc.) in a compassionate and knowledgeable environment.
   c. there is group support for challenging defenses, allowing an individual to realize his or her unique qualities and aspirations.

2. Within the friendship circle, people come to understand the dynamics underlying ethical behaviors with an emphasis on generosity, kindness, and compassion as sound mental health principles. People learn:

   a. to be inclusive and develop a worldview.
   b. to develop transcendent goals, to value people with different customs and beliefs, and to embrace justice, fairness, and equal opportunity for all.
   c. to handle aggression appropriately without externalizing it or internalizing it.
   d. that all feelings are acceptable, but actions require both reality and moral considerations.
   e. that war and violence are not inevitable. The best hope for peace is proper education in psychological principles which leads to ethical behaviors. Dedication to this goal must be coupled with the belief that peace is achievable. Conversely, if one believes that war is inevitable, war becomes a self-fulfilling prophecy.

3. The concepts developed in the friendship circle can be successfully applied to the general culture and society as well.

INDEX

429